These great  t examples of Sh matic vision of the ongings in human his kings, ladies, nobles, soldiers, wretches, and vagabonds are as vital and alive now, in his plays, as they were in his Elizabethan world.

ROMEO AND JULIET: Charged with idealism and threatened in the midst of their overwhelming, voluptuous love for each other.

JULIUS CAESAR: Political prophet and wise man who must die, in one of the most dramatic comments on political interaction ever written.

HAMLET: Prince of Denmark, fighting his conscience and the ghost of his murdered father, in a world as great as it is disillusioning.

MACBETH: Monstrous in battle, noble in defeat, obsessed with a vision of his power; a warning against the evils of disorder in high places.

Ben Jonson's assessment of Shakespeare has never been more true: **"He was not of an age, but for all time."**

FOUR
TRAGEDIES

By William Shakespeare

CAMBRIDGE TEXT AND GLOSSARIES
COMPLETE AND UNABRIDGED

Edited by   WILLIAM ALDIS WRIGHT
Introductions by   MARK VAN DOREN
Synopses by   J. WALKER MCSPADDEN
Illustrations by   LOUIS L. GLANZMAN

ROMEO AND JULIET

JULIUS CAESAR

HAMLET

MACBETH

WASHINGTON SQUARE PRESS
PUBLISHED BY POCKET BOOKS NEW YORK

ACKNOWLEDGMENTS

From *Shakespeare* by Mark Van Doren by permission of the publishers, Henry Holt and Company, Inc., and George Allen and Unwin, Ltd. Copyright, 1939, by Mark Van Doren.

From *Shakespearian Synopses* by J. Walker McSpadden by permission of the publishers, Thomas Y. Crowell and Company. Copyright, 1902, 1923, by Thomas Y. Crowell and Company. Copyright, 1930, by J. Walker McSpadden.

A Washington Square Press/Pocket Books Publication
POCKET BOOKS, a Simon & Schuster division of
GULF & WESTERN CORPORATION
1230 Avenue of the Americas, New York, N.Y. 10020

ISBN: 0-671-41447-X

First Pocket Books printing July, 1939

90   89   88   87   86   85   84   83   82   81   80

Table of Contents

Macbeth   Page

ROMEO AND JULIET

INTRODUCTION TO

Romeo and Juliet

BY

MARK VAN DOREN

WHEN Juliet learns that Romeo has killed Tybalt she cries out that he is a beautiful tyrant, a fiend angelical, a dove-feathered raven, a wolfish lamb, a damned saint, an honorable villain. This echoes Romeo's outcry upon the occasion of Tybalt's first brawl in the streets of Verona: brawling love, loving hate, heavy lightness, serious vanity, chaos of forms, feather of lead, bright smoke, cold fire, sick health, still-waking sleep—Romeo had feasted his tongue upon such opposites, much in the manner of Lucrece when wanton modesty, lifeless life, and cold fire were the only terms that could express her mind's disorder. Of Romeo's lines, says Dr. Johnson, "neither the sense nor the occasion is very evident. He is not yet in love with an enemy, and to love one and hate another is no such uncommon state as can deserve all this toil of antithesis." And of the pathetic strains in Romeo and Juliet generally Dr. Johnson adds that they "are always polluted with some unexpected depravations. His persons, however distressed, have a conceit left them in their misery, a miserable conceit."

Romeo and Juliet, in other words, is still a youthful play; its author, no less than its hero and heroine, is furiously literary. He has written at last a tragedy which is crowded with life, and which will become one of the best-known stories in the world; but it is crowded at the same time with clevernesses, it keeps the odor of ink. Images of poison and the grave are common throughout the dialogue, and they fit the fable. The frame of the author's mind is equally fitted, however, by a literary imagery. There is much about words, books, and reading; as indeed there is in Hamlet, but with a difference. The servant who delivers Capulet's invitations

3

to the feast cannot distinguish the names on his list, and must
have Romeo's help (i, ii). Lady Capulet commands Juliet to

> Read o'er the volume of young Paris' face
> And find delight writ there with beauty's pen; . . .
> This precious book of love, this unbound lover,
> To beautify him, only lacks a cover.   [i, iii]

Romeo's first kiss to Juliet, she remarks, is given "by the
book" (i, v). Love can suggest to Romeo (ii, ii) the way of
schoolboys with their books. Mercutio with his last breath
accuses Tybalt of fighting by "the book of arithmetic" (iii, i).
Juliet, continuing in her rage against Romeo because he has
killed her cousin, demands to know:

> Was ever book containing such vile matter
> So fairly bound?   [iii, ii]

And words seem to be tangible things. Romeo wishes his
name were written down so that he could tear it (ii, ii); when
the Nurse tells him how Juliet has cried out upon his name
it is to him

> As if that name,
> Shot from the deadly level of a gun,
> Did murder her.   [iii, iii]

And the lovers take eloquent turns (iii, ii, iii) at playing var-
iations on "that word 'banished,'" which can "mangle" them
and is indeed but "death mis-term'd."

Even the wit of Romeo and his friends—or, as Dr. Johnson
puts it, "the airy sprightliness" of their "juvenile elegance"—
has a somewhat printed sound. When Romeo, going to the
ball, wants to say that the burden of his passion for Rosaline
weighs him down and makes him less wanton than his friends
he resorts once again to the literary idiom:

> For I am proverb'd with a grandsire phrase.   [i, iv]

Not that the wit of these young gentlemen is poor. It is
Shakespeare's best thus far, and it is as brisk as early morning;
the playful youths are very knowing and proud, and speak
always—until the sudden moment when lightness goes out of
the play like a lamp—as if there were no language but that of
sunrise and spring wind.

Lightness goes out suddenly with the death of Mercutio.

Yet everything is sudden in this play. Its speed is as great as that of *Macbeth*, though it carries no such weight of tragedy. The impatience of the lovers for each other and the brevity of their love are answered everywhere; by Juliet's complaint at the unwieldly slowness with which the Nurse returns from Romeo, by Capulet's testiness as he rushes the preparations for the wedding, by the celerity of the catastrophe once its fuse has been laid.

It is a tragedy in which the catastrophe is everything and so must be both sudden and surprising. Death is not anticipated by as much as anticipates the ends of Shakespeare's major tragedies: that is to say, by all that has been said or done. A few premonitions are planted. The Prologue warns us that the lovers are star-cross'd, misadventur'd and death-mark'd. Romeo's mind misgives him as he arrives at Capulet's feast, and he imagines

> Some consequence yet hanging in the stars.   [I, iv]

Juliet's couplet when she learns her lover's name,

> My only love sprung from my only hate!
> Too early seen unknown, and known too late!   [I, v]

and her experience of second sight as Romeo descends from her chamber:

> O God, I have an ill-divining soul!
> Methinks I see thee, now thou art below,
> As one dead in the bottom of a tomb   [III, v]

are there to light the way towards a woeful conclusion. And Friar Laurence's moral is clearly underlined:

> These violent delights have violent ends,
> And in their triumph die, like fire and powder,
> Which as they kiss consume.   [II, vi]

But such things are significantly few, and they are external to the principal tragic effect, which is that of a lightning flash against the night.

Night is the medium through which the play is felt and in which the lovers are most at home—night, together with certain fires that blaze in its depths for contrast and romance. *Romeo and Juliet* maintains a brilliant shutter-movement of black and white, of cloud and lightning, of midnight and

morning. We first hear of Romeo as one who cherishes the
torch of his love for Rosaline in "an artificial night" of his own
making; he pens himself in his chamber, "locks fair daylight
out," and is for having the world "black and portentous" (i, i).
If day is life, as Friar Laurence says it is, then life is for Romeo
the enemy of love, which can exist in its purity only by itself,
in the little death of a private darkness. Hidden in that darkness it can shine for the knowing lover with a brightness unknown to comets, stars, and suns. When he first sees Juliet he
exclaims:

> O, she doth teach the torches to burn bright!
> It seems she hangs upon the cheek of night
> As a rich jewel in an Ethiop's ear.   [i, v]

"Blind is his love and best befits the dark," jests Benvolio
(ii, i) as he searches with Mercutio for Romeo in Capulet's
garden; but Benvolio does not understand the power that il-
luminates his friend's progress. In the next scene, standing with
Romeo under the balcony, we reach the lighted goal.

> It is the east, and Juliet is the sun. . . .
> Two of the fairest stars in all the heaven,
> Having some business, do entreat her eyes
> To twinkle in their spheres till they return.
> What if her eyes were there, they in her head?
> The brightness of her cheek would shame those stars,
> As daylight doth a lamp; her eyes in heaven
> Would through the airy region stream so bright
> That birds would sing and think it were not night.

Juliet and love are Romeo's life, and there is no light but they.
Juliet may be disquieted by the thought of so much haste:

> It is too rash, too unadvis'd, too sudden,
> Too like the lightning, which doth cease to be
> Ere one can say it lightens.

But Romeo can only cry, "O blessed, blessed night!" There
follows a scene in which Friar Laurence salutes and blesses
the morning. Yet his voice does not obliterate our memory of
many good-nights the lovers had called to each other, and it is
soon (iii, v) Juliet's turn to bless the night that she and
Romeo have had with each other. She cannot admit that day
is coming. Dawn is some mistake, "some meteor." Day, if it is

indeed here, will be as death. And when the Nurse convinces her that darkness is done she sighs:

> Then, window, let day in, and let life out.

For her too love has become the only light; something that shines with its own strength and from its own source, and needs night that it may be known. "O comfort-killing Night, image of hell!" Lucrece had wailed. But night is comfort here, and day—when kinsmen fight, when unwelcome weddings are celebrated, when families wake up to find their daughters dead—is the image of distress. "O day! O day! O day! O hateful day!" howls the Nurse when she finds Juliet stretched out on her bed. She means a particular day, but she has described all days for the death-mark'd lovers. It is perhaps their tragedy that they have been moved to detest day, life, and sun.

At any rate their career derives its brilliance from the contrast we are made to feel between their notion of day and night and the normal thought about such things. Normality is their foe, as it is at last their nemesis; the artificial night of Juliet's feigned death becomes the long night of common death in which no private planets shine. The word normality carries here no moral meaning. It has to do merely with notions about love and life; the lovers' notion being pathetically distinguished from those of other persons who are not in love and so consider themselves realistic or practical. One of the reasons for the fame of *Romeo and Juliet* is that it has so completely and clearly isolated the experience of romantic love. It has let such love speak for itself; and not alone in the celebrated wooing scenes, where the hero and heroine express themselves with a piercing directness, but indirectly also, and possibly with still greater power, in the whole play in so far as the whole play is built to be their foil. Their deep interest for us lies in their being alone in a world which does not understand them; and Shakespeare has devoted much attention to that world.

Its inhabitants talk only of love. The play is saturated with the subject. Yet there is always a wide difference between what the protagonists intend by the term and what is intended by others. The beginning dialogue by Sampson and Gregory, servants, is pornographic on the low level of puns about maidenheads, of horse-humor and hired-man wit. Mercutio will be more indecent (ii, i, iv) on the higher level of a gentleman's cynicism. Mercutio does not believe in love, as perhaps the servants clumsily do; he believes only in sex, and his excellent mind has sharpened the distinction to a very dirty point. He drives hard against the sentiment that has softened his friend and rendered him unfit for the society of young men who really know the world. When Romeo with an effort matches one of his witticisms he is delighted:

> Now art thou sociable, now art thou Romeo, now art thou
> what thou art, by art as well as by nature.   [II, iv]

He thinks that Romeo has returned to the world of artful wit, by which he means cynical wit; he does not know that Romeo is still "dead" and "fishified," and that he himself will soon be mortally wounded under the arm of his friend—who, because love has stupefied him, will be capable of speaking the inane line, "I thought all for the best" (III, i). Romeo so far remembers the code of his class as to admit for a moment that love has made him "effeminate." Mercutio would have applauded this, but he has been carried out to become worms' meat and Romeo will have the rest of the play to himself as far as his friends and contemporaries are concerned. There will be no one about him henceforth who can crack sentences like whips or set the hound of his fancy on the magic scent of Queen Mab.

The older generation is another matter. Romeo and Juliet will have them with them to the end, and will be sadly misunderstood by them. The Capulets hold still another view of love. Their interest is in "good" marriages, in sensible choices. They are match-makers, and believe they know best how their daughter should be put to bed. This also is cynicism, though it be without pornography; at least the young heart of Juliet sees it so. Her father finds her sighs and tears merely ridiculous: "Evermore show'ring?" She is "a wretched puling fool, a whining mammet," a silly girl who does not know what is good for her. Capulet is Shakespeare's first portrait in a long gallery of fussy, tetchy, stubborn, unteachable old men: the Duke of York in *Richard II*, Polonius, Lafeu, Menenius. He is tart-tongued, breathy, wordy, pungent, and speaks with a naturalness unknown in Shakespeare's plays before this, a naturalness consisting in a perfect harmony between his phrasing and its rhythm:

How how, how how, chop-logic! What is this?
"Proud," and "I thank you," and "I thank you not;"
And yet "not proud." Mistress minion, you,
Thank me no thankings, nor proud me no prouds,
But fettle your fine joints 'gainst Thursday next,
To go with Paris to Saint Peter's Church,
Or I will drag thee on a hurdle thither.   [III, v]

We hear his voice in everything he says, as when for instance
the Nurse has told him to go to bed lest he be sick tomorrow
from so much worry about the wedding, and he argues:

No, not a whit! What! I have watch'd ere now
All night for lesser cause, and ne'er been sick.   [IV, iv]

His speaking role has great reality, along with an abrasive
force which takes the temper out of Juliet's tongue.

The Nurse, a member of the same generation, and in Juliet's
crisis as much her enemy as either parent is, for she too urges
the marriage with Paris (III, v), adds to practicality a certain
prurient interest in love-business, the details of which she
mumbles toothlessly, reminiscently, with the indecency of age.
Her famous speech concerning Juliet's age (I, iii), which still
exceeds the speeches of Capulet in the virtue of dramatic
naturalness, runs on so long in spite of Lady Capulet's attempts to stop it because she has become fascinated with the
memory of her husband's broad jest:

NURSE.   And since that time it is eleven years;
                For then she could stand high-lone; nay, by the
                    rood,
                She could have run and waddled all about;
                For even the day before, she broke her brow;
                And then my husband—God be with his soul!
                'A was a merry man—took up the child.
                "Yea," quoth he, "dost thou fall upon thy face?
                Thou wilt fall backward when thou hast more wit;
                Wilt thou not, Jule?" and, by my holidame,
                The pretty wretch left crying and said, "Ay,"
                To see, now, how a jest shall come about!
                I warrant, an I should live a thousand years,
                I never should forget it. "Wilt thou not, Jule?"
                    quoth he;
                And, pretty fool, it stinted and said, "Ay."
LADY CAPULET.   Enough of this; I pray thee, hold thy peace.
NURSE.   Yes, madam; yet I cannot choose but laugh,
                To think it should leave crying and say, "Ay."

And yet, I warrant, it had upon its brow
A bump as big as a young cockerel's stone;
A perilous knock; and it cried bitterly.
"Yea," quoth my husband, "fall'st upon thy face?
Thou wilt fall backward when thou comest to age;
Wilt thou not, Jule?" It stinted and said, "Ay."

The Nurse's delight in the reminiscence is among other things
lickerish, which the delight of Romeo and Juliet in their love
never is, any more than it is prudent like the Capulets, or
pornographic like Mercutio. Their delight is solemn, their behavior holy, and nothing is more natural than that in their
first dialogue (I, v) there should be talk of palmers, pilgrims,
saints, and prayers.

It is of course another kind of holiness than that which appears in Friar Laurence, who nevertheless takes his own part
in the endless conversation which the play weaves about the
theme of love. The imagery of his first speech is by no accident erotic:

> I must up-fill this osier cage of ours
> With baleful weeds and precious-juiced flowers.
> The earth, that's nature's mother, is her tomb;
> What is her burying grave, that is her womb;
> And from her womb children of divers kind
> We sucking on her natural bosom find.   [II, iii]

The Friar is closer to the lovers in sympathy than any other
person of the play. Yet this language is as alien to their mood
as that of Capulet or the Nurse; or as Romeo's recent agitation
over Rosaline is to his ecstasy with Juliet. The lovers are alone.
Their condition is unique. Only by the audience is it understood.

Few other plays, even by Shakespeare, engage the audience
so intimately. The hearts of the hearers, surrendered early, are
handled with the greatest care until the end, and with the
greatest human respect. No distinction of Shakespeare is so
hard to define as this distinction of his which consists of knowing the spectator through and through, and of valuing what is
there. The author of *Romeo and Juliet* watches us as affec-
tionately as he watches his hero and heroine; no sooner has he
hurt our feelings than he has saved them, no sooner are we
outraged than we are healed. The author of *King Lear* will
work to the same end on a grander scale. Here he works lyri-
cally, through our sentiments, which he keeps in trust. Capulet

is an old fool, but we can pity him when the false death of Juliet strikes him dumb at last. As for that false death, our being in on the secret does not prevent us from being touched by it, or from needing the relief which the musicians stand by to give. Five short words at Juliet's bier—"O my love! my wife!"—make up for all of Romeo's young errors. Juliet's appeal after her father has stormed out of the room:

> Is there no pity sitting in the clouds,
> That sees into the bottom of my grief?   [III, v]

is not to the outer world, it is to us. The tension of the entire play, while we await the kiss of fire and powder which will consume its most precious persons, is maintained at an endurable point by the simplicity with which sorrow is made lyric. Even the conceits of Romeo and Juliet sound like things that they and they alone would say, for we know their fancies to be on fire, and we have been close to the flame. Tolstoy, wishing to deny Shakespeare's supposed "talent for depicting character," said it was nothing but a knack with the emotions. "However unnatural the positions may be in which he places his characters, however improper to them the language which he makes them speak, however featureless they are, the very play of emotion, its increase, and alteration, and the combination of many contrary feelings, as expressed correctly and powerfully in some of Shakespeare's scenes, and in the play of good actors, evokes even, if only for a time, sympathy with the persons represented." Shakespeare, in other words, was merely a great poet with a correct and powerful understanding of the surrendered heart, the listening mind; it is the audience, whom he spares nothing yet handles gently, that he makes over in his own image. Which of the two things he does, create characters or create comprehenders of character, may not ultimately matter. At least it is clear that one who has witnessed *Romeo and Juliet* has been taken apart and put together again; has been strangely yet normally moved; has learned a variety of good things about himself; and has been steadily happy in the knowledge.

The Story of the Play

ACT I

THE VERONESE houses of Montague and Capulet have had a feud of long standing, which has brought about continued street-brawls between retainers of the families, from the highest relatives to the lowest servants. The old Capulet gives a feast to which all his friends are bidden. Naturally the Montagues are not included in the list. But Romeo, the heir of the latter house, is persuaded to don a mask and present himself at the festivities, in order to catch a glimpse of Rosaline, a flame of his. Romeo, however, has scant eyes for Rosaline; he discovers another young girl whose beauty and grace set his heart beating as it never beat before. He inquires her name and is dismayed to learn that she is Juliet, the heiress of the Capulets. Meanwhile Tybalt, nephew to Lady Capulet, discovers the identity of Romeo, and is barely dissuaded by old Capulet—whose hospitality overrides his anger—from drawing upon the Montague.

ACT II

JULIET has likewise discovered the name of the handsome young stranger, who carried off her affections by storm at the banquet. Melancholy and lovelorn, she repairs to her balcony, and there confides to the moon and stars the secret of her heart. But it happens that Romeo is underneath the balcony and hears her confess her love for him. Overjoyed, he reveals his presence, and the maiden is constrained to make a further avowal. The lovers resolve on a speedy and secret marriage, which is brought to pass the very next day in the cell of Friar Laurence, a friend of Romeo's.

ACT III

ON THE DAY of the wedding two of Romeo's friends, Benvolio and Mercutio, while walking through the streets of Verona,

are accosted by Tybalt, who is seeking an encounter with
Romeo because of the latter's presence at the Capulets' during
the feast. A quarrel ensues, and at its height Romeo appears.
Tybalt rails at him but Romeo answers softly, for he is just
returned from his wedding and the Capulets are no longer so
hateful in his eyes The others, however, cannot understand
his weakness. and Mercutio, exasperated, fights Tybalt in his
stead. Mercutio is slain. Romeo, in just vengeance, then turns
upon and slays Tybalt By a mandate of the Prince of Verona,
Romeo is banished He flees the land, leaving Juliet the weeping bride of one night.

Juliet's father knowing nothing of her secret nuptials, is
resolved to wed her to her kinsman the young Paris.

ACT IV

IN HER DESPAIR Juliet consults the friendly Friar Laurence,
who advises her to appear to consent to a marriage with Paris,
but on her nuptial morn to drink a potion which the Friar
prepares for her This will give her, he says, the semblance of
death; she will be laid away in the burial vault, and Romeo
will be sent for to rescue her. She takes the drug as the Friar
directs and her parents, heartbroken, believe her dead and
consign her to the tomb.

ACT V

BAD NEWS travels more swiftly than good. Before the Friar
has had the opportunity to notify Romeo of the sham death,
other messengers advise him that Juliet is really no more.
Romeo, frantic with grief, procures a deadly poison and goes
to Juliet's tomb to die beside his wife. At the door of the
tomb he meets Paris, who forces him to fight. Paris is slain.
Romeo enters the tomb, drinks the poison, and breathes his
last. A few moments later Juliet awakes from her trance, sees
her lover's dead body and learns the truth from Friar Laurence,
who has but now arrived at the tomb. She seizes Romeo's
dagger and kills herself. The double tragedy so affects the
heads of the houses of Capulet and Montague that they become reconciled as through a bloody sacrifice.

J. WALKER MCSPADDEN

List of Characters

ESCALUS, *prince of Verona*

PARIS, *a young nobleman, kinsman to the prince*

MONTAGUE, CAPULET, *heads of two houses at variance with each other*

An old man, of the Capulet family

ROMEO, *son to* MONTAGUE

MERCUTIO, *kinsman to the prince, and friend to* ROMEO

BENVOLIO, *nephew to* MONTAGUE, *and friend to* ROMEO

TYBALT, *nephew to* LADY CAPULET

FRIAR LAURENCE, *a Franciscan*

FRIAR JOHN, *of the same order*

BALTHASAR, *servant to* ROMEO

SAMPSON, GREGORY, *servants to* CAPULET

PETER, *servant to* JULIET'S *nurse*

ABRAHAM, *servant to* MONTAGUE

An Apothecary

Three Musicians

Page to PARIS; another Page: an Officer

LADY MONTAGUE, *wife to* MONTAGUE

LADY CAPULET, *wife to* CAPULET

JULIET, *daughter to* CAPULET

Nurse to JULIET

Citizens of Verona; kinsfolk of both houses; Maskers, Guards, Watchmen, and Attendants

Chorus

SIR MONTAGUE

SIR CAPULET

ROMEO

JULIET

TYBALT

FRIAR
LAURENCE

Romeo and Juliet

The Prologue

Enter CHORUS.]
CHORUS. Two households, both alike in dignity,
 In fair Verona, where we lay our scene,
From ancient grudge break to new mutiny,
 Where civil blood makes civil hands unclean.
From forth the fatal loins of these two foes
 A pair of star-cross'd lovers take their life;
Whose misadventured piteous overthrows
 Do with their death bury their parents' strife.
The fearful passage of their death-mark'd love,
 And the continuance of their parents' rage,
Which, but their children's end, nought could remove,
 Is now the two hours' traffic of our stage;
The which if you with patient ears attend,
What here shall miss, our toil shall strive to mend.

Romeo and Juliet

ACT I

S C E N E I — VERONA. *A public place.*

Enter SAMPSON *and* GREGORY, *of the house of*
     CAPULET, *with swords and bucklers.*]

SAMPSON. Gregory, on my word, we'll not carry coals.

GREGORY. No, for then we should be colliers.

SAMPSON. I mean, an we be in choler, we'll draw.

GREGORY. Aye, while you live, draw your neck out o' the collar.

SAMPSON. I strike quickly, being moved.

GREGORY. But thou art not quickly moved to strike.

SAMPSON. A dog of the house of Montague moves me.

GREGORY. To move is to stir, and to be valiant is to stand: therefore, if thou art moved, thou runn'st away.

SAMPSON. A dog of that house shall move me to stand: I will take the wall of any man or maid of Montague's.

GREGORY. That shows thee a weak slave; for the weakest goes to the wall.

SAMPSON. 'Tis true; and therefore women, being the weaker vessels, are ever thrust to the wall: therefore I will push Montague's men from the wall and thrust his maids to the wall.

GREGORY. The quarrel is between our masters and us their men.

SAMPSON. 'Tis all one, I will show myself a tyrant: when I have fought with the men, I will be cruel with the maids; I will cut off their heads.

GREGORY. The heads of the maids?

SAMPSON. Aye, the heads of the maids, or their maidenheads; take it in what sense thou wilt.

GREGORY. They must take it in sense that feel it.

SAMPSON. Me they shall feel while I am able to stand: and 'tis known I am a pretty piece of flesh.

17

GREGORY. 'Tis well thou art not fish; if thou hadst, thou hadst
been poor John. Draw thy tool; here comes two of the house
of Montagues.

Enter ABRAHAM *and* BALTHASAR.]

SAMPSON. My naked weapon is out: quarrel; I will back thee.

GREGORY. How! turn thy back and run?

SAMPSON. Fear me not.

GREGORY. No, marry; I fear thee!

SAMPSON. Let us take the law of our sides; let them begin.

GREGORY. I will frown as I pass by, and let them take it as
they list.

SAMPSON. Nay, as they dare. I will bite my thumb at them;
which is a disgrace to them, if they bear it.

ABRAHAM. Do you bite your thumb at us, sir?

SAMPSON. I do bite my thumb, sir.

ABRAHAM. Do you bite your thumb at us, sir?

SAMPSON. [*Aside to* GREGORY] Is the law of our side, if I say
aye?

GREGORY. No.

SAMPSON. No, sir, I do not bite my thumb at you, sir; but I
bite my thumb, sir.

GREGORY. Do you quarrel, sir?

ABRAHAM. Quarrel, sir! no, sir.

SAMPSON. But if you do, sir, I am for you: I serve as good a
man as you.

ABRAHAM. No better.

SAMPSON. Well, sir.

Enter BENVOLIO.]

GREGORY. [*Aside to* SAMPSON] Say 'better': here comes one of
my master's kinsmen.

SAMPSON. Yes, better, sir.

ABRAHAM. You lie.

SAMPSON. Draw, if you be men. Gregory, remember thy swashing blow.   [*They fight.*

BENVOLIO. Part, fools!   [*Beating down their weapons.*
Put up your swords; you know not what you do.

Enter TYBALT.]

TYBALT. What, art thou drawn among these heartless hinds?
Turn thee, Benvolio, look upon thy death.

BENVOLIO. I do but keep the peace; put up thy sword,
Or manage it to part these men with me.

TYBALT. What, drawn, and talk of peace! I hate the word,
　　As I hate hell, all Montagues, and thee:
　　Have at thee, coward!　　　　　　　　　　*[They fight.*
*Enter several of both houses, who join the fray; then
　　　　enter* CITIZENS *and* PEACE-OFFICERS, *with clubs.*]
FIRST OFFICER. Clubs, bills, and partisans! strike! beat them
　　down!
　　Down with the Capulets! down with the Montagues!
Enter old CAPULET *in his gown, and* LADY CAPULET.]
CAPULET. What noise is this? Give me my long sword, ho!
LADY CAPULET. A crutch, a crutch! why call you for a sword?
CAPULET. My sword, I say! Old Montague is come,
　　And flourishes his blade in spite of me.
Enter old MONTAGUE *and* LADY MONTAGUE.]
MONTAGUE. Thou villain Capulet!—Hold me not, let me go.
LADY MONTAGUE. Thou shalt not stir one foot to seek a foe.
Enter PRINCE ESCALUS, *with his train.*]
PRINCE ESCALUS. Rebellious subjects, enemies to peace,
　　Profaners of this neighbor-stained steel,—
　　Will they not hear? What, ho! you men, you beasts,
　　That quench the fire of your pernicious rage
　　With purple fountains issuing from your veins,
　　On pain of torture, from those bloody hands
　　Throw your mistemper'd weapons to the ground,
　　And hear the sentence of your moved prince.
　　Three civil brawls, bred of an airy word,
　　By thee, old Capulet, and Montague,
　　Have thrice disturb'd the quiet of our streets,
　　And made Verona's ancient citizens
　　Cast by their grave beseeming ornaments,
　　To wield old partisans, in hands as old,
　　Canker'd with peace, to part your canker'd hate:
　　If ever you disturb our streets again,
　　Your lives shall pay the forfeit of the peace.
　　For this time, all the rest depart away:
　　You, Capulet, shall go along with me;
　　And, Montague, come you this afternoon,
　　To know our farther pleasure in this case,
　　To old Free-town, our common judgment-place.
　　Once more, on pain of death, all men depart.
　　　　　　　　　　[Exeunt all but MONTAGUE, LADY
　　　　　　　　　　MONTAGUE, *and* BENVOLIO.

MONTAGUE. Who set this ancient quarrel new abroach?
  Speak, nephew, were you by when it began?
BENVOLIO. Here were the servants of your adversary
  And yours close fighting ere I did approach:
  I drew to part them: in the instant came
  The fiery Tybalt, with his sword prepared;
  Which, as he breathed defiance to my ears,
  He swung about his head, and cut the winds,
  Who, nothing hurt withal, hiss'd him in scorn:
  While we were interchanging thrusts and blows,
  Came more and more, and fought on part and part,
  Till the prince came, who parted either part.
LADY MONTAGUE. O, where is Romeo? saw you him to-day?
  Right glad I am he was not at this fray.
BENVOLIO. Madam, an hour before the worshipp'd sun
  Peer'd forth the golden window of the east,
  A troubled mind drove me to walk abroad;
  Where, underneath the grove of sycamore
  That westward rooteth from the city's side,
  So early walking did I see your son:
  Towards him I made; but he was ware of me,
  And stole into the covert of the wood:
  I, measuring his affections by my own,
  Which then most sought where most might not be found,
  Being one too many by my weary self,
  Pursued my humor, not pursuing his,
  And gladly shunn'd who gladly fled from me.
MONTAGUE. Many a morning hath he there been seen,
  With tears augmenting the fresh morning's dew,
  Adding to clouds more clouds with his deep sighs:
  But all so soon as the all-cheering sun
  Should in the farthest east begin to draw
  The shady curtains from Aurora's bed,
  Away from light steals home my heavy son,
  And private in his chamber pens himself,
  Shuts up his windows, locks fair daylight out,
  And makes himself an artificial night:
  Black and portentous must this humor prove,
  Unless good counsel may the cause remove.
BENVOLIO. My noble uncle, do you know the cause?
MONTAGUE. I neither know it nor can learn of him.
BENVOLIO. Have you importuned him by any means?

MONTAGUE. Both by myself and many other friends:
  But he, his own affections' counsellor,
  Is to himself—I will not say how true—
  But to himself so secret and so close,
  So far from sounding and discovery,
  As is the bud bit with an envious worm,
  Ere he can spread his sweet leaves to the air,
  Or dedicate his beauty to the sun.
  Could we but learn from whence his sorrows grow,
  We would as willingly give cure as know.

Enter ROMEO.]

BENVOLIO. See, where he comes: so please you step aside,
  I'll know his grievance, or be much denied.

MONTAGUE. I would thou wert so happy by thy stay,
  To hear true shrift. Come, madam, let's away.

                              [*Exeunt* MONTAGUE *and* LADY.

BENVOLIO. Good morrow, cousin.

ROMEO. Is the day so young?

BENVOLIO. But new struck nine.

ROMEO. Aye me! sad hours seem long.
  Was that my father that went hence so fast?

BENVOLIO. It was. What sadness lengthens Romeo's hours?

ROMEO. Not having that which, having, makes them short.

BENVOLIO. In love?

ROMEO. Out—

BENVOLIO. Of love?

ROMEO. Out of her favor, where I am in love.

BENVOLIO. Alas, that love, so gentle in his view,
  Should be so tyrannous and rough in proof!

ROMEO. Alas, that love, whose view is muffled still,
  Should without eyes see pathways to his will!
  Where shall we dine? Oh me! What fray was here?
  Yet tell me not, for I have heard it all.
  Here's much to do with hate, but more with love:
  Why, then, O brawling love! O loving hate!
  O any thing, of nothing first create!
  O heavy lightness! serious vanity!
  Mis-shapen chaos of well-seeming forms!
  Feather of lead, bright smoke, cold fire, sick health!
  Still-waking sleep, that is not what it is!
  This love feel I, that feel no love in this.
  Dost thou not laugh?

BENVOLIO. No, coz, I rather weep.

ROMEO. Good heart, at what?

BENVOLIO. At thy good heart's oppression.

ROMEO. Why, such is love's transgression.
Griefs of mine own lie heavy in my breast;
Which thou wilt propagate, to have it prest
With more of thine: this love that thou hast shown
Doth add more grief to too much of mine own.
Love is a smoke raised with the fume of sighs;
Being purged, a fire sparkling in lovers' eyes;
Being vex'd, a sea nourish'd with lovers' tears;
What is it else? a madness most discreet,
A choking gall and a preserving sweet.
Farewell, my coz.

BENVOLIO. Soft! I will go along:
And if you leave me so, you do me wrong.

ROMEO. Tut, I have lost myself; I am not here;
This is not Romeo, he's some other where.

BENVOLIO. Tell me in sadness, who is that you love?

ROMEO. What, shall I groan and tell thee?

BENVOLIO. Groan, why, no;
But sadly tell me who.

ROMEO. Bid a sick man in sadness make his will:
Ah, word ill urged to one that is so ill!
In sadness, cousin, I do love a woman.

BENVOLIO. I aim'd so near when I supposed you loved.

ROMEO. A right good mark-man! And she's fair I love.

BENVOLIO. A right fair mark, fair coz, is soonest hit.

ROMEO. Well, in that hit you miss: she'll not be hit
With Cupid's arrow; she hath Dian's wit,
And in strong proof of chastity well arm'd,
From love's weak childish bow she lives unharm'd.
She will not stay the siege of loving terms,
Nor bide the encounter of assailing eyes,
Nor ope her lap to saint-seducing gold:
O, she is rich in beauty, only poor
That, when she dies, with beauty dies her store.

BENVOLIO. Then she hath sworn that she will still live chaste?

ROMEO. She hath, and in that sparing makes huge waste;
For beauty, starved with her severity,
Cuts beauty off from all posterity.
She is too fair, too wise, wisely too fair,

To merit bliss by making me despair:
She hath forsworn to love; and in that vow
Do I live dead, that live to tell it now.
BENVOLIO. Be ruled by me, forget to think of her.
ROMEO. O, teach me how I should forget to think.
BENVOLIO. By giving liberty unto thine eyes;
Examine other beauties.
ROMEO. 'Tis the way
To call hers, exquisite, in question more:
These happy masks that kiss fair ladies' brows,
Being black, put us in mind they hide the fair;
He that is stricken blind cannot forget
The precious treasure of his eyesight lost:
Show me a mistress that is passing fair,
What doth her beauty serve but as a note
Where I may read who pass'd that passing fair?
Farewell: thou canst not teach me to forget.
BENVOLIO. I'll pay that doctrine, or else die in debt.

[Exeunt.

SCENE II — *A street.*

Enter CAPULET, PARIS, *and* SERVANT.]
CAPULET. But Montague is bound as well as I,
In penalty alike; and 'tis not hard, I think,
For men so old as we to keep the peace.
PARIS. Of honorable reckoning are you both;
And pity 'tis you lived at odds so long.
But now, my lord, what say you to my suit?
CAPULET. But saying o'er what I have said before:
My child is yet a stranger in the world;
She hath not seen the change of fourteen years:
Let two more summers wither in their pride
Ere we may think her ripe to be a bride.
PARIS. Younger than she are happy mothers made.
CAPULET. And too soon marr'd are those so early made.
The earth hath swallow'd all my hopes but she,
She is the hopeful lady of my earth:
But woo her, gentle Paris, get her heart;
My will to her consent is but a part;
An she agree, within her scope of choice
Lies my consent and fair according voice.

This night I hold an old accustom'd feast,
Whereto I have invited many a guest,
Such as I love; and you among the store,
One more, most welcome, makes my number more.
At my poor house look to behold this night
Earth-treading stars that made dark heaven light:
Such comfort as do lusty young men feel
When well-apparell'd April on the heel
Of limping winter treads, even such delight
Among fresh female buds shall you this night
Inherit at my house; hear all, all see,
And like her most whose merit most shall be:
Which on more view, of many mine being one
May stand in number, though in reckoning none.
Come, go with me. Go, sirrah, trudge about
Through fair Verona; find those persons out
Whose names are written there, and to them say,
My house and welcome on their pleasure stay.

[*Exeunt* CAPULET *and* PARIS.

SERVANT. Find them out whose names are written here! It is
written that the shoemaker should meddle with his yard
and the tailor with his last, the fisher with his pencil and
the painter with his nets; but I am sent to find those persons
whose names are here writ, and can never find what names
the writing person hath here writ. I must to the learned. In
good time.

Enter BENVOLIO *and* ROMEO.]

BENVOLIO. Tut, man, one fire burns out another's burning.
    One pain is lessen'd by another's anguish;
Turn giddy, and be holp by backward turning;
    One desperate grief cures with another's languish:
Take thou some new infection to thy eye,
And the rank poison of the old will die.

ROMEO. Your plaintain-leaf is excellent for that.

BENVOLIO. For what, I pray thee?

ROMEO. For your broken shin.

BENVOLIO. Why, Romeo, art thou mad?

ROMEO. Not mad, but bound more than a madman is;
    Shut up in prison, kept without my food,
    Whipt and tormented and—God-den, good fellow.

SERVANT. God gi' god-den. I pray, sir, can you read?

ROMEO. Aye, mine own fortune in my misery.

SERVANT. Perhaps you have learned it without book: but, I pray, can you read anything you see?

ROMEO. Aye, if I know the letters and the language.

SERVANT. Ye say honestly: rest you merry!

ROMEO. Stay, fellow; I can read. [*Reads.*

'Signior Martino and his wife and daughters; County Anselme and his beauteous sisters; the lady widow of Vitruvio; Signior Placentio and his lovely nieces; Mercutio and his brother Valentine; mine uncle Capulet, his wife, and daughters; my fair niece Rosaline; Livia; Signior Valentio and his cousin Tybalt: Lucio and the lively Helena.'

A fair assembly: whither should they come?

SERVANT. Up.

ROMEO. Whither?

SERVANT. To supper; to our house.

ROMEO. Whose house?

SERVANT. My master's.

ROMEO. Indeed, I should have ask'd you that before.

SERVANT. Now I'll tell you without asking: my master is the great rich Capulet; and if you be not of the house of Montagues, I pray, come and crush a cup of wine. Rest you merry! [*Exit.*

BENVOLIO. At this same ancient feast of Capulet's
Sups the fair Rosaline whom thou so lovest,
With all the admired beauties of Verona:
Go thither, and with unattainted eye
Compare her face with some that I shall show,
And I will make thee think thy swan a crow.

ROMEO. When the devout religion of mine eye
Maintains such falsehood, then turn tears to fires;
And these, who, often drown'd, could never die,
Transparent heretics, be burnt for liars!
One fairer than my love! the all-seeing sun
Ne'er saw her match since first the world begun.

BENVOLIO. Tut, you saw her fair, none else being by,
Herself poised with herself in either eye:
But in that crystal scales let there be weigh'd
Your lady's love against some other maid,
That I will show you shining at this feast,
And she shall scant show well that now seems best.

ROMEO. I'll go along, no such sight to be shown,
But to rejoice in splendor of mine own. [*Exeunt.*

SCENE III — *A room in* CAPULET'S *house.*

Enter LADY CAPULET *and* NURSE.]

LADY CAPULET. Nurse, where's my daughter? call her forth to
    me.

NURSE. Now, by my maidenhead at twelve year old,
    I bade her come. What, lamb! what, lady-bird!—
    God forbid!—Where's this girl? What, Juliet!

Enter JULIET.]

JULIET. How now! who calls?

NURSE. Your mother.

JULIET. Madam, I am here. What is your will?

LADY CAPULET. This is the matter. Nurse, give leave awhile,
    We must talk in secret:—nurse, come back again;
    I have remember'd me, thou's hear our counsel.
    Thou know'st my daughter's of a pretty age.

NURSE. Faith, I can tell her age unto an hour.

LADY CAPULET. She's not fourteen.

NURSE. I'll lay fourteen of my teeth,—
    And yet, to my teen be it spoken, I have but four,—
    She is not fourteen. How long is it now
    To Lammas-tide?

LADY CAPULET. A fortnight and odd days.

NURSE. Even or odd, of all days in the year,
    Come Lammas-eve at night shall she be fourteen.
    Susan and she—God rest all Christian souls!—
    Were of an age: well, Susan is with God;
    She was too good for me:—but, as I said,
    On Lammas-eve at night shall she be fourteen;
    That shall she, marry; I remember it well.
    'Tis since the earthquake now eleven years;
    And she was wean'd,—I never shall forget it—
    Of all the days of the year, upon that day:
    For I had then laid wormwood to my dug,
    Sitting in the sun under the dove-house wall;
    My lord and you were then at Mantua:—
    Nay, I do bear a brain:—but, as I said,
    When it did taste the wormwood on the nipple
    Of my dug, and felt it bitter, pretty fool,
    To see it tetchy, and fall out with the dug!
    Shake, quoth the dove-house: 'twas no need, I trow,

To bid me trudge.
And since that time it is eleven years;
For then she could stand high-lone; nay, by the rood,
She could have run and waddled all about;
And even the day before, she broke her brow:
And then my husband,—God be with his soul!
A' was a merry man—took up the child:
'Yea,' quoth he, 'dost thou fall upon thy face?
Thou wilt fall backward when thou hast more wit;
Wilt thou not, Jule?' and, by my holidame,
The pretty wretch left crying, and said 'Aye.'
To see now how a jest shall come about!
I warrant, an I should live a thousand years,
I never should forget it: 'Wilt thou not, Jule?' quoth he;
And, pretty fool, it stinted, and said 'Aye.'

LADY CAPULET. Enough of this; I pray thee, hold thy peace.
NURSE. Yes, madam: yet I cannot choose but laugh,
To think it should leave crying, and say 'Aye':
And yet, I warrant, it had upon its brow
A bump as big as a young cockerel's stone;
A perilous knock; and it cried bitterly.
'Yea,' quoth my husband, 'fall'st upon thy face?
Thou wilt fall backward when thou comest to age;
Wilt thou not, Jule?' It stinted, and said 'Aye.'

JULIET. And stint thou too, I pray thee, nurse, say I.
NURSE. Peace, I have done. God mark thee to his grace!
Thou wast the prettiest babe that e'er I nursed:
An I might live to see thee married once,
I have my wish.

LADY CAPULET. Marry, that 'marry' is the very theme
I came to talk of. Tell me, daughter Juliet,
How stands your disposition to be married?

JULIET. It is an honor that I dream not of.
NURSE. An honor! were not I thine only nurse,
I would say thou hadst suck'd wisdom from thy teat.

LADY CAPULET. Well, think of marriage now; younger than
you
Here in Verona, ladies of esteem,
Are made already mothers. By my count,
I was your mother much upon these years
That you are now a maid. Thus then in brief;
The valiant Paris seeks you for his love.

NURSE. A man, young lady! lady, such a man
    As all the world—why, he's a man of wax.
LADY CAPULET. Verona's summer hath not such a flower.
NURSE. Nay, he's a flower; in faith, a very flower.
LADY CAPULET. What say you? can you love the gentleman?
    This night you shall behold him at our feast:
    Read o'er the volume of young Paris' face,
    And find delight writ there with beauty's pen;
    Examine every married lineament,
    And see how one another lends content;
    And what obscured in this fair volume lies
    Find written in the margent of his eyes.
    This precious book of love, this unbound lover,
    To beautify him, only lacks a cover:
    The fish lives in the sea; and 'tis much pride
    For fair without the fair within to hide:
    That book in many's eyes doth share the glory,
    That in gold clasps locks in the golden story:
    So shall you share all that he doth possess,
    By having him making yourself no less.
NURSE. No less! nay, bigger: women grow by men.
LADY CAPULET. Speak briefly, can you like of Paris' love?
JULIET. I'll look to like, if looking liking move:
    But no more deep will I endart mine eye
    Than your consent gives strength to make it fly.
Enter a SERVINGMAN.]
SERVINGMAN. Madam, the guests are come, supper served up,
    you called, my young lady asked for, the nurse cursed in
    the pantry, and every thing in extremity. I must hence to
    wait; I beseech you, follow straight.
LADY CAPULET. We follow thee. [*Exit* SERVINGMAN.] Juliet, the
    county stays.
NURSE. Go, girl, seek happy nights to happy days.   [*Exeunt.*

SCENE IV — *A street.*

Enter ROMEO, MERCUTIO, BENVOLIO, *with five or
    six other* MASKERS, *and* TORCH-BEARERS.]
ROMEO. What, shall this speech be spoke for our excuse?
    Or shall we on without apology?
BENVOLIO. The date is out of such prolixity:
    We'll have no Cupid hoodwink'd with a scarf,

Bearing a Tartar's painted bow of lath,
Scaring the ladies like a crow-keeper;
Nor no without-book prologue, faintly spoke
After the prompter, for our entrance:
But, let them measure us by what they will,
We'll measure them a measure, and be gone.

ROMEO. Give me a torch: I am not for this ambling;
Being but heavy, I will bear the light.

MERCUTIO. Nay, gentle Romeo, we must have you dance.

ROMEO. Not I, believe me: you have dancing shoes
With nimble soles: I have a soul of lead
So stakes me to the ground, I cannot move.

MERCUTIO. You are a lover; borrow Cupid's wings,
And soar with them above a common bound.

ROMEO. I am too sore enpierced with his shaft
To soar with his light feathers, and so bound,
I cannot bound a pitch above dull woe;
Under love's heavy burthen do I sink.

MERCUTIO. And, to sink in it, should you burthen love;
Too great oppression for a tender thing.

ROMEO. Is love a tender thing? it is too rough,
Too rude, too boisterous, and it pricks like thorn.

MERCUTIO. If love be rough with you, be rough with love;
Prick love for pricking, and you beat love down.
Give me a case to put my visage in:
A visor for a visor! what care I
What curious eye doth quote deformities?
Here are the beetle-brows shall blush for me.

BENVOLIO. Come, knock and enter, and no sooner in
But every man betake him to his legs.

ROMEO. A torch for me: let wantons light of heart
Tickle the senseless rushes with their heels;
For I am proverb'd with a grandsire phrase;
I'll be a candle-holder, and look on.
The game was ne'er so fair, and I am done.

MERCUTIO. Tut, dun's the mouse, the constable's own word
If thou art dun, we'll draw thee from the mire
Of this six-reverence love, wherein thou stick'st
Up to the ears. Come, we burn daylight, ho.

ROMEO. Nay, that's not so.

MERCUTIO. I mean, sir, in delay
We waste our lights in vain, like lamps by day.

Take our good meaning, for our judgment sits
Five times in that ere once in our five wits.
ROMEO. And we mean well, in going to this mask;
But 'tis no wit to go.
MERCUTIO. Why, may one ask?
ROMEO. I dreamt a dream to-night.
MERCUTIO. And so did I.
ROMEO. Well, what was yours?
MERCUTIO. That dreamers often lie.
ROMEO. In bed asleep, while they do dream things true.
MERCUTIO. O, then, I see Queen Mab hath been with you.
 She is the fairies' midwife, and she comes
In shape no bigger than an agate-stone
On the fore-finger of an alderman,
Drawn with a team of little atomies
Athwart men's noses as they lie asleep:
Her wagon-spokes made of long spinners' legs;
The cover, of the wings of grasshoppers;
Her traces, of the smallest spider's web;
Her collars, of the moonshine's watery beams;
Her whip, of cricket's bones; the lash, of film;
Her wagoner, a small gray-coated gnat,
Not half so big as a round little worm
Prick'd from the lazy finger of a maid:
Her chariot is an empty hazel-nut,
Made by the joiner squirrel or old grub,
Time out o' mind the fairies' coachmakers.
And in this state she gallops night by night
Through lovers' brains, and then they dream of love;
O'er courtiers' knees, that dream on court'sies straight;
O'er lawyers' fingers, who straight dream on fees;
O'er ladies' lips, who straight on kisses dream,
Which oft the angry Mab with blisters plagues,
Because their breaths with sweetmeats tainted are:
Sometimes she gallops o'er a courtier's nose,
And then dreams he of smelling out a suit;
And sometime comes she with a tithe-pig's tail
Tickling a parson's nose as a' lies asleep,
Then dreams he of another benefice:
Sometime she driveth o'er a soldier's neck,
And then dreams he of cutting foreign throats,
Of breaches, ambuscadoes, Spanish blades,

Of healths five fathom deep; and then anon
Drums in his ear, at which he starts and wakes,
And being thus frighted swears a prayer or two,
And sleeps again. This is that very Mab
That plats the manes of horses in the night,
And bakes the elf-lock in four sluttish hairs,
Which once untangled much misfortune bodes:
This is the hag, when maids lie on their backs,
That presses them and learns them first to bear,
Making them women of good carriage:
This is she—

ROMEO. Peace, peace, Mercutio, peace!
  Thou talk'st of nothing.

MERCUTIO. True, I talk of dreams;
  Which are the children of an idle brain,
  Begot of nothing but vain fantasy,
  Which is as thin of substance as the air,
  And more inconstant than the wind, who wooes
  Even now the frozen bosom of the north,
  And, being anger'd, puffs away from thence,
  Turning his face to the dew-dropping south.

BENVOLIO. This wind you talk of blows us from ourselves;
  Supper is done, and we shall come too late.

ROMEO. I fear, too early: for my mind misgives
  Some consequence, yet hanging in the stars,
  Shall bitterly begin his fearful date
  With this night's revels, and expire the term
  Of a despised life closed in my breast,
  By some vile forfeit of untimely death:
  But He, that hath the steerage of my course,
  Direct my sail! On, lusty gentlemen.

BENVOLIO. Strike, drum.   [*Exeunt.*

SCENE V—*A hall in* CAPULET'S *house.*

MUSICIANS *waiting. Enter* SERVINGMEN, *with napkins.*]

FIRST SERVINGMAN. Where's Potpan, that he helps not to take
away? he shift a trencher! he scrape a trencher!

SECOND SERVINGMAN. When good manners shall lie all in one
or two men's hands, and they unwashed too, 'tis a foul
thing.

FIRST SERVINGMAN. Away with the joint-stools, remove the

court-cupboard, look to the plate. Good thou, save me a
piece of marchpane; and, as thou lovest me, let the porter
let in Susan Grindstone and Nell. Antony, and Potpan!

SECOND SERVINGMAN. Aye, boy, ready.

FIRST SERVINGMAN. You are looked for and called for, asked
for and sought for, in the great chamber.

THIRD SERVINGMAN. We cannot be here and there too.
Cheerly, boys; be brisk a while, and the longer liver take
all.   [*They retire behind.*

Enter CAPULET, *with* JULIET *and others of his
house, meeting the* GUESTS *and* MASKERS.]

CAPULET. Welcome, gentlemen! ladies that have their toes
Unplagued with corns will have a bout with you:
Ah ha, my mistresses! which of you all
Will now deny to dance? She that makes dainty,
She, I'll swear, hath corns; am I come near ye now?
Welcome, gentlemen! I have seen the day
That I have worn a visor, and could tell
A whispering tale in a fair lady's ear,
Such as would please: 'tis gone, 'tis gone, 'tis gone:
You are welcome, gentlemen! Come, musicians, play.
A hall, a hall! give room! and foot it, girls.
                        [*Music plays, and they dance.*
More light, you knaves; and turn the tables up,
And quench the fire, the room is grown too hot.
Ah, sirrah, this unlook'd-for sport comes well.
Nay, sit, nay, sit, good cousin Capulet;
For you and I are past our dancing days:
How long is 't now since last yourself and I
Were in a mask?

SECOND CAPULET. By'r lady, thirty years.

CAPULET. What, man! 'tis not so much, 'tis not so much:
'Tis since the nuptial of Lucentio,
Come Pentecost as quickly as it will,
Some five and twenty years; and then we mask'd.

SECOND CAPULET. 'Tis more, 'tis more: his son is elder, sir;
His son is thirty.

CAPULET. Will you tell me that?
His son was but a ward two years ago.

ROMEO. [*To a* SERVINGMAN] What lady's that, which doth
enrich the hand
Of yonder knight?

SERVINGMAN. I know not, sir.

ROMEO. O, she doth teach the torches to burn bright!
   It seems she hangs upon the cheek of night
   Like a rich jewel in an Ethiop's ear;
   Beauty too rich for use, for earth too dear!
   So shows a snowy dove trooping with crows,
   As yonder lady o'er her fellows shows.
   The measure done, I'll watch her place of stand,
   And, touching hers, make blessed my rude hand.
   Did my heart love till now? forswear it, sight!
   For I ne'er saw true beauty till this night.

TYBALT. This, by his voice, should be a Montague.
   Fetch me my rapier, boy. What, dares the slave
   Come hither, cover'd with an antic face,
   To fleer and scorn at our solemnity?
   Now, by the stock and honor of my kin,
   To strike him dead I hold it not a sin.

CAPULET. Why, how now, kinsman! wherefore storm you so?

TYBALT. Uncle, this is a Montague, our foe;
   A villain, that is hither come in spite,
   To scorn at our solemnity this night.

CAPULET. Young Romeo is it?

TYBALT. 'Tis he, that villain Romeo.

CAPULET. Content thee, gentle coz, let him alone,
   He bears him like a portly gentleman;
   And, to say truth, Verona brags of him
   To be a virtuous and well-govern'd youth:
   I would not for the wealth of all this town
   Here in my house do him disparagement:
   Therefore be patient, take no note of him:
   It is my will, the which if thou respect,
   Show a fair presence and put off these frowns,
   An ill-beseeming semblance for a feast.

TYBALT. It fits, when such a villain is a guest:
   I'll not endure him.

CAPULET. He shall be endured:
   What, goodman boy! I say, he shall: go to;
   Am I the master here, or you? go to.
   You'll not endure him! God shall mend my soul,
   You'll make a mutiny among my guests!
   You will set cock-a-hoop! you'll be the man!

TYBALT. Why, uncle, 'tis a shame.

CAPULET. Go to, go to;
    You are a saucy boy: is 't so, indeed?
    This trick may chance to scathe you, I know what:
    You must contrary me! marry, 'tis time.
    Well said, my hearts! You are a princox; go:
    Be quiet, or—More light, more light! For shame!
    I'll make you quiet. What, cheerly, my hearts!

TYBALT. Patience perforce with willful choler meeting
    Makes my flesh tremble in their different greeting.
    I will withdraw; but this intrusion shall,
    Now seeming sweet, convert to bitterest gall.   [*Exit.*

ROMEO. [*To* JULIET] If I profane with my unworthiest hand
    This holy shrine, the gentle fine is this,
    My lips, two blushing pilgrims, ready stand
    To smooth that rough touch with a tender kiss.

JULIET. Good pilgrim, you do wrong your hand too much,
    Which mannerly devotion shows in this;
    For saints have hands that pilgrims' hands do touch,
    And palm to palm is holy palmers' kiss.

ROMEO. Have not saints lips, and holy palmers too?

JULIET. Aye, pilgrim, lips that they must use in prayer.

ROMEO. O, then, dear saint, let lips do what hands do;
    They pray, grant thou, lest faith turn to despair.

JULIET. Saints do not move, though grant for prayers' sake.

ROMEO. Then move not, while my prayer's effect I take.
    Thus from my lips by thine my sin is purged.
                           [*Kissing her.*

JULIET. Then have my lips the sin that they have took.

ROMEO. Sin from my lips? O trespass sweetly urged!
    Give me my sin again.

JULIET. You kiss by the book.

NURSE. Madam, your mother craves a word with you.

ROMEO. What is her mother?

NURSE. Marry, bachelor,
    Her mother is the lady of the house,
    And a good lady, and wise and virtuous:
    I nursed her daughter, that you talk'd withal;
    I tell you, he that can lay hold of her
    Shall have the chinks.

ROMEO. Is she a Capulet?
    O dear account! my life is my foe's debt.

BENVOLIO. Away, be gone; the sport is at the best.

ROMEO. Aye, so I fear; the more is my unrest.

CAPULET. Nay, gentlemen, prepare not to be gone;
We have a trifling foolish banquet towards.
Is it e'en so? why, then, I thank you all;
I thank you, honest gentlemen; good night.
More torches here! Come on then, let's to bed.
Ah, sirrah, by my fay, it waxes late:
I'll to my rest.   [*Exeunt all but* JULIET *and* NURSE.

JULIET. Come hither, nurse. What is yond gentleman?

NURSE. The son and heir of old Tiberio.

JULIET. What's he that now is going out of door?

NURSE. Marry, that, I think, be young Petruchio.

JULIET. What's he that follows there, that would not dance?

NURSE. I know not.

JULIET. Go ask his name. If he be married,
My grave is like to be my wedding bed.

NURSE. His name is Romeo, and a Montague,
The only son of your great enemy.

JULIET. My only love sprung from my only hate!
Too early seen unknown, and known too late!
Prodigious birth of love it is to me,
That I must love a loathed enemy.

NURSE. What's this? what's this?

JULIET. A rhyme I learn'd even now
Of one I danced withal.   [*One calls within* 'JULIET.'

NURSE. Anon, anon!
Come let's away; the strangers all are gone.   [*Exeunt*

ACT II

Prologue

Enter CHORUS.]

CHORUS. Now old desire doth in his death-bed lie,
    And young affection gapes to be his heir;
That fair for which love groan'd for and would die,
    With tender Juliet match'd, is now not fair.
Now Romeo is beloved and loves again,
    Alike bewitched by the charm of looks,
But to his foe supposed he must complain,
    And she steals love's sweet bait from fearful hooks:
Being held a foe, he may not have access
    To breathe such vows as lovers use to swear;
And she as much in love, her means much less
    To meet her new beloved any where:
But passion lends them power, time means, to meet,
Tempering extremities with extreme sweet.   [*Exit.*

SCENE I — *A lane by the wall of* CAPULET'S *orchard.*

Enter ROMEO, *alone.*]

ROMEO. Can I go forward when my heart is here?
    Turn back, dull earth, and find thy center out.
            [*He climbs the wall, and leaps down within it.*
Enter BENVOLIO *with* MERCUTIO.]

BENVOLIO. Romeo! my cousin Romeo!

MERCUTIO. He is wise;
    And, on my life, hath stol'n him home to bed.

BENVOLIO. He ran this way, and leap'd this orchard wall;
    Call, good Mercutio.

MERCUTIO. Nay, I'll conjure too.
    Romeo! humors! madman! passion! lover!
    Appear thou in the likeness of a sigh:
    Speak but one rhyme, and I am satisfied;
    Cry but 'aye me!' pronounce but 'love' and 'dove;'
    Speak to my gossip Venus one fair word,
    One nick-name for her purblind son and heir,
    Young Adam Cupid, he that shot so trim

When King Cophetua loved the beggar-maid!
He heareth not, he stirreth not, he moveth not;
The ape is dead, and I must conjure him.
I conjure thee by Rosaline's bright eyes,
By her high forehead and her scarlet lip,
By her fine foot, straight leg and quivering thigh,
And the demesnes that there adjacent lie,
That in thy likeness thou appear to us!

BENVOLIO. An if he hear thee, thou wilt anger him.

MERCUTIO. This cannot anger him; 'twould anger him
To raise a spirit in his mistress' circle
Of some strange nature, letting it there stand
Till she had laid it and conjured it down;
That were some spite: my invocation
Is fair and honest, and in his mistress' name
I conjure only but to raise up him.

BENVOLIO. Come, he hath hid himself among these trees,
To be consorted with the humorous night:
Blind is his love, and best befits the dark.

MERCUTIO. If love be blind, love cannot hit the mark.
Now will he sit under a medlar-tree,
And wish his mistress were that kind of fruit
As maids call medlars when they laugh alone.
O, Romeo, that she were, O, that she were
An open et cetera, thou a poperin pear!
Romeo, good night: I'll to my truckle-bed;
This field-bed is too cold for me to sleep:
Come, shall we go?

BENVOLIO. Go then, for 'tis in vain.
To seek him here that means not to be found.　　[*Exeunt.*

S C E N E II — CAPULET'S *orchard.*

Enter ROMEO.]

ROMEO. He jests at scars that never felt a wound.
　　　　　　　　[JULIET *appears above at a window.*
But, soft! what light through yonder window breaks?
It is the east, and Juliet is the sun!
Arise, fair sun, and kill the envious moon,
Who is already sick and pale with grief,
That thou her maid are far more fair than she:
Be not her maid, since she is envious;

Her vestal livery is but sick and green,
And none but fools do wear it; cast it off.
It is my lady; O, it is my love!
O, that she knew she were!
She speaks, yet she says nothing: what of that?
Her eye discourses, I will answer it.
I am too bold, 'tis not to me she speaks:
Two of the fairest stars in all the heaven,
Having some business, do entreat her eyes
To twinkle in their spheres till they return.
What if her eyes were there, they in her head?
The brightness of her cheek would shame those stars,
As daylight doth a lamp; her eyes in heaven
Would through the airy region stream so bright
That birds would sing and think it were not night.
See, how she leans her cheek upon her hand!
O, that I were a glove upon that hand,
That I might touch that cheek!

JULIET. Aye me!

ROMEO. She speaks:
O, speak again, bright angel! for thou art
As glorious to this night, being o'er my head,
As is a winged messenger of heaven
Unto the white-upturned wondering eyes
Of mortals that fall back to gaze on him,
When he bestrides the lazy-pacing clouds
And sails upon the bosom of the air.

JULIET: O Romeo, Romeo! wherefore art thou Romeo?
Deny thy father and refuse thy name;
Or, if thou wilt not, be but sworn my love,
And I'll no longer be a Capulet.

ROMEO. [*Aside*] Shall I hear more, or shall I speak at this?

JULIET. 'Tis but thy name that is my enemy;
Thou art thyself, though not a Montague.
What's Montague? it is nor hand, nor foot,
Nor arm, nor face, nor any other part
Belonging to a man. O, be some other name!
What's in a name? that which we call a rose
By any other name would smell as sweet;
So Romeo would, were he not Romeo call'd,
Retain that dear perfection which he owes
Without that title. Romeo, doff thy name,

And for thy name, which is no part of thee,
Take all myself.

ROMEO. I take thee at thy word:
Call me but love, and I'll be new baptized;
Henceforth, I never will be Romeo.

JULIET. What man art thou, that, thus bescreen'd in night
So stumblest on my counsel?

ROMEO. By a name
I know not how to tell thee who I am:
My name, dear saint, is hateful to myself,
Because it is an enemy to thee;
Had I it written, I would tear the word.

JULIET. My ears have yet not drunk a hundred words
Of thy tongue's uttering, yet I know the sound:
Art thou not Romeo, and a Montague?

ROMEO. Neither, fair maid, if either thee dislike.

JULIET. How camest thou hither, tell me, and wherefore?
The orchard walls are high and hard to climb,
And the place death, considering who thou art,
If any of my kinsmen find thee here.

ROMEO. With love's light wings did I o'er-perch these walls,
For stony limits cannot hold love out:
And what love can do, that dares love attempt;
Therefore thy kinsmen are no let to me.

JULIET. If they do see thee, they will murder thee.

ROMEO. Alack, there lies more peril in thine eye
Than twenty of their swords: look thou but sweet,
And I am proof against their enmity.

JULIET. I would not for the world they saw thee here.

ROMEO. I have night's cloak to hide me from their eyes;
And but thou love me, let them find me here:
My life were better ended by their hate,
Than death prorogued, wanting of thy love.

JULIET. By whose direction found'st thou out this place?

ROMEO. By love, that first did prompt me to inquire;
He lent me counsel, and I lent him eyes.
I am no pilot; yet, wert thou as far
As that vast shore wash'd with the farthest sea,
I would adventure for such merchandise.

JULIET. Thou know'st the mask of night is on my face,
Else would a maiden blush bepaint my cheek
For that which thou hast heard me speak to-night.

Fain would I dwell on form, fain, fain deny
What I have spoke: but farewell compliment!
Dost thou love me? I know thou wilt say 'Aye,'
And I will take thy word: yet, if thou swear'st,
Thou mayst prove false: at lovers' perjuries,
They say, Jove laughs. O gentle Romeo,
If thou dost love, pronounce it faithfully:
Or if thou think'st I am too quickly won,
I'll frown and be perverse and say thee nay,
So thou wilt woo; but else, not for the world.
In truth, fair Montague, I am too fond;
And therefore thou mayst think my 'havior light:
But trust me, gentleman, I'll prove more true
Than those that have more cunning to be strange.
I should have been more strange, I must confess,
But that thou overheard'st, ere I was ware,
My true love's passion: therefore pardon me,
And not impute this yielding to light love,
Which the dark night hath so discovered.

ROMEO. Lady, by yonder blessed moon I swear,
That tips with silver all these fruit-tree tops,—

JULIET. O, swear not by the moon, th' inconstant moon,
That monthly changes in her circled orb,
Lest that thy love prove likewise variable.

ROMEO. What shall I swear by?

JULIET. Do not swear at all;
Or, if thou wilt, swear by thy gracious self,
Which is the god of my idolatry,
And I'll believe thee.

ROMEO. If my heart's dear love—

JULIET. Well, do not swear: although I joy in thee,
I have no joy of this contract to-night:
It is too rash, too unadvis'd, too sudden,
Too like the lightning, which doth cease to be
Ere one can say 'It lightens.' Sweet, good night!
This bud of love, by summer's ripening breath,
May prove a beauteous flower when next we meet.
Good night, good night! as sweet repose and rest
Come to thy heart as that within my breast!

ROMEO. O, wilt thou leave me so unsatisfied?

JULIET. What satisfaction canst thou have to-night?

ROMEO. The exchange of thy love's faithful vow for mine.

JULIET. I gave thee mine before thou didst request it:
    And yet I would it were to give again.
ROMEO. Wouldst thou withdraw it? for what purpose, love?
JULIET. But to be frank, and give it thee again.
    And yet I wish but for the thing I have:
    My bounty is as boundless as the sea,
    My love as deep; the more I give to thee,
    The more I have, for both are infinite.
    I hear some noise within; dear love, adieu!
                                    [NURSE *calls within.*
    Anon, good nurse! Sweet Montague, be true.
    Stay but a little, I will come again.   [*Exit.*
ROMEO. O blessed, blessed night; I am afeard,
    Being in night, all this is but a dream,
    Too flattering-sweet to be substantial.
Re-enter JULIET, *above.*]
JULIET. Three words, dear Romeo, and good night indeed.
    If that thy bent of love be honorable,
    Thy purpose marriage, send me word to-morrow,
    By one that I'll procure to come to thee,
    Where and what time thou wilt perform the rite,
    And all my fortunes at thy foot I'll lay,
    And follow thee my lord throughout the world.
NURSE. [*Within*] Madam!
JULIET. I come, anon.—But if thou mean'st not well,
    I do beseech thee—
NURSE. [*Within*] Madam!
JULIET. By and by, I come:—
    To cease thy suit, and leave me to my grief:
    To-morrow will I send.
ROMEO. So thrive my soul,—
JULIET. A thousand times good night!   [*Exit.*
ROMEO. A thousand times the worse, to want thy light.
    Love goes toward love, as schoolboys from their books,
    But love from love, toward school with heavy looks.
                                    [*Retiring slowly.*
Re-enter JULIET, *above.*]
JULIET. Hist! Romeo, hist!—O, for a falconer's voice,
    To lure this tassel-gentle back again!
    Bondage is hoarse, and may not speak aloud;
    Else would I tear the cave where Echo lies,
    And make her airy tongue more hoarse than mine,

With repetition of my Romeo's name.
Romeo!
ROMEO. It is my soul that calls upon my name:
How silver-sweet sound lovers' tongues by night,
Like softest music to attending ears!
JULIET. Romeo!
ROMEO. My dear?
JULIET. At what o'clock to-morrow
Shall I send to thee?
ROMEO. At the hour of nine.
JULIET. I will not fail: 'tis twenty years till then.
I have forgot why I did call thee back.
ROMEO. Let me stand here till thou remember it.
JULIET. I shall forget, to have thee still stand there,
Remembering how I love thy company.
ROMEO. And I'll still stay, to have thee still forget,
Forgetting any other home but this.
JULIET. 'Tis almost morning; I would have thee gone:
And yet no farther than a wanton's bird,
Who lets it hop a little from her hand,
Like a poor prisoner in his twisted gyves,
And with a silk thread plucks it back again,
So loving-jealous of his liberty.
ROMEO. I would I were thy bird.
JULIET. Sweet, so would I:
Yet I should kill thee with much cherishing.
Good night, good night! parting is such sweet sorrow
That I shall say good night till it be morrow.   [*Exit.*
ROMEO. Sleep dwell upon thine eyes, peace in thy breast!
Would I were sleep and peace, so sweet to rest!
Hence will I to my ghostly father's cell,
His help to crave, and my dear hap to tell.   [*Exit.*

SCENE III — FRIAR LAURENCE'S *cell.*

Enter FRIAR LAURENCE, *with a basket.*]
FRIAR LAURENCE. The gray-eyed morn smiles on the frowning
night,
Chequering the eastern clouds with streaks of light;
And flecked darkness like a drunkard reels
From forth day's path and Titan's fiery wheels:
Now, ere the sun advance his burning eye,

The day to cheer and night's dank dew to dry,
I must up-fill this osier cage of ours
With baleful weeds and precious-juiced flowers.
The earth that's nature's mother is her tomb;
What is her burying grave, that is her womb:
And from her womb children of divers kind
We sucking on her natural bosom find,
Many for many virtues excellent,
None but for some, and yet all different.
O, mickle is the powerful grace that lies
In herbs, plants, stones, and their true qualities:
For nought so vile that on the earth doth live,
But to the earth some special good doth give;
Nor aught so good, but, strain'd from that fair use,
Revolts from true birth, stumbling on abuse:
Virtue itself turns vice, being misapplied,
And vice sometime's by action dignified.
Within the infant rind of this small flower
Poison hath residence, and medicine power:
For this, being smelt, with that part cheers each part,
Being tasted, slays all senses with the heart.
Two such opposed kings encamp them still
In man as well as herbs, grace and rude will:
And where the worser is predominant,
Full soon the canker death eats up that plant.
Enter ROMEO.]

ROMEO. Good morrow, father.

FRIAR LAURENCE. Benedicite!
What early tongue so sweet saluteth me?
Young son, it argues a distemper'd head
So soon to bid good morrow to thy bed:
Care keeps his watch in every old man's eye,
And where care lodges, sleep will never lie;
But where unbruised youth with unstuff'd brain
Doth couch his limbs, there golden sleep doth reign:
Therefore thy earliness doth me assure
Thou art up-roused by some distemperature;
Or if not so, then here I hit it right,
Our Romeo hath not been in bed to-night.

ROMEO. That last is true; the sweeter rest was mine.

FRIAR LAURENCE. God pardon sin! wast thou with Rosaline?

ROMEO. With Rosaline, my ghostly father? no;

I have forgot that name and that name's woe.

FRIAR LAURENCE. That's my good son: but where hast thou
 been then?

ROMEO. I'll tell thee ere thou ask it me again.
 I have been feasting with mine enemy;
 Where on a sudden one hath wounded me,
 That's by me wounded: both our remedies
 Within thy help and holy physic lies:
 I bear no hatred, blessed man, for, lo,
 My intercession likewise steads my foe.

FRIAR LAURENCE. Be plain, good son, and homely in thy drift;
 Riddling confession finds but riddling shrift.

ROMEO. Then plainly know my heart's dear love is set
 On the fair daughter of rich Capulet:
 As mine on hers, so hers is set on mine;
 And all combined, save what thou must combine
 By holy marriage: when, and where, and how,
 We met, we woo'd and made exchange of vow,
 I'll tell thee as we pass; but this I pray,
 That thou consent to marry us to-day.

FRIAR LAURENCE. Holy Saint Francis, what a change is here!
 Is Rosaline, that thou didst love so dear,
 So soon forsaken? young men's love then lies
 Not truly in their hearts, but in their eyes.
 Jesu Maria, what a deal of brine
 Hath wash'd thy sallow cheeks for Rosaline!
 How much salt water thrown away in waste,
 To season love, that of it doth not taste!
 The sun not yet thy sighs from heaven clears,
 Thy old groans ring yet in mine ancient ears;
 Lo, here upon thy cheek the stain doth sit
 Of an old tear that is not wash'd off yet:
 If e'er thou wast thyself and these woes thine,
 Thou and these woes were all for Rosaline:
 And art thou changed? pronounce this sentence then:
 Women may fall when there's no strength in men.

ROMEO. Thou chid'st me oft for loving Rosaline.

FRIAR LAURENCE. For doting, not for loving, pupil mine.

ROMEO. And bad'st me bury love.

FRIAR LAURENCE.   Not in a grave,
 To lay one in, another out to have.

ROMEO. I pray thee, chide not: she whom I love now

Doth grace for grace and love for love allow;
The other did not so.
FRIAR LAURENCE. O, she knew well
Thy love did read by rote and could not spell.
But come, young waverer, come, go with me,
In one respect I'll thy assistant be;
For this alliance may so happy prove,
To turn your households' rancor to pure love.
ROMEO. O, let us hence; I stand on sudden haste.
FRIAR LAURENCE. Wisely and slow: they stumble that run fast.
                                                    [*Exeunt.*

SCENE IV — *A street.*

Enter BENVOLIO *and* MERCUTIO.]
MERCUTIO. Where the devil should this Romeo be?
Came he not home to-night?
BENVOLIO. Not to his father's; I spoke with his man.
MERCUTIO. Ah, that same pale hard-hearted wench, that
Rosaline,
Torments him so that he will sure run mad.
BENVOLIO. Tybalt, the kinsman to old Capulet,
Hath sent a letter to his father's house.
MERCUTIO. A challenge, on my life.
BENVOLIO. Romeo will answer it.
MERCUTIO. Any man that can write may answer a letter.
BENVOLIO. Nay, he will answer the letter's master, how he
dares, being dared.
MERCUTIO. Alas, poor Romeo, he is already dead! stabbed
with a white wench's black eye: shot through the ear with
a love-song; the very pin of his heart cleft with the blind
bow-boy's butt-shaft: and is he a man to encounter Tybalt?
BENVOLIO. Why, what is Tybalt?
MERCUTIO. More than prince of cats, I can tell you. O, he's
the courageous captain of compliments. He fights as you
sing prick-song, keeps time, distance and proportion; rests
me his minim rest, one, two, and the third in your bosom:
the very butcher of a silk button, a duelist, a duelist; a
gentleman of the very first house, of the first and second
cause: ah, the immortal passado! the punto reverso! the
hai!
BENVOLIO. The what?

MERCUTIO. The pox of such antic, lisping, affecting fantasticoes; these new tuners of accents! 'By Jesu, a very good
blade! a very tall man; a very good whore!' Why, is not
this a lamentable thing, grandsire, that we should be thus
afflicted with these strange flies, these fashion-mongers,
these perdona-mi's, who stand so much on the new form
that they cannot sit at ease on the old bench? O, their
bones, their bones!

Enter ROMEO.]

BENVOLIO. Here comes Romeo, here comes Romeo.

MERCUTIO. Without his roe, like a dried herring: O flesh,
flesh, how art thou fishified! Now is he for the numbers that
Petrarch flowed in: Laura to his lady was but a kitchen-
wench; marry, she had a better love to be-rhyme her; Dido,
a dowdy; Cleopatra, a gipsy; Helen and Hero, hildings and
harlots; Thisbe, a gray eye or so, but not to the purpose.
Signior Romeo, bon jour! there's a French salutation to your
French slop. You gave us the counterfeit fairly last night.

ROMEO. Good morrow to you both. What counterfeit did I
give you?

MERCUTIO. The slip, sir, the slip; can you not conceive?

ROMEO. Pardon, good Mercutio, my business was great; and
in such a case as mine a man may strain courtesy.

MERCUTIO. That's as much as to say, Such a case as yours constrains a man to bow in the hams.

ROMEO. Meaning, to court'sy.

MERCUTIO. Thou hast most kindly hit it.

ROMEO. A most courteous exposition.

MERCUTIO. Nay, I am the very pink of courtesy.

ROMEO. Pink for flower.

MERCUTIO. Right.

ROMEO. Why, then is my pump well flowered.

MERCUTIO. Well said: follow me this jest now, till thou hast
worn out thy pump, that, when the single sole of it is worn,
the jest may remain, after the wearing, solely singular.

ROMEO. O single-soled jest, solely singular for the singleness!

MERCUTIO. Come between us, good Benvolio; my wits faint.

ROMEO. Switch and spurs, switch and spurs; or I'll cry a
match.

MERCUTIO. Nay, if thy wits run the wild-goose chase, I have
done; for thou hast more of the wild-goose in one of thy

wits than, I am sure, I have in my whole five: was I with
you there for the goose?

ROMEO. Thou wast never with me for anything when thou
wast not there for the goose.

MERCUTIO. I will bite thee by the ear for that jest.

ROMEO. Nay, good goose, bite not.

MERCUTIO. Thy wit is a very bitter sweeting; it is a most
sharp sauce.

ROMEO. And is it not well served in to a sweet goose?

MERCUTIO. O, here's a wit of cheveril, that stretches from an
inch narrow to an ell broad!

ROMEO. I stretch it out for that word 'broad;' which added
to the goose, proves thee far and wide a broad goose.

MERCUTIO. Why, is not this better now than groaning for
love? now art thou sociable, now art thou Romeo; now art
thou what thou art, by art as well as by nature: for this
driveling love is like a great natural, that runs lolling up
and down to hide his bauble in a hole.

BENVOLIO. Stop there, stop there.

MERCUTIO. Thou desirest me to stop in my tale against the
hair.

BENVOLIO. Thou wouldst else have made thy tale large.

MERCUTIO. O, thou art deceived; I would have made it short:
for I was come to the whole depth of my tale, and meant
indeed to occupy the argument no longer.

ROMEO. Here's goodly gear!

Enter NURSE *and* PETER.]

MERCUTIO. A sail, a sail!

BENVOLIO. Two, two; a shirt and a smock.

NURSE. Peter!

PETER. Anon?

NURSE. My fan, Peter.

MERCUTIO. Good Peter, to hide her face; for her fan's the
fairer of the two.

NURSE. God ye good morrow, gentlemen.

MERCUTIO. God ye good den, fair gentlewoman.

NURSE. Is it good den?

MERCUTIO. 'Tis no less, I tell you; for the bawdy hand of the
dial is now upon the prick of noon.

NURSE. Out upon you! what a man are you!

ROMEO. One, gentlewoman, that God hath made himself to
mar.

NURSE. By my troth, it is well said; 'for himself to mar,' quoth
a'? Gentlemen, can any of you tell me where I may find the
young Romeo?

ROMEO. I can tell you; but young Romeo will be older when
you have found him than he was when you sought him: I
am the youngest of that name, for fault of a worse.

NURSE. You say well.

MERCUTIO. Yea, is the worst well? very well took, i' faith;
wisely, wisely.

NURSE. If you be he, sir, I desire some confidence with you.

BENVOLIO. She will indite him to some supper.

MERCUTIO. A bawd, a bawd, a bawd! So ho!

ROMEO. What hast thou found?

MERCUTIO. No hare, sir; unless a hare, sir, in a lenten pie, that
is something stale and hoar ere it be spent.   [Sings.

> An old hare hoar,
> And an old hare hoar,
> Is very good meat in lent:
> But a hare that is hoar,
> Is too much for a score,
> When it hoars ere it be spent.

Romeo, will you come to your father's? we'll to dinner
thither.

ROMEO. I will follow you.

MERCUTIO. Farewell, ancient lady; farewell, [Singing] 'lady,
lady, lady.'   [Exeunt MERCUTIO and BENVOLIO.

NURSE. Marry, farewell! I pray you, sir, what saucy merchant
was this, that was so full of his ropery?

ROMEO. A gentleman, nurse, that loves to hear himself talk,
and will speak more in a minute than he will stand to in a
month.

NURSE. An a' speak any thing against me, I'll take him down,
an a' were lustier than he is, and twenty such Jacks; and if
I cannot, I'll find those that shall. Scurvy knave! I am none
of his flirt-gills; I am none of his skains-mates. [Turning to
PETER] And thou must stand by too, and suffer every knave
to use me at his pleasure?

PETER. I saw no man use you at his pleasure; if I had, my
weapon should quickly have been out, I warrant you: I
dare draw as soon as another man, if I see occasion in a
good quarrel and the law on my side.

NURSE. Now, afore God, I am so vexed that every part about

me quivers. Scurvy knave! Pray you, sir, a word: and as I
told you, my young lady bade me inquire you out; what she
bade me say, I will keep to myself: but first let me tell ye,
if ye should lead her into a fool's paradise, as they say, it
were a very gross kind of behavior, as they say: for the
gentlewoman is young, and therefore, if you should deal
double with her, truly it were an ill thing to be offered to
any gentlewoman, and very weak dealing.

ROMEO. Nurse, commend me to thy lady and mistress. I protest unto thee—

NURSE. Good heart, and, i' faith, I will tell her as much: Lord,
Lord, she will be a joyful woman.

ROMEO. What wilt thou tell her, nurse? thou dost not mark
me.

NURSE. I will tell her, sir, that you do protest; which, as I take
it, is a gentlemanlike offer.

ROMEO. Bid her devise
Some means to come to shrift this afternoon;
And there she shall at Friar Laurence' cell
Be shrived and married. Here is for thy pains.

NURSE. No, truly, sir; not a penny.

ROMEO. Go to; I say you shall.

NURSE. This afternoon, sir? well, she shall be there.

ROMEO. And stay, good nurse, behind the abbey-wall:
Within this hour my man shall be with thee,
And bring thee cords made like a tackled stair;
Which to the high top-gallant of my joy
Must be my convoy in the secret night.
Farewell; be trusty, and I'll quit thy pains:
Farewell; commend me to thy mistress.

NURSE. Now God in heaven bless thee! Hark you, sir.

ROMEO. What say'st thou, my dear nurse?

NURSE. Is your man secret? Did you ne'er hear say,
Two may keep counsel, putting one away?

ROMEO. I warrant thee, my man's as true as steel.

NURSE. Well, sir; my mistress is the sweetest lady—Lord,
Lord! when 'twas a little prating thing—O, there is a nobleman in town, one Paris, that would fain lay knife aboard;
but she, good soul, had as lieve see a toad, a very toad, as
see him. I anger her sometimes, and tell her that Paris is
the properer man; but, I'll warrant you, when I say so, she

looks as pale as any clout in the versal world. Doth not
rosemary and Romeo begin both with a letter?

ROMEO. Aye, nurse; what of that? both with an R.

NURSE. Ah, mocker! that's the dog's name; R is for the—No;
I know it begins with some other letter—and she hath the
prettiest sententious of it, of you and rosemary, that it would
do you good to hear it.

ROMEO. Commend me to thy lady.

NURSE. Aye, a thousand times. [*Exit* ROMEO.] Peter!

PETER. Anon?

NURSE. Peter, take my fan, and go before, and apace.

[*Exeunt.*

SCENE V — CAPULET'S *orchard.*

Enter JULIET.]

JULIET. The clock struck nine when I did send the nurse:
In half an hour she promised to return.
Perchance she cannot meet him: that's not so.
O, she is lame! love's heralds should be thoughts,
Which ten times faster glide than the sun's beams,
Driving back shadows over louring hills:
Therefore do nimble-pinion'd doves draw love,
And therefore hath the wind-swift Cupid wings.
Now is the sun upon the highmost hill
Of this day's journey, and from nine till twelve
Is three long hours; yet she is not come.
Had she affections and warm youthful blood,
She would be as swift in motion as a ball;
My words would bandy her to my sweet love,
And his to me:
But old folks, many feign as they were dead;
Unwieldy, slow, heavy and pale as lead.

Enter NURSE, *with* PETER.]

O God, she comes! O honey nurse, what news?
Hast thou met with him? Send thy man away.

NURSE. Peter, stay at the gate.   [*Exit* PETER.

JULIET. Now, good sweet nurse,—O Lord, why look'st thou
sad?
Though news be sad, yet tell them merrily;
If good, thou shamest the music of sweet news
By playing it to me with so sour a face.

NURSE. I am a-weary; give me leave awhile.
    Fie, how my bones ache! what a jaunce have I had!
JULIET. I would thou hadst my bones and I thy news:
    Nay, come, pray thee, speak; good, good nurse, speak.
NURSE. Jesu, what haste? can you not stay awhile?
    Do you not see that I am out of breath?
JULIET. How art thou out of breath, when thou hast breath
    To say to me that thou art out of breath?
    The excuse that thou dost make in this delay
    Is longer than the tale thou dost excuse.
    Is thy news good, or bad? answer to that;
    Say either, and I'll stay the circumstance:
    Let me be satisfied, is't good or bad?
NURSE. Well, you have made a simple choice; you know not
    how to choose a man: Romeo! no, not he; though his face
    be better than any man's, yet his leg excels all men's; and
    for a hand, and a foot, and a body, though they be not to
    be talked on, yet they are past compare: he is not the flower
    of courtesy, but, I'll warrant him, as gentle as a lamb. Go
    thy ways, wench; serve God. What, have you dined at
    home?
JULIET. No, no: but all this did I know before.
    What says he of our marriage? what of that?
NURSE. Lord, how my head aches! what a head have I!
    It beats as it would fall in twenty pieces.
    My back o' t'other side,—ah, my back, my back!
    Beshrew your heart for sending me about,
    To catch my death with jauncing up and down!
JULIET. I' faith, I am sorry that thou art not well.
    Sweet, sweet, sweet nurse, tell me, what says my love?
NURSE. Your love says, like an honest gentleman, and a cour-
    teous, and a kind, and a handsome, and I warrant, a virtu-
    ous,—Where is your mother?
JULIET. Where is my mother! why, she is within;
    Where should she be? How oddly thou repliest!
    'Your love says, like an honest gentleman,
    Where is your mother?'
NURSE.   O God's lady dear!
    Are you so hot? marry, come up, I trow;
    Is this the poultice for my aching bones?
    Henceforward do your messages yourself.
JULIET. Here's such a coil! come, what says Romeo?

NURSE. Have you got leave to go to shrift to-day?

JULIET. I have.

NURSE. Then hie you hence to Friar Laurence' cell;
   There stays a husband to make you a wife:
   Now comes the wanton blood up in your cheeks,
   They'll be in scarlet straight at any news.
   Hie you to church; I must another way,
   To fetch a ladder, by the which your love
   Must climb a bird's nest soon when it is dark;
   I am the drudge, and toil in your delight;
   But you shall bear the burthen soon at night.
   Go; I'll to dinner; hie you to the cell.

JULIET. Hie to high fortune! Honest nurse, farewell.

                        [*Exeunt.*

SCENE VI — FRIAR LAURENCE'S *cell.*

Enter FRIAR LAURENCE *and* ROMEO.]

FRIAR LAURENCE. So smile the heavens upon this holy act
   That after-hours with sorrow chide us not!

ROMEO. Amen, amen! but come what sorrow can,
   It cannot countervail the exchange of joy
   That one short minute gives me in her sight:
   Do thou but close our hands with holy words,
   Then love-devouring death do what he dare,
   It is enough I may but call her mine.

FRIAR LAURENCE. These violent delights have violent ends,
   And in their triumph die; like fire and powder
   Which as they kiss consume: the sweetest honey
   Is loathsome in his own deliciousness,
   And in the taste confounds the appetite:
   Therefore, love moderately; long love doth so;
   Too swift arrives as tardy as too slow.

Enter JULIET.]

   Here comes the lady. O, so light a foot
   Will ne'er wear out the everlasting flint.
   A lover may bestride the gossamer
   That idles in the wanton summer air,
   And yet not fall; so light is vanity.

JULIET. Good even to my ghostly confessor.

FRIAR LAURENCE. Romeo shall thank thee, daughter, for us
    both.

JULIET. As much to him, else is his thanks too much.
ROMEO. Ah, Juliet, if the measure of thy joy
    Be heap'd like mine, and that thy skill be more
    To blazon it, then sweeten with thy breath
    This neighbor air, and let rich music's tongue
    Unfold the imagined happiness that both
    Receive in either by this dear encounter.
JULIET. Conceit, more rich in matter than in words,
    Brags of his substance, not of ornament:
    They are but beggars that can count their worth;
    But my true love is grown to such excess,
    I cannot sum up sum of half my wealth.
FRIAR LAURENCE. Come, come with me, and we will make
    short work;
    For, by your leaves, you shall not stay alone
    Till holy church incorporate two in one.   *[Exeunt.*

ACT III

Scene I — *A public place.*

Enter MERCUTIO, BENVOLIO, PAGE, *and* SERVANTS.]

BENVOLIO. I pray thee, good Mercutio, let's retire:
The day is hot, the Capulets abroad,
And, if we meet, we shall not 'scape a brawl;
For now these hot days is the mad blood stirring.

MERCUTIO. Thou art like one of those fellows that when he
enters the confines of a tavern claps me his sword upon the
table, and says 'God send me no need of thee!' and by the
operation of the second cup draws it on the drawer, when
indeed there is no need.

BENVOLIO. Am I like such a fellow?

MERCUTIO. Come, come, thou art as hot a Jack in thy mood as
any in Italy, and as soon moved to be moody, and as soon
moody to be moved.

BENVOLIO. And what to?

MERCUTIO. Nay, an there were two such, we should have none
shortly, for one would kill the other. Thou! why, thou wilt
quarrel with a man that hath a hair more, or a hair less, in
his beard than thou hast: thou wilt quarrel with a man for
cracking nuts, having no other reason but because thou
hast hazel eyes; what eye, but such an eye, would spy out
such a quarrel? thy head is as full of quarrels as an egg is
full of meat, and yet thy head hath been beaten as addle
as an egg for quarreling: thou hast quarreled with a man
for coughing in the street, because he hath wakened thy
dog that hath lain asleep in the sun: didst thou not fall out
with a tailor for wearing his new doublet before Easter?
with another, for tying his new shoes with old riband? and
yet thou wilt tutor me from quarreling!

BENVOLIO. An I were so apt to quarrel as thou art, any man
should buy the fee-simple of my life for an hour and a
quarter.

MERCUTIO. The fee-simple! O simple!

Enter TYBALT *and others.*]

BENVOLIO. By my head, here come the Capulets.

MERCUTIO. By my heel, I care not.

TYBALT. Follow me close, for I will speak to them.
Gentlemen, good den: a word with one of you.

MERCUTIO. And but one word with one of us? couple it with
something; make it a word and a blow.

TYBALT. You shall find me apt enough to that, sir, an you will
give me occasion.

MERCUTIO. Could you not take some occasion without giving?

TYBALT. Mercutio, thou consort'st with Romeo,—

MERCUTIO. Consort! what, dost thou make us minstrels? an
thou make minstrels of us, look to hear nothing but discords: here's my fiddlestick; here's that shall make you
dance. 'Zounds, consort!

BENVOLIO. We talk here in the public haunt of men:
Either withdraw into some private place,
Or reason coldly of your grievances,
Or else depart; here all eyes gaze on us.

MERCUTIO. Men's eyes were made to look, and let them gaze;
I will not budge for no man's pleasure, I.

Enter ROMEO.]

TYBALT. Well, peace be with you, sir: here comes my man.

MERCUTIO. But I'll be hang'd, sir, if he wear your livery:
Marry, go before to field, he'll be your follower;
Your worship in that sense may call him man.

TYBALT. Romeo, the love I bear thee can afford
No better term than this,—thou art a villain.

ROMEO. Tybalt, the reason that I have to love thee
Doth much excuse the appertaining rage
To such a greeting: villain am I none;
Therefore farewell; I see thou know'st me not.

TYBALT. Boy, this shall not excuse the injuries
That thou hast done me; therefore turn and draw.

ROMEO. I do protest, I never injured thee.
But love thee better than thou canst devise
Till thou shalt know the reason of my love:
And so, good Capulet,—which name I tender
As dearly as mine own,—be satisfied.

MERCUTIO. O calm, dishonorable, vile submission!
Alla stoccata carries it away.   [*Draws.*
Tybalt, you rat-catcher, will you walk?

TYBALT. What wouldst thou have with me?

MERCUTIO. Good king of cats, nothing but one of your nine
lives, that I mean to make bold withal, and, as you shall

use me hereafter, dry-beat the rest of the eight. Will you
pluck your sword out of his pilcher by the ears? make haste,
lest mine be about your ears ere it be out.

TYBALT. I am for you.   [Drawing.

ROMEO. Gentle Mercutio, put thy rapier up.

MERCUTIO. Come, sir, your passado.   [They fight.

ROMEO. Draw, Benvolio; beat down their weapons.
Gentlemen, for shame, forbear this outrage!
Tybalt, Mercutio, the prince expressly hath
Forbid this bandying in Verona streets:
Hold, Tybalt! good Mercutio!

> [TYBALT under ROMEO's arm stabs MERCUTIO
> and flies with his followers.

MERCUTIO.   I am hurt;
A plague o' both your houses! I am sped:
Is he gone, and hath nothing?

BENVOLIO.   What, art thou hurt?

MERCUTIO. Aye, aye, a scratch, a scratch; marry, 'tis enough.
Where is my page? Go, villain, fetch a surgeon.

> [Exit PAGE.

ROMEO. Courage, man; the hurt cannot be much.

MERCUTIO. No, 'tis not so deep as a well, nor so wide as a
church-door; but 'tis enough, 'twill serve: ask for me to-
morrow, and you shall find me a grave man. I am pep-
pered, I warrant, for this world. A plague o' both your
houses! 'Zounds, a dog, a rat, a mouse, a cat, to scratch a
man to death! a braggart, a rogue, a villain, that fights by
the book of arithmetic! Why the devil came you between
us? I was hurt under your arm.

ROMEO. I thought all for the best.

MERCUTIO. Help me into some house, Benvolio,
Or I shall faint. A plague o' both your houses!
They have made worms' meat of me: I have it,
And soundly too: your houses!

> [Exeunt MERCUTIO and BENVOLIO.

ROMEO. This gentleman, the prince's near ally,
My very friend, hath got this mortal hurt
In my behalf; my reputation stain'd
With Tybalt's slander,—Tybalt, that an hour
Hath been my kinsman: O sweet Juliet,
Thy beauty hath made me effeminate,
And in my temper soften'd valor's steel!

Re-enter BENVOLIO.]

BENVOLIO. O Romeo, Romeo, brave Mercutio's dead!
    That gallant spirit hath aspired the clouds,
    Which too untimely here did scorn the earth.

ROMEO. This day's black fate on more days doth depend;
    This but begins the woe others must end.

Re-enter TYBALT.]

BENVOLIO. Here comes the furious Tybalt back again.

ROMEO. Alive, in triumph! and Mercutio slain!
    Away to heaven, respective lenity,
    And fire-eyed fury be my conduct now!
    Now, Tybalt, take the 'villain' back again
    That late thou gavest me; for Mercutio's soul
    Is but a little way above our heads,
    Staying for thine to keep him company:
    Either thou, or I, or both, must go with him.

TYBALT. Thou, wretched boy, that didst consort him here,
    Shalt with him hence.

ROMEO.   This shall determine that.
                   [*They fight;* TYBALT *falls.*

BENVOLIO. Romeo, away, be gone!
    The citizens are up, and Tybalt slain:
    Stand not amazed: the prince will doom thee death
    If thou art taken: hence, be gone, away!

ROMEO. O, I am fortune's fool!

BENVOLIO. Why dost thou stay?   [*Exit* ROMEO.

Enter CITIZENS, *&c.*]

FIRST CITIZEN. Which way ran he that kill'd Mercutio?
    Tybalt, that murderer, which way ran he?

BENVOLIO. There lies that Tybalt.

FIRST CITIZEN.   Up, sir, go with me;
    I charge thee in the prince's name, obey.

Enter PRINCE, *attended;* MONTAGUE, CAPULET,
      their WIVES, *and others.*]

PRINCE. Where are the vile beginners of this fray?

BENVOLIO. O noble prince, I can discover all.
    The unlucky manage of this fatal brawl:
    There lies the man, slain by young Romeo,
    That slew thy kinsman, brave Mercutio.

LADY CAPULET. Tybalt, my cousin! O my brother's child!
    O prince! O cousin! husband! O, blood is spilt
    Of my dear kinsman! Prince, as thou art true,

For blood of ours, shed blood of Montague.
O cousin, cousin!

PRINCE. Benvolio, who began this bloody fray?

BENVOLIO. Tybalt, here slain, whom Romeo's hand did slay;
Romeo that spoke him fair, bid him bethink
How nice the quarrel was, and urged withal
Your high displeasure: all this uttered
With gentle breath, calm look, knees humbly bow'd,
Could not take truce with the unruly spleen
Of Tybalt deaf to peace, but that he tilts
With piercing steel at bold Mercutio's breast;
Who, all as hot, turns deadly point to point,
And, with a martial scorn, with one hand beats
Cold death aside, and with the other sends
It back to Tybalt, whose dexterity
Retorts it: Romeo he cries aloud,
'Hold, friends! friends, part!' and, swifter than his tongue,
His agile arm beats down their fatal points,
And 'twixt them rushes; underneath whose arm
An envious thrust from Tybalt hit the life
Of stout Mercutio, and then Tybalt fled:
But by and by comes back to Romeo,
Who had but newly entertain'd revenge,
And to 't they go like lightning: for, ere I
Could draw to part them, was stout Tybalt slain;
And, as he fell, did Romeo turn and fly;
This is the truth, or let Benvolio die.

LADY CAPULET. He is a kinsman to the Montague,
Affection makes him false, he speaks not true:
Some twenty of them fought in this black strife,
And all those twenty could but kill one life.
I beg for justice, which thou, prince, must give;
Romeo slew Tybalt, Romeo must not live.

PRINCE. Romeo slew him, he slew Mercutio;
Who now the price of his dear blood doth owe?

MONTAGUE. Not Romeo, prince, he was Mercutio's friend;
His fault concludes but what the law should end,
The life of Tybalt.

PRINCE.   And for that offense
Immediately we do exile him hence:
I have an interest in your hate's proceeding,
My blood for your rude brawls doth lie a-bleeding;

But I'll amerce you with so strong a fine,
That you shall all repent the loss of mine:
I will be deaf to pleading and excuses;
Nor tears nor prayers shall purchase out abuses:
Therefore use none: let Romeo hence in haste,
Else, when he's found, that hour is his last.
Bear hence this body, and attend our will:
Mercy but murders, pardoning those that kill.   [*Exeunt.*

SCENE II — CAPULET's *orchard.*

Enter JULIET.]

JULIET. Gallop apace, you fiery-footed steeds,
   Towards Phœbus' lodging: such a wagoner
As Phaethon would whip you to the west,
And bring in cloudy night immediately.
Spread thy close curtain, love-performing night,
That runaways' eyes may wink, and Romeo
Leap to these arms, untalk'd of and unseen.
Lovers can see to do their amorous rites
By their own beauties; or, if love be blind,
It best agrees with night. Come, civil night,
Thou sober-suited matron, all in black,
And learn me how to lose a winning match,
Play'd for a pair of stainless maidenhoods:
Hood my unmann'd blood bating in my cheeks
With thy black mantle, till strange love grown bold
Think true love acted simple modesty.
Come, night, come, Romeo, come, thou day in night;
For thou wilt lie upon the wings of night
Whiter than new snow on a raven's back.
Come, gentle night, come, loving, black-brow'd night,
Give me my Romeo; and, when he shall die,
Take him and cut him out in little stars,
And he will make the face of heaven so fine,
That all the world will be in love with night,
And pay no worship to the garish sun.
O, I have bought the mansion of a love,
But not possess'd it, and, though I am sold,
Not yet enjoy'd; so tedious is this day
As is the night before some festival
To an impatient child that hath new robes

And may not wear them. O, here comes my nurse,
And she brings news, and every tongue that speaks
But Romeo's name speaks heavenly eloquence.

Enter NURSE, *with cords.*]

Now, nurse, what news? What hast thou there? the cords
That Romeo bid thee fetch?

NURSE.   Aye, aye, the cords.   [*Throws them down.*
JULIET. Aye me! what news? why dost thou wring thy hands?
NURSE. Ah, well-a-day! he's dead, he's dead, he's dead.
We are undone, lady, we are undone.
Alack the day! he's gone, he's kill'd, he's dead.
JULIET. Can heaven be so envious?
NURSE.   Romeo can,
Though heaven cannot. O Romeo, Romeo!
Who ever would have thought it? Romeo!
JULIET. What devil art thou that dost torment me thus?
This torture should be roar'd in dismal hell.
Hath Romeo slain himself? say thou but 'I,'
And that bare vowel 'I' shall poison more
Than the death-darting eye of cockatrice:
I am not I, if there be such an I,
Or those eyes shut, that make thee answer 'I.'
If he be slain, say 'I'; or if not, no:
Brief sounds determine of my weal or woe.
NURSE. I saw the wound, I saw it with mine eyes—
God save the mark!—here on his manly breast:
A piteous corse, a bloody piteous corse;
Pale, pale as ashes, all bedaub'd in blood,
All in gore blood: I swounded at the sight.
JULIET. O, break, my heart! poor bankrupt, break at once!
To prison, eyes, ne'er look on liberty!
Vile earth, to earth resign, end motion here,
And thou and Romeo press one heavy bier!
NURSE. O Tybalt, Tybalt, the best friend I had!
O courteous Tybalt! honest gentleman!
That ever I should live to see thee dead!
JULIET. What storm is this that blows so contrary?
Is Romeo slaughter'd, and is Tybalt dead?
My dear-loved cousin, and my dearer lord?
Then, dreadful trumpet, sound the general doom!
For who is living, if those two are gone?
NURSE. Tybalt is gone, and Romeo banished;

    Romeo that kill'd him, he is banished.

JULIET. O God! did Romeo's hand shed Tybalt's blood?

NURSE. It did, it did; alas the day, it did!

JULIET. O serpent heart, hid with a flowering face!
    Did ever dragon keep so fair a cave?
    Beautiful tyrant! fiend angelical!
    Dove-feather'd raven! wolvish-ravening lamb!
    Despised substance of divinest show!
    Just opposite to what thou justly seem'st,
    A damned saint, an honorable villain!
    O nature, what hadst thou to do in hell,
    When thou didst bower the spirit of a fiend
    In mortal paradise of such sweet flesh?
    Was ever book containing such vile matter
    So fairly bound? O, that deceit should dwell
    In such a gorgeous palace!

NURSE.   There's no trust,
    No faith, no honesty in men; all perjured,
    All forsworn, all naught, all dissemblers.
    Ah, where's my man? give me some aqua vitæ:
    These griefs, these woes, these sorrows make me old.
    Shame come to Romeo!

JULIET. Blister'd be thy tongue
    For such a wish! he was not born to shame:
    Upon his brow shame is ashamed to sit;
    For 'tis a throne where honor may be crown'd
    Sole monarch of the universal earth.
    O, what a beast was I to chide at him!

NURSE. Will you speak well of him that kill'd your cousin?

JULIET. Shall I speak ill of him that is my husband?
    Ah, poor my lord, what tongue shall smooth thy name,
    When I, thy three-hours wife, have mangled it?
    But wherefore, villain, didst thou kill my cousin?
    That villain cousin would have kill'd my husband:
    Back, foolish tears, back to your native spring;
    Your tributary drops belong to woe,
    Which you mistaking offer up to joy.
    My husband lives, that Tybalt would have slain;
    And Tybalt's dead, that would have slain my husband:
    All this is comfort; wherefore weep I then?
    Some word there was, worser than Tybalt's death,
    That murder'd me: I would forget it fain;

But, O, it presses to my memory,
Like damned guilty deeds to sinners' minds:
'Tybalt is dead, and Romeo banished;'
That 'banished,' that one word 'banished,'
Hath slain ten thousand Tybalts. Tybalt's death
Was woe enough, if it had ended there:
Or, if sour woe delights in fellowship,
And needly will be rank'd with other griefs,
Why follow'd not, when she said 'Tybalt's dead,'
Thy father, or thy mother, nay, or both,
Which modern lamentation might have moved?
But with a rear-ward following Tybalt's death,
'Romeo is banished:' to speak that word,
Is father, mother, Tybalt, Romeo, Juliet,
All slain, all dead. 'Romeo is banished.'
There is no end, no limit, measure, bound,
In that word's death; no words can that woe sound.
Where is my father, and my mother, nurse?
NURSE. Weeping and wailing over Tybalt's corse:
Will you go to them? I will bring you thither.
JULIET. Wash they his wounds with tears: mine shall be spent,
When theirs are dry, for Romeo's banishment.
Take up those cords: poor ropes, you are beguiled,
Both you and I; for Romeo is exiled:
He made you for a highway to my bed;
But I, a maid, die maiden-widowed.
Come, cords; come, nurse; I'll do my wedding-bed;
And death, not Romeo, take my maidenhead!
NURSE. Hie to your chamber: I'll find Romeo
To comfort you: I wot well where he is.
Hark ye, your Romeo will be here at night:
I'll to him; he is hid at Laurence' cell.
JULIET. O, find him! give this ring to my true knight,
And bid him come to take his last farewell.   [Exeunt.

SCENE III — FRIAR LAURENCE'S cell.

Enter FRIAR LAURENCE.]
FRIAR LAURENCE. Romeo, come forth; come forth, thou fearful
    man:
Affliction is enamor'd of thy parts,
And thou art wedded to calamity.

Enter ROMEO.]

ROMEO. Father, what news? what is the prince's doom?
  What sorrow craves acquaintance at my hand,
  That I yet know not?

FRIAR LAURENCE.   Too familiar
  Is my dear son with such sour company:
  I bring thee tidings of the prince's doom.

ROMEO. What less than dooms-day is the prince's doom?

FRIAR LAURENCE. A gentler judgment vanish'd from his lips,
  Not body's death, but body's banishment.

ROMEO. Ha, banishment! be merciful, say 'death;'
  For exile hath more terror in his look,
  Much more than death: do not say 'banishment.'

FRIAR LAURENCE. Here from Verona art thou banished:
  Be patient, for the world is broad and wide.

ROMEO. There is no world without Verona walls,
  But purgatory, torture, hell itself.
  Hence banished is banish'd from the world,
  And world's exile is death: then 'banished'
  Is death mis-term'd: calling death 'banished,'
  Thou cut'st my head off with a golden axe,
  And smilest upon the stroke that murders me.

FRIAR LAURENCE. O deadly sin! O rude unthankfulness!
  Thy fault our law calls death; but the kind prince,
  Taking thy part, hath rush'd aside the law,
  And turn'd that black word death to banishment:
  This is dear mercy, and thou seest it not.

ROMEO. 'Tis torture, and not mercy: heaven is here,
  Where Juliet lives; and every cat and dog
  And little mouse, every unworthy thing,
  Live here in heaven and may look on her,
  But Romeo may not: more validity,
  More honorable state, more courtship lives
  In carrion-flies than Romeo: they may seize
  On the white wonder of dear Juliet's hand,
  And steal immortal blessing from her lips;
  Who, even in pure and vestal modesty,
  Still blush, as thinking their own kisses sin;
  But Romeo may not; he is banished:
  This may flies do, but I from this must fly:
  They are free men, but I am banished:
  And say'st thou yet, that exile is not death?

Hadst thou no poison mix'd, no sharp-ground knife,
No sudden mean of death, though ne'er so mean,
But 'banished' to kill me?—'Banished'?
O friar, the damned use that word in hell;
Howling attends it: how hast thou the heart,
Being a divine, a ghostly confessor,
A sin-absolver, and my friend profess'd,
To mangle me with that word 'banished'?

FRIAR LAURENCE. Thou fond mad man, hear me but speak a
word.

ROMEO. O, thou wilt speak again of banishment.

FRIAR LAURENCE. I'll give thee armor to keep off that word;
Adversity's sweet milk, philosophy,
To comfort thee, though thou art banished.

ROMEO. Yet 'banished'? Hang up philosophy!
Unless philosophy can make a Juliet,
Displant a town, reverse a prince's doom,
It helps not, it prevails not: talk no more.

FRIAR LAURENCE. O, then I see that madmen have no ears.

ROMEO. How should they, when that wise men have no eyes?

FRIAR LAURENCE. Let me dispute with thee of thy estate.

ROMEO. Thou canst not speak of that thou dost not feel:
Wert thou as young as I, Juliet thy love,
An hour but married, Tybalt murdered,
Doting like me, and like me banished,
Then might'st thou speak, then might'st thou tear thy hair,
And fall upon the ground, as I do now,
Taking the measure of an unmade grave.

[Knocking within.

FRIAR LAURENCE. Arise; one knocks; good Romeo, hide thyself.

ROMEO. Not I; unless the breath of heart-sick groans
Mist-like infold me from the search of eyes.   [Knocking.

FRIAR LAURENCE. Hark, how they knock! Who's there? Romeo
arise;
Thou wilt be taken.—Stay awhile!—Stand up; [Knocking.
Run to my study.—By and by!—God's will,
What simpleness is this!—I come, I come!   [Knocking.
Who knocks so hard? whence come you? what's your will?

NURSE. [Within] Let me come in, and you shall know my
errand;
I come from Lady Juliet.

FRIAR LAURENCE.   Welcome, then.

Enter NURSE.]

NURSE. O holy friar, O, tell me, holy friar,
    Where is my lady's lord, where's Romeo?
FRIAR LAURENCE. There on the ground, with his own tears
    made drunk.
NURSE. O, he is even in my mistress' case,
    Just in her case!
FRIAR LAURENCE. O woeful sympathy!
    Piteous predicament!
NURSE.   Even so lies she,
    Blubbering and weeping, weeping and blubbering.
    Stand up, stand up; stand, an you be a man:
    For Juliet's sake, for her sake, rise and stand;
    Why should you fall into so deep an O?
ROMEO. Nurse!
NURSE. Ah sir! ah sir! Well, death's the end of all.
ROMEO. Spakest thou of Juliet? how is it with her?
    Doth she not think me an old murderer,
    Now I have stain'd the childhood of our joy
    With blood removed but little from her own?
    Where is she? and how doth she? and what says
    My conceal'd lady to our cancel'd love?
NURSE. O, she says nothing, sir, but weeps and weeps;
    And now falls on her bed; and then starts up,
    And Tybalt calls; and then on Romeo cries,
    And then down falls again.
ROMEO.   As if that name,
    Shot from the deadly level of a gun,
    Did murder her, as that name's cursed hand
    Murder'd her kinsman. O, tell me, friar, tell me,
    In what vile part of this anatomy
    Doth my name lodge? tell me, that I may sack
    The hateful mansion.   [*Drawing his sword.*
FRIAR LAURENCE.   Hold thy desperate hand:
    Art thou a man? thy form cries out thou art:
    Thy tears are womanish; thy wild acts denote
    The unreasonable fury of a beast:
    Unseemly woman in a seeming man!
    Or ill-beseeming beast in seeming both!
    Thou hast amazed me: by my holy order,
    I thought thy disposition better temper'd.
    Hast thou slain Tybalt? wilt thou slay thyself?

And slay thy lady that in thy life lives,
By doing damned hate upon thyself?
Why rail'st thou on thy birth, the heaven and earth?
Since birth and heaven and earth, all three do meet
In thee at once, which thou at once wouldst lose.
Fie, fie, thou shamest thy shape, thy love, thy wit;
Which, like a usurer, abound'st in all,
And usest none in that true use indeed
Which should bedeck thy shape, thy love, thy wit:
Thy noble shape is but a form of wax,
Digressing from the valor of a man;
Thy dear love sworn, but hollow perjury,
Killing that love which thou hast vow'd to cherish;
Thy wit, that ornament to shape and love,
Mis-shapen in the conduct of them both,
Like powder in a skilless soldier's flask,
Is set a-fire by thine own ignorance,
And thou dismember'd with thine own defense.
What, rouse thee, man! thy Juliet is alive,
For whose dear sake thou wast but lately dead;
There art thou happy: Tybalt would kill thee,
But thou slew'st Tybalt; there art thou happy too:
The law, that threaten'd death, becomes thy friend,
And turns it to exile; there art thou happy:
A pack of blessings lights upon thy back;
Happiness courts thee in her best array;
But, like a misbehaved and sullen wench,
Thou pout'st upon thy fortune and thy love:
Take heed, take heed, for such die miserable.
Go, get thee to thy love, as was decreed,
Ascend her chamber, hence and comfort her:
But look thou stay not till the watch be set,
For then thou canst not pass to Mantua;
Where thou shalt live till we can find a time
To blaze your marriage, reconcile your friends,
Beg pardon of the prince, and call thee back
With twenty hundred thousand times more joy
Than thou went'st forth in lamentation.
Go before, nurse: commend me to thy lady,
And bid her hasten all the house to bed,
Which heavy sorrow makes them apt unto:
Romeo is coming.

NURSE. O Lord, I could have stay'd here all the night
  To hear good counsel: O, what learning is!
  My lord, I'll tell my lady you will come.
ROMEO. Do so, and bid my sweet prepare to chide.
NURSE. Here, sir, a ring she bid me give you, sir:
  Hie you, make haste, for it grows very late.   [*Exit.*
ROMEO. How well my comfort is revived by this!
FRIAR LAURENCE. Go hence; good night; and here stands all
    your state:
  Either be gone before the watch be set,
  Or by the break of day disguised from hence:
  Sojourn in Mantua; I'll find out your man,
  And he shall signify from time to time
  Every good hap to you that chances here:
  Give me thy hand; 'tis late: farewell; good night.
ROMEO. But that a joy past joy calls out on me,
  It were a grief, so brief to part with thee:
  Farewell.   [*Exeunt.*

SCENE IV — *A room in* CAPULET'S *house.*

Enter CAPULET, LADY CAPULET, *and* PARIS.]
CAPULET. Things have fall'n out, sir, so unluckily,
  That we have had no time to move our daughter.
  Look you, she loved her kinsman Tybalt dearly,
  And so did I. Well, we were born to die.
  'Tis very late; she'll not come down to-night:
  I promise you, but for your company,
  I would have been a-bed an hour ago.
PARIS. These times of woe afford no time to woo.
  Madam, good night; commend me to your daughter.
LADY CAPULET. I will, and know her mind early to-morrow;
  To-night she's mew'd up to her heaviness.
CAPULET. Sir Paris, I will make a desperate tender
  Of my child's love: I think she will be ruled
  In all respects by me; nay more, I doubt it not.
  Wife, go you to her ere you go to bed;
  Acquaint her here of my son Paris' love;
  And bid her, mark you me, on Wednesday next—
  But, soft! what day is this?
PARIS.   Monday, my lord.
CAPULET. Monday! ha, ha! Well, Wednesday is too soon;

O' Thursday let it be: o' Thursday, tell her,
She shall be married to this noble earl.
Will you be ready? do you like this haste?
We'll keep no great ado; a friend or two;
For, hark you, Tybalt being slain so late,
It may be thought we held him carelessly,
Being our kinsman, if we revel much:
Therefore we'll have some half-a-dozen friends,
And there an end. But what say you to Thursday?
PARIS. My lord, I would that Thursday were to-morrow.
CAPULET. Well, get you gone: o' Thursday be it then.
Go you to Juliet ere you go to bed,
Prepare her, wife, against this wedding-day.
Farewell, my lord. Light to my chamber, ho!
Afore me, it is so very very late,
That we may call it early by and by:
Good night.   [*Exeunt.*

SCENE V — CAPULET's *orchard.*

Enter ROMEO *and* JULIET, *above, at the window.*]
JULIET. Wilt thou be gone? it is not yet near day:
It was the nightingale, and not the lark,
That pierced the fearful hollow of thine ear;
Nightly she sings on yond pomegranate-tree:
Believe me, love, it was the nightingale.
ROMEO. It was the lark, the herald of the morn,
No nightingale: look, love, what envious streaks
Do lace the severing clouds in yonder east:
Night's candles are burnt out, and jocund day
Stands tiptoe on the misty mountain tops:
I must be gone and live, or stay and die.
JULIET. Yond light is not day-light, I know it, I:
It is some meteor that the sun exhales,
To be to thee this night a torch-bearer,
And light thee on thy way to Mantua:
Therefore stay yet; thou need'st not to be gone.
ROMEO. Let me be ta'en, let me be put to death;
I am content, so thou wilt have it so.
I'll say yon gray is not the morning's eyes,
'Tis but the pale reflex of Cynthia's brow;
Nor that is not the lark, whose notes do beat

The vaulty heaven so high above our heads:
I have more care to stay than will to go:
Come, death, and welcome! Juliet wills it so.
How is't, my soul? let's talk: it is not day.
JULIET. It is, it is: hie hence, be gone, away!
It is the lark that sings so out of tune,
Straining harsh discords and unpleasing sharps.
Some say the lark makes sweet division;
This doth not so, for she divideth us:
Some say the lark and loathed toad change eyes;
O, now I would they had changed voices too!
Since arm from arm that voice doth us affray,
Hunting thee hence with hunts-up to the day.
O, now be gone; more light and light it grows.
ROMEO. More light and light: more dark and dark our woes!
Enter NURSE, *to the chamber.*]
NURSE. Madam!
JULIET. Nurse?
NURSE. Your lady mother is coming to your chamber:
The day is broke; be wary, look about.   [*Exit.*
JULIET. Then, window, let day in, and let life out.
ROMEO. Farewell, farewell! one kiss, and I'll descend.
                                              [*Descends.*
JULIET. Art thou gone so? my lord, my love, my friend!
I must hear from thee every day in the hour,
For in a minute there are many days:
O, by this count I shall be much in years
Ere I again behold my Romeo!
ROMEO. Farewell!
I will omit no opportunity
That may convey my greetings, love, to thee.
JULIET. O, think'st thou we shall ever meet again?
ROMEO. I doubt it not; and all these woes shall serve
For sweet discourses in our time to come.
JULIET. O God! I have an ill-divining soul.
Methinks I see thee, now thou art below,
As one dead in the bottom of a tomb:
Either my eyesight fails or thou look'st pale.
ROMEO. And trust me, love, in my eye so do you:
Dry sorrow drinks our blood. Adieu, adieu!   [*Exit.*
JULIET. O fortune, fortune! all men call thee fickle:
If thou art fickle, what dost thou with him

That is renown'd for faith? Be fickle, fortune;
For then, I hope, thou wilt not keep him long,
But send him back.

LADY CAPULET. [*Within*] Ho, daughter! are you up?

JULIET. Who is't that calls? it is my lady mother!
Is she not down so late, or up so early?
What unaccustom'd cause procures her hither?

Enter LADY CAPULET.]

LADY CAPULET. Why, how now, Juliet!

JULIET.   Madam, I am not well.

LADY CAPULET. Evermore weeping for your cousin's death?
What, wilt thou wash him from his grave with tears?
An if thou couldst, thou couldst not make him live;
Therefore have done: some grief shows much of love,
But much of grief shows still some want of wit.

JULIET. Yet let me weep for such a feeling loss.

LADY CAPULET. So shall you feel the loss, but not the friend
Which you weep for.

JULIET.   Feeling so the loss,
I cannot choose but ever weep the friend.

LADY CAPULET. Well, girl, thou weep'st not so much for his
death
As that the villain lives which slaughter'd him.

JULIET. What villain, madam?

LADY CAPULET.   That same villain, Romeo.

JULIET. [*Aside*] Villain and he be many miles asunder.
God pardon him! I do, with all my heart;
And yet no man like he doth grieve my heart.

LADY CAPULET. That is because the traitor murderer lives.

JULIET. Aye, madam, from the reach of these my hands:
Would none but I might venge my cousin's death!

LADY CAPULET. We will have vengeance for it, fear thou not:
Then weep no more. I'll send to one in Mantua,
Where that same banish'd runagate doth live,
Shall give him such an unaccustom'd dram
That he shall soon keep Tybalt company:
And then, I hope, thou wilt be satisfied.

JULIET. Indeed, I never shall be satisfied
With Romeo, till I behold him—dead—
Is my poor heart so for a kinsman vex'd.
Madam, if you could find out but a man
To bear a poison, I would temper it,

That Romeo should, upon receipt thereof,
Soon sleep in quiet. O, how my heart abhors
To hear him named, and cannot come to him,
To wreck the love I bore my cousin
Upon his body that hath slaughter'd him!

LADY CAPULET. Find thou the means, and I'll find such a man.
But now I'll tell thee joyful tidings, girl.

JULIET. And joy comes well in such a needy time:
What are they, I beseech your ladyship?

LADY CAPULET. Well, well, thou hast a careful father, child;
One who, to put thee from thy heaviness,
Hath sorted out a sudden day of joy,
That thou expect'st not, nor I look'd not for.

JULIET. Madam, in happy time, what day is that?

LADY CAPULET. Marry, my child, early next Thursday morn,
The gallant, young, and noble gentleman,
The County Paris, at Saint Peter's Church,
Shall happily make thee there a joyful bride.

JULIET. Now, by Saint Peter's Church, and Peter too,
He shall not make me there a joyful bride.
I wonder at this haste; that I must wed
Ere he that should be husband comes to woo.
I pray you, tell my lord and father, madam,
I will not marry yet; and, when I do, I swear,
It shall be Romeo, whom you know I hate,
Rather than Paris. These are news indeed!

LADY CAPULET. Here comes your father; tell him so yourself,
And see how he will take it at your hands.

Enter CAPULET *and* NURSE.]

CAPULET. When the sun sets, the air doth drizzle dew;
But for the sunset of my brother's son
It rains downright.
How now! a conduit, girl? what, still in tears?
Evermore showering? In one little body
Thou counterfeit'st a bark, a sea, a wind:
For still thy eyes, which I may call the sea,
Do ebb and flow with tears; the bark thy body is,
Sailing in this salt flood; the winds, thy sighs;
Who raging with thy tears, and they with them,
Without a sudden calm will overset
Thy tempest-tossed body. How now, wife!
Have you deliver'd to her our decree?

LADY CAPULET. Aye, sir; but she will none, she gives you
      thanks.
   I would the fool were married to her grave!
CAPULET. Soft! take me with you, take me with you, wife,
      How! will she none? doth she not give us thanks?
      Is she not proud? doth she not count her blest,
      Unworthy as she is, that we have wrought
      So worthy a gentleman to be her bridegroom?
JULIET. Not proud, you have, but thankful that you have:
      Proud can I never be of what I hate;
      But thankful even for hate that is meant love.
CAPULET. How, how! how, how! chop-logic! What is this?
      'Proud,' and 'I thank you,' and 'I thank you not;'
      And yet 'not proud:' mistress minion, you,
      Thank me no thankings, nor proud me no prouds,
      But fettle your fine joints 'gainst Thursday next,
      To go with Paris to Saint Peter's Church,
      Or I will drag thee on a hurdle thither.
      Out, you green-sickness carrion! out, you baggage!
      You tallow-face!
LADY CAPULET.   Fie, fie! what, are you mad?
JULIET. Good father, I beseech you on my knees,
      Hear me with patience but to speak a word.
CAPULET. Hang thee, young baggage! disobedient wretch!
      I tell thee what: get thee to church o' Thursday,
      Or never after look me in the face:
      Speak not, reply not, do not answer me;
      My fingers itch. Wife, we scarce thought us blest
      That God had lent us but this only child;
      But now I see this one is one too much,
      And that we have a curse in having her:
      Out on her, hilding!
NURSE.   God in heaven bless her!
      You are to blame, my lord, to rate her so.
CAPULET. And why, my lady wisdom? hold your tongue,
      Good prudence; smatter with your gossips, go.
NURSE. I speak no treason.
CAPULET.   O, God ye god-den.
NURSE. May not one speak?
CAPULET.   Peace, you mumbling fool!
      Utter you gravity o'er a gossip's bowl;
      For here we need it not.

LADY CAPULET. You are too hot.
CAPULET. God's bread! it makes me mad:
  Day, night, hour, tide, time, work, play,
  Alone, in company, still my care hath been
  To have her match'd: and having now provided
  A gentleman of noble parentage,
  Of fair demesnes, youthful, and nobly train'd,
  Stuff'd, as they say, with honorable parts,
  Proportion'd as one's thought would wish a man;
  And then to have a wretched puling fool,
  A whining mammet, in her fortune's tender,
  To answer 'I'll not wed; I cannot love,
  I am too young; I pray you, pardon me.'
  But, an you will not wed, I'll pardon you:
  Graze where you will, you shall not house with me:
  Look to't, think on't, I do not use to jest.
  Thursday is near; lay hand on heart, advise:
  An you be mine, I'll give you to my friend;
  An you be not, hang, beg, starve, die in the streets
  For, by my soul, I'll ne'er acknowledge thee,
  Nor what is mine shall never do thee good:
  Trust to't, bethink you; I'll not be forsworn. [*Exit.*
JULIET. Is there no pity sitting in the clouds,
  That sees into the bottom of my grief?
  O, sweet my mother, cast me not away!
  Delay this marriage for a month, a week;
  Or, if you do not, make the bridal bed
  In that dim monument where Tybalt lies.
LADY CAPULET. Talk not to me, for I'll not speak a word:
  Do as thou wilt, for I have done with thee. [*Exit.*
JULIET. O God!—O nurse, how shall this be prevented?
  My husband is on earth, my faith in heaven;
  How shall that faith return again to earth,
  Unless that husband send it me from heaven
  By leaving earth? comfort me, counsel me.
  Alack, alack, that heaven should practice stratagems
  Upon so soft a subject as myself!
  What say'st thou? hast thou not a word of joy?
  Some comfort, nurse.
NURSE. Faith, here it is.
  Romeo is banish'd and all the world to nothing,
  That he dares ne'er come back to challenge you;

Or, if he do, it needs must be by stealth.
Then, since the case so stands as now it doth,
I think it best you married with the county.
O, he's a lovely gentleman!
Romeo's a dishclout to him: an eagle, madam,
Hath not so green, so quick, so fair an eye
As Paris hath. Beshrew my very heart,
I think you are happy in this second match,
For it excels your first: or if it did not,
Your first is dead, or 'twere as good he were
As living here and you no use of him.

JULIET. Speakest thou from thy heart?

NURSE.   And from my soul too;
Else beshrew them both.

JULIET.   Amen!

NURSE.   What?

JULIET. Well, thou hast comforted me marvelous much.
Go in, and tell my lady I am gone,
Having displeased my father, to Laurence' cell,
To make confession and to be absolved.

NURSE. Marry, I will, and this is wisely done.   [*Exit.*

JULIET. Ancient damnation! O most wicked fiend!
It is more sin to wish me thus forsworn,
Or to dispraise my lord with that same tongue
Which she hath praised him with above compare
So many thousand times? Go, counselor;
Thou and my bosom henceforth shall be twain.
I'll to the friar, to know his remedy:
If all else fail, myself have power to die.   [*Exit.*

ACT IV

S c e n e   I — Friar Laurence's *cell.*

Enter Friar Laurence *and* Paris.]

FRIAR LAURENCE. On Thursday, sir? the time is very short.

PARIS. My father Capulet will have it so;
  And I am nothing slow to slack his haste.

FRIAR LAURENCE You say you do not know the lady's mind:
  Uneven is the course; I like it not.

PARIS. Immoderately she weeps for Tybalt's death,
  And therefore have I little talk'd of love,
  For Venus smiles not in a house of tears.
  Now, sir, her father counts it dangerous
  That she doth give her sorrow so much sway,
  And in his wisdom hastes our marriage,
  To stop the inundation of her tears,
  Which, too much minded by herself alone,
  May be put from her by society:
  Now do you know the reason of this haste.

FRIAR LAURENCE. [*Aside*] I would I knew not why it should
    be slow'd.
  Look, sir, here comes the lady toward my cell.

Enter JULIET.]

PARIS. Happily met, my lady and my wife!

JULIET. That may be, sir, when I may be a wife.

PARIS. That may be must be, love, on Thursday next.

JULIET. What must be shall be.

FRIAR LAURENCE.   That's a certain text.

PARIS. Come you to make confession to this father?

JULIET. To answer that, I should confess to you.

PARIS. Do not deny to him that you love me.

JULIET. I will confess to you that I love him.

PARIS. So will ye, I am sure, that you love me.

JULIET. If I do so, it will be of more price,
  Being spoke behind your back, than to your face.

PARIS. Poor soul, thy face is much abused with tears.

JULIET. The tears have got small victory by that;
  For it was bad enough before their spite.

PARIS. Thou wrong'st it more than tears with that report.

JULIET. That is no slander, sir, which is a truth,
And what I spake, I spake it to my face.

PARIS. Thy face is mine, and thou hast slander'd it.

JULIET. It may be so, for it is not mine own.
Are you at leisure, holy father, now;
Or shall I come to you at evening mass?

FRIAR LAURENCE. My leisure serves me, pensive daughter, now.
My lord, we must entreat the time alone.

PARIS. God shield I should disturb devotion!
Juliet, on Thursday early will I rouse ye:
Till then, adieu, and keep this holy kiss.   [*Exit.*

JULIET. O, shut the door, and when thou hast done so,
Come weep with me; past hope, past cure, past help!

FRIAR LAURENCE. Ah, Juliet, I already know thy grief;
It strains me past the compass of my wits:
I hear thou must, and nothing may prorogue it,
On Thursday next be married to this county.

JULIET. Tell me not, friar, that thou hear'st of this,
Unless thou tell me how I may prevent it:
If in thy wisdom thou canst give no help,
Do thou but call my resolution wise,
And with this knife I'll help it presently.
God join'd my heart and Romeo's, thou our hands;
And ere this hand, by thee to Romeo's seal'd,
Shall be the label to another deed,
Or my true heart with treacherous revolt
Turn to another, this shall slay them both:
Therefore, out of thy long-experienced time,
Give me some present counsel; or, behold,
'Twixt my extremes and me this bloody knife
Shall play the umpire, arbitrating that
Which the commission of thy years and art
Could to no issue of true honor bring.
Be not so long to speak; I long to die,
If what thou speak'st speak not of remedy.

FRIAR LAURENCE. Hold, daughter: I do spy a kind of hope,
Which craves as desperate an execution
As that is desperate which we would prevent.
If, rather than to marry County Paris,
Thou hast the strength of will to slay thyself,

Then is it likely thou wilt undertake
A thing like death to chide away this shame,
That copest with death himself to 'scape from it;
And, if thou darest, I'll give thee remedy.

JULIET. O, bid me leap, rather than marry Paris,
From off the battlements of yonder tower;
Or walk in thievish ways; or bid me lurk
Where serpents are; chain me with roaring bears;
Or shut me nightly in a charnel-house,
O'er-cover'd quite with dead men's rattling bones,
With reeky shanks and yellow chapless skulls;
Or bid me go into a new-made grave,
And hide me with a dead man in his shroud;
Things that to hear them told, have made me tremble;
And I will do it without fear or doubt,
To live an unstain'd wife to my sweet love.

FRIAR LAURENCE. Hold, then; go home, be merry, give consent
To marry Paris Wednesday is to-morrow;
To-morrow night look that thou lie alone,
Let not thy nurse lie with thee in thy chamber:
Take thou this vial, being then in bed,
And this distilled liquor drink thou off:
When presently through all thy veins shall run
A cold and drowsy humor; for no pulse
Shall keep his native progress, but surcease:
No warmth, no breath, shall testify thou livest;
The roses in thy lips and cheeks shall fade
To paly ashes; thy eyes' windows fall,
Like death, when he shuts up the day of life;
Each part, deprived of supple government,
Shall, stiff and stark and cold, appear like death:
And in this borrow'd likeness of shrunk death
Thou shalt continue two and forty hours,
And then awake as from a pleasant sleep.
Now, when the bridegroom in the morning comes
To rouse thee from thy bed, there art thou dead:
Then, as the manner of our country is,
In thy best robes uncover'd on the bier
Thou shalt be borne to that same ancient vault
Where all the kindred of the Capulets lie.
In the mean time, against thou shalt awake,
Shall Romeo by my letters know our drift;

And hither shall he come: and he and I
Will watch thy waking, and that very night
Shall Romeo bear thee hence to Mantua.
And this shall free thee from this present shame,
If no inconstant toy nor womanish fear
Abate thy valor in the acting it.

JULIET. Give me, give me! O, tell me not of fear!

FRIAR LAURENCE. Hold; get you gone, be strong and pros-
    perous
In this resolve; I'll send a friar with speed
To Mantua, with my letters to thy lord.

JULIET. Love give me strength! and strength shall help afford.
    Farewell, dear father!   [*Exeunt.*

SCENE II — *Hall in* CAPULET'S *house.*

Enter CAPULET, LADY CAPULET, NURSE,
    and two SERVINGMEN.]

CAPULET. So many guests invite as here are writ.
                                [*Exit* FIRST SERVANT.
Sirrah, go hire me twenty cunning cooks.

SECOND SERVANT. You shall have none ill, sir, for I'll try if they
    can lick their fingers.

CAPULET. How canst thou try them so?

SECOND SERVANT. Marry, sir, 'tis an ill cook that cannot lick
    his own fingers: therefore he that cannot lick his fingers
    goes not with me.

CAPULET. Go, be gone.   [*Exit* SECOND SERVANT.
We shall be much unfurnish'd for this time.
What, is my daughter gone to Friar Laurence?

NURSE. Aye, forsooth.

CAPULET. Well, he may chance to do some good on her:
A peevish self-will'd harlotry it is.

Enter JULIET.]

NURSE. See where she comes from shrift with merry look.

CAPULET. How now, my headstrong! where have you been
    gadding?

JULIET. Where I have learn'd me to repent the sin
Of disobedient opposition
To you and your behests, and am enjoin'd
By holy Laurence to fall prostrate here,
To beg your pardon! pardon, I beseech you!

Henceforward I am ever ruled by you.
CAPULET. Send for the county; go tell him of this:
   I'll have this knot knit up to-morrow morning.
JULIET. I met the youthful lord at Laurence' cell,
   And gave him what becomed love I might,
   Not stepping o'er the bounds of modesty.
CAPULET. Why, I am glad on't; this is well: stand up:
   This is as't should be. Let me see the county;
   Aye, marry, go, I say, and fetch him hither.
   Now, afore God, this reverend holy friar,
   All our whole city is much bound to him.
JULIET. Nurse, will you go with me into my closet,
   To help me sort such needful ornaments
   As you think fit to furnish me to-morrow?
LADY CAPULET. No, not till Thursday; there is time enough.
CAPULET. Go, nurse, go with her: we'll to church to-morrow.
                            [*Exeunt* JULIET *and* NURSE.
LADY CAPULET. We shall be short in our provision:
   'Tis now near night.
CAPULET.   Tush, I will stir about,
   And all things shall be well, I warrant thee, wife:
   Go thou to Juliet, help to deck up her;
   I'll not to bed to-night; let me alone;
   I'll play the housewife for this once. What, ho!
   They are all forth: well, I will walk myself
   To County Paris, to prepare him up
   Against to-morrow: my heart is wondrous light,
   Since this same wayward girl is so reclaim'd.   [*Exeunt.*

SCENE III — JULIET'S *chamber.*

Enter JULIET *and* NURSE.]
JULIET. Aye, those attires are best: but, gentle nurse,
   I pray thee, leave me to myself to-night;
   For I have need of many orisons
   To move the heavens to smile upon my state,
   Which, well thou know'st, is cross and full of sin.
Enter LADY CAPULET.]
LADY CAPULET. What, are you busy, ho? need you my help?
JULIET. No, madam; we have cull'd such necessaries
   As are behoveful for our state to-morrow:
   So please you, let me now be left alone,

And let the nurse this night sit up with you,
For I am sure you have your hands full all
In this so sudden business.

LADY CAPULET.   Good night!
Get thee to bed and rest, for thou hast need.

[*Exeunt* LADY CAPULET *and* NURSE.

JULIET. Farewell! God knows when we shall meet again.
I have a faint cold fear thrills through my veins,
That almost freezes up the heart of life:
I'll call them back again to comfort me.
Nurse!—What should she do here?
My dismal scene I needs must act alone.
Come, vial.
What if this mixture do not work at all?
Shall I be married then to-morrow morning?
No, no: this shall forbid it. Lie thou there.

[*Laying down a dagger.*

What if it be a poison, which the friar
Subtly hath minister'd to have me dead,
Lest in this marriage he should be dishonor'd,
Because he married me before to Romeo?
I fear it is; and yet, methinks, it should not,
For he hath still been tried a holy man.
How if, when I am laid into the tomb,
I wake before the time that Romeo
Come to redeem me? there's a fearful point,
Shall I not then be stifled in the vault,
To whose foul mouth no healthsome air breathes in,
And there die strangled ere my Romeo comes?
Or, if I live, is it not very like,
The horrible conceit of death and night,
Together with the terror of the place,
As in a vault, an ancient receptacle,
Where for these many hundred years the bones
Of all my buried ancestors are pack'd;
Where bloody Tybalt, yet but green in earth,
Lies festering in his shroud; where, as they say,
At some hours in the night spirits resort;
Alack, alack, is it not like that I
So early waking, what with loathsome smells
And shrieks like mandrakes' torn out of the earth,
That living mortals hearing them run mad:

Or, if I wake, shall I not be distraught,
Environed with all these hideous fears?
And madly play with my forefathers' joints?
And pluck the mangled Tybalt from his shroud?
And, in this rage, with some great kinsman's bone,
As with a club, dash out my desperate brains?
O, look! methinks I see my cousin's ghost
Seeking out Romeo, that did spit his body
Upon a rapier's point: stay, Tybalt, stay!
Romeo, I come! this do I drink to thee.

> [*She falls upon her bed, within the curtains.*

SCENE IV — *Hall in* CAPULET'S *house.*

Enter LADY CAPULET *and* NURSE.]

LADY CAPULET. Hold, take these keys, and fetch more spices, nurse.

NURSE. They call for dates and quinces in the pastry.

Enter CAPULET.]

CAPULET. Come, stir, stir, stir! the second cock hath crow'd,
　The curfew-bell hath rung, 'tis three o'clock:
　Look to the baked meats, good Angelica:
　Spare not for cost.

NURSE.　　　　　　Go, you cot-quean, go,
　Get you to bed; faith, you'll be sick to-morrow
　For this night's watching.

CAPULET. No, not a whit! What! I have watch'd ere now
　All night for lesser cause, and ne'er been sick.

LADY CAPULET. Aye, you have been a mouse-hunt in your time;
　But I will watch you from such watching now.

> [*Exeunt* LADY CAPULET *and* NURSE.

CAPULET. A jealous-hood, a jealous-hood!

Enter three or four SERVINGMEN, *with spits, and logs, and baskets.*]

　　　　　　　　　　　Now, fellow,
What's there?

FIRST SERVINGMAN. Things for the cook, sir, but I know not what.

CAPULET. Make haste, make haste. [*Exit* FIRST SERVINGMAN.
　Sirrah, fetch drier logs:
　Call Peter, he will show thee where they are.

SECOND SERVINGMAN. I have a head, sir, that will find out logs,
and never trouble Peter for the matter.

CAPULET. Mass, and well said; a merry whoreson, ha!
Thou shalt be logger-head.   [*Exit* SECOND SERVINGMAN.
Good faith, 'tis day:
The county will be here with music straight,
For so he said he would. [*Music within*] I hear him near.
Nurse! Wife! What, ho! What, nurse, I say!

Re-enter NURSE.]
Go waker Juliet, go and trim her up;
I'll go and chat with Paris: hie, make haste,
Make haste: the bridegroom he is come already:
Make haste, I say.   [*Exeunt.*

SCENE V — JULIET's *chamber.*

Enter NURSE.]

NURSE. Mistress! what, mistress! Juliet! fast, I warrant her,
she:
Why, lamb! why, lady! fie, you slug-a-bed!
Why, love, I say! madam! sweet-heart! why, bride!
What, not a word? you take your pennyworths now;
Sleep for a week; for the next night, I warrant,
The County Paris hath set up his rest
That you shall rest but little. God forgive me,
Marry, and amen, how sound is she asleep!
I needs must wake her. Madam, madam, madam!
Aye, let the county take you in your bed;
He'll fright you up, i' faith. Will it not be?
                                [*Undraws the curtains.*
What, dress'd! and in your clothes! and down again!
I must needs wake you. Lady! lady! lady!
Alas, alas! Help, help! my lady's dead!
O, well-a-day, that ever I was born!
Some aqua vitæ, ho! My lord, my lady!

Enter LADY CAPULET.]

LADY CAPULET. What noise is here?

NURSE.   O lamentable day!

LADY CAPULET. What is the matter?

NURSE.   Look, look! O heavy day!

LADY CAPULET. O me, O me! My child, my only life,

    Revive, look up, or I will die with thee.
    Help! help! call help.

Enter CAPULET.]

CAPULET. For shame, bring Juliet forth; her lord is come.

NURSE. She's dead, deceased, she's dead; alack the day!

LADY CAPULET. Alack the day, she's dead, she's dead, she's
    dead!

CAPULET. Ha! let me see her. Out, alas! she's cold;
    Her blood is settled and her joints are stiff;
    Life and these lips have long been separated;
    Death lies on her like an untimely frost
    Upon the sweetest flower of all the field.

NURSE. O lamentable day!

LADY CAPULET.   O woeful time!

CAPULET. Death, that hath ta'en her hence to make me wail,
    Ties up my tongue and will not let me speak.

Enter FRIAR LAURENCE *and* PARIS, *with* MUSICIANS.]

FRIAR LAURENCE. Come, is the bride ready to go to church?

CAPULET. Ready to go, but never to return.
    O son, the night before thy wedding-day
    Hath death lain with thy wife: see, there she lies,
    Flower as she was, deflowered by him.
    Death is my son-in-law, death is my heir;
    My daughter he hath wedded: I will die,
    And leave him all; life, living, all is Death's.

PARIS. Have I thought long to see this morning's face,
    And doth it give me such a sight as this?

LADY CAPULET. Accurst, unhappy, wretched, hateful day!
    Most miserable hour that e'er time saw
    In lasting labor of his pilgrimage!
    But one, poor one, one poor and loving child,
    But one thing to rejoice and solace in,
    And cruel death hath catch'd it from my sight!

NURSE. O woe! O woeful, woeful, woeful day!
    Most lamentable day, most woeful day,
    That ever, ever, I did yet behold!
    O day! O day! O day! O hateful day!
    Never was seen so black a day as this:
    O woeful day, O woeful day!

PARIS. Beguiled, divorced, wronged, spited, slain!
    Most detestable death, by thee beguiled,
    By cruel cruel thee quite overthrown!

O love! O life! not life, but love in death!

CAPULET. Despised, distressed, hated, martyr'd, kill'd!
Uncomfortable time, why camest thou now
To murder, murder our solemnity?
O child! O child! my soul, and not my child!
Dead art thou! Alack, my child is dead;
And with my child my joys are buried!

FRIAR LAURENCE. Peace, ho, for shame! confusion's cure lives
  not
In these confusions. Heaven and yourself
Had part in this fair maid; now heaven hath all,
And all the better is it for the maid:
Your part in her you could not keep from death;
But heaven keeps his part in eternal life.
The most you sought was her promotion,
For 'twas your heaven she should be advanced:
And weep ye now, seeing she is advanced
Above the clouds, as high as heaven itself?
O, in this love, you love your child so ill,
That you run mad, seeing that she is well:
She's not well married that lives married long,
But she's best married that dies married young.
Dry up your tears, and stick your rosemary
On this fair corse, and, as the custom is,
In all her best array bear her to church:
For though fond nature bids us all lament,
Yet nature's tears are reason's merriment.

CAPULET. All things that we ordained festival,
Turn from their office to black funeral:
Our instruments to melancholy bells;
Our wedding cheer to a sad burial feast;
Our solemn hymns to sullen dirges change;
Our bridal flowers serve for a buried corse,
And all things change them to the contrary.

FRIAR LAURENCE. Sir, go you in; and, madam, go with him;
And go, Sir Paris; every one prepare
To follow this fair corse unto her grave:
The heavens do lour upon you for some ill;
Move them no more by crossing their high will.

　　　　　　[*Exeunt* CAPULET, LADY CAPULET, PARIS, *and* FRIAR.

FIRST MUSICIAN. Faith, we may put up our pipes, and be gone.

NURSE. Honest good fellows, ah, put up, put up;

For, well you know, this is a pitiful case.   [*Exit.*

FIRST MUSICIAN. Aye, by my troth, the case may be amended. *Enter* PETER.]

PETER. Musicians, O, musicians, 'Heart's ease, Heart's ease.' O, an you will have me live, play 'Heart's ease.'

FIRST MUSICIAN. Why 'Heart's ease'?

PETER. O, musicians, because my heart itself plays 'My heart is full of woe:' O, play me some merry dump, to comfort me.

FIRST MUSICIAN. Not a dump we; 'tis no time to play now.

PETER. You will not then?

FIRST MUSICIAN. No.

PETER. I will then give it you soundly.

FIRST MUSICIAN. What will you give us?

PETER. No money, on my faith, but the gleek; I will give you the minstrel.

FIRST MUSICIAN. Then will I give you the serving-creature.

PETER. Then will I lay the serving-creature's dagger on your pate. I will carry no crochets; I'll re you, I'll fa you; do you note me?

FIRST MUSICIAN. An you re us and fa us, you note us.

SECOND MUSICIAN. Pray you, put up your dagger, and put out your wit.

PETER. Then have at you with my wit! I will dry-beat you with an iron wit, and put up my iron dagger. Answer me like men:

> 'When griping grief the heart doth wound
>   And doleful dumps the mind oppress,
>   Then music with her silver sound'—

why 'silver sound'? why 'music with her silver sound'?— What say you, Simon Catling?

FIRST MUSICIAN. Marry, sir, because silver hath a sweet sound.

PETER. Pretty! What say you, Hugh Rebeck?

SECOND MUSICIAN. I say, 'silver sound,' because musicians sound for silver.

PETER. Pretty too! What say you, James Soundpost?

THIRD MUSICIAN. Faith, I know not what to say.

PETER. O, I cry you mercy; you are the singer: I will say for you. It is 'music with her silver sound,' because musicians have no gold for sounding:

> 'Then music with her silver sound
>   With speedy help doth lend redress.'   [*Exit.*

FIRST MUSICIAN. What a pestilent knave is this same!

SECOND MUSICIAN. Hang him, Jack! Come, we'll in here; tarry
for the mourners, and stay dinner.   [*Exeunt.*

ACT V

Scene I — Mantua. *A street.*

Enter ROMEO.]

ROMEO. If I may trust the flattering truth of sleep,
My dreams presage some joyful news at hand:
My bosom's lord sits lightly in his throne,
And all this day an unaccustom'd spirit
Lifts me above the ground with cheerful thoughts.
I dreamt my lady came and found me dead—
Strange dream, that gives a dead man leave to think!—
And breathed such life with kisses in my lips,
That I revived and was an emperor.
Ah me! how sweet is love itself possess'd,
When but love's shadows are so rich in joy!

Enter BALTHASAR, *booted.*]

News from Verona! How now, Balthasar!
Dost thou not bring me letters from the friar?
How doth my lady? Is my father well?
How fares my Juliet? that I ask again;
For nothing can be ill, if she be well.

BALTHASAR. Then she is well, and nothing can be ill:
Her body sleeps in Capels' monument,
And her immortal part with angels lives.
I saw her laid low in her kindred's vault,
And presently took post to tell it you:
O, pardon me for bringing these ill news,
Since you did leave it for my office, sir.

ROMEO. Is it e'en so? then I defy you, stars!
Thou know'st my lodging: get me ink and paper,
And hire post-horses; I will hence to-night.

BALTHASAR. I do beseech you, sir, have patience:
Your looks are pale and wild, and do import
Some misadventure.

ROMEO.   Tush, thou art deceived:
Leave me, and do the thing I bid thee do.
Hast thou no letters to me from the friar?

BALTHASAR. No, my good lord.

ROMEO.   No matter; get thee gone,

And hire those horses: I'll be with thee straight.

[*Exit* BALTHASAR.

Well, Juliet, I will lie with thee to-night.
Let's see for means:—O mischief, thou art swift
To enter in the thoughts of desperate men!
I do remember an apothecary,
And hereabouts a' dwells, which late I noted
In tatter'd weeds, with overwhelming brows,
Culling of simples; meager were his looks;
Sharp misery had worn him to the bones:
And in his needy shop a tortoise hung,
An alligator stuff'd and other skins
Of ill-shaped fishes; and about his shelves
A beggarly account of empty boxes,
Green earthen pots, bladders and musty seeds,
Remnants of packthread and old cakes of roses,
Were thinly scatter'd, to make up a show.
Noting this penury, to myself I said,
An if a man did need a poison now,
Whose sale is present death in Mantua,
Here lives a caitiff wretch would sell it him.
O, this same thought did but forerun my need,
And this same needy man must sell it me.
As I remember, this should be the house:
Being holiday, the beggar's shop is shut.
What, ho! apothecary!

Enter APOTHECARY.]

APOTHECARY.   Who calls so loud?
ROMEO. Come hither, man. I see that thou art poor;
    Hold, there is forty ducats: let me have
    A dram of poison; such soon-speeding gear
    As will disperse itself through all the veins,
    That the life-weary taker may fall dead,
    And that the trunk may be discharged of breath
    As violently as hasty powder fired
    Doth hurry from the fatal cannon's womb.
APOTHECARY. Such mortal drugs I have; but Mantua's law
    Is death to any he that utters them.
ROMEO. Art thou so bare and full of wretchedness,
    And fear'st to die? famine is in thy cheeks,
    Need and oppression starveth in thy eyes,
    Contempt and beggary hangs upon thy back,

The world is not thy friend, nor the world's law:
The world affords no law to make thee rich;
Then be not poor, but break it, and take this.
APOTHECARY. My poverty, but not my will, consents.
ROMEO. I pay thy poverty and not thy will.
APOTHECARY. Put this in any liquid thing you will,
And drink it off; and, if you had the strength
Of twenty men, it would dispatch you straight.
ROMEO. There is thy gold, worse poison to men's souls,
Doing more murder in this loathsome world,
Than these poor compounds that thou mayst not sell:
I sell thee poison, thou hast sold me none.
Farewell: buy food, and get thyself in flesh.
Come, cordial and not poison, go with me,
To Juliet's grave; for there must I use thee. [*Exeunt.*

Scene II — Friar Laurence's *cell.*

Enter Friar John.]
FRIAR JOHN. Holy Franciscan friar! brother, ho!
Enter FRIAR LAURENCE.]
FRIAR LAURENCE. This same should be the voice of Friar John.
Welcome from Mantua: what says Romeo?
Or, if his mind be writ, give me his letter.
FRIAR JOHN. Going to find a bare-foot brother out,
One of our order, to associate me,
Here in this city visiting the sick,
And finding him, the searchers of the town,
Suspecting that we both were in a house
Where the infectious pestilence did reign,
Seal'd up the doors and would not let us forth;
So that my speed to Mantua there was stay'd.
FRIAR LAURENCE. Who bare my letter then to Romeo?
FRIAR JOHN. I could not send it,—here it is again,—
Nor get a messenger to bring it thee,
So fearful were they of infection.
FRIAR LAURENCE. Unhappy fortune! by my brotherhood,
The letter was not nice, but full of charge
Of dear import, and the neglecting it
May do much danger. Friar John, go hence;
Get me an iron crow and bring it straight
Unto my cell.

FRIAR JOHN. Brother, I'll go and bring it thee.   [Exit.
FRIAR LAURENCE. Now must I to the monument alone;
     Within this three hours will fair Juliet wake:
     She will beshrew me much that Romeo
     Hath had no notice of these accidents;
     But I will write again to Mantua,
     And keep her at my cell till Romeo come:
     Poor living corse, closed in a dead man's tomb!   [Exit.

SCENE III — *A churchyard; in it a monument
          belonging to the* CAPULETS.

Enter PARIS *and his* PAGE, *bearing flowers and a torch.*]
PARIS. Give me thy torch, boy: hence, and stand aloof:
     Yet put it out, for I would not be seen.
     Under yond yew-trees lay thee all along,
     Holding thine ear close to the hollow ground;
     So shall no foot upon the churchyard tread,
     Being loose, unfirm, with digging up of graves,
     But thou shalt hear it: whistle then to me,
     As signal that thou hear'st something approach.
     Give me those flowers. Do as I bid thee, go.
PAGE. [*Aside*] I am almost afraid to stand alone
     Here in the churchyard; yet I will adventure.   [*Retires.*
PARIS. Sweet flower, with flowers thy bridal bed I strew,—
     O woe! thy canopy is dust and stones;—
     Which with sweet water nightly I will dew,
     Or, wanting that, with tears distill'd by moans:
     The obsequies that I for thee will keep
     Nightly shall be to strew thy grave and weep.
                              [*The* PAGE *whistles.*
     The boy gives warning something doth approach.
     What cursed foot wanders this way to-night,
     To cross my obsequies and true love's rite?
     What, with a torch! Muffle me, night, a while.   [*Retires.*
Enter ROMEO *and* BALTHASAR, *with a torch, mattock, &c.*]
ROMEO. Give me that mattock and the wrenching iron.
     Hold, take this letter; early in the morning
     See thou deliver it to my lord and father.
     Give me the light: upon thy life, I charge thee,
     Whate'er thou hear'st or seest, stand all aloof,
     And do not interrupt me in my course.

Why I descend into this bed of death
Is partly to behold my lady's face,
But chiefly to take thence from her dead finger
A precious ring, a ring that I must use
In dear employment: therefore hence, be gone:
But if thou, jealous, dost return to pry
In what I farther shall intend to do,
By heaven, I will tear thee joint by joint
And strew this hungry churchyard with thy limbs:
The time and my intents are savage-wild,
More fierce and more inexorable by far
Than empty tigers or the roaring sea.

BALTHASAR. I will be gone, sir, and not trouble you.

ROMEO. So shalt thou show me friendship. Take thou that:
Live, and be prosperous: and farewell, good fellow.

BALTHASAR. [*Aside*] For all this same, I'll hide me hereabout:
His looks I fear, and his intents I doubt.　　　　[*Retires.*

ROMEO. Thou detestable maw, thou womb of death,
Gorged with the dearest morsel of the earth,
Thus I enforce thy rotten jaws to open,
And in despite I'll cram thee with more food.
　　　　　　　　　　　　　　　[*Opens the tomb.*

PARIS. This is that banish'd haughty Montague
That murder'd my love's cousin, with which grief,
It is supposed, the fair creature died,
And here is come to do some villanous shame
To the dead bodies: I will apprehend him.
　　　　　　　　　　　　　　[*Comes forward.*
Stop thy unhallow'd toil, vile Montague!
Can vengeance be pursued further than death?
Condemned villain, I do apprehend thee:
Obey, and go with me; for thou must die.

ROMEO. I must indeed, and therefore came I hither.
Good gentle youth, tempt not a desperate man;
Fly hence and leave me: think upon these gone;
Let them affright thee. I beseech thee, youth,
Put not another sin upon my head,
By urging me to fury: O, be gone!
By heaven, I love thee better than myself,
For I come hither arm'd against myself:
Stay not, be gone: live, and hereafter say,
A madman's mercy bid thee run away.

PARIS. I do defy thy conjurations
  And apprehend thee for a felon here.
ROMEO. Wilt thou provoke me? then have at thee, boy!
                                        [*They fight.*
PAGE. O Lord, they fight! I will go call the watch.   [*Exit.*
PARIS. O, I am slain! [*Falls*] If thou be merciful,
  Open the tomb, lay me with Juliet.   [*Dies.*
ROMEO. In faith, I will. Let me peruse this face:
  Mercutio's kinsman, noble County Paris!
  What said my man, when my betossed soul
  Did not attend him as we rode? I think
  He told me Paris should have married Juliet:
  Said he not so? or did I dream it so?
  Or am I mad, hearing him talk of Juliet,
  To think it was so? O, give me thy hand,
  One writ with me in sour misfortune's book!
  I'll bury thee in a triumphant grave;
  A grave? O, no, a lantern, slaughter'd youth;
  For here lies Juliet, and her beauty makes
  This vault a feasting presence full of light.
  Death, lie thou there, by a dead man interr'd.
                    [*Laying* PARIS *in the monument.*
  How oft when men are at the point of death
  Have they been merry! which their keepers call
  A lightning before death: O, how may I
  Call this a lightning? O my love! my wife!
  Death, that hath suck'd the honey of thy breath,
  Hath had no power yet upon thy beauty:
  Thou art not conquer'd; beauty's ensign yet
  Is crimson in thy lips and in thy cheeks,
  And death's pale flag is not advanced there.
  Tybalt, liest thou there in thy bloody sheet?
  O, what more favor can I do to thee
  Than with that hand that cut thy youth in twain
  To sunder his that was thine enemy?
  Forgive me, cousin! Ah, dear Juliet,
  Why art thou yet so fair? shall I believe
  That unsubstantial death is amorous,
  And that the lean abhorred monster keeps
  Thee here in dark to be his paramour?
  For fear of that, I still will stay with thee,
  And never from this palace of dim night

Depart again: here, here will I remain
With worms that are thy chamber-maids; O, here
Will I set up my everlasting rest,
And shake the yoke of inauspicious stars
From this world-wearied flesh. Eyes, look your last!
Arms, take your last embrace! and, lips, O you
The doors of breath, seal with a righteous kiss
A dateless bargain to engrossing death!
Come, bitter conduct, come, unsavory guide!
Thou desperate pilot, now at once run on
The dashing rocks thy sea-sick weary bark.
Here's to my love! [*Drinks*] O true apothecary!
Thy drugs are quick. Thus with a kiss I die.   [*Dies.*

Enter, at the other end of the churchyard, FRIAR
      LAURENCE, *with a lantern, crow, and spade.*]

FRIAR LAURENCE. Saint Francis be my speed! how oft to-night
   Have my old feet stumbled at graves! Who's there?

BALTHASAR. Here's one, a friend, and one that knows you
   well.

FRIAR LAURENCE. Bliss be upon you! Tell me, good my friend,
   What torch is yond that vainly lends his light
   To grubs and eyeless skulls? as I discern,
   It burneth in the Capel's monument.

BALTHASAR. It doth so, holy sir; and there's my master,
   One that you love.

FRIAR LAURENCE.   Who is it?

BALTHASAR.   Romeo.

FRIAR LAURENCE. How long hath he been there?

BALTHASAR.   Full half an hour.

FRIAR LAURENCE. Go with me to the vault.

BALTHASAR.   I dare not, sir:
   My master knows not but I am gone hence;
   And fearfully did menace me with death,
   If I did stay to look on his intents.

FRIAR LAURENCE. Stay, then; I'll go alone: fear comes upon
      me;
   O, much I fear some ill unlucky thing.

BALTHASAR. As I did sleep under this yew-tree here,
   I dreamt my master and another fought,
   And that my master slew him.

FRIAR LAURENCE.   Romeo!   [*Advances.*
   Alack, alack, what blood is this, which stains

The stony entrance of this sepulcher?
What means these masterless and gory swords
To lie discolor'd by this place of peace?   [*Enters the tomb.*
Romeo! O, pale! who else? what, Paris too?
And steep'd in blood? Ah, what an unkind hour
Is guilty of this lamentable chance!
The lady stirs.   [JULIET *wakes.*

JULIET. O comfortable friar! where is my lord?
I do remember well where I should be,
And there I am: where is my Romeo?   [*Noise within.*

FRIAR LAURENCE. I hear some noise. Lady, come from that nest
Of death, contagion and unnatural sleep:
A greater power than we can contradict
Hath thwarted our intents: come, come away:
Thy husband in thy bosom there lies dead;
And Paris too: come, I'll dispose of thee
Among a sisterhood of holy nuns:
Stay not to question, for the watch is coming;
Come, go, good Juliet; I dare no longer stay.

JULIET. Go, get thee hence, for I will not away.
                           [*Exit* FRIAR LAURENCE.
What's here? a cup, closed in my true love's hand?
Poison, I see, hath been his timeless end:
O churl! drunk all, and left no friendly drop
To help me after? I will kiss thy lips;
Haply some poison yet doth hang on them,
To make me die with a restorative.   [*Kisses him.*
Thy lips are warm.

FIRST WATCHMAN. [*Within*] Lead, boy: which way?

JULIET. Yea, noise? then I'll be brief. O happy dagger!
                           [*Snatching* ROMEO's *dagger.*
This is thy sheath [*Stabs herself*]; there rust, and let me die.
                           [*Falls on* ROMEO's *body, and dies.*

Enter WATCHMAN, *with the* PAGE *of* PARIS.]

PAGE. This is the place; there, where the torch doth burn.

FIRST WATCHMAN. The ground is bloody; search about the churchyard:
Go, some of you, who'er you find attach.
Pitiful sight! here lies the county slain;
And Juliet bleeding, warm, and newly dead,
Who here hath lain this two days buried.

Go, tell the prince: run to the Capulets:
Raise up the Montagues: some others search:
We see the ground whereon these woes do lie;
But the true ground of all these piteous woes
We cannot without circumstance descry.

Re-enter some of the WATCHMEN, *with* BALTHASAR.]

SECOND WATCHMAN. Here's Romeo's man; we found him in
the churchyard.

FIRST WATCHMAN. Hold him in safety, till the prince come
hither.

Re-enter FRIAR LAURENCE, *and another* WATCHMAN.]

THIRD WATCHMAN. Here is a friar, that trembles, sighs and
weeps:
We took this mattock and this spade from him,
As he was coming from this churchyard's side.

FIRST WATCHMAN. A great suspicion: stay the friar too.

Enter the PRINCE *and* ATTENDANTS.]

PRINCE. What misadventure is so early up,
That calls our person from our morning rest?

Enter CAPULET, LADY CAPULET, *and others.*]

CAPULET. What should it be that they so shriek abroad?

LADY CAPULET. The people in the street cry Romeo,
Some Juliet, and some Paris, and all run
With open outcry toward our monument.

PRINCE. What fear is this that startles in our ears?

FIRST WATCHMAN. Sovereign, here lies the County Paris slain;
And Romeo dead; and Juliet, dead before
Warm and new kill'd.

PRINCE. Search, seek, and know how this foul murder comes.

FIRST WATCHMAN. Here is a friar, and slaughter'd Romeo's
man,
With instruments upon them fit to open
These dead men's tombs.

CAPULET. O heavens! O wife, look how our daughter bleeds!
This dagger hath mista'en, for, lo, his house
Is empty on the back of Montague,
And it mis-sheathed in my daughter's bosom!

LADY CAPULET. O me! this sight of death is as a bell
That warns my old age to a sepulcher.

Enter MONTAGUE *and others.*]

PRINCE. Come, Montague; for thou art early up,
To see thy son and heir more early down.

MONTAGUE. Alas, my liege, my wife is dead to-night;
    Grief of my son's exile hath stopp'd her breath:
    What further woe conspires against mine age?
PRINCE. Look, and tnou shalt see.
MONTAGUE. O thou untaught! what manners is in this,
    To press before thy father to a grave?
PRINCE. Seal up the mouth of outrage for a while,
    Till we can clear these ambiguities,
    And know their spring, their head, their true descent;
    And then will I be general of your woes,
    And lead you even to death: meantime forbear,
    And let mischance be slave to patience.
    Bring forth the parties of suspicion.
FRIAR LAURENCE. I am the greatest, able to do least,
    Yet most suspected, as the time and place
    Doth make against me, of this direful murder;
    And here I stand, both to impeach and purge
    Myself condemned and myself excused.
PRINCE. Then say at once what thou dost know in this.
FRIAR LAURENCE. I will be brief, for my short date of breath
    Is not so long as is a tedious tale.
    Romeo, there dead, was husband to that Juliet;
    And she, there dead, that Romeo's faithful wife:
    I married them; and their stol'n marriage day
    Was Tybalt's dooms-day, whose untimely death
    Banish'd the new-made bridegroom from this city;
    For whom, and not for Tybalt, Juliet pined.
    You, to remove that siege of grief from her,
    Betroth'd and would have married her perforce
    To County Paris: then comes she to me,
    And with wild looks bid me devise some means
    To rid her from this second marriage,
    Or in my cell there would she kill herself.
    Then gave I her, so tutor'd by my art,
    A sleeping potion; which so took effect
    As I intended, for it wrought on her
    The form of death: meantime I writ to Romeo,
    That he should hither come as this dire night,
    To help to take her from her borrow'd grave,
    Being the time the potion's force should cease.
    But he which bore my letter, Friar John,
    Was stay'd by accident, and yesternight

Return'd my letter back. Then all alone
At the prefixed hour of her waking
Came I to take her from her kindred's vault,
Meaning to keep her closely at my cell
Till I conveniently could send to Romeo;
But when I came, some minute ere the time
Of her awaking here untimely lay
The noble Paris and true Romeo dead.
She wakes and I entreated her come forth,
And bear this work of heaven with patience:
But then a noise did scare me from the tomb,
And she too desperate would not go with me,
But, as it seems, did violence on herself.
All this I know and to the marriage
Her nurse is privy and, if aught in this
Miscarried by my fault, let my old life
Be sacrificed some hour before his time
Unto the rigor of severest law.

PRINCE. We still have known thee for a holy man.
Where's Romeo's man? what can he say in this?

BALTHASAR I brought my master news of Juliet's death,
And then in post he came from Mantua
To this same place, to this same monument.
This letter he early bid me give his father,
And threaten'd me with death, going in the vault,
If I departed not and left him there.

PRINCE. Give me the letter; I will look on it.
Where is the county's page, that raised the watch?
Sirrah, what made your master in this place?

PAGE. He came with flowers to strew his lady's grave;
And bid me stand aloof, and so I did:
Anon comes one with light to ope the tomb;
And by and by my master drew on him;
And then I ran away to call the watch.

PRINCE. This letter doth make good the friar's words,
Their course of love, the tidings of her death:
And here he writes that he did buy a poison
Of a poor 'pothecary, and therewithal
Came to this vault to die and lie with Juliet.
Where be these enemies? Capulet! Montague!
See, what a scourge is laid upon your hate,
That heaven finds means to kill your joys with love!

And I, for winking at your discords too,
Have lost a brace of kinsmen: all are punishe'd.

CAPULET. O brother Montague, give me thy hand:
This is my daughter's jointure, for no more
Can I demand.

MONTAGUE.   But I can give thee more:
For I will raise her statue in pure gold;
That while Verona by that name is known,
There shall no figure at such rate be set
As that of true and faithful Juliet.

CAPULET. As rich shall Romeo's by his lady's lie;
Poor sacrifices of our enmity!

PRINCE. A glooming peace this morning with it brings;
The sun for sorrow will not show his head:
Go hence, to have more talk of these sad things;
Some shall be pardon'd and some punished:
For never was a story of more woe
Than this of Juliet and her Romeo.   [*Exeunt.*

JULIUS CAESAR

INTRODUCTION TO

Julius Caesar

BY

MARK VAN DOREN

SHAKESPEARE idealized Plutarch's Brutus, but not in the direction of his own Henry V. The Roman conspirator has become an exemplary gentleman, and the chief sign of this is his set of scruples. His imagination is indeed so selfless, and his consideration of other men so full and kind, as almost to smother his powers and render him inactive. He is not very much like Hamlet, whose inaction, if inaction it is, has its paradoxical dynamics. But he is a sober step in that direction —too sober for the kind of success his creator, with a nimble bound back into the northern scene, is next to achieve.

If Brutus is less interesting than Hamlet, if his internal complications diminish rather than exhibit his dramatic force, the principal reason may be that Shakespeare has kept himself too conscious of a remote Roman grandeur in the scene. In Plutarch he seems always to have recognized an artist whom it would be rash to change, but his respect for the biographer was in the present case perhaps too solemn. The accommodation of his style to an ancient and alien atmosphere is amazingly complete, and there is in *Julius Caesar* a perfection of form which even he will never surpass. But the accommodation is something of a tour de force, and the perfection is of that sort which limits rather than releases poetry. *Julius Caesar* is more rhetoric than poetry, just as its persons are more orators than men. They all have something of the statue in them, for they express their author's idea of antiquity rather than his knowledge of life. They have the clarity and simplicity of worked marble, and are the easiest of Shakespeare's people to understand if one expects everything from speeches, and if one is innocent of the distinction between men and public men. The characters of *Julius Caesar* are public men. Even Antony and Caesar are. But Shakespeare's deepest interest is in the private man. And though he tries to find that man in Brutus he does not do so, because he has already submitted Brutus, like everybody else in the play, to the smoothing and simplifying process of a certain style. This style is in its way wonderful, but the hero who follows Brutus will accomplish infinitely greater wonders in no style at all, or at any rate in none that can be named; unless its name is Shakespeare's English.

Julius Caesar is least notable among Shakespeare's better plays for the distinctions of its speech. All of its persons tend to talk alike; their training has been forensic and therefore uniform, so that they can say anything with both efficiency and ease. With Marullus's first speech in the opening scene the play swings into its style: a style which will make it appear that nobody experiences the least difficulty in saying what he thinks. The phrasing is invariably flawless from the oral point of view; the breathing is right; no thought is too long for order or too short for roundness. Everything is brilliantly and surely said; the effects are underlined, the i's are firmly dotted. Speeches have tangible outlines, like plastic objects, and the drift from one of them to another has never to be guessed, for it is clearly stated.

The characters are accomplished in all the practical arts of statement. Not merely in the Forum is Brutus an orator—"I pause for a reply" (iii, ii)—but in his private tent, quarreling with Cassius. Dryden admired the famous quarrel scene (iv, iii) because it was "masculine," and his admiration was sound; yet the epithet implies a limitaton of effect. The thump and rap of the repartee remind us once more that public men are training their tongues against each other; the dialogue, for all its power, could do with some relief by way of things half said or never said. Brutus and Cassius say it all —with knowledge, too, of how it will be taken. Along with the rest here they are artists in declamation.

Rhetorical questions abound in *Julius Caesar*:

> Wherefore rejoice? What conquest brings he home?
> What tributaries follow him to Rome
> To grace in captive bonds his chariot-wheels? . . .
> And do you now put on your best attire?
> And do you now cull out a holiday?

And do you now strew flowers in his way
That comes in triumph over Pompey's blood?   [I, i]

There they are piled in parallel formation, and this is frequently the case. Antony knows best the trick of letting them forth singly, with the force of simple assertion:

Did this in Caesar seem ambitious?   [III, ii]

You will compel me, then, to read the will?   [III, ii]

Portia, the public wife of a public man, goes so far as to answer one of hers:

Is Brutus sick? . . .
                    No, my Brutus;
You have some sick offence within your mind.   [II, i]

But all in their various ways know how to ask them, and how not to pause for a reply unless the pause too will be effective.

So are they tutored in the music of monosyllables. No play of Shakespeare's has so many, so superbly used. The seasoned orator strings short words together as often as he can—for an effect of artlessness, of sincerity that only speaks right on, and also because there is a secret pleasure in demonstrating the discipline of his tongue. It takes skill to deliver monosyllables in an agreeable and natural rhythm, and a rhetorician likes nothing better than problems of skill. In *Julius Caesar* there may be in one place as many as thirty monosyllables together.

And when the fit was on him, I did mark
How he did shake—'t is true, this god did shake.   [I, ii]

When went there by an age, since the great flood,
But it was fam'd with more than with one man?
When could they say, till now, that talk'd of Rome . . .
                                                          [I, ii]

I will come home to you; or, if you will,
Come home to me, and I will wait for you.
I will do so; till then, think of the world.   [I, ii]

                    What's to do?
A piece of work that will make sick men whole.
But are not some whole that we must make sick?   [II, i]

          Let me know some cause,
Lest I be laugh'd at when I tell them so.
The cause is in my will; I will not come.   [II, ii]

If thou dost bend and pray and fawn for him,
I spurn thee like a cur out of my way.   [III, i]

'T is good you know not that you are his heirs;
For, if you should, O, what would come of it!   [III, ii]

I pray you, sirs, lie in my tent and sleep;
It may be I shall raise you by and by. . . .
I will not have it so: lie down, good sirs. . . .
I know young bloods look for a time of rest. . . .
I will not hold thee long. If I do live,
I will be good to thee.   [IV, iii]

They may occur in orations or they may crop out in discourse;
they may be triumphs by the orator Antony—

> But, as you know me all, a plain blunt man
> That love my friend;

> But here I am to speak what I do know;
> And I must pause till it come back to me—

or they may be the last words of a dying man:

> I kill'd not thee with half so good a will.

They may serve any purpose at the moment. But the purpose
they serve at all times is to pour into the ear an unimpeded
stream of eloquence, a smooth current of artful sound. And
once again it is to be noted that monosyllables are no one
speaker's monopoly. The craft is native to them all.

So is the loftier craft of framing superlatives, of condensing
infinite compliment into a finite phrase. Antony, being the
best orator, does best at this:

> With the most noble blood of all this world   [III, i]

> The choice and master spirits of this age   [III, i]

> Thou art the ruins of the noblest man
> That ever lived in the tide of times   [III, i]

> This was the noblest Roman of them all.   [V, v]

But the second best of Brutus is impressive:

> That struck the foremost man of all this world   [IV, iii]
> The last of all the Romans, fare thee well!
> It is impossible that ever Rome
> Should breed thy fellow.   [V, iii]

And again the gift is common to the cast.

Their voices are not differentiated then. Nor are their states of mind. Brutus anticipates Hamlet, Othello, Lear, and Macbeth when he soliloquizes concerning the disorder in his soul:

> Between the acting of a dreadful thing
> And the first motion, all the interim is
> Like a phantasma or a hideous dream.
> The Genius and the mortal instruments
> Are then in council; and the state of a man,
> Like to a little kingdom, suffers then
> The nature of an insurrection.   [II, i]

This is fine, like everything else in *Julius Caesar*, but it is rotund and political, and it was relatively easy for Brutus to say; nor is it impossible to imagine another man's saying it. It is not, like comparable speeches in the tragedies ahead, cut to the individual, and cut with so keen a knife that the individual is dissected in the process and seems to bleed his words. Brutus addresses us through a wrapping of rhetoric, of public speech. And this wrapping is around the imageries of blood and sleep which are so prominent in the play—so prominent, and yet, if one remembers *Macbeth*, so remote from contact with us. The blood that smears the entire surface of *Macbeth* is physical; we see, feel, and smell it. Not so with Caesar's blood; it is "noble" and "costly" because Caesar was the foremost man of all the world, but it remains a metaphor, a political metaphor, distant from the experience of our senses. It may be significant that it can pour from Caesar's statue as well as from his body (II, ii), and that when he falls at the base of Pompey's statue it too runs red. There is as much real blood in *Julius Caesar* as there is in stone. And Brutus, once more ancestor to Macbeth, cannot sleep. At home before the assassination, in his tent on the eve of battle, and facing death in his last hour, his lids are heavy, his bones want rest. Yet the fact is not ghastly as in the case of one who will murder Sleep itself, and whose resulting exhaustion will visit itself upon the audience. The fatigue of Brutus is the noble tiredness of a great man, and we respect it; but our pity for the sufferer is not tinged with fear. This is the noblest Roman of them all, and even in distress he keeps his distance.

In such an atmosphere Caesar has little chance to be himself, yet Shakespeare has permitted him to make the most of it. Caesar is not a noble Roman, not one of Plutarch's men.

He is that rarity in the play, an Elizabethan personality; he
is one of Shakespeare's men. While he lasts he reveals himself in his irregularity, not in his symmetry, in picturesqueness
rather than in pose. His monosyllables—for he speaks them
too—tell us that he is deficient in one of the senses:

> Come on my right hand, for this ear is deaf; [I, ii]

that he changes his mind suddenly, with no reason given:

> He is a dreamer; let us leave him. Pass; [I, ii]
>
> The cause is in my will; I will not come; [II, ii]

and that he is inordinately vain:

> But there's but one in all doth hold his place.
> So in the world; . . . and that I am he. [III, i]

His enemies tell us that he has the falling sickness (I, ii), that
he is gullible to flattery (II, i), that he is superstitious grown
of late and loves to be regaled with wondrous tales of unicorns, bears, lions, and elephants (II, i). He appears, indeed,
only in his singularity; and he appears but briefly before he
falls at the hands of men so completely unlike him that the
difference alone might pass as motive for their hatred. Their
hatred is of a man not noble, a man who has not suppressed
himself. And for a similar reason they distrust Antony, who
revels long o' nights (II, ii) and whose orator's tongue flicks
unfairly with the serpent speed of irony. They cannot cope
with his irony; it is a thing to which solemn men feel superior, and so, since they are not only solemn but innocent, it is
a thrust they cannot parry. It is what destroys them, along
with much mischance and the heaped mountain of their
blunders. They never know him as we do; they do not hear
him, for example, prick down the character of Lepidus with
epigrams as merciless as bullets (IV, i). They never know the
force that is coiled behind his charm. Nor do we know it as
we shall in *Antony and Cleopatra*. But it is here, if only
briefly as in the case of the eccentric Caesar.

The blunders of Brutus and Cassius, but particularly of
Brutus, are many and pathetic. If they do not achieve the
dignity of tragic error, of heroic fault, the trouble is with the
men who make them; their virtues are not positive enough.
This is less true of Cassius, who misconstrues everything at
Philippi and so brings on the catastrophe (v, iii). Through-

out the play he has been the sharper figure. Caesar defines him in negative terms—"he hears no music" and "loves no plays" as Antony does, and "seldom he smiles" (I, ii)—and yet it is from the same source that we learn something we never forget: "a lean and hungry look . . . such men are dangerous." His voice is lean and hungry too, as his mind is rank and practical; when Brutus sees Antony after the assassination he thinks of nothing but assuring him of his "kind love, good thoughts, and reverence," whereas Cassius is only waiting till he can ask:

> But what compact mean you to have with us? [III, i]

Brutus has no patience with the poet who sneaks in at Philippi:

> What should the wars do with these jigging fools?

But Cassius rasps out an angrier rebuke:

> Ha, ha! how vilely doth this cynic rhyme! [IV, iii]

He is the angrier of the two when they quarrel, and therefore he is dramatically the more interesting. He has more flaws than Brutus, who indeed has none except the dramatic one of an impenetrable and inexpressible nobility.

The mistakes of Brutus are the mistakes of a man whose nobility muffles his intelligence. His conquest of himself has extended to his wit; his excellence is not inconsistent with a certain lethargy of mind. He knows this well enough:

> I am not gamesome; I do lack some part
> Of that quick spirit that is in Antony. [I, ii]

His honesty is absolute and disarming, so that he will not wait as Cassius does for Caesar to compare him unfavorably with the one brilliant person of the play. But honesty in him is humorless and edgeless; it rings a little dully in our ears, and even a little smugly:

> There is no terror, Cassius, in your threats,
> For I am arm'd so strong in honesty
> That they pass by me as the idle wind,
> Which I respect not. [IV, iii]

He would not call this boasting; he would call it the truth, as indeed it is; but the fact that it is, and that he is the speaker, tells us everything about him. Neither would he ad-

mit that his behavior to Messala when Messala brings him the
news of Portia's death is a piece of acting.

BRUTUS.   Now, as you are a Roman, tell me true.
MESSALA. Then like a Roman bear the truth I tell:
          For certain she is dead, and by strange manner.
BRUTUS.   Why, farewell, Portia. We must die, Messala.
          With meditating that she must die once,
          I have the patience to endure it now.
MESSALA. Even so great men great losses should endure.
CASSIUS. I have as much of this in art as you,
          But yet my nature could not bear it so.
BRUTUS.   Well, to our work alive. What do you think
          Of marching to Philippi presently?   [IV, iii]

He would call it a demonstration of how Stoic gentlemen
should conduct themselves. And in truth it is. Brutus already
knows of Portia's death, for we have heard him telling Cassius
of it. Cassius then is assisting him in the act, and Messala is
being impressed as he should be. It is not vanity. It is virtue,
it is true manhood demonstrating itself for the benefit of
others. But to say as much is again to say that Brutus is hu-
morlessly good. If his duty is to know himself, his performance fails. Nobility has numbed him until he cannot see himself for his principles. When his principles are expressing
themselves they are beautiful in their clarity; his consideration for the tired boy Lucius is exquisite (IV, iii), and his last
compliment to mankind should have been deserved:

          My heart doth joy that yet in all my life
          I found no man but he was true to me.   [V, v]

But when he speaks to himself he knows not who is there; he
addresses a strange audience, and fumbles. The reasoning
with which he convinces himself that Caesar should be murdered is woefully inadequate.

                    So Caesar may;
          Then, lest he may, prevent.   [II, i]

The soliloquy of which these pitiful phrases are a part is rid-
dled with rank fallacy. The fine man is a coarse thinker, the
saint of self-denial has little self left to deny.

     Shakespeare has done all that could be done with such a
man, but what could be done was limited. The hero is heavy
in the poet's hands; his reticence prevents intimacy, so that

his blunders—as a conspirator with respect to Antony and as a general with respect to the time for attack—are difficult to excuse, they do not arouse in us any instinct to insist that to fail as such a man fails is to be glorious after all. Even the gentleness which will not let him desire Antony's death is in the last analysis confused. He is not mad, or haunted, or inspired, or perplexed in the extreme. He is simply confused. And the grounds of confusion in a man so negative are not to be known. Neither perhaps are they to be known in a man like Hamlet who uncovers something in himself with every word he utters. Yet we know the man—so well that his very attempts to evade us bring him closer. Hamlet may seldom mean what he says; and Shakespeare will never commit the error of exposing him in thought as he exposes Brutus; but we shall be instantly aware of what he means, at any rate to us, and we shall not fail to measure the disturbance in a too much changed mind.

The Story of the Play

ACT I

JULIUS CAESAR returns victorious from foreign wars and, according to custom, the citizens of Rome escort him in triumph to the Capitol. So overjoyed are they that Mark Antony deems the day propitious to offer him a kingly crown. This is thrice offered and thrice refused. But even in the hour of Caesar's greatest triumph forces are at work against him. Cassius has gathered together a band of conspirators, who finally persuade Brutus, a high-minded Roman, to join them, under the belief that the death of Caesar will be for the country's good.

ACT II

UPON his entry into Rome, Caesar had been warned by a soothsayer to "beware the ides of March." So on the dawn of this portentous day, he is minded to remain at home, especially since his wife has been the victim of ominous dreams. But the conspirators have foreseen his hesitancy and therefore come in a body to urge his attendance at the senate-house. Ashamed of his fears, he yields and goes with them.

ACT III

ONCE in the senate-house, the conspirators, under guise of presenting a petition, press about Caesar; and presently each one stabs him, Brutus thrusting last of all. Caesar murmurs, "And *thou*, Brutus?" and expires.

Mark Antony, Caesar's steadfast friend, flies at the first scent of danger, but returns to dissemble with the slayers of Caesar. He pleads friendliness for their cause, but begs permission to speak at the burial of the slain leader. Brutus generously consents to this, despite his friends' disapproval, stipulating only that he himself speak first, and that Antony in his oration make no charges. Antony declares himself satisfied.

Brutus accordingly makes a short speech to the citizens, in which he pleads the general welfare as sufficient cause and excuse for the slaying of Caesar. Antony follows him in a skilful harangue, full of praise for Caesar; and though referring to Brutus and his party as "honourable men," he turns the term into a reproach and byword. The populace, which but a moment before was applauding Brutus to the echo, now turns in fury against him. The conspirators are forced to flee the city.

ACT IV

Upon the death of Caesar two factions arise and take the field against each other. The first is the army of Brutus and Cassius. The second comprises the forces of a newly formed triumvirate, consisting of Mark Antony, Octavius Caesar, and Lepidus. Both armies converge towards the Plains of Philippi. One night while Brutus is lying awake and restless in his tent, the ghost of Caesar appears and tells him, "Thou shalt see me at Philippi."

ACT V

The forces meet at Philippi and engage in battle. But from the first the troops of Brutus and Cassius are dispirited—unconsciously influenced by the forebodings that have come to both their leaders. With his own "good sword, that ran through Caesar's bowels," Cassius causes himself to be killed by his servant Pindarus. Later in the day Brutus runs on his sword and dies. The triumvirate are victorious, and Caesar may "now be still."

J. Walker McSpadden

List of Characters

Julius Caesar,

Octavius Caesar,
Marcus Antonius,
M. Æmil. Lepidus, } *Triumvirs after the death of Julius Caesar*

Cicero,
Publius,
Popilius Lena, } *Senators*

Marcus Brutus,
Cassius,
Casca,
Trebonius,
Ligarius,
Decius Brutus,
Metellus Cimber,
Cinna, } *Conspirators against Julius Caesar*

Flavius *and* Marullus, Tribunes

Artemidorus of Cnidos, *a teacher of Rhetoric*

A Soothsayer

Cinna, *a poet*

Another Poet

Lucilius, Titinius Messala, Young Cato, *and* Volumnius,—*Friends to* Brutus *and* Cassius

Varro, Clitus, Claudius, Strato, Lucius, Dardanius,—*Servants to* Brutus

Pindarus, *Servant to* Cassius

Calpurnia, *Wife to* Caesar

Portia, *Wife to* Brutus

Senators, Citizens, Guards, Attendants, &c.

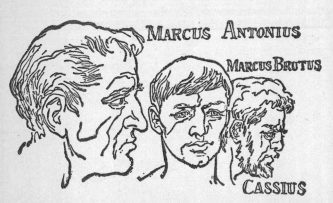

MARCUS ANTONIUS

MARCUS BRUTUS

CASSIUS

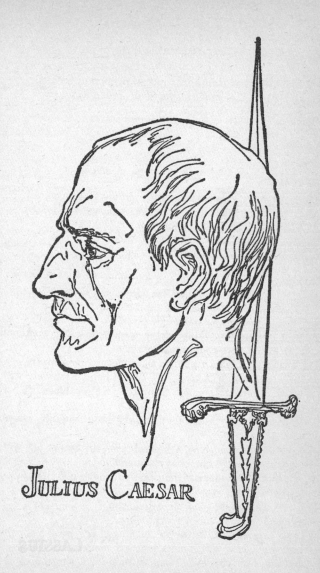

JULIUS CAESAR

Julius Caesar

SCENE — *Rome; the neighborhood of* SARDIS;
the neighborhood of PHILIPPI.

ACT I

SCENE I — ROME. *A street.*

Enter FLAVIUS, MARULLUS, *and certain* COMMONERS.]

FLAVIUS. Hence! home, you idle creatures, get you home:
  Is this a holiday? what! know you not,
  Being mechanical, you ought not walk
  Upon a laboring day without the sign
  Of your profession? Speak, what trade art thou?

FIRST COMMONER. Why, sir, a carpenter.

MARULLUS. Where is thy leather apron and thy rule?
  What dost thou with thy best apparel on?
  You, sir, what trade are you?

SECOND COMMONER. Truly, sir, in respect of a fine workman,
  I am but, as you would say, a cobbler.

MARULLUS. But what trade art thou? answer me directly.

SECOND COMMONER. A trade, sir, that, I hope, I may use with
  a safe conscience; which is indeed, sir, a mender of bad
  soles.

MARULLUS. What trade, thou knave? thou naughty knave,
  what trade?

SECOND COMMONER. Nay, I beseech you, sir, be not out with
  me: yet, if you be out, sir, I can mend you.

MARULLUS. What mean'st thou by that? mend me, thou saucy
  fellow!

SECOND COMMONER. Why, sir, cobble you.

FLAVIUS. Thou art a cobbler, art thou?

SECOND COMMONER. Truly, sir, all that I live by is with the
  awl: I meddle with no tradesman's matters, nor women's
  matters, but with awl. I am indeed, sir, a surgeon to old

shoes; when they are in great danger, I re-cover them. As proper men as ever trod upon neats-leather have gone upon my handiwork.

FLAVIUS. But wherefore art not in thy shop to-day?
Why dost thou lead men about the streets?

SECOND COMMONER. Truly, sir, to wear out their shoes, to get myself into more work. But indeed, sir, we make holiday, to see Cæsar and to rejoice in his triumph.

MARULLUS. Wherefore rejoice? What conquest brings he home?
What tributaries follow him to Rome,
To grace in captive bonds his chariot-wheels?
You blocks, you stones, you worse than senseless things!
O you hard hearts, you cruel men of Rome,
Knew you not Pompey? Many a time and oft
Have you climb'd up to walls and battlements,
To towers and windows, yea, to chimney-tops,
Your infants in your arms, and there have sat
The live-long day with patient expectation
To see great Pompey pass the streets of Rome:
And when you saw his chariot but appear,
Have you not made an universal shout,
That Tiber trembled underneath her banks
To hear the replication of your sounds
Made in her concave shores?
And do you now put on your best attire?
And do you now cull out a holiday?
And do you now strew flowers in his way
That comes in triumph over Pompey's blood?
Be gone!
Run to your houses, fall upon your knees,
Pray to the gods to intermit the plague
That needs must light on this ingratitude.

FLAVIUS. Go, go, good countrymen, and, for this fault,
Assemble all the poor men of your sort;
Draw them to Tiber banks and weep your tears
Into the channel, till the lowest stream
Do kiss the most exalted shores of all.

                              [*Exeunt all the* COMMONERS.

See, whether their basest metal be not moved;
They vanish tongue-tied in their guiltiness.

Go you down that way towards the Capitol;
This way will I: disrobe the images,
If you do find them deck'd with ceremonies.

MARULLUS. May we do so?
You know it is the feast of Lupercal.

FLAVIUS. It is no matter: let no images
Be hung with Cæsar's trophies. I'll about,
And drive away the vulgar from the streets:
So do you too, where you perceive them thick.
These growing feathers pluck'd from Cæsar's wing
Will make him fly an ordinary pitch,
Who else would soar above the view of men
And keep us all in servile fearfulness.   [Exeunt.

SCENE II — A public place.

Flourish. Enter CÆSAR; ANTONY, for the course;
    CALPURNIA, PORTIA, DECIUS, CICERO,
    BRUTUS, CASSIUS, and CASCA; a great
    crowd following, among them a SOOTH-
    SAYER.]

CÆSAR. Calpurnia!

CASCA.   Peace, ho! Cæsar speaks.   [Music ceases.

CÆSAR.   Calpurnia!

CALPURNIA. Here, my lord.

CÆSAR. Stand you directly in Antonius' way,
When he doth run his course. Antonius!

ANTONY. Cæsar, my lord?

CÆSAR. Forget not, in your speed, Antonius,
To touch Calpurnia; for our elders say,
The barren, touched in this holy chase,
Shake off their sterile curse.

ANTONY.   I shall remember:
When Cæsar says 'do this,' it is perform'd.

CÆSAR. Set on, and leave no ceremony out.   [Flourish.

SOOTHSAYER. Cæsar!

CÆSAR. Ha! who calls?

CASCA. Bid every noise be still: peace yet again!

CÆSAR. Who is it in the press that calls on me?
I hear a tongue, shriller than all the music,
Cry 'Cæsar.' Speak; Cæsar is turn'd to hear.

SOOTHSAYER. Beware the ides of March.

CÆSAR.   What man is that?

BRUTUS. A soothsayer bids you beware the ides of March.

CÆSAR. Set him before me; let me see his face.

CASSIUS. Fellow, come from the throng; look upon Cæsar.

CÆSAR. What say'st thou to me now? speak once again.

SOOTHSAYER. Beware the ides of March.

CÆSAR. He is a dreamer; let us leave him: pass.

> [*Sennet. Exeunt all but* BRUTUS *and* CASSIUS.

CASSIUS. Will you go see the order of the course?

BRUTUS. Not I.

CASSIUS. I pray you, do.

BRUTUS. I am not gamesome: I do lack some part
Of that quick spirit that is in Antony.
Let me not hinder, Cassius, your desires;
I'll leave you.

CASSIUS. Brutus, I do observe you now of late:
I have not from your eyes that gentleness
And show of love as I was wont to have:
You bear too stubborn and too strange a hand
Over your friend that loves you.

BRUTUS.   Cassius,
Be not deceived: if I have veil'd my look,
I turn the trouble of my countenance
Merely upon myself. Vexed I am
Of late with passions of some difference,
Conceptions only proper to myself,
Which give some soil perhaps to my behaviors;
But let not therefore my good friends be grieved—
Among which number, Cassius, be you one—
Nor construe any further my neglect
Than that poor Brutus with himself at war
Forgets the shows of love to other men.

CASSIUS. Then, Brutus, I have much mistook your passion;
By means whereof this breast of mine hath buried
Thoughts of great value, worthy cogitations.
Tell me, good Brutus, can you see your face?

BRUTUS. No, Cassius; for the eye sees not itself
But by reflection, by some other things.

CASSIUS. 'Tis just:
And it is very much lamented, Brutus,
That you have no such mirrors as will turn
Your hidden worthiness into your eye,

That you might see your shadow. I have heard
Where many of the best respect in Rome,
Except immortal Cæsar, speaking of Brutus,
And groaning underneath this age's yoke,
Have wish'd that noble Brutus had his eyes.

BRUTUS. Into what dangers would you lead me, Cassius,
That you would have me seek into myself
For that which is not in me?

CASSIUS. Therefore, good Brutus, be prepared to hear:
And since you know you cannot see yourself
So well as by reflection, I your glass
Will modestly discover to yourself
That of yourself which you yet know not of.
And be not jealous on me, gentle Brutus:
Were I a common laughter, or did use
To stale with ordinary oaths my love
To every new protester; if you know
That I do fawn on men and hug them hard,
And after scandal them; or if you know
That I profess myself in banqueting
To all the rout, then hold me dangerous.

[Flourish and shout.

BRUTUS. What means this shouting? I do fear, the people
Choose Cæsar for their king.

CASSIUS.   Aye, do you fear it?
Then must I think you would not have it so.

BRUTUS. I would not, Cassius, yet I love him well.
But wherefore do you hold me here so long?
What is it that you would impart to me?
If it be aught toward the general good,
Set honor in one eye and death i' the other,
And I will look on both indifferently:
For let the gods so speed me as I love
The name of honor more than I fear death.

CASSIUS. I know that virtue to be in you, Brutus,
As well as I do know your outward favor.
Well, honor is the subject of my story.
I cannot tell what you and other men
Think of this life, but, for my single self,
I had as lief not be as live to be
In awe of such a thing as I myself.
I was born free as Cæsar; so were you:

We both have fed as well, and we can both
Endure the winter's cold as well as he:
For once, upon a raw and gusty day,
The troubled Tiber chafing with her shores,
Cæsar said to me, 'Darest thou, Cassius, now
Leap in with me into this angry flood,
And swim to yonder point?' Upon the word,
Accoutered as I was, I plunged in
And bade him follow: so indeed he did.
The torrent roar'd, and we did buffet it
With lusty sinews, throwing it aside
And stemming it with hearts of controversy;
But ere we could arrive the point proposed,
Cæsar cried 'Help me, Cassius, or I sink!'
I, as Æneas our great ancestor
Did from the flames of Troy upon his shoulder
The old Anchises bear, so from the waves of Tiber
Did I the tired Cæsar: and this man
Is now become a god, and Cassius is
A wretched creature, and must bend his body
If Cæsar carelessly but nod on him.
He had a fever when he was in Spain,
And when the fit was on him, I did mark
How he did shake: 'tis true, this god did shake;
His coward lips did from their color fly,
And that same eye whose bend doth awe the world
Did lose his luster: I did hear him groan:
Aye, and that tongue of his that bade the Romans
Mark him and write his speeches in their books,
Alas, it cried, 'Give me some drink, Titinius,'
As a sick girl. Ye gods! it doth amaze me
A man of such a feeble temper should
So get the start of the majestic world
And bear the palm alone.   [*Shout. Flourish.*

BRUTUS. Another general shout!
I do believe that these applauses are
For some new honors that are heap'd on Cæsar.
CASSIUS. Why, man, he doth bestride the narrow world
Like a Colossus, and we petty men
Walk under his huge legs and peep about
To find ourselves dishonorable graves.
Men at some time are masters of their fates:

The fault, dear Brutus, is not in our stars,
But in ourselves, that we are underlings.
Brutus, and Cæsar: what should be in that Cæsar?
Why should that name be sounded more than yours?
Write them together, yours is as fair a name;
Sound them, it doth become the mouth as well;
Weigh them, it is as heavy; conjure with 'em,
Brutus will start a spirit as soon as Cæsar.
Now, in the names of all the gods at once,
Upon what meat doth this our Cæsar feed,
That he is grown so great? Age, thou are shamed!
Rome, thou hast lost the breed of noble bloods!
When went there by an age, since the great flood,
But it was famed with more than with one man?
When could they say till now that talk'd of Rome
That her wide walls encompass'd but one man?
Now is it Rome indeed, and room enough,
When there is in it but one only man.
O, you and I have heard our fathers say
There was a Brutus once that would have brook'd
The eternal devil to keep his state in Rome
As easily as a king.

BRUTUS. That you do love me, I am nothing jealous;
What you would work me to, I have some aim:
How I have thought of this and of these times,
I shall recount hereafter; for this present,
I would not, so with love I might entreat you,
Be any further moved. What you have said
I will consider; what you have to say
I will with patience hear, and find a time
Both meet to hear and answer such high things.
Till then, my noble friend, chew upon this:
Brutus had rather be a villager
Then to repute himself a son of Rome
Under these hard conditions as this time
Is like to lay upon us.

CASSIUS. I am glad that my weak words
Have struck but thus much show of fire from Brutus.

BRUTUS. The games are done, and Cæsar is returning.

CASSIUS. As they pass by, pluck Casca by the sleeve;
And he will, after his sour fashion, tell you
What hath proceeded worthy note to-day.

Re-enter CÆSAR *and his train.*]

BRUTUS. I will do so: but, look you, Cassius,
   The angry spot doth glow on Cæsar's brow,
   And all the rest look like a chidden train:
   Calpurnia's cheek is pale, and Cicero
   Looks with such ferret and such fiery eyes
   As we have seen him in the Capitol,
   Being cross'd in conference by some senators.

CASSIUS. Casca will tell us what the matter is.

CÆSAR. Antonius!

ANTONY. Cæsar?

CÆSAR. Let me have men about me that are fat,
   Sleek-headed men, and such as sleep o' nights:
   Yond Cassius has a lean and hungry look;
   He thinks too much: such men are dangerous.

ANTONY. Fear him not, Cæsar; he's not dangerous;
   He is a noble Roman, and well given.

CÆSAR. Would he were fatter! but I fear him not:
   Yet if my name were liable to fear,
   I do not know the man I should avoid
   So soon as that spare Cassius. He reads much;
   He is a great observer, and he looks
   Quite through the deeds of men: he loves no plays,
   As thou dost, Antony; he hears no music:
   Seldom he smiles, and smiles in such a sort
   As if he mock'd himself, and scorn'd his spirit
   That could be moved to smile at any thing.
   Such men as he be never at heart's ease
   Whiles they behold a greater than themselves,
   And therefore are they very dangerous.
   I rather tell thee what is to be fear'd
   Than what I fear; for always I am Cæsar.
   Come on my right hand, for this ear is deaf,
   And tell me truly what thou think'st of him.
      [*Sennet. Exeunt* CÆSAR *and all his train but* CASCA.

CASCA. You pull'd me by the cloak; would you speak with me?

BRUTUS. Aye, Casca; tell us what hath chanced to-day,
   That Cæsar looks so sad.

CASCA. Why, you were with him, were you not?

BRUTUS. I should not then ask Casca what had chanced.

CASCA. Why, there was a crown offered him: and being offered him, he put it by with the back of his hand, thus: and then the people fell a-shouting.

BRUTUS. What was the second noise for?

CASCA. Why, for that too.

CASSIUS. They shouted thrice: what was the last cry for?

CASCA. Why, for that too.

BRUTUS. Was the crown offered him thrice?

CASCA. Aye, marry, was't, and he put it by thrice, every time gentler than other; and at every putting by mine honest neighbors shouted.

CASSIUS. Who offered him the crown?

CASCA. Why, Antony.

BRUTUS. Tell us the manner of it, gentle Casca.

CASCA. I can as well be hang'd as tell the manner of it: it was mere foolery; I did not mark it. I saw Mark Antony offer him a crown: yet 'twas not a crown neither, 'twas one of these coronets: and, as I told you, he put it by once: but for all that, to my thinking, he would fain have had it. Then he offered it to him again; then he put it by again: but, to my thinking, he was very loath to lay his fingers off it. And then he offered it the third time; he put it the third time by: and still as he refused it, the rabblement hooted and clapped their chopped hands and threw up their sweaty night-caps and uttered such a deal of stinking breath because Cæsar refused the crown, that it had almost choked Cæsar; for he swounded and fell down at it: and for mine own part, I durst not laugh, for fear of opening my lips and receiving the bad air.

CASSIUS. But, soft, I pray you: what, did Cæsar swound?

CASCA. He fell down in the market-place and foamed at mouth and was speechless.

BRUTUS. 'Tis very like: he hath the falling-sickness.

CASSIUS. No, Cæsar hath it not: but you, and I,
And honest Casca, we have the falling-sickness.

CASCA. I know not what you mean by that, but I am sure Cæsar fell down. If the tag-rag people did not clap him and kiss him according as he pleased and displeased them, as they used to do the players in the theater, I am no true man.

BRUTUS. What said he when he came unto himself?

CASCA. Marry, before he fell down, when he perceived the common herd was glad he refused the crown, he plucked me ope his doublet and offered them his throat to cut. An I had been a man of any occupation, if I would not have taken him at a word, I would I might go to hell among the rogues. And so he fell. When he came to himself again, he said, if he had done or said anything amiss, he desired their worships to think it was his infirmity. Three or four wenches, where I stood, cried 'Alas, good soul!' and forgave him with all their hearts: but there's no heed to be taken of them; if Cæsar had stabbed their mothers, they would have done no less.

BRUTUS. And after that, he came, thus sad, away?

CASCA. Aye.

CASSIUS. Did Cicero say any thing?

CASCA. Aye, he spoke Greek.

CASSIUS. To what effect?

CASCA. Nay, an I tell you that, I'll ne'er look you i' the face again: but those that understood him smiled at one another and shook their heads; but for mine own part, it was Greek to me. I could tell you more news too: Marullus and Flavius, for pulling scarfs off Cæsar's images, are put to silence. Fare you well. There was more foolery yet, if I could remember it.

CASSIUS. Will you sup with me to-night, Casca?

CASCA. No, I am promised forth.

CASSIUS. Will you dine with me to-morrow?

CASCA. Aye, if I be alive, and your mind hold, and your dinner worth the eating.

CASSIUS. Good; I will expect you.

CASCA. Do so: farewell, both.   [*Exit.*

BRUTUS. What a blunt fellow is this grown to be!
He was quick metal when he went to school.

CASSIUS. So is he now in execution
Of any bold or noble enterprise,
However he puts on this tardy form.
This rudeness is a sauce to his good wit,
Which gives men stomach to digest his words
With better appetite.

BRUTUS. And so it is. For this time I will leave you:
To-morrow, if you please to speak with me,
I will come home to you, or, if you will,
Come home to me and I will wait for you.

CASSIUS. I will do so: till then, think of the world.

[*Exit* BRUTUS.

Well, Brutus, thou art noble; yet, I see,
Thy honorable metal may be wrought
From that it is disposed: therefore, it is meet
That noble minds keep ever with their likes;
For who so firm that cannot be seduced?
Cæsar doth bear me hard; but he loves Brutus:
If I were Brutus now and he were Cassius,
He should not humor me. I will this night,
In several hands, in at his windows throw,
As if they came from several citizens,
Writings, all tending to the great opinion
That Rome holds of his name, wherein obscurely
Cæsar's ambition shall be glanced at:
And after this let Cæsar seat him sure;
For we will shake him, or worse days endure.   [*Exit.*

SCENE III — *A street.*

Thunder and lightning. Enter, from opposite sides,
    CASCA, *with his sword drawn, and* CICERO.]

CICERO. Good even, Casca: brought you Cæsar home?
    Why are you breathless? and why stare you so?
CASCA. Are not you moved, when all the sway of earth
    Shakes like a thing unfirm? O Cicero,
    I have seen tempests, when the scolding winds
    Have rived the knotty oaks, and I have seen
    The ambitious ocean swell and rage and foam,
    To be exalted with the threatening clouds;
    But never till to-night, never till now,
    Did I go through a tempest dropping fire.
    Either there is a civil strife in heaven,
    Or else the world too saucy with the gods
    Incenses them to send destruction.
CICERO. Why, saw you a thing more wonderful?
CASCA. A common slave—you know him well by sight—
    Held up his left hand, which did flame and burn
    Like twenty torches join'd, and yet his hand
    Not sensible of fire remain'd unscorch'd.
    Besides—I ha' not since put up my sword—
    Against the Capitol I met a lion,

Who glared upon me and went surly by
Without annoying me: and there were drawn
Upon a heap a hundred ghastly women
Transformed with their fear, who swore they saw
Men all in fire walk up and down the streets.
And yesterday the bird of night did sit
Even at noon-day upon the market-place,
Hooting and shrieking. When these prodigies
Do so conjointly meet, let not men say
'These are their reasons: they are natural:'
For, I believe, they are portentous things
Unto the climate that they point upon.

CICERO. Indeed, it is a strange-disposed time:
But men may construe things after their fashion,
Clean from the purpose of the things themselves.
Comes Cæsar to the Capitol to-morrow?

CASCA. He doth; for he did bid Antonius
Send word to you he would be there to-morrow.

CICERO. Good night then, Casca: this disturbed sky
Is not to walk in.

CASCA.   Farewell, Cicero.   [*Exit* CICERO.
Enter CASSIUS.]

CASSIUS. Who's there?

CASCA.   A Roman.

CASSIUS.   Casca, by your voice.

CASCA. Your ear is good. Cassius, what night is this!

CASSIUS. A very pleasing night to honest men.

CASCA. Who ever knew the heavens menace so?

CASSIUS. Those that have known the earth so full of faults.
For my part, I have walk'd about the streets,
Submitting me unto the perilous night,
And thus unbraced, Casca, as you see,
Have bared my bosom to the thunder-stone;
And when the cross blue lightning seem'd to open
The breast of heaven, I did present myself
Even in the aim and very flash of it.

CASCA. But wherefore did you so much tempt the heavens?
It is the part of men to fear and tremble
When the most mighty gods by tokens send
Such dreadful heralds to astonish us.

CASSIUS. You are dull, Casca, and those sparks of life
That should be in a Roman you do want,

Or else you use not. You look pale and gaze
And put on fear and cast yourself in wonder,
To see the strange impatience of the heavens:
But if you would consider the true cause
Why all these fires, why all these gliding ghosts,
Why birds and beasts from quality and kind,
Why old men fool and children calculate,
Why all these things change from their ordinance,
Their natures and preformed faculties,
To monstrous quality, why, you shall find
That heaven hath infused them with these spirits
To make them instruments of fear and warning
Unto some monstrous state.
Now could I, Casca, name to thee a man
Most like this dreadful night,
That thunders, lightens, opens graves, and roars
As doth the lion in the Capitol,
A man no mightier than thyself or me
In personal action, yet prodigious grown
And fearful, as these strange eruptions are.

CASCA. 'Tis Cæsar that you mean; is it not, Cassius?

CASSIUS. Let it be who it is: for Romans now
Have thews and limbs like to their ancestors;
But, woe the while! our fathers' minds are dead,
And we are govern'd with our mothers' spirits;
Our yoke and sufferance show us womanish.

CASCA. Indeed they say the senators to-morrow
Mean to establish Cæsar as a king;
And he shall wear his crown by sea and land,
In every place save here in Italy.

CASSIUS. I know where I will wear this dagger then:
Cassius from bondage will deliver Cassius.
Therein, ye gods, you make the weak most strong;
Therein, ye gods, you tyrants do defeat:
Nor stony tower, nor walls of beaten brass,
Nor airless dungeon, nor strong links of iron,
Can be retentive to the strength of spirit;
But life, being weary of these worldly bars,
Never lacks power to dismiss itself.
If I know this, know all the world besides,
That part of tyranny that I do bear

I can shake off at pleasure.   [*Thunder still.*

CASCA.   So can I:
　So every bondman in his own hand bears
　The power to cancel his captivity.

CASSIUS. And why should Cæsar be a tyrant then?
　Poor man! I know he would not be a wolf
　But that he sees the Romans are but sheep:
　He were no lion, were not Romans hinds.
　Those that with haste will make a mighty fire
　Begin it with weak straws: what trash is Rome,
　With rubbish and what offal, when it serves
　For the base matter to illuminate
　So vile a thing as Cæsar! But, O grief,
　Where hast thou led me? I perhaps speak this
　Before a willing bondman; then I know
　My answer must be made. But I am arm'd,
　And dangers are to me indifferent.

CASCA. You speak to Casca, and to such a man
　That is no fleering tell-tale. Hold, my hand:
　Be factious for redress of all these griefs,
　And I will set this foot of mine as far
　As who goes farthest.

CASSIUS.   There's a bargain made.
　Now know you, Casca, I have moved already
　Some certain of the noblest-minded Romans
　To undergo with me an enterprise
　Of honorable-dangerous consequence;
　And I do know, by this they stay for me
　In Pompey's porch: for now, this fearful night,
　There is no stir or walking in the streets,
　And the complexion of the element
　In favor's like the work we have in hand,
　Most bloody, fiery, and most terrible.

Enter CINNA.]

CASCA. Stand close awhile, for here comes one in haste.

CASSIUS. 'Tis Cinna; I do know know him by his gait;
　Here is a friend. Cinna, where haste you so?

CINNA. To find out you. Who's that? Metellus Cimber?

CASSIUS. No, it is Casca; one incorporate
　To our attempts. Am I not stay'd for, Cinna?

CINNA. I am glad on 't. What a fearful night is this!
　There's two or three of us have seen strange sights.

CASSIUS. Am I not stay'd for? tell me.
CINNA.   Yes, you are.
    Cassius, if you could
    But win the noble Brutus to our party—
CASSIUS. Be you content: good Cinna, take this paper,
    And look you lay it in the prætor's chair,
    Where Brutus may but find it, and throw this
    In at his window; set this up with wax
    Upon old Brutus' statue: all this done,
    Repair to Pompey's porch, here you shall find us.
    Is Decius Brutus and Trebonius there?
CINNA. All but Metellus Cimber; and he's gone
    To seek you at your house. Well, I will hie,
    And so bestow these papers as you bade me.
CASSIUS. That done, repair to Pompey's theater   [*Exit* CINNA.
    Come, Casca, you and I will yet ere day
    See Brutus at his house: three parts of him
    Is ours already, and the man entire
    Upon the next encounter yields him ours.
CASCA. O, he sits high in all the people's hearts;
    And that which would appear offense in us
    His countenance, like richest alchemy,
    Will change to virtue and to worthiness.
CASSIUS. Him and his worth and our great need of him
    You have right well conceited. Let us go,
    For it is after midnight, and ere day
    We will awake him and be sure of him.   [*Exeunt.*

ACT II

Scene I — Rome. Brutus's *orchard*.

Enter Brutus.]

BRUTUS. What, Lucius, ho!
 I cannot, by the progress of the stars,
 Give guess how near to day. Lucius, I say!
 I would it were my fault to sleep so soundly.
 When, Lucius, when? awake. I say! what, Lucius!

Enter LUCIUS.]

LUCIUS. Call'd you, my lord?

BRUTUS. Get me a taper in my study, Lucius:
 When it is lighted, come and call me here.

LUCIUS. I will, my lord.   [*Exit.*

BRUTUS. It must be by his death: and, for my part,
 I know no personal cause to spurn at him,
 But for the general. He would be crown'd:
 How that might change his nature, there's the question:
 It is the bright day that brings forth the adder;
 And that craves wary walking. Crown him?—that;—
 And then, I grant, we put a sting in him,
 That at his will he may do danger with.
 The abuse of greatness is when it disjoins
 Remorse from power: and, to speak truth of Cæsar,
 I have not known when his affections sway'd
 More than his reason. But 'tis a common proof,
 That lowliness is young ambition's ladder,
 Whereto the climber-upward turns his face;
 But when he once attains the upmost round,
 He then unto the ladder turns his back,
 Looks in the clouds, scorning the base degrees
 By which he did ascend: so Cæsar may;
 Then, lest he may, prevent. And, since the quarrel
 Will bear no color for the thing he is,
 Fashion it thus; that what he is, augmented,
 Would run to these and these extremities:
 And therefore think him as a serpent's egg
 Which hatch'd would as his kind grow mischievous,
 And kill him in the shell.

Re-enter LUCIUS.]

LUCIUS. The taper burneth in your closet, sir.
　Searching the window for a flint I found
　This paper thus seal'd up, and I am sure
　It did not lie there when I went to bed.

　　　　　　　　　　　　　　[*Gives him the letter.*

BRUTUS. Get you to bed again; it is not day.
　Is not to-morrow, boy, the ides of March?

LUCIUS. I know not, sir.

BRUTUS. Look in the calendar and bring me word.

LUCIUS. I will, sir.　　　　　　　　　　　[*Exit.*

BRUTUS. The exhalations whizzing in the air
　Give so much light that I may read by them.

　　　　　　　　　　　[*Opens the letter and reads.*

　'Brutus, thou sleep'st: awake and see thyself.
　Shall Rome, &c. Speak, strike, redress.
　Brutus, thou sleep'st: awake.'
　Such instigations have been often dropp'd
　Where I have took them up.
　'Shall Rome, &c.' Thus must I piece it out:
　Shall Rome stand under one man's awe? What, Rome?
　My ancestors did from the streets of Rome
　The Tarquin drive, when he was call'd a king.
　'Speak, strike, redress.' Am I entreated
　To speak and strike? O Rome, I make thee promise,
　If the redress will follow, thou receivest
　Thy full petition at the hand of Brutus!

Re-enter LUCIUS.]

LUCIUS. Sir, March is wasted fifteen days.　[*Knocking within.*

BRUTUS. 'Tis good. Go to the gate; somebody knocks.

　　　　　　　　　　　　　　[*Exit* LUCIUS.

　Since Cassius first did whet me against Cæsar
　I have not slept.
　Between the acting of a dreadful thing
　And the first motion, all the interim is
　Like a phantasma or a hideous dream:
　The genius and the mortal instruments
　Are then in council, and the state of man,
　Like to a little kingdom, suffers then
　The nature of an insurrection.

Re-enter LUCIUS.]

LUCIUS. Sir, 'tis your brother Cassius at the door,

Who doth desire to see you.

BRUTUS.   Is he alone?

LUCIUS. No, sir, there are more with him.

BRUTUS.   Do you know them?

LUCIUS. No, sir: their hats are pluck'd about their ears,
    And half their faces buried in their cloaks,
    That by no means I may discover them
    By any mark of favor.

BRUTUS.   Let them enter.   [*Exit* LUCIUS.
    They are the faction. O conspiracy,
    Shamest thou to show thy dangerous brow by night,
    When evils are most free? O, then, by day
    Where wilt thou find a cavern dark enough
    To mask thy monstrous visage? Seek none, conspiracy;
    Hide it in smiles and affability:
    For if thou path, thy native semblance on,
    Not Erebus itself were dim enough
    To hide thee from prevention.

Enter the conspirators, CASSIUS, CASCA, DECIUS,
        CINNA, METELLUS CIMBER, *and* TREBONIUS.]

CASSIUS. I think we are too bold upon your rest:
    Good morrow, Brutus; do we trouble you?

BRUTUS. I have been up this hour, awake all night.
    Know I these men that come along with you?

CASSIUS. Yes, every man of them; and no man here
    But honors you; and everyone doth wish
    You had but that opinion of yourself
    Which every noble Roman bears of you.
    This is Trebonius.

BRUTUS.   He is welcome hither.

CASSIUS. This, Decius Brutus.

BRUTUS.   He is welcome too.

CASSIUS. This, Casca; this, Cinna; and this, Metellus Cimber.

BRUTUS. They are all welcome.
    What watchful cares do interpose themselves
    Betwixt your eyes and night?

CASSIUS. Shall I entreat a word?   [*They whisper.*

DECIUS. Here lies the east: does not the day break here?

CASCA. No.

CINNA. O, pardon, sir, it doth, and yon gray lines
    That fret the clouds are messengers of day.

CASCA. You shall confess that you are both deceived.

Here, as I point my sword, the sun arises;
Which is a great way growing on the south,
Weighing the youthful season of the year.
Some two months hence up higher toward the north
He first presents his fire, and the high east
Stands at the Capitol, directly here.

BRUTUS. Give me your hands all over, one by one.

CASSIUS. And let us swear our resolution.

BRUTUS. No, not an oath: if not the face of men,
The sufferance of our souls, the time's abuse,—
If these be motives weak, break off betimes,
And every man hence to his idle bed;
So let high-sighted tyranny range on
Till each man drop by lottery. But if these,
As I am sure they do, bear fire enough
To kindle cowards and to steel with valor
The melting spirits of women, then, countrymen,
What need we any spur but our own cause
To prick us to redress? what other bond
Than secret Romans that have spoke the word,
And will not palter? and what other oath
Than honesty to honesty engaged
That this shall be or we will fall for it?
Swear priests and cowards and men cautelous,
Old feeble carrions and such suffering souls
That welcome wrongs; unto bad causes swear
Such creatures as men doubt: but do not stain
The even virtue of our enterprise,
Nor the insuppressive mettle of our spirits,
To think that or our cause or our performance
Did need an oath; when every drop of blood
That every Roman bears, and nobly bears,
Is guilty of a several bastardy
If he do break the smallest particle
Of any promise that hath pass'd from him.

CASSIUS. But what of Cicero? shall we sound him?
I think he will stand very strong with us.

CASCA. Let us not leave him out.

CINNA.   No, by no means.

METELLUS. O, let us have him, for his silver hairs
Will purchase us a good opinion,
And buy men's voices to commend our deeds:

It shall be said his judgment ruled our hands;
Our youths and wildness shall no whit appear,
But all be buried in his gravity.

BRUTUS. O, name him not: let us not break with him,
For he will never follow any thing
That other men begin.

CASSIUS.　　　　　　　　Then leave him out.

CASCA. Indeed he is not fit.

DECIUS. Shall no man else be touch'd but only Cæsar?

CASSIUS. Decius, well urged: I think it is not meet
Mark Antony, so well beloved of Cæsar,
Should outlive Cæsar: we shall find of him
A shrewd contriver; and you know his means,
If he improve them, may well stretch so far
As to annoy us all: which to prevent,
Let Anthony and Cæsar fall together.

BRUTUS. Our course will seem too bloody, Caius Cassius,
To cut the head off and then hack the limbs,
Like wrath in death and envy afterwards;
For Antony is but a limb of Cæsar:
Let us be sacrificers, but not butchers, Caius.
We all stand up against the spirit of Cæsar,
And in the spirit of men there is no blood:
O, that we then could come by Cæsar's spirit,
And not dismember Cæsar! But, alas,
Cæsar must bleed for it! And, gentle friends,
Let's kill him boldly, but not wrathfully;
Let's carve him as a dish fit for the gods,
Not hew him as a carcass fit for hounds:
And let our hearts, as subtle masters do,
Stir up their servants to an act of rage
And after seem to chide 'em. This shall make
Our purpose necessary and not envious:
Which so appearing to the common eyes,
We shall be call'd purgers, not murderers.
And for Mark Antony, think not of him;
For he can do no more than Cæsar's arm
When Cæsar's head is off.

CASSIUS　　　　　　　　Yet I fear him,
For in the ingrafted love he bears to Cæsar—

BRUTUS. Alas, good Cassius, do not think of him:
If he love Cæsar, all that he can do

Is to himself, take thought and die for Cæsar:
And that were much he should, for he is given
To sports, to wildness and much company.

TREBONIUS. There is no fear in him; let him not die;
For he will live and laugh at this hereafter.   [*Clock strikes.*

BRUTUS. Peace! count the clock.

CASSIUS.   The clock hath stricken three.

TREBONIUS. 'Tis time to part.

CASSIUS.   But it is doubtful yet
Whether Cæsar will come forth to-day or no;
For he is superstitious grown of late,
Quite from the main opinion he held once
Of fantasy, of dreams and ceremonies:
It may be these apparent prodigies,
The unaccustom'd terror of this night
And the persuasion of his augurers,
May hold him from the Capitol to-day.

DECIUS. Never fear that: if he be so resolved,
I can o'ersway him; for he loves to hear
That unicorns may be betray'd with trees
And bears with glasses, elephants with holes,
Lions with toils and men with flatterers:
But when I tell him he hates flatterers,
He says he does, being then most flattered.
Let me work;
For I can give his humor the true bent,
And I will bring him to the Capitol.

CASSIUS. Nay, we will all of us be there to fetch him.

BRUTUS. By the eighth hour: is that the uttermost?

CINNA. Be that the uttermost, and fail not then.

METELLUS. Caius Ligarius doth bear Cæsar hard,
Who rated him for speaking well of Pompey:
I wonder none of you have thought of him.

BRUTUS. Now, good Metellus, go along by him:
He loves me well, and I have given him reasons;
Send him but hither, and I'll fashion him.

CASSIUS. The morning comes upon 's: we'll leave you, Brutus:
And, friends, disperse yourselves: but all remember
What you have said and show yourselves true Romans.

BRUTUS. Good gentlemen, look fresh and merrily;
Let not our looks put on our purposes;
But bear it as our Roman actors do,

With untired spirits and formal constancy:
And so, good morrow to you every one.

                                      [Exeunt all but BRUTUS.

Boy! Lucius! Fast asleep! It is no matter;
Enjoy the honey-heavy dew of slumber:
Thou hast no figures nor no fantasies,
Which busy care draws in the brains of men;
Therefore thou sleep'st so sound.

Enter PORTIA.]

PORTIA.   Brutus, my lord!
BRUTUS. Portia, what mean you? wherefore rise you now?
  It is not for your health thus to commit
  Your weak condition to the raw cold morning.
PORTIA. Nor for yours neither. You've ungently, Brutus,
  Stole from my bed: and yesternight at supper
  You suddenly arose and walk'd about,
  Musing and sighing, with your arms across;
  And when I ask'd you what the matter was,
  You stared upon me with ungentle looks:
  I urged you further; then you scratch'd your head,
  And too impatiently stamp'd with your foot:
  Yet I insisted, yet you answer'd not,
  But with an angry wafture of your hand
  Gave sign for me to leave you: so I did,
  Fearing to strengthen that impatience
  Which seem'd too much enkindled, and withal
  Hoping it was but an effect of humor,
  Which sometime hath his hour with every man.
  It will not let you eat, nor talk, nor sleep,
  And, could it work so much upon your shape
  As it hath much prevail'd on your condition,
  I should not know you, Brutus. Dear my lord,
  Make me acquainted with your cause of grief.
BRUTUS. I am not well in health, and that is all.
PORTIA. Brutus is wise, and, were he not in health,
  He would embrace the means to come by it.
BRUTUS. Why, so I do: good Portia, go to bed.
PORTIA. Is Brutus sick, and is it physical
  To walk unbraced and suck up the humors
  Of the dank morning? What, is Brutus sick,
  And will he steal out of his wholesome bed,
  To dare the vile contagion of the night,

And tempt the rheumy and unpurged air
To add unto his sickness? No, my Brutus;
You have some sick offense within your mind,
Which by the right and virtue of my place
I ought to know of: and, upon my knees,
I charm you, by my once commended beauty,
By all your vows of love and that great vow
Which did incorporate and make us one,
That you unfolded to me, yourself, your half,
Why you are heavy, and what men to-night
Have had resort to you; for here have been
Some six or seven, who did hide their faces
Even from darkness.

BRUTUS.   Kneel not, gentle Portia.

PORTIA. I should not need, if you were gentle Brutus.
Within the bond of marriage, tell me, Brutus,
Is it excepted I should know no secrets
That appertain to you? Am I yourself
But, as it were, in sort or limitation,
To keep with you at meals, comfort your bed,
And talk to you sometimes? Dwell I but in the suburbs
Of your good pleasure? If it be no more,
Portia is Brutus' harlot, not his wife.

BRUTUS. You are my true and honorable wife,
As dear to me as are the ruddy drops
That visit my sad heart.

PORTIA. If this were true, then should I know this secret.
I grant I am a woman, but withal
A woman that Lord Brutus took to wife:
I grant I am a woman, but withal
A woman well reputed, Cato's daughter.
Think you I am no stronger than my sex,
Being so father'd and so husbanded?
Tell me your counsels, I will not disclose 'em:
I have made strong proof of my constancy,
Giving myself a voluntary wound
Here in the thigh: can I bear that with patience
And not my husband's secrets?

BRUTUS.   O ye gods,
Render me worthy of this noble wife!   [*Knocking within.*
Hark, hark! one knocks: Portia, go in a while;
And by and by thy bosom shall partake

The secrets of my heart:
All my engagements I will construe to thee,
All the charactery of my sad brows.
Leave me with haste. [*Exit* PORTIA.] Lucius, who's that
knocks?

Re-enter LUCIUS *with* LIGARIUS.]

LUCIUS. Here is a sick man that would speak with you.

BRUTUS. Caius Ligarius, that Metellus spake of.
Boy, stand aside. Caius Ligarius! how?

LIGARIUS. Vouchsafe good morrow from a feeble tongue.

BRUTUS. O, what a time have you chose out, brave Caius,
To wear a kerchief! Would you were not sick!

LIGARIUS. I am not sick, if Brutus have in hand
Any exploit worthy the name of honor.

BRUTUS. Such an exploit have I in hand, Ligarius,
Had you a healthful ear to hear of it.

LIGARIUS. By all the gods that Romans bow before,
I here discard my sickness! Soul of Rome!
Brave son, derived from honorable loins!
Thou, like an exorcist, hast conjured up
My mortified spirit. Now bid me run,
And I will strive with things impossible,
Yea, get the better of them. What's to do?

BRUTUS. A piece of work that will make sick men whole.

LIGARIUS. But are not some whole that we must make sick?

BRUTUS. That must we also. What it is, my Caius,
I shall unfold to thee, as we are going
To whom it must be done.

LIGARIUS.   Set on your foot,
And with a heart new-fired I follow you,
To do I know not what: but it sufficeth
That Brutus leads me on.

BRUTUS.   Follow me then.   [*Exeunt.*

SCENE II — CAESAR'S *house.*

Thunder and lightning. Enter CÆSAR, *in his night-gown.*]

CÆSAR. Nor heaven nor earth have been at peace to-night:
Thrice hath Calpurnia in her sleep cried out,
'Help, ho! they murder Cæsar!' Who's within?

Enter a SERVANT.]

SERVANT. My lord?

CÆSAR. Go bid the priests do present sacrifice,
  And bring me their opinions of success.
SERVANT. I will, my lord.   [Exit.
Enter CALPURNIA.]
CALPURNIA. What mean you, Cæsar? think you to walk forth?
  You shall not stir out of your house to-day.
CÆSAR. Cæsar shall forth: the things that threaten'd me
  Ne'er look'd but on my back; when they shall see
  The face of Cæsar, they are vanished.
CALPURNIA. Cæsar, I never stood on ceremonies,
  Yet now they fright me. There is one within,
  Besides the things that we have heard and seen,
  Recounts most horrid sights seen by the watch.
  A lioness hath whelped in the streets;
  And graves have yawn'd, and yielded up their dead;
  Fierce fiery warriors fight upon the clouds,
  In ranks and squadrons and right form of war,
  Which drizzled blood upon the Capitol;
  The noise of battle hurtled in the air,
  Horses did neigh and dying men did groan,
  And ghosts did shriek and squeal about the streets.
  O Cæsar! these things are beyond all use,
  And I do fear them.
CÆSAR.   What can be avoided
  Whose end is purposed by the mighty gods?
  Yet Cæsar shall go forth; for these predictions
  Are to the world in general as to Cæsar.
CALPURNIA. When beggars die, there are no comets seen;
  The heavens themselves blaze forth the death of princes.
CÆSAR. Cowards die many times before their death;
  The valiant never taste of death but once.
  Of all the wonders that I yet have heard,
  It seems to me most strange that men should fear;
  Seeing that death, a necessary end,
  Will come when it will come.
Re-enter SERVANT.]
                     What say the augurers?
SERVANT. They would not have you to stir forth to-day.
  Plucking the entrails of an offering forth,
  They could not find a heart within the beast.
CÆSAR. The gods do this in shame of cowardice:
  Cæsar should be a beast without a heart

If he should stay at home to-day for fear.
No, Cæsar shall not: danger knows full well
That Cæsar is more dangerous than he:
We are two lions litter'd in one day,
And I the elder and more terrible:
And Cæsar shall go forth.

CALPURNIA.   Alas, my lord,
Your wisdom is consumed in confidence.
Do not go forth to-day: call it my fear
That keeps you in the house and not your own.
We'll send Mark Antony to the senate-house,
And he shall say you are not well to-day:
Let me, upon my knee, prevail in this.

CÆSAR. Mark Antony shall say I am not well,
And, for thy humor, I will stay at home.

Enter DECIUS.]

Here's Decius Brutus, he shall tell them so.

DECIUS. Cæsar, all hail! good morrow, worthy Cæsar:
I come to fetch you to the senate-house.

CÆSAR. And you are come in very happy time,
To bear my greeting to the senators
And tell them that I will not come to-day:
Cannot, is false, and that I dare not, falser:
I will not come to-day: tell them so, Decius.

CALPURNIA. Say he is sick.

CÆSAR.   Shall Cæsar send a lie?
Have I in conquest stretch'd mine arm so far,
To be afeard to tell graybeards the truth?
Decius, go tell them Cæsar will not come.

DECIUS. Most mighty Cæsar, let me know some cause,
Lest I be laugh'd at when I tell them so.

CÆSAR. The cause is in my will: I will not come;
That is enough to satisfy the senate.
But, for your private satisfaction,
Because I love you, I will let you know.
Calpurnia here, my wife, stays me at home:
She dreamt to-night she saw my statuë,
Which like a fountain with an hundred spouts
Did run pure blood, and many lusty Romans
Came smiling and did bathe their hands in it:
And these does she apply for warnings and portents
And evils imminent, and on her knee

Hath begg'd that I will stay at home to-day.

DECIUS. This dream is all amiss interpreted;
It was a vision fair and fortunate:
Your statue spouting blood in many pipes,
In which so many smiling Romans bathed,
Signifies that from you great Rome shall suck
Reviving blood, and that great men shall press
For tinctures, stains, relics and cognizance.
This by Calpurnia's dream is signified.

CÆSAR. And this way have you well expounded it.

DECIUS. I have, when you have heard what I can say:
And know it now: the senate have concluded
To give this day a crown to mighty Cæsar.
If you shall send them word you will not come,
Their minds may change. Besides, it were a mock
Apt to be render'd, for some one to say
'Break up the senate till another time,
When Cæsar's wife shall meet with better dreams.'
If Cæsar hide himself, shall they not whisper
'Lo, Cæsar is afraid'?
Pardon me, Cæsar, for my dear dear love
To your proceeding bids me tell you this,
And reason to my love is liable.

CÆSAR. How foolish do your fears seem now, Calpurnia!
I am ashamed I did yield to them.
Give me my robe, for I will go.

Enter PUBLIUS, BRUTUS, LIGARIUS, METELLUS,
        CASCA, TREBONIUS, *and* CINNA.]

And look where Publius is come to fetch me.

PUBLIUS. Good morrow, Cæsar.

CÆSAR.   Welcome, Publius.
What, Brutus, are you stirr'd so early too?
Good morrow, Casca. Caius Ligarius,
Cæsar was ne'er so much your enemy
As that same ague which hath made you lean.
What is 't o'clock?

BRUTUS.   Cæsar, 'tis strucken eight.

CÆSAR. I thank you for your pains and courtesy.

Enter ANTONY.]

See! Antony, that revels long o' nights,
Is notwithstanding up. Good morrow, Antony.

ANTONY. So to most noble Cæsar.

CÆSAR.   Bid them prepare within:
I am to blame to be thus waited for.
Now, Cinna: now, Metellus: what, Trebonius!
I have an hour's talk in store for you;
Remember that you call on me to-day:
Be near me, that I may remember you.

TREBONIUS. Cæsar, I will [*Aside*] And so near will I be,
That your best friends shall wish I had been further.

CÆSAR. Good friends go in and taste some wine with me;
And we like friends will straightway go together.

BRUTUS. [*Aside*] That every like is not the same, O Cæsar,
The heart of Brutus yearns to think upon!   [*Exeunt.*

SCENE III — *A street near the* CAPITOL.

Enter ARTEMIDORUS, *reading a paper.*]

ARTEMIDORUS. 'Cæsar, beware of Brutus; take heed of Cassius;
come not near Casca; have an eye to Cinna; trust not Trebonius; mark well Metellus Cimber: Decius Brutus loves
thee not: thou hast wronged Caius Ligarius. There is but
one mind in all these men, and it is bent against Cæsar. If
you beest not immortal, look about you: security gives way
to conspiracy. The mighty gods defend thee!

                                    Thy lover, ARTEMIDORUS.'
Here will I stand till Cæsar pass along,
And as a suitor will I give him this.
My heart laments that virtue cannot live
Out of the teeth of emulation.
If thou read this, O Cæsar, thou mayst live:
If not, the Fates with traitors do contrive.   [*Exit.*

SCENE IV — *Another part of the same street, before
the house of* BRUTUS.

Enter PORTIA *and* LUCIUS.]

PORTIA. I prithee, boy, run to the senate-house;
Stay not to answer me, but get thee gone.
Why dost thou stay?

LUCIUS.   To know my errand, madam.

PORTIA. I would have had thee there, and here again,
Ere I can tell thee what thou shouldst do there.

O constancy, be strong upon my side!
Set a huge mountain 'tween my heart and tongue!
I have a man's mind, but a woman's might.
How hard it is for women to keep counsel!
Art thou here yet?

LUCIUS.　　　　　　　Madam, what should I do?
Run to the Capitol, and nothing else?
And so return to you, and nothing else?

PORTIA. Yes, bring me word, boy, if thy lord look well,
For he went sickly forth: and take good note
What Cæsar doth, what suitors press to him.
Hark, boy! what noise is that?

LUCIUS. I hear none, madam.

PORTIA.　　　　　　Prithee, listen well:
I heard a bustling rumor like a fray,
And the wind brings it from the Capitol.

LUCIUS. Sooth, madam, I hear nothing.

Enter the SOOTHSAYER.]

PORTIA.　　　　　　Come hither, fellow:
Which way hast thou been?

SOOTHSAYER.　　　　At mine own house, good lady.

PORTIA. What is 't o'clock?

SOOTHSAYER.　　　　About the ninth hour, lady.

PORTIA. Is Cæsar yet gone to the Capitol?

SOOTHSAYER. Madam, not yet: I go to take my stand,
To see him pass on to the Capitol.

PORTIA. Thou hast some suit to Cæsar, hast thou not?

SOOTHSAYER. That I have, lady: if it will please Cæsar
To be so good to Cæsar as to hear me,
I shall beseech him to befriend himself.

PORTIA. Why, know'st thou any harm's intended towards him?

SOOTHSAYER. None that I know will be, much that I fear may
chance.
Good morrow to you. Here the street is narrow:
The throng that follows Cæsar at the heels,
Of senators, of prætors, common suitors,
Will crowd a feeble man almost to death:
I'll get me to a place more void and there
Speak to great Cæsar as he comes along.　　　　[*Exit.*

PORTIA. I must go in. Aye me, how weak a thing
The heart of woman is! O Brutus,
The heavens speed thee in thine enterprise!

Sure, the boy heard me. Brutus hath a suit
That Cæsar will not grant. O, I grow faint.
Run, Lucius, and commend me to my lord;
Say I am merry: come to me again,
And bring me word what he doth say to thee.

[*Exeunt severally.*

ACT III

Scene I — Rome. *Before the* Capitol; *the Senate sitting above.*

A crowd of people; among them Artemidorus *and
     the* Soothsayer. *Flourish. Enter* Cæsar,
     Brutus, Cassius, Casca, Decius, Metel-
     lus, Trebonius, Cinna, Antony, Lepidus,
     Popilius, Publius, *and others.*]

Cæsar. The ides of March are come.

soothsayer. Aye, Cæsar; but not gone.

artemidorus. Hail, Cæsar! read this schedule.

decius. Trebonius doth desire you to o'er-read,
     At your best leisure, this his humble suit.

artemidorus. O Cæsar, read mine first; for mine's a suit
     That touches Cæsar nearer: read it, great Cæsar.

cæsar. What touches us ourself shall be last served.

artemidorus. Delay not, Cæsar; read it instantly.

cæsar. What, is the fellow mad?

publius.   Sirrah, give place.

cassius. What, urge you your petitions in the street?
     Come to the Capitol.

cæsar *goes up to the Senate-house, the rest following.*]

popilius. I wish your enterprise to-day may thrive.

cassius. What enterprise, Popilius?

popilius.   Fare you well. [*Advances to* cæsar.

brutus. What said Popilius Lena?

cassius. He wish'd to-day our enterprise might thrive.
     I fear our purpose is discovered.

brutus. Look, how he makes to Cæsar: mark him.

cassius. Casca, be sudden, for we fear prevention.
     Brutus, what shall be done? If this be known,
     Cassius or Cæsar never shall turn back,
     For I will slay myself.

brutus.   Cassius, be constant:
     Popilius Lena speaks not of our purposes;
     For, look, he smiles, and Cæsar does not change.

cassius. Trebonius knows his time; for, look you, Brutus,

He draws Mark Antony out of the way.

[*Exeunt* ANTONY *and* TREBONIUS.

DECIUS. Where is Metellus Cimber? Let him go,
And presently prefer his suit to Cæsar.

BRUTUS. He is address'd: press near and second him.

CINNA. Casca, you are the first that rears your hand.

CÆSAR. Are we all ready? What is now amiss
That Cæsar and his senate must redress?

METELLUS. Most high, most mighty and most puissant Cæsar,
Metellus Cimber throws before thy seat
An humble heart:— [*Kneeling.*

CÆSAR.   I must prevent thee, Cimber.
These couchings and these lowly courtesies
Might fire the blood of ordinary men,
And turn pre-ordinance and first decree
Into the law of children. Be not fond,
To think that Cæsar bears such rebel blood
That will be thaw'd from the true quality
With that which melteth fools, I mean, sweet words,
Low-crooked court'sies and base spaniel-fawning.
Thy brother by decree is banished:
If thou dost bend and pray and fawn for him,
I spurn thee like a cur out of my way.
Know, Cæsar doth not wrong, nor without cause
Will he be satisfied.

METELLUS. Is there no voice more worthy than my own,
To sound more sweetly in great Cæsar's ear
For the repealing of my banish'd brother?

BRUTUS. I kiss thy hand, but not in flattery, Cæsar,
Desiring thee that Publius Cimber may
Have an immediate freedom of repeal.

CÆSAR. What, Brutus!

CASSIUS.   Pardon, Cæsar; Cæsar, pardon:
As low as to thy foot doth Cassius fall,
To beg enfranchisement for Publius Cimber.

CÆSAR. I could be well moved, if I were as you;
If I could pray to move, prayers would move me:
But I am constant as the northern star,
Of whose true-fix'd and resting quality
There is no fellow in the firmament.
The skies are painted with unnumber'd sparks;
They are all fire and every one doth shine;

But there's but one in all doth hold his place:
So in the world; 'tis furnish'd well with men,
An men are flesh and blood, and apprehensive;
Yet in the number I do know but one
That unassailable holds on his rank,
Unshaked of motion: and that I am he,
Let me a little show it, even in this;
That I was constant Cimber should be banish'd,
And constant do remain to keep him so.

CINNA. O, Cæsar,—

CÆSAR.   Hence! wilt thou lift up Olympus?

DECIUS. Great Cæsar,—

CÆSAR.   Doth not Brutus bootless kneel?

CASCA. Speak, hands, for me!

> [CASCA *first, then the other Conspirators
> and* MARCUS BRUTUS *stab* CÆSAR.

CÆSAR. Et tu, Brute? Then fall, Cæsar!   [*Dies.*

CINNA. Liberty! freedom! Tyranny is dead!
Run hence, proclaim, cry it about the streets.

CASSIUS. Some to the common pulpits, and cry out
'Liberty, freedom and enfranchisement!'

BRUTUS. People, and senators, be not affrighted;
Fly not; stand still: ambition's debt is paid.

CASCA. Go to the pulpit, Brutus.

DECIUS. And Cassius too.

BRUTUS. Where's Publius?

CINNA. Here, quite confounded with this mutiny.

METELLUS. Stand fast together, lest some friend of Cæsar's
Should chance—

BRUTUS. Talk not of standing. Publius, good cheer;
There is no harm intended to your person,
Nor to no Roman else: so tell them, Publius.

CASSIUS. And leave us, Publius; lest that the people
Rushing on us should do your age some mischief.

BRUTUS. Do so: and let no man abide his deed
But we the doers.

Re-enter TREBONIUS.]

CASSIUS. Where is Antony?

TREBONIUS.   Fled to his house amazed:
Men, wives and children stare, cry out and run
As it were doomsday.

BRUTUS.   Fates, we will know your pleasures:

That we shall die, we know; 'tis but the time,
And drawing days out, that men stand upon.

CASSIUS. Why, he that cuts off twenty years of life
Cuts off so many years of fearing death.

BRUTUS. Grant that, and then is death a benefit:
So are we Cæsar's friends, that have abridged
His time of fearing death. Stoop, Romans, stoop,
And let us bathe our hands in Cæsar's blood
Up to the elbows, and besmear our swords:
Then walk we forth, even to the market-place,
And waving our red weapons o'er our heads,
Let's all cry 'Peace, freedom and liberty!'

CASSIUS. Stoop then, and wash. How many ages hence
Shall this our lofty scene be acted over
In states unborn and accents yet unknown!

BRUTUS. How many times shall Cæsar bleed in sport,
That now on Pompey's basis lies along
No worthier than the dust!

CASSIUS.   So oft as that shall be,
So often shall the knot of us be call'd
The men that gave their country liberty.

DECIUS. What, shall we forth?

CASSIUS.   Aye, every man away:
Brutus shall lead, and we will grace his heels
With the most boldest and best hearts of Rome.

Enter a SERVANT.]

BRUTUS. Soft! who comes here? A friend of Antony's.

SERVANT. Thus, Brutus, did my master bid me kneel;
Thus did Mark Antony bid me fall down;
And, being prostrate, thus he bade me say:
Brutus is noble, wise, valiant and honest;
Cæsar was mighty, bold, royal and loving:
Say I love Brutus and I honor him;
Say I fear'd Cæsar, honor'd him and loved him.
If Brutus will vouchsafe that Antony
May safely come to him and be resolved
How Cæsar hath deserved to lie in death,
Mark Antony shall not love Cæsar dead
So well as Brutus living, but will follow
The fortunes and affairs of noble Brutus
Through the hazards of this untrod state
With all true faith. So says my master Antony.

BRUTUS. Thy master is a wise and valiant Roman;
  I never thought him worse.
  Tell him, so please him come unto this place,
  He shall be satisfied and, by my honor,
  Depart untouch'd.

SERVANT.   I'll fetch him presently.   [*Exit.*

BRUTUS. I know that we shall have him well to friend.

CASSIUS. I wish we may: but yet have I a mind
  That fears him much, and my misgiving still
  Falls shrewdly to the purpose.

Re-enter ANTONY.]

BRUTUS. But here comes Antony. Welcome, Mark Antony.

ANTONY. O mighty Cæsar! dost thou lie so low?
  Are all thy conquests, glories, triumphs, spoils,
  Shrunk to this little measure? Fare thee well.
  I know not, gentlemen, what you intend,
  Who else must be let blood, who else is rank:
  If I myself, there is no hour so fit
  As Cæsar's death hour, nor no instrument
  Of half that worth as those your swords, made rich
  With the most noble blood of all this world.
  I do beseech ye, if you bear me hard,
  Now, whilst your purpled hands do reek and smoke,
  Fulfill your pleasure. Live a thousand years,
  I shall not find myself so apt to die:
  No place will please me so, no mean of death,
  As here by Cæsar, and by you cut off,
  The choice and master spirits of this age.

BRUTUS. O Antony, beg not your death of us.
  Though now we must appear bloody and cruel,
  As, by our hands and this our present act,
  You see we do; yet see you but our hands
  And this the bleeding business they have done:
  Our hearts you see not; they are pitiful;
  And pity to the general wrong of Rome—
  As fire drives out fire, so pity pity—
  Hath done this deed on Cæsar. For your part,
  To you our swords have leaden points, Mark Antony;
  Our arms in strength of malice, and our hearts
  Of brothers' temper, do receive you in
  With all kind love, good thoughts and reverence.

CASSIUS. Your voice shall be as strong as any man's
   In the disposing of new dignities.
BRUTUS. Only be patient till we have appeased
   The multitude, beside themselves with fear,
   And then we will deliver you the cause
   Why I, that did love Cæsar when I struck him,
   Have thus proceeded.
ANTONY.   I doubt not of your wisdom.
   Let each man render me his bloody hand:
   First, Marcus Brutus, will I shake with you;
   Next, Caius Cassius, do I take your hand;
   Now, Decius Brutus, yours; now yours, Metellus;
   Yours, Cinna; and, my valiant Casca, yours;
   Though last, not least in love, yours, good Trebonius.
   Gentlemen all,—alas, what shall I say?
   My credit now stands on such slippery ground,
   That one of two bad ways you must conceit me,
   Either a coward or a flatterer.
   That I did love thee, Cæsar, O, 'tis true:
   If then thy spirit look upon us now,
   Shall it not grieve thee dearer than thy death,
   To see thy Antony making his peace,
   Shaking the bloody fingers of thy foes,
   Most noble! in the presence of thy corse?
   Had I as many eyes as thou hast wounds,
   Weeping as fast as they stream forth thy blood,
   It would become me better than to close
   In terms of friendship with thine enemies.
   Pardon me, Julius! Here wast thou bay'd, brave heart;
   Here didst thou fall, and here thy hunters stand,
   Sign'd in thy spoil and crimson'd in thy lethe.
   O world, thou wast the forest to this hart;
   And this, indeed, O world, the heart of thee.
   How like a deer strucken by many princes
   Dost thou here lie!
CASSIUS. Mark Antony,—
ANTONY.   Pardon me, Caius Cassius:
   The enemies of Cæsar shall say this;
   Then, in a friend, it is cold modesty.
CASSIUS. I blame you not for praising Cæsar so;
   But what compact mean you to have with us?

Will you be prick'd in number of our friends,
Or shall we on, and not depend on you?

ANTONY. Therefore I took your hands, but was indeed
Sway'd from the point by looking down on Cæsar.
Friends am I with you all and love you all,
Upon this hope that you shall give me reasons
Why and wherein Cæsar was dangerous.

BRUTUS. Or else were this a savage spectacle:
Our reasons are so full of good regard
That were you, Antony, the son of Cæsar,
You should be satisfied.

ANTONY.   That's all I seek:
And am moreover suitor that I may
Produce his body to the market-place,
And in the pulpit, as becomes a friend,
Speak in the order of his funeral.

BRUTUS. You shall, Mark Antony.

CASSIUS.   Brutus, a word with you.
[Aside to BRUTUS] You know not what you do: do not
    consent
That Antony speak in his funeral:
Know you how much the people may be moved
By that which he will utter?

BRUTUS.   By your pardon:
I will myself into the pulpit first,
And show the reason of our Cæsar's death:
What Antony shall speak, I will protest
He speaks by leave and by permission,
And that we are contented Cæsar shall
Have all true rites and lawful ceremonies.
It shall advantage more than do us wrong.

CASSIUS. I know not what may fall; I like it not.

BRUTUS. Mark Antony, here, take you Cæsar's body.
You shall not in your funeral speech blame us,
But speak all good you can devise of Cæsar,
And say you do 't by our permission;
Else shall you not have any hand at all
About his funeral: and you shall speak
In the same pulpit whereto I am going,
After my speech is ended.

ANTONY.   Be it so;
I do desire no more.

BRUTUS. Prepare the body then, and follow us.

                              [Exeunt all but ANTONY.

ANTONY. O, pardon me, thou bleeding piece of earth,
   That I am meek and gentle with these butchers!
   Thou art the ruins of the noblest man
   That ever lived in the tide of times.
   Woe to the hand that shed this costly blood!
   Over thy wounds now do I prophesy,
   Which like dumb mouths do ope their ruby lips
   To beg the voice and utterance of my tongue,
   A curse shall light upon the limbs of men;
   Domestic fury and fierce civil strife
   Shall cumber all the parts of Italy;
   Blood and destruction shall be so in use,
   And dreadful objects so familiar,
   That mothers shall but smile when they behold
   Their infants quarter'd with the hands of war;
   All pity choked with custom of fell deeds:
   And Cæsar's spirit ranging for revenge,
   With Ate by his side come hot from hell,
   Shall in these confines with a monarch's voice
   Cry 'Havoc,' and let slip the dogs of war;
   That this foul deed shall smell above the earth
   With carrion men, groaning for burial.

Enter a SERVANT.]

   You serve Octavius Cæsar, do you not?

SERVANT. I do, Mark Antony.

ANTONY. Cæsar did write for him to come to Rome.

SERVANT. He did receive his letters, and is coming;
   And bid me say to you by word of mouth—
   O Cæsar!   *[Seeing the body.*

ANTONY. Thy heart is big; get thee apart and weep.
   Passion, I see, is catching, for mine eyes,
   Seeing those beads of sorrow stand in thine,
   Began to water. Is thy master coming?

SERVANT. He lies to-night within seven leagues of Rome.

ANTONY. Post back with speed, and tell him what hath
      chanced;
   Here is a mourning Rome, a dangerous Rome,
   No Rome of safety for Octavius yet;
   Hie hence, and tell him so. Yet stay awhile;
   Thou shalt not back till I have borne this corse

Into the market-place: there shall I try,
In my oration, how the people take
The cruel issue of these bloody men;
According to the which, thou shalt discourse
To young Octavius of the state of things.
Lend me your hand.   [*Exeunt with* CÆSAR'S *body.*

SCENE II — *The* FORUM.

Enter BRUTUS *and* CASSIUS, *and a throng of* CITIZENS.]
CITIZENS. We will be satisfied; let us be satisfied.
BRUTUS. Then follow me, and give me audience, friends.
    Cassius, go you into the other street,
    And part the numbers.
    Those that will hear me speak, let 'em stay here;
    Those that will follow Cassius, go with him;
    And public reasons shall be rendered
    Of Cæsar's death.
FIRST CITIZEN.   I will hear Brutus speak.
SECOND CITIZEN. I will hear Cassius; and compare their rea-
    sons,
    When severally we hear them rendered.
            [*Exit* CASSIUS, *with some of the* CITIZENS.
                    BRUTUS *goes into the pulpit.*
THIRD CITIZEN. The noble Brutus is ascended: silence!
BRUTUS. Be patient till the last.
    Romans, countrymen, and lovers! hear me for my cause,
    and be silent, that you may hear: believe me for mine
    honor, and have respect to mine honor, that you may be-
    lieve: censure me in your wisdom, and awake your senses,
    that you may the better judge. If there be any in this
    assembly, any dear friend of Cæsar's, to him I say that
    Brutus' love to Cæsar was no less than his. If then that
    friend demand why Brutus rose against Cæsar, this is my
    answer: not that I loved Cæsar less, but that I loved Rome
    more. Had you rather Cæsar were living, and die all slaves,
    than that Cæsar were dead, to live all freemen? As Cæsar
    loved me, I weep for him; as he was fortunate, I rejoice at
    it; as he was valiant, I honor him; but as he was ambitious,
    I slew him. There is tears for his love; joy for his fortune;
    honor for his valor; and death for his ambition. Who is here
    so base that would be a bondman? If any, speak; for him

have I offended. Who is here so rude that would not be a
Roman? If any, speak; for him have I offended. Who is
here so vile that will not love his country? if any, speak;
for him have I offended. I pause for a reply.

ALL. None, Brutus, none.

BRUTUS. Then none have I offended. I have done no more to
Cæsar than you shall do to Brutus. The question of his
death is enrolled in the Capitol; his glory not extenuated,
wherein he was worthy, nor his offenses enforced, for which
he suffered death.

Enter ANTONY *and others, with* CÆSAR'S *body.*]

Here comes his body, mourned by Mark Antony: who,
though he had no hand in his death, shall receive the benefit of his dying, a place in the commonwealth; as which
of you shall not? With this I depart,—that, as I slew my
best lover for the good of Rome, I have the same dagger
for myself, when it shall please my country to need my
death.

ALL. Live, Brutus! live, live!

FIRST CITIZEN. Bring him with triumph home unto his house.

SECOND CITIZEN. Give him a statue with his ancestors.

THIRD CITIZEN. Let him be Cæsar.

FOURTH CITIZEN.   Cæsar's better parts
Shall be crown'd in Brutus.

FIRST CITIZEN. We'll bring him to his house with shouts and
clamors.

BRUTUS. My countrymen,—

SECOND CITIZEN.   Peace! silence! Brutus speaks.

FIRST CITIZEN. Peace, ho!

BRUTUS. Good countrymen, let me depart alone,
And, for my sake, stay here with Antony:
Do grace to Cæsar's corse, and grace his speech
Tending to Cæsar's glories, which Mark Antony
By our permission is allow'd to make.
I do entreat you, not a man depart,
Save I alone, till Antony have spoke.   [*Exit.*

FIRST CITIZEN. Stay, ho! and let us hear Mark Antony.

THIRD CITIZEN. Let him go up into the public chair;
We'll hear him. Noble Antony, go up.

ANTONY. For Brutus' sake, I am beholding to you.
                    [*Goes into the pulpit.*

FOURTH CITIZEN. What does he say of Brutus?

THIRD CITIZEN.   He says, for Brutus' sake,
　He finds himself beholding to us all.
FOURTH CITIZEN. 'Twere best he speak no harm of Brutus here.
FIRST CITIZEN. This Cæsar was a tyrant.
THIRD CITIZEN.   Nay, that's certain:
　We are blest that Rome is rid of him.
SECOND CITIZEN. Peace! let us hear what Antony can say.
ANTONY. You gentle Romans,—
ALL.   Peace, ho! let us hear him.
ANTONY. Friends, Romans, countrymen, lend me your ears;
　I come to bury Cæsar, not to praise him.
　The evil that men do lives after them;
　The good is oft interred with their bones;
　So let it be with Cæsar. The noble Brutus
　Hath told you Cæsar was ambitious:
　If it were so, it was a grievous fault,
　And grievously hath Cæsar answer'd it.
　Here, under leave of Brutus and the rest,—
　For Brutus is an honorable man;
　So are they all, all honorable men,—
　Come I to speak in Cæsar's funeral.
　He was my friend, faithful and just to me:
　But Brutus says he was ambitious;
　And Brutus is an honorable man.
　He hath brought many captives home to Rome,
　Whose ransoms did the general coffers fill:
　Did this in Cæsar seem ambitious?
　When that the poor have cried, Cæsar hath wept:
　Ambition should be made of sterner stuff:
　Yet Brutus says he was ambitious;
　And Brutus is an honorable man.
　You all did see that on the Lupercal
　I thrice presented him a kingly crown,
　Which he did thrice refuse: was this ambition?
　Yet Brutus says he was ambitious;
　And, sure, he is an honorable man.
　I speak not to disprove what Brutus spoke,
　But here I am to speak what I do know.
　You all did love him once, not without cause:
　What cause withholds you then to mourn for him?
　O judgment! thou art fled to brutish beasts,
　And men have lost their reason. Bear with me;

My heart is in the coffin there with Cæsar,
And I must pause till it come back to me.

FIRST CITIZEN. Methinks there is much reason in his sayings.

SECOND CITIZEN. If thou consider rightly of the matter,
Cæsar has had great wrong.

THIRD CITIZEN.   Has he, masters?
I fear there will a worse come in his place.

FOURTH CITIZEN. Mark'd ye his words? He would not take the
crown;
Therefore 'tis certain he was not ambitious.

FIRST CITIZEN. If it be found so, some will dear abide it.

SECOND CITIZEN. Poor soul! his eyes are red as fire with weeping.

THIRD CITIZEN. There's not a nobler man in Rome than Antony.

FOURTH CITIZEN. Now mark him, he begins again to speak.

ANTONY. But yesterday the word of Cæsar might
Have stood against the world: now lies he there,
And none so poor to do him reverence.
O masters, if I were disposed to stir
Your hearts and minds to mutiny and rage,
I should do Brutus wrong and Cassius wrong,
Who, you all know, are honorable men:
I will not do them wrong; I rather choose
To wrong the dead, to wrong myself and you,
Than I will wrong such honorable men.
But here's a parchment with the seal of Cæsar;
I found it in his closet; 'tis his will:
Let but the commons hear this testament—
Which, pardon me, I do not mean to read—
And they would go and kiss dead Cæsar's wounds
And dip their napkins in his sacred blood,
Yea, beg a hair of him for memory,
And, dying, mention it within their wills,
Bequeathing it as a rich legacy
Unto their issue.

FOURTH CITIZEN. We'll hear the will: read it, Mark Antony.

ALL. The will, the will! we will hear Cæsar's will.

ANTONY. Have patience, gentle friends, I must not read it;
It is not meet you know how Cæsar loved you.
You are not wood, you are not stones, but men;
And, being men, hearing the will of Cæsar,

It will inflame you, it will make you mad:
'Tis good you know not that you are his heirs;
For if you should, O, what would come of it!
FOURTH CITIZEN. Read the will; we'll hear it, Antony;
You shall read us the will, Cæsar's will.
ANTONY. Will you be patient? will you stay awhile?
I have o'ershot myself to tell you of it:
I fear I wrong the honorable men
Whose daggers have stabb'd Cæsar; I do fear it.
FOURTH CITIZEN. They were traitors: honorable men!
ALL. The will! the testament!
SECOND CITIZEN. They were villains, murderers: the will! read
   the will.
ANTONY. You will compel me then to read the will?
Then make a ring about the corse of Cæsar,
And let me show you him that made the will.
Shall I descend? and will you give me leave?
ALL. Come down.
SECOND CITIZEN. Descend.   [He comes down from the pulpit.
THIRD CITIZEN. You shall have leave.
FOURTH CITIZEN. A ring; stand round.
FIRST CITIZEN. Stand from the hearse, stand from the body.
SECOND CITIZEN. Room for Antony, most noble Antony.
ANTONY. Nay, press not so upon me; stand far off
ALL. Stand back. Room! Bear back.
ANTONY. If you have tears, prepare to shed them now.
You all do know this mantle: I remember
The first time ever Cæsar put it on;
'Twas on a summer's evening, in his tent,
That day he overcame the Nervii:
Look, in this place ran Cassius' dagger through:
See what a rent the envious Casca made:
Through this the well-beloved Brutus stabb'd;
And as he pluck'd his cursed steel away,
Mark how the blood of Cæsar follow'd it,
As rushing out of doors, to be resolved
If Brutus so unkindly knock'd, or no:
For Brutus, as you know, was Cæsar's angel:
Judge, O you gods, how dearly Cæsar loved him!
This was the most unkindest cut of all;
For when the noble Cæsar saw him stab,
Ingratitude, more strong than traitors' arms,

Quite vanquish'd him: then burst his mighty heart;
And, in his mantle muffling up his face,
Even at the base of Pompey's statuë,
Which all the while ran blood, great Cæsar fell.
O, what a fall was there, my countrymen!
Then I, and you, and all of us fell down,
Whilst bloody treason flourish'd over us.
O, now you weep, and I perceive you feel
The dint of pity: these are gracious drops.
Kind souls, what, weep you when you but behold
Our Cæsar's vesture wounded? Look you here,
Here is himself, marr'd, as you see, with traitors.

FIRST CITIZEN. O piteous spectacle!

SECOND CITIZEN. O noble Cæsar!

THIRD CITIZEN. O woeful day!

FOURTH CITIZEN. O traitors, villains!

FIRST CITIZEN. O most bloody sight!

SECOND CITIZEN. We will be revenged.

ALL. Revenge! About! Seek! Burn! Fire! Kill!
Slay! Let not a traitor live!

ANTONY. Stay, countrymen.

FIRST CITIZEN. Peace there! hear the noble Antony.

SECOND CITIZEN. We'll hear him, we'll follow him, we'll die
with him.

ANTONY. Good friends, sweet friends, let me not stir you up
To such a sudden flood of mutiny.
They that have done this deed are honorable;
What private griefs they have, alas, I know not,
That made them do it: they are wise and honorable,
And will, no doubt, with reasons answer you.
I come not, friends, to steal away your hearts:
I am no orator, as Brutus is;
But, as you know me all, a plain blunt man,
That loves my friend; and that they know full well
That gave me public leave to speak of him:
For I have neither wit, nor words, nor worth,
Action, nor utterance, nor the power of speech,
To stir men's blood: I only speak right on;
I tell you that which you yourselves do know;
Show you sweet Cæsar's wounds, poor poor dumb mouths,
And bid them speak for me: but were I Brutus,
And Brutus Antony, there were an Antony

Would ruffle up your spirits, and put a tongue
In every wound of Cæsar, that should move
The stones of Rome to rise and mutiny.

ALL. We'll mutiny.

FIRST CITIZEN. We'll burn the house of Brutus.

THIRD CITIZEN. Away, then! come, seek the conspirators.

ANTONY. Yet hear me, countrymen: yet hear me speak.

ALL. Peace, ho! Hear Antony. Most noble Antony!

ANTONY. Why, friends, you go to do you know not what:
Wherein hath Cæsar thus deserved your loves?
Alas, you know not; I must tell you then:
You have forgot the will I told you of.

ALL. Most true: the will! Let's stay and hear the will.

ANTONY. Here is the will, and under Cæsar's seal.
To every Roman citizen he gives,
To every several man, seventy-five drachmas.

SECOND CITIZEN. Most noble Cæsar! we'll revenge his death.

THIRD CITIZEN. O royal Cæsar!

ANTONY.   Hear me with patience.

ALL. Peace, ho!

ANTONY. Moreover, he hath left you all his walks,
His private arbors and new-planted orchards,
On this side Tiber; he hath left them you,
And to your heirs for ever; common pleasures,
To walk abroad and recreate yourselves.
Here was a Cæsar! when comes such another?

FIRST CITIZEN. Never, never. Come, away, away!
We'll burn his body in the holy place,
And with the brands fire the traitors' houses.
Take up the body.

SECOND CITIZEN. Go fetch fire.

THIRD CITIZEN. Pluck down benches.

FOURTH CITIZEN. Pluck down forms, windows, any thing.

                    [*Exeunt* CITIZENS *with the body.*

ANTONY. Now let it work. Mischief, thou art afoot,
Take thou what course thou wilt.

Enter a SERVANT.]

                             How now, fellow!

SERVANT. Sir, Octavius is already come to Rome.

ANTONY. Where is he?

SERVANT. He and Lepidus are at Cæsar's house.

ANTONY. And thither will I straight to visit him.
  He comes upon a wish. Fortune is merry,
  And in this mood will give us any thing.
SERVANT. I heard him say, Brutus and Cassius
  Are rid like madmen through the gates of Rome.
ANTONY. Belike they had some notice of the people,
  How I had moved them. Bring me to Octavius.   [*Exeunt.*

SCENE III — *A street.*

Enter CINNA *the poet.*]
CINNA. I dreamt to-night that I did feast with Cæsar,
  And things unluckily charge my fantasy:
  I have no will to wander forth of doors,
  Yet something leads me forth.
Enter CITIZENS.]
FIRST CITIZEN. What is your name?
SECOND CITIZEN. Whither are you going?
THIRD CITIZEN. Where do you dwell?
FOURTH CITIZEN. Are you a married man or a bachelor?
SECOND CITIZEN. Answer every man directly.
FIRST CITIZEN. Aye, and briefly.
FOURTH CITIZEN. Aye, and wisely.
THIRD CITIZEN. Aye, and truly, you were best.
CINNA. What is my name? Whither am I going? Where do I
  dwell? Am I a married man or a bachelor? Then to answer
  every man directly and briefly, wisely and truly: wisely I
  say, I am a bachelor.
SECOND CITIZEN. That's as much as to say, they are fools that
  marry: you'll bear me a bang for that, I fear. Proceed; di-
  rectly.
CINNA. Directly, I am going to Cæsar's funeral.
FIRST CITIZEN. As a friend or an enemy?
CINNA. As a friend.
SECOND CITIZEN. That matter is answered directly.
FOURTH CITIZEN. For your dwelling, briefly.
CINNA. Briefly, I dwell by the Capitol.
THIRD CITIZEN. Your name, sir, truly.
CINNA. Truly, my name is Cinna.
FIRST CITIZEN. Tear him to pieces; he's a conspirator.
CINNA. I am Cinna the poet, I am Cinna the poet.

FOURTH CITIZEN. Tear him for his bad verses, tear him for his bad verses.

CINNA. I am not Cinna the conspirator.

FOURTH CITIZEN. It is no matter, his name's Cinna; pluck but his name out of his heart, and turn him going.

THIRD CITIZEN. Tear him, tear him! Come, brands, ho! fire-brands: to Brutus', to Cassius'; burn all: some to Decius' house, and some of Casca's; some to Ligarius': away, go!

                                  [*Exeunt.*

ACT IV

SCENE I — *A house in* ROME.

ANTONY, OCTAVIUS, *and* LEPIDUS, *seated at a table.*]

ANTONY. These many then shall die; their names are prick'd.

OCTAVIUS. Your brother too must die; consent you, Lepidus?

LEPIDUS. I do consent—

OCTAVIUS.   Prick him down, Antony.

LEPIDUS. Upon condition Publius shall not live,
   Who is your sister's son, Mark Antony.

ANTONY. He shall not live; look, with a spot I damn him.
   But, Lepidus, go you to Cæsar's house;
   Fetch the will hither, and we shall determine
   How to cut off some charge in legacies.

LEPIDUS. What, shall I find you here?

OCTAVIUS. Or here, or at the Capitol.   [*Exit* LEPIDUS.

ANTONY. This is a slight unmeritable man,
   Meet to be sent on errands: is it fit,
   The three-fold world divided, he should stand
   One of the three to share it?

OCTAVIUS.   So you thought him,
   And took his voice who should be prick'd to die
   In our black sentence and proscription.

ANTONY. Octavius, I have seen more days than you:
   And though we lay these honors on this man,
   To ease ourselves of divers slanderous loads,
   He shall but bear them as the ass bears gold,
   To groan and sweat under the business,
   Either led or driven, as we point the way;
   And having brought out treasure where we will,
   Then take we down his load and turn him off,
   Like to the empty ass, to shake his ears
   And graze in commons.

OCTAVIUS.   You may do your will:
   But he's a tried and valiant soldier.

ANTONY. So is my horse, Octavius, and for that
   I do appoint him store of provender:
   It is a creature that I teach to fight,
   To wind, to stop, to run directly on,

His corporal motion govern'd by my spirit.
And, in some taste, is Lepidus but so;
He must be taught, and train'd, and bid go forth;
A barren-spirited fellow; one that feeds
On abjects, orts and imitations,
Which, out of use and staled by other men,
Begin his fashion: do not talk of him
But as a property. And now, Octavius,
Listen great things: Brutus and Cassius
Are levying powers: we must straight make head:
Therefore let our alliance be combined,
Our best friends made, our means stretch'd;
And let us presently go sit in council,
How covert matters may be best disclosed,
And open perils surest answered.

OCTAVIUS. Let us do so: for we are at the stake,
And bay'd about with many enemies;
And some that smile have in their hearts, I fear,
Millions of mischiefs.   [*Exeunt.*

SCENE II—*Camp near* SARDIS. *Before* BRUTUS' *tent.*

Drum. Enter BRUTUS, LUCILIUS, LUCIUS, *and* SOLDIERS;
        TITINIUS *and* PINDARUS *meet them.*]

BRUTUS. Stand, ho!

LUCILIUS. Give the word, ho! and stand.

BRUTUS. What now, Lucilius! is Cassius near?

LUCILIUS. He is at hand; and Pindarus is come
To do you salutation from his master.

BRUTUS. He greets me well. Your master, Pindarus,
In his own change, or by ill officers,
Hath given me some worthy cause to wish
Things done undone: but if he be at hand,
I shall be satisfied.

PINDARUS.   I do not doubt
But that my noble master will appear
Such as he is, full of regard and honor.

BRUTUS. He is not doubted. A word, Lucilius,
How he received you: let me be resolved.

LUCILIUS. With courtesy and with respect enough;
But not with such familiar instances,

Nor with such free and friendly conference,
As he hath used of old.

BRUTUS.   Thou hast described
A hot friend cooling: ever note, Lucilius,
When love begins to sicken and decay,
It useth an enforced ceremony.
There are no tricks in plain and simple faith:
But hollow men, like horses hot at hand,
Make gallant show and promise of their mettle;
But when they should endure the bloody spur,
They fall their crests and like deceitful jades
Sink in the trial. Comes his army on?

LUCILIUS. They mean this night in Sardis to be quarter'd;
The great part, the horse in general,
Are come with Cassius.   [*Low march within.*

BRUTUS. Hark! he is arrived:
March gently on to meet him.
Enter CASSIUS *and his powers.*]

CASSIUS. Stand, ho!

BRUTUS. Stand, ho! Speak the word along.

FIRST SOLDIER. Stand!

SECOND SOLDIER. Stand!

THIRD SOLDIER. Stand!

CASSIUS. Most noble brother, you have done me wrong.

BRUTUS. Judge me, you gods! wrong I mine enemies?
And, if not so, how should I wrong a brother?

CASSIUS. Brutus, this sober form of yours hides wrongs;
And when you do them—

BRUTUS.   Cassius, be content;
Speak your griefs softly: I do know you well.
Before the eyes of both our armies here,
Which should perceive nothing but love from us,
Let us not wrangle: bid them move away;
Then in my tent, Cassius, enlarge your griefs,
And I will give you audience.

CASSIUS.   Pindarus,
Bid our commanders lead their charges off
A little from this ground.

BRUTUS. Lucilius, do you the like, and let no man
Come to our tent till we have done our conference.
Let Lucius and Titinius guard our door.   [*Exeunt.*

SCENE III — BRUTUS' *tent.*

Enter BRUTUS *and* CASSIUS.]

CASSIUS. That you have wrong'd me doth appear in this:
  You have condemn'd and noted Lucius Pella
  For taking bribes here of the Sardians;
  Wherein my letters, praying on his side,
  Because I knew the man, were slighted off.

BRUTUS. You wrong'd yourself to write in such a case.

CASSIUS. In such a time as this it is not meet
  That every nice offense should bear his comment.

BRUTUS. Let me tell you, Cassius, you yourself
  Are much condemn'd to have an itching palm,
  To sell and mart your offices for gold
  To undeservers.

CASSIUS.   I an itching palm!
  You know that you are Brutus that speaks this,
  Or, by the gods, this speech were else your last.

BRUTUS. The name of Cassius honors this corruption,
  And chastisement doth therefore hide his head.

CASSIUS. Chastisement!

BRUTUS. Remember March, the ides of March remember:
  Did not great Julius bleed for justice' sake?
  What villain touch'd his body, that did stab,
  And not for justice? What, shall one of us,
  That struck the foremost man of all this world
  But for supporting robbers, shall we now
  Contaminate our fingers with base bribes,
  And sell the mighty space of our large honors
  For so much trash as may be grasped thus?
  I had rather be a dog, and bay the moon,
  Than such a Roman.

CASSIUS.   Brutus, bait not me;
  I'll not endure it: you forget yourself,
  To hedge me in; I am a soldier, I,
  Older in practice, abler than yourself
  To make conditions.

BRUTUS.   Go to; you are not, Cassius.

CASSIUS. I am.

BRUTUS. I say you are not.

CASSIUS. Urge me no more, I shall forget myself;
  Have mind upon your health, tempt me no farther.

BRUTUS. Away, slight man!

CASSIUS. Is 't possible?

BRUTUS.   Hear me, for I will speak.
  Must I give way and room to your rash choler?
  Shall I be frighted when a madman stares?

CASSIUS. O ye gods, ye gods! must I endure all this?

BRUTUS. All this! aye, more: fret till your proud heart break;
  Go show your slaves how choleric you are,
  And make your bondmen tremble. Must I budge?
  Must I observe you? must I stand and crouch
  Under your testy humor? By the gods,
  You shall digest the venom of your spleen,
  Though it do split you; for, from this day forth,
  I'll use you for my mirth, yea, for my laughter,
  When you are waspish.

CASSIUS.   Is it come to this?

BRUTUS. You say you are a better soldier:
  Let it appear so; make your vaunting true,
  And it shall please me well: for mine own part,
  I shall be glad to learn of noble men.

CASSIUS. You wrong me every way; you wrong me, Brutus; I
  said, an elder soldier, not a better:
  Did I say, better?

BRUTUS.   If you did, I care not.

CASSIUS. When Cæsar lived, he durst not thus have moved me.

BRUTUS. Peace, peace! you durst not so have tempted him.

CASSIUS. I durst not!

BRUTUS. No.

CASSIUS. What, durst not tempt him!

BRUTUS.   For your life you durst not.

CASSIUS. Do not presume too much upon my love;
  I may do that I shall be sorry for.

BRUTUS. You have done that you should be sorry for.
  There is no terror, Cassius, in your threats;
  For I am arm'd so strong in honesty,
  That they pass by me as the idle wind
  Which I respect not. I did send to you
  For certain sums of gold, which you denied me:
  For I can raise no money by vile means:
  By heaven, I had rather coin my heart,

And drop my blood for drachmas, than to wring
From the hard hands of peasants their vile trash
By any indirection. I did send
To you for gold to pay my legions,
Which you denied me: was that done like Cassius?
Should I have answer'd Caius Cassius so?
When Marcus Brutus grows so covetous,
To lock such rascal counters from his friends,
Be ready, gods, with all your thunderbolts,
Dash him to pieces!

CASSIUS.   I denied you not.

BRUTUS. You did.

CASSIUS.   I did not: he was but a fool
That brought my answer back. Brutus hath rived my heart:
A friend should bear his friend's infirmities,
But Brutus makes mine greater than they are.

BRUTUS. I do not, till you practise them on me.

CASSIUS. You love me not.

BRUTUS.   I do not like your faults.

CASSIUS. A friendly eye could never see such faults.

BRUTUS. A flatterer's would not, though they do appear
As huge as high Olympus.

CASSIUS. Come, Antony, and young Octavius, come,
Revenge yourselves alone on Cassius,
For Cassius is aweary of the world;
Hated by one he loves; braved by his brother;
Check'd like a bondman; all his faults observed,
Set in a note-book, learn'd and conn'd by rote,
To cast into my teeth. O, I could weep
My spirit from mine eyes! There is my dagger,
And here my naked breast; within, a heart
Dearer than Plutus' mine, richer than gold:
If that thou be'st a Roman, take it forth;
I, that denied thee gold, will give my heart:
Strike, as thou didst at Cæsar; for I know,
When thou didst hate him worst, thou lovedst him better
Than ever thou lovedst Cassius.

BRUTUS.   Sheathe your dagger:
Be angry when you will, it shall have scope;
Do what you will, dishonor shall be humor.
O Cassius, you are yoked with a lamb,
That carries anger as the flint bears fire,

Who, much enforced, shows a hasty spark
And straight is cold again.

CASSIUS.   Hath Cassius lived
To be but mirth and laughter to his Brutus,
When grief and blood ill-temper'd vexed him?

BRUTUS. When I spoke that, I was ill-temper'd too.

CASSIUS. Do you confess so much? Give me your hand.

BRUTUS. And my heart too.

CASSIUS. O Brutus!

BRUTUS.   What's the matter?

CASSIUS. Have not you love enough to bear with me,
When that rash humor which my mother gave me
Makes me forgetful?

BRUTUS.   Yes, Cassius, and from henceforth.
When you are over-earnest with your Brutus,
He'll think your mother chides, and leave you so.

POET. [*Within*] Let me go in to see the generals;
There is some grudge between 'em; 'tis not meet
They be alone.

LUCILIUS. [*Within*] You shall not come to them.

POET. [*Within*] Nothing but death shall stay me.

Enter POET, *followed by* LUCILIUS, TITINIUS, *and*
       LUCIUS.]

CASSIUS. How now! what's the matter?

POET. For shame, you generals! what do you mean?
Love, and be friends, as two such men should be;
For I have seen more years, I'm sure, than ye.

CASSIUS. Ha, ha, how vilely doth this cynic rhyme!

BRUTUS. Get your hence, sirrah; saucy fellow, hence!

CASSIUS. Bear with him, Brutus; 'tis his fashion.

BRUTUS. I'll know his humor when he knows his time:
What should the wars do with these jigging fools?
Companion, hence!

CASSIUS.   Away, way, be gone!   [*Exit* POET.

BRUTUS. Lucilius and Titinius, bid the commanders
Prepare to lodge their companies to-night.

CASSIUS. And come yourselves, and bring Messala with you
Immediately to us.   [*Exeunt* LUCILIUS *and* TITINIUS.

BRUTUS.   Lucius, a bowl of wine!   [*Exit* LUCIUS.

CASSIUS. I did not think you could have been so angry.

BRUTUS. O Cassius, I am sick of many griefs.

CASSIUS. Of your philosophy you make no use,
  If you give place to accidental evils.
BRUTUS. No man bears sorrow better: Portia is dead.
CASSIUS. Ha! Portia!
BRUTUS. She is dead.
CASSIUS. How 'scaped I killing when I cross'd you so?
  O insupportable and touching loss!
  Upon what sickness?
BRUTUS.   Impatient of my absence,
  And grief that young Octavius with Mark Antony
  Have made themselves so strong: for with her death
  That tidings came: with this she fell distract,
  And, her attendants absent, swallow'd fire.
CASSIUS. And died so?
BRUTUS.   Even so.
CASSIUS.   O ye immortal gods!
Re-enter LUCIUS, *with wine and taper.*]
BRUTUS. Speak no more of her. Give me a bowl of wine.
  In this I bury all unkindness, Cassius.   [*Drinks.*
CASSIUS. My heart is thirsty for that noble pledge.
  Fill, Lucius, till the wine o'erswell the cup;
  I cannot drink too much of Brutus' love.   [*Drinks.*
BRUTUS. Come in, Titinius!   [*Exit* LUCIUS.
Re-enter TITINIUS, *with* MESSALA.]
  Welcome, good Messala.
  Now sit we close about this taper here,
  And call in question our necessities.
CASSIUS. Portia, art thou gone?
BRUTUS.   No more, I pray you.
  Messala, I have here received letters,
  That young Octavius and Mark Antony
  Come down upon us with a mighty power,
  Bending their expedition toward Philippi.
MESSALA. Myself have letters of the self-same tenor.
BRUTUS. With what addition?
MESSALA. That by proscription and bills of outlawry
  Octavius, Antony and Lepidus,
  Have put to death an hundred senators.
BRUTUS. Therein our letters do not well agree;
  Mine speak of seventy senators that died
  By their proscriptions, Cicero being one.
CASSIUS. Cicero one!

MESSALA.   Cicero is dead,
  And by that order of proscription.
  Had you your letters from your wife, my lord?
BRUTUS. No, Messala.
MESSALA. Nor nothing in your letters writ of her?
BRUTUS. Nothing, Messala.
MESSALA. That, methinks, is strange.
BRUTUS. Why ask you? hear you aught of her in yours?
MESSALA. No, my lord.
BRUTUS. Now, as you are a Roman, tell me true.
MESSALA. Then like a Roman bear the truth I tell:
  For certain she is dead, and by strange manner.
BRUTUS. Why, farewell, Portia. We must die, Messala:
  With meditating that she must die once
  I have the patience to endure it now.
MESSALA. Even so great men great losses should endure.
CASSIUS. I have as much of this in art as you,
  But yet my nature could not bear it so.
BRUTUS. Well, to our work alive. What do you think
  Of marching to Philippi presently?
CASSIUS. I do not think it good.
BRUTUS.   Your reason?
CASSIUS.   This it is:
  'Tis better that the enemy seek us:
  So shall he waste his means, weary his soldiers,
  Doing himself offense; whilst we lying still
  Are full of rest, defense and nimbleness.
BRUTUS. Good reasons must of force give place to better.
  The people 'twixt Philippi and this ground
  Do stand but in a forced affection,
  For they have grudged us contribution:
  The enemy, marching along by them,
  By them shall make a fuller number up,
  Come on refresh'd, new-added and encouraged;
  From which advantage shall we cut him off
  If at Philippi we do face him there,
  These people at our back.
CASSIUS.   Hear me, good brother.
BRUTUS. Under your pardon. You must note beside
  That we have tried the utmost of our friends,
  Our legions are brim-full, our cause is ripe:
  The enemy increaseth every day;

We, at the height, are ready to decline.
There is a tide in the affairs of men
Which taken at the flood leads on to fortune;
Omitted, all the voyage of their life
Is bound in shallows and in miseries.
On such a full sea are we now afloat,
And we must take the current when it serves,
Or lose our ventures.

CASSIUS.   Then, with your will, go on;
We'll along ourselves and meet them at Philippi.

BRUTUS. The deep of night is crept upon our talk,
And nature must obey necessity;
Which we will niggard with a little rest.
There is no more to say?

CASSIUS.   No more. Good night:
Early to-morrow will we rise and hence.

BRUTUS. Lucius! [Re-enter LUCIUS] My gown. [Exit LUCIUS.]
Farewell, good Messala:
Good night, Titinius: noble, noble Cassius,
Good night, and good repose.

CASSIUS.   O my dear brother!
This was an ill beginning of the night:
Never come such division 'tween our souls!
Let it not, Brutus.

BRUTUS.   Every thing is well.

CASSIUS. Good night, my lord.

BRUTUS.   Good night, good brother.

TITINIUS, MESSALA. Good night, Lord Brutus.

BRUTUS. Farewell, every one.   [Exeunt all but BRUTUS.
Re-enter LUCIUS, with the gown.]
Give me the gown. Where is thy instrument?

LUCIUS. Here in the tent.

BRUTUS.   What, thou speak'st drowsily?
Poor knave, I blame thee not; thou art o'er-watch'd.
Call Claudius and some other of my men;
I'll have them sleep on cushions in my tent.

LUCIUS. Varro and Claudius!
Enter VARRO and CLAUDIUS.]

VARRO. Calls my lord?

BRUTUS. I pray you, sirs, lie in my tent and sleep;
It may be I shall raise you by and by
On business to my brother Cassius.

VARRO. So please you, we will stand and watch your pleasure.
BRUTUS. I will not have it so: lie down, good sirs;
  It may be I shall otherwise bethink me.
  Look, Lucius, here's the book I sought for so;
  I put it in the pocket of my gown.

                          [VARRO *and* CLAUDIUS *lie down.*
LUCIUS. I was sure your lordship did not give it me.
BRUTUS. Bear with me, good boy, I am much forgetful.
  Canst thou hold up thy heavy eyes awhile,
  And touch thy instrument a strain or two?
LUCIUS. Aye, my lord, an 't please you.
BRUTUS.   It does, my boy:
  I trouble thee too much, but thou art willing.
LUCIUS. It is my duty, sir.
BRUTUS. I should not urge thy duty past thy might;
  I know young bloods look for a time of rest.
LUCIUS. I have slept, my lord, already.
BRUTUS. It was well done; and thou shalt sleep again.
  I will not hold thee long: if I do live,
  I will be good to thee.   [*Music, and a song.*
  This is a sleepy tune. O murderous slumber,
  Lay'st thou thy leaden mace upon my boy,
  That plays thee music? Gentle knave, good night;
  I will not do thee so much wrong to wake thee:
  If thou dost nod, thou break'st thy instrument;
  I'll take it from thee; and, good boy, good night.
  Let me see, let me see; is not the leaf turn'd down
  Where I left reading? Here it is, I think.   [*Sits down.*
Enter the GHOST OF CÆSAR.]
  How ill this taper burns! Ha! who comes here?
  I think it is the weakness of mine eyes
  That shapes this monstrous apparition.
  It comes upon me. Art thou any thing?
  Art thou some god, some angel, or some devil,
  That makest my blood cold, and my hair to stare?
  Speak to me what thou art.
GHOST. Thy evil spirit, Brutus.
BRUTUS.   Why comest thou?
GHOST. To tell thee thou shalt see me at Philippi.
BRUTUS. Well; then I shall see thee again?
GHOST. Aye, at Philippi.
BRUTUS. Why, I will see thee at Philippi then.   [*Exit* GHOST.

Now I have taken heart thou vanishest.
Ill spirit, I would hold more talk with thee.
Boy, Lucius! Varro! Claudius! Sirs, awake!
Claudius!

LUCIUS. The strings, my lord, are false.

BRUTUS. He thinks he still is at his instrument.
Lucius, awake!

LUCIUS. My lord?

BRUTUS. Didst thou dream, Lucius, that thou so criedst out?

LUCIUS. My lord, I do not know that I did cry.

BRUTUS. Yes, that thou didst: didst thou see any thing?

LUCIUS. Nothing, my lord.

BRUTUS. Sleep again, Lucius. Sirrah, Claudius!
[*To* VARRO] Fellow thou, awake!

VARRO. My lord?

CLAUDIUS. My lord?

BRUTUS. Why did you so cry out, sirs, in your sleep?

VARRO, CLAUDIUS. Did we, my lord?

BRUTUS.   Aye: saw you any thing?

VARRO. No, my lord, I saw nothing.

CLAUDIUS.   Nor I, my lord.

BRUTUS. Go and commend me to my brother Cassius;
Bid him set on his powers betimes before,
And we will follow.

VARRO, CLAUDIUS. It shall be done, my lord.   [*Exeunt.*

ACT V

SCENE I — *The plains of* PHILIPPI.

Enter OCTAVIUS, ANTONY, *and their army.*]

OCTAVIUS. Now, Antony, our hopes are answered:
　You said the enemy would not come down,
　But keep the hills and upper regions;
　It proves not so: their battles are at hand;
　They mean to warn us at Philippi here,
　Answering before we do demand of them.

ANTONY. Tut, I am in their bosoms, and I know
　Wherefore they do it: they could be content
　To visit other places; and come down
　With fearful bravery, thinking by this face
　To fasten in our thoughts that they have courage;
　But 'tis not so.

Enter a MESSENGER.]

MESSENGER.　　Prepare you, generals:
　The enemy comes on in gallant show;
　Their bloody sign of battle is hung out,
　And something to be done immediately.

ANTONY. Octavius, lead your battle softly on,
　Upon the left hand of the even field.

OCTAVIUS. Upon the right hand I; keep thou the left.

ANTONY. Why do you cross me in this exigent?

OCTAVIUS. I do not cross you; but I will do so.　　　[*March.*

Drum. Enter BRUTUS, CASSIUS, *and their army;*
　　　　LUCILIUS, TITINIUS, MESSALA, *and others.*]

BRUTUS. They stand, and would have parley.

CASSIUS. Stand fast, Titinius: we must out and talk.

OCTAVIUS. Mark Antony, shall we give sign of battle?

ANTONY. No, Cæsar, we will answer on their charge.
　Make forth; the generals would have some words.

OCTAVIUS. Stir not until the signal.

BRUTUS. Words before blows: is it so, countrymen?

OCTAVIUS. Not that we love words better, as you do.

BRUTUS. Good words are better than bad strokes, Octavius:

ANTONY. In your bad strokes, Brutus, you give good words:

Witness the hole you made in Cæsar's heart,
Crying 'Long live! hail, Cæsar!'

CASSIUS.   Antony,
The posture of your blows are yet unknown;
But for your words, they rob the Hybla bees,
And leave them honeyless.

ANTONY.   Not stingless too.

BRUTUS. O, yes, and soundless too;
For you have stol'n their buzzing, Antony,
And very wisely threat before you sting.

ANTONY. Villains, you did not so, when your vile daggers
Hack'd one another in the side of Cæsar:
You show'd your teeth like apes, and fawn'd like hounds,
And bow'd like bondmen, kissing Cæsar's feet;
Whilst damned Casca, like a cur, behind
Struck Cæsar on the neck. O you flatterers!

CASSIUS. Flatterers! Now, Brutus, thank yourself:
This tongue had not offended so to-day,
If Cassius might have ruled.

OCTAVIUS. Come, come, the cause: if arguing make us sweat,
The proof of it will turn to redder drops.
Look;
I draw a sword against conspirators;
When think you that the sword goes up again?
Never, till Cæsar's three and thirty wounds
Be well avenged, or till another Cæsar
Have added slaughter to the sword of traitors.

BRUTUS. Cæsar, thou canst not die by traitors' hands,
Unless thou bring'st them with thee.

OCTAVIUS.   So I hope;
I was not born to die on Brutus' sword.

BRUTUS. O, if thou wert the noblest of thy strain,
Young man, thou couldst not die more honorable.

CASSIUS. A peevish schoolboy, worthless of such honor,
Join'd with a masker and a reveler!

ANTONY. Old Cassius still!

OCTAVIUS.   Come, Antony; away!
Defiance, traitors, hurl we in your teeth;
If you dare fight to-day, come to the field:
If not, when you have stomachs.

               [*Exeunt* OCTAVIUS, ANTONY, *and their army.*

CASSIUS. Why, now, blow wind, swell billow, and swim back!
   The storm is up, and all is on the hazard.
BRUTUS. Ho, Lucilius! hark, a word with you.
LUCILIUS. [*Standing forth*]   My lord?
                              [BRUTUS *and* LUCILIUS *converse apart.*
CASSIUS. Messala!
MESSALA. [*Standing forth*] What says my general?
CASSIUS.   Messala,
   This is my birth-day; as this very day
   Was Cassius born. Give me thy hand, Messala:
   Be thou my witness that, against my will,
   As Pompey was, am I compell'd to set
   Upon one battle all our liberties.
   You know that I held Epicurus strong,
   And his opinion: now I change my mind,
   And partly credit things that do presage.
   Coming from Sardis, on our former ensign
   Two mighty eagles fell, and there they perch'd,
   Gorging and feeding from our soldiers' hands;
   Who to Philippi here consorted us:
   This morning are they fled away and gone;
   And in their steads do ravens, crows and kites
   Fly o'er our heads and downward look on us,
   As we were sickly prey: their shadows seem
   A canopy most fatal, under which
   Our army lies, ready to give up the ghost.
MESSALA. Believe not so.
CASSIUS.   I but believe it partly,
   For I am fresh of spirit and resolved
   To met all perils very constantly.
BRUTUS. Even so, Lucilius.
CASSIUS.   Now, most noble Brutus,
   The gods to-day stand friendly, that we may,
   Lovers in peace, lead on our days to age!
   But, since the affairs of men rest still incertain,
   Let's reason with the worst that may befall.
   If we do lose this battle, then is this
   The very last time we shall speak together:
   What are you then determined to do?
BRUTUS. Even by the rule of that philosophy
   By which I did blame Cato for the death
   Which he did give himself: I know not how,

But I do find it cowardly and vile,
For fear of what might fall, so to prevent
The time of life: arming myself with patience
To stay the providence of some high powers
That govern us below.

CASSIUS.   Then, if we lose this battle,
You are contented to be led in triumph
Thorough the streets of Rome?

BRUTUS. No, Cassius, no: think not, thou noble Roman,
That ever Brutus will go bound to Rome;
He bears too great a mind. But this same day
Must end that work the ides of March begun;
And whether we shall meet again I know not.
Therefore our everlasting farewell take.
For ever, and for ever, farewell, Cassius!
If we do meet again, why, we shall smile;
If not, why then this parting was well made.

CASSIUS. For ever and for ever farewell, Brutus!
If we do meet again, we'll smile indeed;
If not, 'tis true this parting was well made.

BRUTUS. Why then, lead on. O, that a man might know
The end of this day's business ere it come!
But it sufficeth that the day will end,
And then the end is known. Come, ho! away! *[Exeunt.*

SCENE II — *The field of battle.*

Alarum. Enter BRUTUS *and* MESSALA.]

BRUTUS. Ride, ride, Messala, ride, and give these bills
Unto the legions on the other side: *[Loud alarum.*
Let them set on at once; for I perceive
But cold demeanor in Octavius' wing,
And sudden push gives them the overthrow.
Ride, ride, Messala: let them all come down.   *[Exeunt.*

SCENE III — *Another part of the field.*

Alarums. Enter CASSIUS *and* TITINIUS.]

CASSIUS. O, look, Titinius, look, the villains fly!
Myself have to mine own turn'd enemy:
This ensign here of mine was turning back;
I slew the coward, and did take it from him.

TITINIUS. O Cassius, Brutus gave the word too early;
  Who, having some advantage on Octavius.
  Took it too eagerly: his soldiers fell to spoil,
  Whilst we by Antony are all enclosed.
Enter PINDARUS.]
PINDARUS. Fly further off, my lord, fly further off;
  Mark Antony is in your tents, my lord:
  Fly, therefore, noble Cassius, fly far off.
CASSIUS. This hill is far enough. Look, look, Titinius;
  Are those my tents where I perceive the fire?
TITINIUS. They are, my lord.
CASSIUS.   Titinius, if thou lovest me,
  Mount thou my horse and hide thy spurs in him,
  Till he have brought thee up to yonder troops
  And here again; that I may rest assured
  Whether yond troops are friend or enemy.
TITINIUS. I will be here again, even with athought.   [*Exit.*
CASSIUS. Go, Pindarus, get higher on that hill;
  My sight was ever thick; regard Titinius,
  And tell me what thou notest about the field.
                          [PINDARUS *ascends the hill.*
  This day I breathed first: time is come round,
  And where I did begin, there shall I end;
  My life is run his compass. Sirrah, what news?
PINDARUS. [*Above*] O my lord!
CASSIUS. What news?
PINDARUS. [*Above*] Titinius is enclosed round about
  With horsemen, that make to him on the spur;
  Yet he spurs on. Now they are almost on him.
  Now, Titinius! Now some light. O, he lights too.
  He's ta'en. [*Shout.*] And, hark! they shout for joy.
CASSIUS. Come down; behold no more.
  O coward that I am, to live so long,
  To see my best friend ta'en before my face!
                          [PINDARUS *descends.*
  Come hither, sirrah:
  In Parthia did I take thee prisoner;
  And then I swore thee, saving of thy life,
  That whatsoever I did bid thee do,
  Thou shouldst attempt it. Come now, keep thine oath;
  Now be a freeman; and with this good sword,
  That ran through Cæsar's bowels, search this bosom.

Stand not to answer: here, take thou the hilts;
And when my face is cover'd, as 'tis now,
Guide thou the sword. [PINDARUS *stabs him.*] Cæsar, thou
   art revenged,
Even with the sword that kill'd thee.   [*Dies.*

PINDARUS. So, I am free; yet would not so have been,
Durst I have done my will. O Cassius!
Far from this country Pindarus shall run,
Where never Roman shall take note of him.   [*Exit.*

Re-enter TITINIUS *with* MESSALA.]

MESSALA. It is but change, Titinius; for Octavius
Is overthrown by noble Brutus' power,
As Cassius' legions are by Antony.

TITINIUS. These tidings will well comfort Cassius.

MESSALA. Where did you leave him?

TITINIUS.   All disconsolate,
With Pindarus his bondman, on this hill.

MESSALA. Is not that he that lies upon the ground?

TITINIUS. He lies not like the living. O my heart!

MESSALA. Is not that he?

TITINIUS.   No, this was he, Messala,
But Cassius is no more. O setting sun,
As in thy red rays thou dost sink to night,
So in his red blood Cassius' day is set,
The sun of Rome is set! Our day is gone;
Clouds, dews and dangers come; our deeds are done!
Mistrust of my success hath done this deed.

MESSALA. Mistrust of good success hath done this deed.
O hateful error, melancholy's child,
Why dost thou show to the apt thoughts of men
The things that are not? O error, soon conceived,
Thou never comest unto a happy birth,
But kill'st the mother that engender'd thee!

TITINIUS. What, Pindarus! where art thou, Pindarus?

MESSALA. Seek him, Titinius, whilst I go to meet
The noble Brutus, thrusting this report
Into his ears: I may say 'thrusting' it,
For piercing steel and darts envenomed
Shall be as welcome to the ears of Brutus
As tidings of this sight.

TITINIUS.   Hie you, Messala,
And I will seek for Pindarus the while.   [*Exit* MESSALA.

Why didst thou send me forth, brave Cassius?
Did I not meet thy friends? and did not they
Put on my brows this wreath of victory,
And bid me give it thee? Didst thou not hear their shouts?
Alas, thou hast misconstrued every thing!
But, hold thee, take this garland on thy brow;
Thy Brutus bid me give it thee, and I
Will do his bidding. Brutus, come apace,
And see how I regarded Caius Cassius.
By your leave, gods: this is a Roman's part.
Come, Cassius' sword, and find Titinius' heart.

                   [Kills himself.

Alarum. Re-enter MESSALA, *with* BRUTUS, *young* CATO,
     and others.]

BRUTUS. Where, where, Messala, doth his body lie?
MESSALA. Lo, yonder, and Titinius mourning it.
BRUTUS. Titinius' face is upward.
CATO.   He is slain.
BRUTUS. O Julius Cæsar, thou art mighty yet!
    Thy spirit walks abroad, and turns our swords
    In our own proper entrails.   *[Low alarums.*
CATO.   Brave Titinius!
    Look, whether he have not crown'd dead Cassius!
BRUTUS. Are yet two Romans living such as these?
    The last of all the Romans, fare thee well!
    It is impossible that ever Rome
    Should breed thy fellow. Friends, I owe more tears
    To this dead man than you shall see me pay.
    I shall find time, Cassius, I shall find time.
    Come therefore, and to Thasos send his body:
    His funerals shall not be in our camp,
    Lest it discomfort us. Lucilius, come,
    And come, young Cato: let us to the field.
    Labeo and Flavius, set our battles on.
    'Tis three o'clock; and, Romans, yet ere night
    We shall try fortune in a second fight.   *[Exeunt.*

       S C E N E   IV — *Another part of the field.*

Alarum. Enter, fighting, SOLDIERS *of both armies; then*
        BRUTUS, *young* CATO, LUCILIUS, *and others.]*
BRUTUS. Yet, countrymen, O, yet hold up your heads!

CATO. What bastard doth not? Who will go with me?
    I will proclaim my name about the field.
    I am the son of Marcus Cato, ho!
    A foe to tyrants and my country's friend;
    I am the son of Marcus Cato, ho!
BRUTUS. And I am Brutus, Marcus Brutus, I;
    Brutus my country's friend; know me for Brutus!   [Exit.
LUCILIUS. O young and noble Cato, art thou down?
    Why, now thou diest as bravely as Titinius,
    And mayst be honor'd, being Cato's son.
FIRST SOLDIER. Yield, or thou diest.
LUCILIUS.   Only I yield to die:
    [Offering money] There is so much that thou wilt kill me
        straight;
    Kill Brutus and be honor'd in his death.
FIRST SOLDIER. We must not. A noble prisoner!
SECOND SOLDIER. Room, ho! Tell Antony, Brutus is ta'en.
FIRST SOLDIER. I'll tell the news. Here comes the general.
Enter ANTONY.]
    Brutus is ta'en, Brutus is ta'en, my lord.
ANTONY. Where is he?
LUCILIUS. Safe, Antony; Brutus is safe enough:
    I dare assure thee that no enemy
    Shall ever take alive the noble Brutus:
    The gods defend him from so great a shame!
    When you do find him, or alive or dead,
    He will be found like Brutus, like himself.
ANTONY. This is not Brutus, friend, but, I assure you,
    A prize no less in worth: keep this man safe,
    Give him all kindness: I had rather have
    Such men my friends than enemies: Go on,
    And see whether Brutus be alive or dead,
    And bring us word unto Octavius' tent
    How every thing is chanced.   [Exeunt.

    SCENE V — Another part of the field.

Enter BRUTUS, DARDANIUS, CLITUS, STRATO,
        and VOLUMNIUS.]
BRUTUS. Come, poor remains of friends, rest on this rock.
CLITUS. Statilius show'd the torch-light, but, my lord,
    He came not back: he is or ta'en or slain.

BRUTUS. Sit thee down, Clitus: slaying is the word;
 It is a deed in fashion. Hark thee, Clitus. [*Whispering.*
CLITUS. What, I, my lord? No, not for all the world.
BRUTUS. Peace then, no words.
CLITUS.   I'll rather kill myself.
BRUTUS. Hark thee, Dardanius.   [*Whispering.*
DARDANIUS.   Shall I do such a deed?
CLITUS. O Dardanius!
DARDANIUS. O Clitus!
CLITUS. What ill request did Brutus make to thee?
DARDANIUS. To kill him, Clitus. Look, he meditates.
CLITUS. Now is that noble vessel full of grief,
 That it runs over even at his eyes.
BRUTUS. Come hither, good Volumnius; list a word.
VOLUMNIUS. What says my lord?
BRUTUS.   Why, this, Volumnius:
 The ghost of Cæsar hath appear'd to me
 Two several times by night; at Sardis once,
 And this last night here in Philippi fields:
 I know my hour is come.
VOLUMNIUS.   Not so, my lord.
BRUTUS. Nay, I am sure it is, Volumnius.
 Thou seest the world, Volumnius, how it goes;
 Our enemies have beat us to the pit: [*Low alarums.*
 It is more worthy to leap in ourselves
 Than tarry till they push us. Good Volumnius,
 Thou know'st that we two went to school together:
 Even for that our love of old, I prithee,
 Hold thou my sword-hilts, whilst I run on it.
VOLUMNIUS. That's not an office for a friend, my lord.
            [*Alarum still.*
CLITUS. Fly, fly, my lord; there is no tarrying here.
BRUTUS. Farewell to you; and you; and you, Volumnius.
 Strato, thou hast been all this while asleep;
 Farewell to thee too, Strato. Countrymen,
 My heart doth joy that yet in all my life
 I found no man but he was true to me.
 I shall have glory by this losing day,
 More than Octavius and Mark Antony
 By this vile conquest shall attain unto.
 So, fare you well at once; for Brutus' tongue
 Hath almost ended his life's history:

Night hangs upon mine eyes; my bones would rest,
That have but labor'd to attain this hour.

　　　　　　　　　[*Alarum Cry within, 'Fly, fly, fly!'*

CLITUS. Fly, my lord, fly.

BRUTUS.　　　　　　　Hence! I will follow.

　　　　　[*Exeunt* CLITUS, DARDANIUS, *and* VOLUMNIUS.

I prithee, Strato, stay thou by thy lord:
Thou art a fellow of a good respect;
Thy life hath had some smatch of honor in it:
Hold then my sword, and turn away thy face,
While I do run upon it. Wilt thou, Strato?

STRATO. Give me your hand first: fare you well, my lord.

BRUTUS. Farewell, good Strato. [*Runs on his sword.*] Cæsar,
　　now be still:
I kill'd not thee with half so good a will.　　　　[*Dies.*

Alarum. Retreat. Enter OCTAVIUS, ANTONY,
　　　　MESSALA, LUCILIUS, *and the army.*]

OCTAVIUS. What man is that?

MESSALA. My master's man. Strato, where is thy master?

STRATO. Free from the bondage you are in, Messala:
　The conquerors can but make a fire of him;
For Brutus only overcame himself,
And no man else hath honor by his death.

LUCILIUS. So Brutus should be found. I thank thee, Brutus,
That thou hast proved Lucilius' saying true.

OCTAVIUS. All that served Brutus, I will entertain them.
Fellow, wilt thou bestow thy time with me?

STRATO. Aye, if Messala will prefer me to you.

OCTAVIUS. Do so, good Messala.

MESSALA. How died my master, Strato?

STRATO. I held the sword, and he did run on it.

MESSALA. Octavius, then take him to follow thee,
That did the latest service to my master.

ANTONY. This was the noblest Roman of them all:
All the conspirators, save only he,
Did that they did in envy of great Cæsar;
He only, in a general honest thought
And common good to all, made one of them.
His life was gentle, and the elements
So mix'd in him that Nature might stand up
And say to all the world 'This was a man!'

OCTAVIUS. According to his virtue let us use him,
　With all respect and rites of burial.
　Within my tent his bones to-night shall lie,
　Most like a soldier, order'd honorably.
　So call the field to rest, and let's away,
　To part the glories of this happy day.　　　　　[*Exeunt.*

HAMLET,

Prince of Denmark

What cause withholds you then to mourn for him?
O judgment! thou art fled to brutish beasts,
And men have lost their reason. Bear with me;

INTRODUCTION TO

Hamlet

BY

MARK VAN DOREN

IT HAS been said of Hamlet that something in his genius
renders him superior to decision and incapable of act,
and it has been pointed out that he dominates the busiest of
all known plays. Both views are right. His antic disposition
has been analyzed as a symptom of abnormality and as a device for seeming mad. Neither theory is without support. He
has been called the best of men and the worst of men. One
judgment is as just as the other. Opinions have differed as to
whether his deepest attention is engaged by the murder of his
father, the marriage of his mother, the villainy of his uncle the
King, the senility of Polonius, the apparent perfidy of Ophelia,
the reliability of Horatio, the meddling of Rosencrantz and
Guildenstern, or the manliness of Fortinbras. Any of them
will do. Scarcely anything can be said that will be untrue of
this brilliant and abounding young man; the first crisis in
whose life is also, to our loss, the last.

It has been said of the play *Hamlet* that its best scene is
the one in which Horatio first sees the ghost, or the one in
which he tells Hamlet of it, or the one in which Hamlet himself sees it and swears his friends to secrecy, or the one in
which Polonius bids farewell to his son and warns his daughter away from the prince, or the one in which Ophelia reports
Hamlet's disorder, or the one in which Polonius explains it to
the King and Queen, or the one in which Hamlet, entering
with a book, seems to Polonius to support the explanation, or
the one in which Hamlet discovers the intentions of Rosencrantz and Guildenstern and discourses to them of his mis-
anthropy, or the one in which he greets the players and con-
ceives a use to which they can be put, or the one in which
Ophelia is loosed to him while the King and Polonius listen as

187

spies, or the one in which he addresses the players on the subject of their art, or the one in which the play he has planned breaks down the King's composure, or the one with the recorders, or the one in which Hamlet cannot kill the King because he is praying, or the one in his mother's closet when Polonius is stabbed and the ghost walks again, or the one in which he makes merry over Polonius's supper of worms, or the one in which he watches Fortinbras march against Poland, or the one in which Ophelia sings mad songs and rouses her brother to revenge, or the one in which, while Laertes plots with the King, the Queen reports Ophelia's death, or the one in the graveyard, or the one with Osric, or the one at the end which leaves only Horatio and Fortinbras alive. Any of them will do. For all of the scenes in *Hamlet* are good, and relative to the play as a whole each one in its turn is best.

The two absolutes are related. Neither the hero nor his play can be taken apart. The joints are invisible. The character of Hamlet would appear to be no character at all because a name cannot be found for it, or—which is the same thing— because too many can be found. Yet no reader or beholder of the play has ever doubted that Hamlet was one man, or doubted that he knew him better than most men. He is so singular in each particular, to paraphrase Florizel's account of Perdita, that all his acts are kings. He is alive to the last syllable, and where there is so much life there is no blank space for labels. So likewise with the tragedy of which he is the heart and brain if not the whole moving body. There is no blank scene in *Hamlet* because it is not made up of scenes; it is one situation and one action, and though like any whole it is composed of parts there is no part whose tissue can be separated from the rest without the sound of tearing. *Hamlet* is a highly organized animal, sensitive and thoroughbred, each of whose sinews overlaps another, each of whose tendons tightens some extremity, and all of whose blood-stream is necessary to the unique, quick life which even the quietest movement expresses.

An attempt to enter the play through any scene of the conventional division will leave us still outside it—aware once more of its unspeakable vitality, but rewarded with no other sight than that of divers muscles rippling under skin. The thing has been put together, but either there are no joints or there are so many that the creature is all curves. Take, for instance, the section of the play which is called Act II, Scene ii. The number of its incidents is not the measure of its fullness, nor is the sum total of the things it tells us about Hamlet the final sum of our experience. The linkage of the incidents, the way they glide into one another without our being warned, is more important than their number; and our experience is not confined to the present Hamlet, or to what is happening around him now. The scene twitches remote corners of a dramatic web whose size we for the moment do not see; we gather that the whole play is implicit here, though we cannot be specific as to what is coming.

Rosencrantz and Guildenstern, two old friends of Hamlet, have arrived at court to keep him company; to draw him on to pleasures in the midst of which, as now the King makes clear, he may disclose the nature of his affliction. The King admits no other explanation than a father's death, and lets it be understood, the Queen concurring, that the motive behind this lawful espionage is a desire to cure the Prince's condition. As Rosencrantz and Guildenstern are led away to find Hamlet and begin their work, Polonius enters to announce that the ambassadors from Norway have returned and to assure the King and Queen that he has found the cause of Hamlet's lunacy. They are eager to hear the cause, but first they must receive the ambassadors, who bring word that old Norway has forbidden Fortinbras to continue the advance on Denmark which has so much troubled the King; and that Fortinbras, marching now against Poland, requests the right to cross Denmark so that he may gain his objective. The King, promising to consider the request at another time, dismisses the ambassadors and turns to Polonius, who with more art than matter, and with promises of brevity which his amusing tediousness belies, develops the theory that Hamlet is mad because Ophelia has repulsed him. The Queen had believed that her overhasty marriage was the cause, but agrees that Polonius's explanation is very likely. The King asks for better proof, whereupon Polonius remarks that Hamlet is in the habit of walking here in the lobby and that Ophelia can be set in his way while the King and her father watch behind an arras. As the King consents, Hamlet, who may have overheard the conclusion of the dialogue, enters reading a book. Polonius asks the King and Queen to be left alone with him, and argues from the nature of the insults he stays to receive that Hamlet is indeed afflicted with love-melancholy; though Hamlet's only state would appear to be boredom with old fools and anxiety for his own safety—"except my life, my life." As Polonius goes out, bewildered yet all the more convinced that he is right and that a meeting between Hamlet and his daughter must take place, Rosencrantz and Guildenstern pass him and are greeted by Hamlet, who plays a game of wit with them until their guard is down and he can ask them bluntly why they have come to Elsinore. They hesitate and temporize, but he forces them to confess that they have been sent for by the King and Queen. At once he tells them he will make everything clear: he has of late lost all his mirth, so that the earth and the great sky above it are to him but foul and pestilent, and man—the beauty of the world, the paragon of animals, the creature nearest the angels and most like a god—delights not him. He has spoken his best prose for the benefit of two fools upon whom he wishes to make a certain impression. But he has been betrayed into the eloquence of truth, and so he breaks off with the abrupt addition that woman delights him neither, though by their smiling they seem to say so. Their only thought, they assure him, is of the poor entertainment such a prince would be able to offer the players who have just come to Elsinore. He is very much interested in the news that players have come, and as a trumpet announces their approach he summons high spirits to inform Rosencrantz and Guildenstern that the King and Queen are deceived: he is but mad north-north-west. In still higher spirits he jests at Polonius who has entered in advance of the players, and when they enter at last he greets them excitedly, pressing one of them to recite Aeneas's speech about Priam's slaughter. The player complies, but is so overcome by the speech that he weeps and cannot go on. Hamlet, dismissing the rest of the troupe to Polonius's care, holds this one member until he consents to play "The Murder of Gonzago" tomorrow night and to learn some dozen or sixteen lines which will be inserted in the text. Then Hamlet, commanding him to follow Polonius and mock him not, and sending away Rosencrantz and Guildenstern with assurances of their welcome to Elsinore, is left alone for the soliloquy which ends the scene. In a mere dream of passion, a fiction, this player here has wept for Hecuba. What would he do had he the motive and the cue for passion that Hamlet has? Is Hamlet a coward that so far he has done nothing to avenge his father's murder? The question enrages him and he falls to cursing the King. But that is nothing. He must act. He still must be indirect, for the spirit he has seen may have been the devil and not his father. So—now he has it—he will act to gain the knowledge he needs. He will put on a play that will make the King blench if he is guilty. And if he but blench, Hamlet will know his course. The play's the thing.

Such a synopsis is circumstantial and would seem to be complete. But it leaves almost everything out. It does not suggest the quality of Rosencrantz and Guildenstern—the combination in them of the sinister and the commonplace— and it does not begin to explore the processes of Hamlet as he discourses with them, or to explain the full meaning for himself of the great speech about earth and man. It does not record the suspicions we may have as we listen to the King's expressed motive for spying on Hamlet; for we can guess that he is lying, but we do not know just what he fears, nor do we know how deeply the Queen is disturbed. It does not render our still unripened sense of a stern and remote significance in the military movements of Fortinbras, whom we perceive we are not being permitted to forget but whose importance as a symbol is to manifest itself much later. It does not balance Polonius on that subtle point of space which he occupies throughout three acts, moving us to consider him simultaneously as ridiculous and pathetic, consequential and a nuisance, the father of Ophelia and the victim with her of the prince's newborn savagery; it does not indicate that his diagnosis can be credited as correct, and it certainly does not examine the whole question of Hamlet's feeling toward the man who was to have been his father-in-law—"and look you mock him not." It does not register our conviction that Hamlet's interest in the players is general as well as particular; he has thought much about the theater, and it may be that he is more at home with actors than with other people. It does not describe the beautiful courtesy, even if it be tempered by mockery, with which he welcomes Rosencrantz and Guildenstern to Elsinore. It fails, in brief, to follow the innumerable nerves which connect this part of the play with every other part, and which converge in the vital organ of the closing soliloquy as extensions of the same nerves converge to produce other soliloquies, other organs, in other areas.

No synopis of *Hamlet,* whole or part, can hope to succeed. The play is its own synopsis, and nothing shorter will do. Neither will anything longer; analysis in this case overruns and outrages art. Shakespeare for once has perfectly translated idea into act. Whatever the idea was, we now have only the play, and it is so clear that it becomes mysterious. For it is nothing but detail. The density of its concreteness is absolute. We do not know why Hamlet does this or that, we only know that he does it, and that we are interested in nothing else while he does it. We can no more understand him than we can doubt him. He is an enigma because he is real. We do not know why he was created or what he means. We simply and amply perceive that he exists.

Hamlet is intellectual, but we do not learn this from his thoughts, for he has none; he does not deliver himself of propositions. Of the many statements he makes there is none which is made for its own sake, and with the sense that it would be true at another time or place. In any situation only the relevant portion of the person speaks; the whole man never does, except in the play as a whole, which can be thought of as his body speaking, or rather his life. He is that unique thing in literature, a credible genius. But the reason is that Shakespeare has kept our view restricted to the surface. Here is an intellectual seen altogether from the outside. We know him as one from the way he behaves, not from the things he says he believes. We may not assume, indeed, that he believes what he says. For one thing he is a soul in agitation, his equilibrium has been lost. This glass of fashion and this mold of form, this noble mind whose harmony was once like that of sweet bells rung in tune, this courtier, soldier, scholar whose disposition has hitherto been generous and free from all contriving, this matchless gentleman who has never been known to overstep the modesty of nature, is not himself save for a few minutes at the end when his calmness comes back like magic and his apology to Laertes can almost avert the catastrophe which every event has prepared. His words elsewhere are wild and whirling; or they are cruel in their kindness; or they are simply cruel. Or they are spoken for a calculated effect—the calculation in most cases being extempore. For Hamlet is immensely sensitive to his environment, and adjusts himself with marvelous quickness to its many changes. His asides are sudden, like needles whose function is to keep both him and us awake to the farthest implications of the danger close at hand. His repartee is pistol-swift, whipped out by one forever abnormally on guard against real or imagined enemies. And his soliloquies are secret mirrors the subdued brilliance of whose shifting planes reflects the predicament that surrounds him, past and future as well as present.

Curiously then we know a man in terms of what he is not; this gentlest of all heroes is never gentle. But it is more complicated than that. Hamlet is an actor. Like any character in whom Shakespeare was greatly interested, he plays a role. He plays indeed many roles, being supreme in tragedy as Falstaff was supreme in comedy. His long interest in the theater has taught him how, but his best tutors now are the pressure of circumstance and the richness of his own nature. Like Falstaff he shows the man he is by being many men. With the exception of Horatio there is no person in the play for whose benefit he has not conceived and studied a part. He acts with the King and Queen, with Ophelia, with Polonius, with the court at large; taking on and putting off each role as occasion dictates, and at the climax of the tragedy wearing all of them simultaneously. For in the scene of the play within the play he has his audiences for the first time together. Now the fiction of Ophelia's Hamlet must harmonize with that of her father's, of the King's, of the Queen's, and with that of the general public. Only a virtuoso would succeed. But Hamlet, not to speak of Shakespeare, is a virtuoso, and he succeeds. No playwright every attempted a subtler scene, or ever achieved it with so little show of labor. The only thing we are conscious of is the intentness with which we follow the waves of meaning across Hamlet's face. The whole meaning of the play is in vibration there, even if we cannot put it in words of our own. There is, of course, no slightest reason why we should desire to do so.

As always in Shakespeare, the style of Hamlet is the man. He is made of mercury and so has many styles, yet they are one if only because they ever are telling us of what he is made. His tongue is as flexible as his mind. It knows its way among all words, all tones, all attitudes. And it is superbly trained. The intellect of its owner is apparent in nothing so much as his literary skill. With no notice at all he can say anything, and be master of what he has said. "Well said, old mole! Canst work i' the earth so fast?" "To be honest, as this world goes, is to be one man pick'd out of ten thousand." "You cannot, sir, take from me anything that I will more willingly part withal." "Then is doomsday near." "Denmark's a prison." "O God, I could be bounded in a nutshell and count myself a king of infinite space, were it not that I have bad dreams." "To be, or not to be: that is the question." "Thus conscience does make cowards of us all." "Get thee to a nunnery, go." "I say, we will have no more marriages." "No, good mother, here's metal more attractive." "You would play upon me, you would seem to know my stops, you would pluck out the heart of my mystery." "I will speak daggers to her, but use none." "I must be cruel, only to be kind." "Not where he eats, but where he is eaten." "I see a cherub that sees them." "Where be your gibes now, your gambols, your songs, your flashes of merriment, that were wont to set the table on a roar? Not one now, to mock your own grinning? Quite chopfallen?" "But I am very sorry, good Horatio, that to Laertes I forgot myself." "But thou wouldst not think how ill all's here about my heart." "If it be now, 't is not to come; if it be not to come, it will be now; if it be not now, yet it will come; the readiness is all." "The rest is silence." The simplicity of such utterances reveals a geat man and a princely artist, an artist too much the master of his medium to be proud of what he can do with it, or even to be conscious that it is there. But Hamlet can be elaborate as well as simple, artful as well as quick. His address to the players says something which he wants them to understand, and the thing it says has been said for all time; yet the man who is speaking enjoys his speech, and may be a little proud of the nobility which knows its way so well among the short words and the long ones, the epigrams and the periods.

Speak the speech, I pray you, as I pronounc'd it to you, trippingly on the tongue; but if you mouth it, as many of your players do, I had as lief the town-crier spoke my lines. Nor do not saw the air too much with your hand, thus, but use all gently; for in the very torrent, tempest, and, as I may say, the whirlwind of passion, you must acquire and beget a temperance that may give it smoothness. O, it offends me to the soul to see a robustious periwig-pated fellow tear a passion to tatters, to very rags, to split the ears of the groundlings, who for the most part are capable of nothing but in-

explicable dumb-shows and noise. I could have such a fellow
whipp'd for o'erdoing Termagant. It out-herods Herod. Pray you,
avoid it. . . . Be not too tame neither, but let your own discretion
be your tutor. Suit the action to the word, the word to the action;
with this special observance, that you o'erstep not the modesty of
nature. For anything so overdone is from the purpose of playing,
whose end, both at the first and now, was and is, to hold, as 't were,
the mirror up to nature; to show virtue her own feature, scorn her
own image, and the very age and body of the time his form and
pressure. Now this overdone, or come tardy off, though it make
the unskilful laugh, cannot but make the judicious grieve; the
censure of the which one must, in your allowance, o'erweigh a
whole theatre of others. O, there be players that I have seen play,
and heard others praise, and that highly, not to speak it profanely
that, neither having the accent of Christians nor the gait of Christian, pagan, nor man, have so strutted and bellowed that I have
thought some of Nature's journeymen had made men and not made
them well, they imitated humanity so abominably.   [III, ii]

"Imitated humanity so abominably," "capable of nothing but
inexplicable dumb-shows and noise." Only a skilled tongue
could say such phrases well, and only a proud tongue would
undertake them at all. A man who can talk like that must be
aware of everything in the world—except perhaps the dis-
proportion between his discourse and its occasion. And of
Shakespeare we are to remember that he never used in his
play the speech which for his hero had seemed to call for so
long a commentary. But then we shall be confirmed in our
belief that the character of Hamlet is the character of an
actor, and that the instinct of Shakespeare as a dramatic poet
is to pour his fullest gifts into such persons. That Hamlet is
histrionic is no less clear than that he is high-strung, cerebral,
magnanimous, and sometimes obscene. Richard II had been
an amateur of the boards, Jaques had been a sentimentalist
spoiling to be a star, and Brutus to his own loss had been no
actor at all. Hamlet is so much of a professional that the
man in him is indistinguishable from the mime. His life as we
have it is so naturally and completely a play that we can
almost think of him as his own author, his own director, and
his own protagonist. We can even think of him as his own
entire cast, he is the plexus of so much humanity, the mirror
in which so many other minds are registered.

We see Hamlet in other persons even more clearly than in
himself. His relation to each of them is immediate and deli-

cate; his least gesture records itself in them—in their concern, their pity, their love, their anger, or their fear. They cannot be indifferent to him, and this is one reason that we cannot. Nor is vanity in him the cause. He has not willed or desired his eminence. It is not in his nature to dominate humanity, and at last destroy it. Yet he does; this gentleman warps every other life to his own, and scatters death like a universal plague. Not quite universal, either. The world of this tragedy, like that of any other tragedy by Shakespeare, is large; Denmark is a prison and its air is close to breathe, but four times we have heard through darkness the brisk tramp of Fortinbras' feet on the bright ice beyond tragedy's frontiers. Fortinbras is Hamlet's frame. He is not completely drawn until his cannon, his drums, and his colors come on with him at the end to announce that human existence will be what it was before Hamlet lived. But then he is firmly drawn; the story of Hamlet, however morbid, has been confined. Another frame, an inner one, is Hamlet's good friend Horatio, who will live on until he has reported Hamlet and his cause aright to the unsatisfied, until he has healed a hero's wounded name. For just as Hamlet with his last breath remembers the state and thinks to give Fortinbras his dying voice for king, so he remembers that his aim had never been to strew the stage of life with corpses; to deliver Rosencrantz and Guildenstern to an English hangman, to feed Polonius to politic worms, to send Ophelia, dripping with tears and muddy death, into unsanctified ground. Within these two frames the spectacle of Hamlet is forever suspended. A merest glance from us, a chance return to any scene, and the whole movement recommences. Hamlet walks again, alone and yet surrounded: a genius of unfathomable depth who yet is in contact at every point of his clear surface with another life as sensitive to his as a still night is to sound. That honor could too much change him, that scruples too fine could distort him into a dealer of coarse death, was both his tragedy and the world's. The world could not let so destructive a man live longer, but when it sacrificed him it lost the light of its fiercest sun.

The Story of the Play

ACT I

HAMLET, Prince of Denmark, is advised by the sentinels of the royal castle of Kronborg, at Elsinore, that an apparition strongly resembling his dead father had appeared on the battlements. Hamlet therefore resolves to encounter the spirit and learn from it, if possible, the true cause of his father's taking-off, about which the Prince has had many suspicions. He meets the Ghost at its next nightly visitation, and in an interview with it his worst fears are confirmed. The late King's brother Claudius, who has ascended the throne and wedded the widowed Queen, had poisoned the King while he slept. Hamlet is enjoined to secrecy and revenge, and the Ghost vanishes. Hamlet's followers are sworn to say nothing of the occurrence.

ACT II

BECAUSE of the news and of the dread task to which he is commissioned, Hamlet is seized with a species of madness, perhaps largely feigned, whereby he may cloak his designs. He writes incoherent and passionate letters to his lady-love, Ophelia, daughter of Polonius, a court dignitary. At this juncture a company of strolling players arrives at the castle and at Hamlet's suggestion a certain play is given before the King and Queen and members of the court.

ACT III

THE PLAY deals with the murder of a Venetian duke, whose wife afterwards weds the murderer. The story closely resembles the circumstances of the King of Denmark's demise. During the play Hamlet is intent not upon the players but upon the countenance and actions of his uncle. The latter, as if struck with a realizing sense of his own crime, as Hamlet suspected, hurriedly leaves. Hamlet no longer doubts the truth of the Ghost's communications, and turns with energy to seek the vengeance which he has sworn to execute.

The queen mother is also much disturbed by the purport of the play, and sends for Hamlet in order to upbraid him. Hamlet answers reproach with reproach, and leaves his mother overwhelmed with shame and self-convicted. But for the opportune arrival of the dead King's spirit, Hamlet might have adopted even more violent measures. Ophelia's father, Polonius, who is spying upon this interview, is slain by Hamlet, who mistakes him for the King.

ACT IV

HAMLET'S banishment is decided upon. Two former school comrades of his are entrusted with a commission to leave him in England, where sealed orders are to bring about the Prince's death. But by a combination of plot and accident the execution is visited instead upon the heads of the two accomplices. Hamlet returns to Denmark. There he is greeted by a strange spectacle—the funeral of a young girl, honored by the presence of the King, Queen, and persons of the court. Hamlet has in fact arrived home just at the time of Ophelia's interment. That unfortunate maiden, through incessant brooding over the madness of her lover, the untimely end of her father, and the continued absence of her brother, Laertes, had become insane. For some days she had wandered about the court singing and strewing flowers, then had strayed to the banks of a stream and been drowned.

ACT V

WHEN Hamlet discovers that it is Ophelia's funeral, he is beside himself with grief. He leaps into the grave and angrily contests with Laertes, who also has just returned, the place of chief mourner. Laertes in turn desires to kill Hamlet, for he regards the Prince as the cause of all the woes that have fallen upon his house.

Seeing the animosity of Laertes, King Claudius thinks he may make use of it to work Hamlet's undoing. He secretly advises Laertes to engage Hamlet in a fencing-match—supposedly friendly. Laertes' foil, however, is to be naked and envenomed. Hamlet, unsuspecting, consents to a trial of skill before the court. The King prepares a poisoned drink for Hamlet, if perchance he shall escape the tipped foil. Laertes and Hamlet fence. After a touch or two for Hamlet, the Queen, to do him honor, toasts him—unwittingly—with the poisoned cup. Laertes wounds Hamlet. In the scuffle they change rapiers, and Hamlet in turn wounds Laertes with the latter's treacherous blade. The Queen dies from the drugged wine. Laertes falls, but before he dies he confesses his guilty design and craves pardon of the Prince. Hamlet turns upon the King with his own dying strength and stabs the usurping monarch to the heart.

J. WALKER McSPADDEN

List of Characters

CLAUDIUS, *king of Denmark*

HAMLET, *son to the late, and nephew to the present king*

POLONIUS, *lord chamberlain*

HORATIO, *friend to* HAMLET

LAERTES, *son to* POLONIUS

VOLTIMAND,
CORNELIUS,
ROSENCRANTZ,
GUILDENSTERN, } *courtiers*
OSRIC,
A Gentleman,

A Priest

MARCELLUS, } *officers*
BERNARDO,

FRANCISCO, *a soldier*

REYNALDO, *servant to* POLONIUS

Players

Two clowns, grave-diggers

FORTINBRAS, *prince of Norway*

A Captain

English Ambassadors

GERTRUDE, *queen of Denmark, and mother to* HAMLET

OPHELIA, *daughter to* POLONIUS

Lords, Ladies, Officers, Soldiers, Sailors, Messengers, and other Attendants

Ghost of Hamlet's Father

CLAUDIUS

HAMLET

LAERTES

OPHELIA

GERTRUDE

Hamlet, Prince of Denmark

Scene — Denmark.

ACT I

Scene I — Elsinore. *A platform before the castle.*

Francisco *at his post. Enter to him* Bernardo.]

BERNARDO. Who's there?

FRANCISCO. Nay, answer me: stand, and unfold yourself.

BERNARDO. Long live the king!

FRANCISCO. Bernardo?

BERNARDO. He.

FRANCISCO. You come most carefully upon your hour.

BERNARDO. 'Tis now struck twelve; get thee to bed, Francisco.

FRANCISCO. For this relief much thanks: 'tis bitter cold,
   And I am sick at heart.

BERNARDO. Have you had quiet guard?

FRANCISCO.   Not a mouse stirring.

BERNARDO. Well, good night.
   If you do meet Horatio and Marcellus,
   The rivals of my watch, bid them make haste.

FRANCISCO. I think I hear them. Stand, ho! Who is there?

Enter HORATIO *and* MARCELLUS.]

HORATIO. Friends to this ground.

MARCELLUS.   And liegemen to the Dane.

FRANCISCO. Give you good night.

MARCELLUS.   O, farewell, honest soldier:
   Who hath relieved you?

FRANCISCO.   Bernardo hath my place.
   Give you good night.   [*Exit.*

MARCELLUS.   Holla! Bernardo!

BERNARDO.   Say,
   What, is Horatio there?

HORATIO.   A piece of him.

202

BERNARDO. Welcome, Horatio; welcome, good Marcellus.

MARCELLUS. What, has this thing appear'd again to-night?

BERNARDO. I have seen nothing.

MARCELLUS. Horatio says 'tis but our fantasy,
　And will not let belief take hold of him
　Touching this dreaded sight, twice seen of us:
　Therefore I have entreated him along
　With us to watch the minutes of this night,
　That if again this apparition come,
　He may approve our eyes and speak to it.

HORATIO. Tush, tush, 'twill not appear.

BERNARDO.　　　　　　　　　　　Sit down a while;
　And let us once again assail your ears,
　That are so fortified against our story,
　What we have two nights seen.

HORATIO.　　　　　　　　　　Well, sit we down,
　And let us hear Bernardo speak of this.

BERNARDO. Last night of all,
　When yond same star that's westward from the pole
　Had made his course to illume that part of heaven
　Where now it burns, Marcellus and myself,
　The bell then beating one,—

Enter GHOST.]

MARCELLUS. Peace, break thee off; look, where it comes again!

BERNARDO. In the same figure, like the king that's dead.

MARCELLUS. Thou art a scholar; speak to it, Horatio.

BERNARDO. Looks it not like the king? mark it, Horatio.

HORATIO. Most like: it harrows me with fear and wonder.

BERNARDO. It would be spoke to.

MARCELLUS.　　　　　　　　　Question it, Horatio.

HORATIO. What art thou, that usurp'st this time of night,
　Together with that fair and warlike form
　In which the majesty of buried Denmark
　Did sometimes march? by heaven I charge thee, speak!

MARCELLUS. It is offended.

BERNARDO.　　　　　　　See, it stalks away!

HORATIO. Stay! speak, speak! I charge thee, speak!

　　　　　　　　　　　　　　　　　[*Exit* GHOST.

MARCELLUS. 'Tis gone, and will not answer.

BERNARDO. How now, Horatio! you tremble and look pale:

Is not this something more than fantasy?
What think you on't?

HORATIO. Before my God, I might not this believe
Without the sensible and true avouch
Of mine own eyes.

MARCELLUS.   Is it not like the king?

HORATIO. As thou art to thyself:
Such was the very armor he had on
When he the ambitious Norway combated;
So frown'd he once, when, in an angry parle,
He smote the sledded Polacks on the ice.
'Tis strange.

MARCELLUS. Thus twice before, and jump at this dead hour,
With martial stalk hath he gone by our watch.

HORATIO. In what particular thought to work I know not;
But, in the gross and scope of my opinion,
This bodes some strange eruption to our state.

MARCELLUS. Good now, sit down, and tell me, he that knows,
Why this same strict and most observant watch
So nightly toils the subject of the land,
And why such daily cast of brazen cannon,
And foreign mart for implements of war;
Why such impress of shipwrights, whose sore task
Does not divide the Sunday from the week;
What might be toward, that this sweaty haste
Doth make the night joint-laborer with the day:
Who is't that can inform me?

HORATIO.   That can I;
At least the whisper goes so. Our last king,
Whose image even but now appear'd to us,
Was, as you know, by Fortinbras of Norway,
Thereto prick'd on by a most emulate pride,
Dared to the combat; in which our valiant Hamlet—
For so this side of our known world esteem'd him—
Did slay this Fortinbras; who by a seal'd compact
Well ratified by law and heraldry,
Did forfeit, with his life, all those his lands
Which he stood seized of, to the conqueror:
Against the which, a moiety competent
Was gaged by our king; which had return'd
To the inheritance of Fortinbras,
Had he been vanquisher; as, by the same covenant

    And carriage of the article design'd,
    His fell to Hamlet. Now, sir, young Fortinbras,
    Of unimproved metal hot and full,
    Hath in the skirts of Norway here and there
    Shark'd up a list of lawless resolutes,
    For food and diet, to some enterprise
    That hath a stomach in't: which is no other—
    As it doth well appear unto our state—
    But to recover of us, by strong hand
    And terms compulsatory, those foresaid lands
    So by his father lost: and this, I take it,
    Is the main motive of our preparations,
    The source of this our watch and the chief head
    Of this post-haste and romage in the land.
BERNARDO. I think it be no other but e'en so:
    Well may it sort, that this portentous figure
    Comes armed through our watch, so like the king
    That was and is the question of these wars.
HORATIO. A mote it is to trouble the mind's eye.
    In the most high and palmy state of Rome,
    A little ere the mightiest Julius fell,
    The graves stood tenantless, and the sheeted dead
    Did squeak and gibber in the Roman streets:
        .   .   .   .
    As stars with trains of fire and dews of blood,
    Disasters in the sun; and the moist star,
    Upon whose influence Neptune's empire stands,
    Was sick almost to doomsday with eclipse:
    And even the like precurse of fierce events,
    As harbingers preceding still the fates
    And prologue to the omen coming on,
    Have heaven and earth together demonstrated
    Unto our climatures and countrymen.
Re-enter GHOST.]
    But soft, behold! lo, where it comes again!
    I'll cross it, though it blast me. Stay, illusion!
    If thou hast any sound, or use of voice,
    Speak to me:
    If there be any good thing to be done,
    That may to thee do ease and grace to me,
    Speak to me:
    If thou art privy to thy country's fate,

Which, happily, foreknowing may avoid,
O, speak!
Or if thou hast uphoarded in thy life
Extorted treasure in the womb of earth,
For which, they say, you spirits oft walk in death,
Speak of it: stay, and speak! [*The cock crows.*] Stop it,
    Marcellus.

MARCELLUS. Shall I strike at it with my partisan?

HORATIO. Do, if it will not stand.

BERNARDO.   'Tis here!

HORATIO.   'Tis here!

MARCELLUS. 'Tis gone!   [*Exit* GHOST.

We do it wrong, being so majestical,
To offer it the show of violence;
For it is, as the air, invulnerable,
And our vain blows malicious mockery.

BERNARDO. It was about to speak, when the cock crew.

HORATIO. And then it started like a guilty thing
Upon a fearful summons. I have heard,
The cock, that is the trumpet to the morn,
Doth with his lofty and shrill-sounding throat
Awake the god of day, and at his warning,
Whether in sea or fire, in earth or air,
The extravagant and erring spirit hies
To his confine: and of the truth herein
This present object made probation.

MARCELLUS. It faded on the crowing of the cock.
Some say that ever 'gainst that season comes
Wherein our Saviour's birth is celebrated,
The bird of dawning singeth all night long:
And then, they say, no spirit dare stir abroad,
The nights are wholesome, then no planets strike,
No fairy takes nor witch hath power to charm,
So hallow'd and so gracious is the time.

HORATIO. So have I heard and do in part believe it.
But look, the morn, in russet mantle clad,
Walks o'er the dew of yon high eastward hill:
Break we our watch up; and by my advice,
Let us impart what we have seen to-night
Unto young Hamlet; for, upon my life,
This spirit, dumb to us, will speak to him:
Do you consent we shall acquaint him with it,

As needful in our loves, fitting our duty?

MARCELLUS. Let's do't, I pray; and I this morning know
Where we shall find him most conveniently.　　　[*Exeunt.*

SCENE II — *A room of state in the castle.*

Flourish. Enter the KING, QUEEN, HAMLET, POLONIUS,
　　LAERTES, VOLTIMAND, CORNELIUS, LORDS, *and*
　　ATTENDANTS.]

KING. Though yet of Hamlet our dear brother's death
The memory be green, and that it us befitted
To bear our hearts in grief and our whole kingdom
To be contracted in one brow of woe,
Yet so far hath discretion fought with nature
That we with wisest sorrow think on him,
Together with remembrance of ourselves.
Therefore our sometime sister, now our queen,
The imperial jointress to this warlike state,
Have we, as 'twere with a defeated joy,—
With an auspicious and a dropping eye,
With mirth in funeral and with dirge in marriage,
In equal scale weighing delight and dole,—
Taken to wife: nor have we herein barr'd
Your better wisdoms, which have freely gone
With this affair along. For all, our thanks.
Now follows, that you know, young Fortinbras,
Holding a weak supposal of our worth,
Or thinking by our late dear brother's death
Our state to be disjoint and out of frame,
Colleagued with this dream of his advantage,
He hath not fail'd to pester us with message,
Importing the surrender of those lands
Lost by his father, with all bonds of law,
To our most valiant brother. So much for him.
Now for ourself, and for this time of meeting:
Thus much the business is: we have here writ
To Norway, uncle of young Fortinbras,—
Who, impotent and bed-rid, scarcely hears
Of this his nephew's purpose,—to suppress
His further gait herein; in that the levies,
The lists and full proportions, are all made
Out of his subject: and we here dispatch

You, good Cornelius, and you, Voltimand,
For bearers of this greeting to old Norway,
Giving to you no further personal power
To business with the king more than the scope
Of these delated articles allow.
Farewell, and let your haste commend your duty.

CORNELIUS. }
VOLTIMAND.} In that and all things will we show our duty.

KING. We doubt it nothing: heartily farewell.

                 [*Exeunt* VOLTIMAND *and* CORNELIUS.

And now, Laertes, what's the news with you?
You told us of some suit; what is't, Laertes?
You cannot speak of reason to the Dane,
And lose your voice: what wouldst thou beg, Laertes,
That shall not be my offer, not thy asking?
The head is not more native to the heart,
The hand more instrumental to the mouth,
Than is the throne of Denmark to thy father.
What wouldst thou have, Laertes?

LAERTES.   My dread lord,
Your leave and favor to return to France,
From whence though willingly I came to Denmark,
To show my duty in your coronation,
Yet now, I must confess, that duty done,
My thoughts and wishes bend again toward France
And bow them to your gracious leave and pardon.

KING. Have you your father's leave? What says Polonius?

POLONIUS. He hath, my lord, wrung from me my slow leave
By laborsome petition, and at last
Upon his will I seal'd my hard consent:
I do beseech you, give him leave to go.

KING. Take thy fair hour, Laertes; time be thine,
And thy best graces spend it at thy will!
But now, my cousin Hamlet, and my son,—

HAMLET. [*Aside*] A little more than kin, and less than kind.

KING. How is it that the clouds still hang on you?

HAMLET. Not so, my lord; I am too much i' the sun.

QUEEN. Good Hamlet, cast thy nighted color off,
And let thine eye look like a friend on Denmark.
Do not for ever with thy vailed lids
Seek for thy noble father in the dust:
Thou know'st 'tis common; all that lives must die,

　　Passing through nature to eternity.
HAMLET. Aye, madam, it is common.
QUEEN.　　　　　　　　　　　　　If it be,
　　Why seems it so particular with thee?
HAMLET. Seems, madam! nay, it is; I know not 'seems.'
　　'Tis not alone my inky cloak, good mother,
　　Nor customary suits of solemn black,
　　Nor windy suspiration of forced breath,
　　No, nor the fruitful river in the eye,
　　Nor the dejected havior of the visage,
　　Together with all forms, moods, shapes of grief,
　　That can denote me truly: these indeed seem,
　　For they are actions that a man might play:
　　But I have that within which passeth show;
　　These but the trappings and the suits of woe.
KING. 'Tis sweet and commendable in your nature, Hamlet,
　　To give these mourning duties to your father:
　　But, you must know, your father lost a father,
　　That father lost, lost his, and the survivor bound
　　In filial obligation for some term
　　To do obsequious sorrow: but to persevere
　　In obstinate condolement is a course
　　Of impious stubbornness; 'tis unmanly grief:
　　It shows a will most incorrect to heaven,
　　A heart unfortified, a mind impatient,
　　An understanding simple and unschool'd:
　　For what we know must be and is as common
　　As any the most vulgar thing to sense,
　　Why should we in our peevish opposition
　　Take it to heart? Fie! 'tis a fault to heaven,
　　A fault against the dead, a fault to nature,
　　To reason most absurd, whose common theme
　　Is death of fathers, and who still hath cried,
　　From the first corse till he that died to-day,
　　'This must be so.' We pray you, throw to earth
　　This unprevailing woe, and think of us
　　As of a father: for let the world take note,
　　You are the most immediate to our throne,
　　And with no less nobility of love
　　Than that which dearest father bears his son
　　Do I impart toward you. For your intent
　　In going back to school in Wittenberg,

It is most retrograde to our desire:
And we beseech you, bend you to remain
Here in the cheer and comfort of our eye,
Our chiefest courtier, cousin and our son.
QUEEN. Let not thy mother lose her prayers, Hamlet:
I pray thee, stay with us; go not to Wittenberg.
HAMLET. I shall in all my best obey you, madam.
KING. Why, 'tis a loving and a fair reply:
Be as ourself in Denmark. Madam, come;
This gentle and unforced accord of Hamlet
Sits smiling to my heart: in grace whereof,
No jocund health that Denmark drinks to-day,
But the great cannon to the clouds shall tell,
And the king's rouse the heaven shall bruit again,
Re-speaking earthly thunder. Come away.
                    [*Flourish. Exeunt all but* HAMLET.

HAMLET. O, that this too too solid flesh would melt,
Thaw and resolve itself into a dew!
Or that the Everlasting had not fix'd
His canon 'gainst self-slaughter! O God! God!
How weary, stale, flat and unprofitable
Seem to me all the uses of this world!
Fie on't! ah fie! 'tis an unweeded garden,
That grows to seed; things rank and gross in nature
Possess it merely. That it should come to this!
But two months dead! nay, not so much, not two:
So excellent a king; that was, to this,
Hyperion to a satyr: so loving to my mother,
That he might not beteem the winds of heaven
Visit her face too roughly. Heaven and earth!
Must I remember? why, she would hang on him,
As if increase of appetite had grown
By what it fed on: and yet, within a month—
Let me not think on't—Frailty, thy name is woman!—
A little month, or ere those shoes were old
With which she follow'd my poor father's body,
Like Niobe, all tears:—why she, even she,—
O God! a beast that wants discourse of reason
Would have mourn'd longer,—married with my uncle,
My father's brother, but no more like my father
Than I to Hercules: within a month;
Ere yet the salt of most unrighteous tears

Had left the flushing in her galled eyes,
She married. O, most wicked speed, to post
With such dexterity to incestuous sheets!
It is not, nor it cannot come to good:
But break, my heart, for I must hold my tongue!

Enter HORATIO, MARCELLUS, *and* BERNARDO.]

HORATIO. Hail to your lordship!

HAMLET.   I am glad to see you well:
  Horatio,—or I do forget myself.

HORATIO. The same, my lord, and your poor servant ever.

HAMLET. Sir, my good friend; I'll change that name with you:
  And what make you from Wittenberg, Horatio?
  Marcellus?

MARCELLUS. My good lord?

HAMLET. I am very glad to see you. [*To* BERNARDO] Good
  even, sir.
  But what, in faith, make you from Wittenberg?

HORATIO. A truant disposition, good my lord.

HAMLET. I would not hear your enemy say so,
  Nor shall you do my ear that violence,
  To make it truster of your own report
  Against yourself: I know you are no truant.
  But what is your affair in Elsinore?
  We'll teach you to drink deep ere you depart.

HORATIO. My lord, I came to see your father's funeral.

HAMLET. I pray thee, do not mock me, fellow-student;
  I think it was to see my mother's wedding.

HORATIO. Indeed, my lord, it follow'd hard upon.

HAMLET. Thrift, thrift, Horatio! the funeral baked-meats
  Did coldly furnish forth the marriage tables.
  Would I had met my dearest foe in heaven
  Or ever I had seen that day, Horatio!
  My father!—methinks I see my father.

HORATIO. O where, my lord?

HAMLET.   In my mind's eye, Horatio.

HORATIO. I saw him once; he was a goodly king.

HAMLET. He was a man, take him for all in all,
  I shall not look upon his like again.

HARATIO. My lord, I think I saw him yesternight.

HAMLET. Saw? who?

HORATIO. My lord, the king your father.

HAMLET.   The king my father!

HORATIO. Season your admiration for a while
  With an attent ear, till I may deliver,
  Upon the witness of these gentlemen,
  This marvel to you.
HAMLET.   For God's love, let me hear.
HORATIO. Two nights together had these gentlemen,
  Marcellus and Bernardo, on their watch,
  In the dead vast and middle of the night,
  Been thus encounter'd. A figure like your father,
  Armed at point exactly, cap-a-pe,
  Appears before them, and with solemn march
  Goes slow and stately by them: thrice he walk'd
  By their oppress'd and fear-surprised eyes,
  Within his truncheon's length; whilst they, distill'd
  Almost to jelly with the act of fear,
  Stand dumb, and speak not to him. This to me
  In dreadful secrecy impart they did;
  And I with them the third night kept the watch:
  Where, as they had deliver'd, both in time,
  Form of the thing, each word made true and good,
  The apparition comes: I knew your father;
  These hands are not more like.
HAMLET.   But where was this?
MARCELLUS. My lord, upon the platform where we watch'd.
HAMLET. Did you not speak to it?
HORATIO.   My lord, I did.
  But answer made it none: yet once methought
  It lifted up its head and did address
  Itself to motion, like as it would speak:
  But even then the morning cock crew loud,
  And at the sound it shrunk in haste away
  And vanish'd from our sight.
HAMLET.   'Tis very strange.
HORATIO. As I do live, my honor'd lord, 'tis true,
  And we did think it writ down in our duty
  To let you know of it.
HAMLET. Indeed, indeed, sirs, but this troubles me.
  Hold you the watch to-night?
MARCELLUS.)
BERNARDO.)   We do, my lord.
HAMLET. Arm'd, say you?

MARCELLUS.　　　　　　　Arm'd, my lord.
BERNARDO.

HAMLET.　　　　　　　　　　　　From top to toe?

MARCELLUS.　My lord, from head to foot.
BERNARDO.

HAMLET. Then saw you not his face?

HORATIO. O, yes, my lord; he wore his beaver up.

HAMLET. What, look'd he frowningly?

HORATIO. A countenance more in sorrow than in anger.

HAMLET. Pale, or red?

HORATIO. Nay, very pale.

HAMLET.　　　　　　　And fix'd his eyes upon you?

HORATIO. Most constantly.

HAMLET.　　　　　　　I would I had been there.

HORATIO. It would have much amazed you.

HAMLET. Very like, very like. Stay'd it long?

HORATIO. While one with moderate haste might tell a hundred.

MARCELLUS.　Longer, longer.
BERNARDO.

HORATIO. Not when I saw't.

HAMLET.　　　　　　　His beard was grizzled? no?

HORATIO. It was, as I have seen it in his life,
　A sable silver'd.

HAMLET.　　　　I will watch to-night;
　Perchance 'twill walk again.

HORATIO.　　　　　　　I warrant it will.

HAMLET. If it assume my noble father's person,
　I'll speak to it, though hell itself should gape
　And bid me hold my peace. I pray you all,
　If you have hitherto conceal'd this sight,
　Let it be tenable in your silence still,
　And whatsoever else shall hap to-night,
　Give it an understanding, but no tongue:
　I will requite your loves. So fare you well:
　Upon the platform, 'twixt eleven and twelve,
　I'll visit you.

ALL.　　　　　Our duty to your honor.

HAMLET. Your loves, as mine to you: farewell.
　　　　　　　　　　　　[Exeunt all but HAMLET.
　My father's spirit in arms! all is not well;
　I doubt some foul play: would the night were come!

Till then sit still, my soul: foul deeds will rise,
Though all the earth o'erwhelm them, to men's eyes.

[*Exit.*

Scene III — *A room in* Polonius's *house.*

Enter Laertes *and* Ophelia.]

LAERTES. My necessaries are embark'd: farewell:
    And, sister, as the winds give benefit
    And convoy is assistant, do not sleep,
    But let me hear from you.
OPHELIA.   Do you doubt that?
LAERTES. For Hamlet, and the trifling of his favor,
    Hold it a fashion, and a toy in blood,
    A violet in the youth of primy nature,
    Forward, not permanent, sweet, not lasting,
    The perfume and suppliance of a minute;
    No more.
OPHELIA.   No more but so?
LAERTES.   Think it no more:
    For nature crescent does not grow alone
    In thews and bulk; but, as this temple waxes,
    The inward service of the mind and soul
    Grows wide withal. Perhaps he loves you now;
    And now no soil nor cautel doth besmirch
    The virtue of his will: but you must fear,
    His greatness weigh'd, his will is not his own;
    For he himself is subject to his birth:
    He may not, as unvalued persons do,
    Carve for himself, for on his choice depends
    The safety and health of this whole state,
    And therefore must his choice be circumscribed
    Unto the voice and yielding of that body
    Whereof he is the head. Then if he says he loves you,
    It fits your wisdom so far to believe it
    As he in his particular act and place
    May give his saying deed; which is no further
    Than the main voice of Denmark goes withal.
    Then weigh what loss your honor may sustain,
    If with too credent ear you list his songs,
    Or lose your heart, or your chaste treasure open
    To his unmaster'd importunity.

Fear it, Ophelia, fear it, my dear sister,
And keep you in the rear of your affection,
Out of the shot and danger of desire.
The chariest maid is prodigal enough,
If she unmask her beauty to the moon:
Virtue itself 'scapes not calumnious strokes:
The canker galls the infants of the spring
Too oft before their buttons be disclosed,
And in the morn and liquid dew of youth
Contagious blastments are most imminent.
Be wary then; best safety lies in fear:
Youth to itself rebels, though none else near.

OPHELIA. I shall the effect of this good lesson keep,
As watchman to my heart. But, good my brother,
Do not, as some ungracious pastors do,
Show me the steep and thorny way to heaven,
Whilst, like puff'd and reckless libertine,
Himself the primrose path of dalliance treads
And recks not his own rede.

LAERTES.   O, fear me not.
I stay too long; but here my father comes.
Enter POLONIUS.]
A double blessing is a double grace;
Occasion smiles upon a second leave.

POLONIUS. Yet here, Laertes! Aboard, aboard, for shame!
The wind sits in the shoulder of your sail,
And you are stay'd for. There; my blessing with thee!
And these few precepts in thy memory
See thou character. Give thy thoughts no tongue,
Nor any unproportion'd thought his act.
Be thou familiar, but by no means vulgar.
Those friends thou hast, and their adoption tried,
Grapple them to thy soul with hoops of steel,
But do not dull thy palm with entertainment
Of each new-hatch'd unfledged comrade. Beware
Of entrance to a quarrel; but being in,
Bear't, that the opposed may beware of thee.
Give every man thy ear, but few thy voice:
Take each man's censure, but reserve thy judgment.
Costly thy habit as thy purse can buy,
But not express'd in fancy; rich, not gaudy:
For the apparel oft proclaims the man;

And they in France of the best rank and station
Are of a most select and generous chief in that.
Neither a borrower nor a lender be:
For loan oft loses both itself and friend,
And borrowing dulls the edge of husbandry.
This above all: to thine own self be true,
And it must follow, as the night the day,
Thou canst not then be false to any man.
Farewell: my blessing season this in thee!

LAERTES. Most humbly do I take my leave, my lord.

POLONIUS. The time invites you; go, your servants tend.

LAERTES. Farewell, Ophelia, and remember well
What I have said to you.

OPHELIA.   'Tis in my memory lock'd,
And you yourself shall keep the key of it.

LAERTES. Farewell.   [Exit.

POLONIUS.   What is't, Ophelia, he hath said to you?

OPHELIA. So please you, something touching the Lord Hamlet.

POLONIUS. Marry, well bethought:
'Tis told me, he hath very oft of late
Given private time to you, and you yourself
Have of your audience been most free and bounteous:
If it be so—as so 'tis put on me,
And that in way of caution—I must tell you,
You do not understand yourself so clearly
As it behoves my daughter and your honor.
What is between you? give me up the truth.

OPHELIA. He hath, my lord, of late made many tenders
Of his affection to me.

POLONIUS. Affection! pooh! you speak like a green girl,
Unsifted in such perilous circumstance.
Do you believe his tenders, as you call them?

OPHELIA. I do not know, my lord, what I should think.

POLONIUS. Marry, I'll teach you: think yourself a baby,
That you have ta'en these tenders for true pay,
Which are not sterling. Tender yourself more dearly;
Or—not to crack the wind of the poor phrase,
Running it thus—you'll tender me a fool.

OPHELIA. My lord, he hath importuned me with love
In honorable fashion.

POLONIUS. Aye, fashion you may call it; go to, go to.

OPHELIA. And hath given countenance to his speech, my lord,

With almost all the holy vows of heaven.

POLONIUS. Aye, springes to catch woodcocks. I do know,
When the blood burns, how prodigal the soul
Lends the tongue vows: these blazes, daughter,
Giving more light than heat, extinct in both,
Even in their promise, as it is a-making,
You must not take for fire. From this time
Be something scanter of your maiden presence;
Set your entreatments at a higher rate
Than a command to parley. For Lord Hamlet,
Believe so much in him, that he is young,
And with a larger tether may he walk
Than may be given you: in few, Ophelia,
Do not believe his vows; for they are brokers,
Not of that dye which their investments show,
But mere implorators of unholy suits,
Breathing like sanctified and pious bawds,
The better to beguile. This is for all:
I would not, in plain terms, from this time forth,
Have you so slander any moment leisure,
As to give words or talk with the Lord Hamlet.
Look to't, I charge you: come your ways.

OPHELIA. I shall obey, my lord.   [*Exeunt.*

SCENE IV — *The platform.*

Enter HAMLET, HORATIO, *and* MARCELLUS.]

HAMLET. The air bites shrewdly; it is very cold.

HORATIO. It is a nipping and an eager air.

HAMLET. What hour now?

HORATIO.   I think it lacks of twelve.

MARCELLUS. No, it is struck.

HORATIO. Indeed? I heard it not: it then draws near the season
Wherein the spirit held his wont to walk.
     [*A flourish of trumpets, and ordnance shot off within.*
What doth this mean, my lord?

HAMLET. The king doth wake to-night, and takes his rouse,
Keeps wassail, and the swaggering up-spring reels;
And as he drains his draughts of Rhenish down,
The kettle-drum and trumpet thus bray out
The triumph of his pledge.

HORATIO.   It is a custom?

HAMLET. Aye, marry, is't:
    But to my mind, though I am native here
    And to the manner born, it is a custom
    More honor'd in the breach than the observance.
    This heavy-headed revel east and west
    Makes us traduced and tax'd of other nations:
    They clepe us drunkards, and with swinish phrase
    Soil our addition; and indeed it takes
    From our achievements, though perform'd at height,
    The pith and marrow of our attribute.
    So, oft it chances in particular men,
    That for some vicious mole of nature in them,
    As, in their birth,—wherein they are not guilty,
    Since nature cannot choose his origin,—
    By the o'ergrowth of some complexion,
    Oft breaking down the pales and forts of reason,
    Or by some habit that too much o'er-leavens
    The form of plausive manners, that these men,—
    Carrying, I say, the stamp of one defect,
    Being nature's livery, or fortune's star,—
    Their virtues else—be they as pure as grace,
    As infinite as man may undergo—
    Shall in the general censure take corruption
    From that particular fault: the dram of eale
    Doth all the noble substance of a doubt
    To his own scandal.
Enter GHOST.]
HORATIO.   Look, my lord it comes!
HAMLET. Angels and ministers of grace defend us!
    Be thou a spirit of health or goblin damn'd,
    Bring with thee airs from heaven or blasts from hell,
    Be thy intents wicked or charitable,
    Thou comest in such a questionable shape
    That I will speak to thee: I'll call thee Hamlet,
    King, father, royal Dane: O, answer me!
    Let me not burst in ignorance; but tell
    Why thy canonized bones, hearsed in death,
    Have burst their cerements; why the sepulchre,
    Wherein we saw thee quietly inurn'd,
    Hath oped his ponderous and marble jaws,
    To cast thee up again. What may this mean,
    That thou, dead corse, again, in complete steel,

Revisit'st thus the glimpses of the moon,
Making night hideous; and we fools of nature
So horridly to shake our disposition
With thoughts beyond the reaches of our souls?
Say, why is this? wherefore? what should we do?

                    [GHOST *beckons* HAMLET.

HORATIO. It beckons you to go away with it,
  As if it some impartment did desire
  To you alone.

MARCELLUS. Look, with what courteous action
  It waves you to a more removed ground:
  But do not go with it.

HORATIO.   No, by no means.

HAMLET. It will not speak; then I will follow it.

HORATIO. Do not, my lord.

HAMLET.   Why, what should be the fear?
  I do not set my life at a pin's fee;
  And for my soul, what can it do to that,
  Being a thing immortal as itself?
  It waves me forth again: I'll follow it.

HORATIO. What if it tempt you toward the flood, my lord,
  Or to the dreadful summit of the cliff
  That beetles o'er his base into the sea,
  And there assume some other horrible form,
  Which might deprive your sovereignty of reason
  And draw you into madness? think of it:
  The very place puts toys of desperation,
  Without more motive, into every brain
  That looks so many fathoms to the sea
  And hears it roar beneath.

HAMLET.   It waves me still.
  Go on; I'll follow thee.

MARCELLUS. You shall not go, my lord.

HAMLET.   Hold off your hands.

HORATIO. Be ruled; you shall not go.

HAMLET.   My fate cries out,
  And makes each petty artery in this body
  As hardy as the Nemean lion's nerve.
  Still am I call'd, unhand me, gentlemen;
  By heaven, I'll make a ghost of him that lets me:
  I say, away! Go on; I'll follow thee.

                    [*Exeunt* GHOST *and* HAMLET.

HORATIO. He waxes desperate with imagination.

MARCELLUS. Let's follow; 'tis not fit thus to obey him.

HORATIO. Have after. To what issue will this come?

MARCELLUS. Something is rotten in the state of Denmark.

HORATIO. Heaven will direct it.

MARCELLUS.　　　　　　　　　　Nay, let's follow him.　[*Exeunt.*

SCENE V — *Another part of the platform.*

Enter GHOST *and* HAMLET.]

HAMLET. Whither wilt thou lead me? speak; I'll go no further.

GHOST. Mark me.

HAMLET.　　　　　　I will.

GHOST.　　　　　　　　　My hour is almost come,
　　When I to sulphurous and tormenting flames
　　Must render up myself.

HAMLET.　　　　　　　　　　Alas, poor ghost!

GHOST. Pity me not, but lend thy serious hearing
　　To what I shall unfold.

HAMLET.　　　　　　　　Speak; I am bound to hear.

GHOST. So art thou to revenge, when thou shalt hear.

HAMLET. What?

GHOST. I am thy father's spirit;
　　Doom'd for a certain term to walk the night,
　　And for the day confined to fast in fires,
　　Till the foul crimes done in my days of nature
　　Are burnt and purged away. But that I am forbid
　　To tell the secrets of my prison-house,
　　I could a tale unfold whose lightest word
　　Would harrow up thy soul, freeze thy young blood,
　　Make thy two eyes, like stars, start from their spheres,
　　Thy knotted and combined locks to part
　　And each particular hair to stand on end,
　　Like quills upon the fretful porpentine:
　　But this eternal blazon must not be
　　To ears of flesh and blood. List, list, O, list!
　　If thou didst ever thy dear father love—

HAMLET. O God!

GHOST. Revenge his foul and most unnatural murder.

HAMLET.　　　　　　　　　　　　　Murder!

GHOST. Murder most foul, as in the best it is,
　　But this most foul, strange, and unnatural.

HAMLET. Haste me to know't, that I, with wings as swift
   As meditation or the thoughts of love,
   May sweep to my revenge.
GHOST.   I find thee apt;
   And duller shouldst thou be than the fat weed
   That roots itself in ease on Lethe wharf,
   Wouldst thou not stir in this. Now, Hamlet, hear:
   'Tis given out that, sleeping in my orchard,
   A serpent stung me; so the whole ear of Denmark
   Is by a forged process of my death
   Rankly abused: but know, thou noble youth,
   The serpent that did sting thy father's life
   Now wears his crown.
HAMLET.   O my prophetic soul!
   My uncle!
GHOST. Aye, that incestuous, that adulterate beast,
   With witchcraft of his wit, with traitorous gifts,—
   O wicked wit and gifts, that have the power
   So to seduce!—won to his shameful lust
   The will of my most seeming-virtuous queen:
   O Hamlet, what a falling-off was there!
   From me, whose love was of that dignity
   That it went hand in hand even with the vow
   I made to her in marriage; and to decline
   Upon a wretch, whose natural gifts were poor
   To those of mine!
   But virtue, as it never will be moved,
   Though lewdness court it in a shape of heaven,
   So lust, though to a radiant angel link'd,
   Will sate itself in a celestial bed
   And prey on garbage.
   But, soft! methinks I scent the morning air;
   Brief let me be. Sleeping within my orchard,
   My custom always of the afternoon,
   Upon my secure hour thy uncle stole,
   With juice of cursed hebenon in a vial,
   And in the porches of my ears did pour
   The leperous distilment; whose effect
   Holds such an enmity with blood of man
   That swift as quicksilver it courses through
   The natural gates and alleys of the body;
   And with a sudden vigor it doth posset

And curd, like eager droppings into milk,
The thin and wholesome blood: so did it mine;
And a most instant tetter bark'd about,
Most lazar-like, with vile and loathsome crust,
All my smooth body.
Thus was I, sleeping, by a brother's hand
Of life, of crown, of queen, at once dispatch'd:
Cut off even in the blossoms of my sin,
Unhousel'd, disappointed, unaneled;
No reckoning made, but sent to my account
With all my imperfections on my head:
O, horrible! O, horrible! most horrible!
If thou hast nature in thee, bear it not;
Let not the royal bed of Denmark be
A couch for luxury and damned incest.
But, howsoever thou pursuest this act,
Taint not thy mind, nor let thy soul contrive
Against thy mother aught: leave her to heaven,
And to those thorns that in her bosom lodge,
To prick and sting her. Fare thee well at once!
The glow-worm shows the matin to be near,
And 'gins to pale his uneffectual fire:
Adieu, adieu, adieu! remember me.   [*Exit.*

HAMLET. O all you host of heaven! O earth! what else?
And shall I couple hell? O, fie! Hold, hold, my heart;
And you, my sinews, grow not instant old,
But bear me stiffly up. Remember thee!
Aye, thou poor ghost, while memory holds a seat
In this distracted globe. Remember thee!
Yea, from the table of my memory
I'll wipe away all trivial fond records,
All saws of books, all forms, all pressures past,
That youth and observation copied there;
And thy commandment all alone shall live
Within the book and volume of my brain,
Unmix'd with baser matter: yes, by heaven!
O most pernicious woman!
O villain, villain, smiling, damned villain!
My tables,—meet it is I set it down,
That one may smile, and smile, and be a villain;
At least I'm sure it may be so in Denmark.   [*Writing.*
So, uncle, there you are. Now to my word;

It is 'Adieu, adieu! remember me.'
I have sworn't.

HORATIO.   }
MARCELLUS. } [*Within*] My lord, my lord!

Enter HORATIO *and* MARCELLUS.]

MARCELLUS.   Lord Hamlet!

HORATIO.   Heaven secure him!

HAMLET. So be it!

MARCELLUS. Illo, ho, ho, my lord!

HAMLET. Hillo, ho, ho, boy! come, bird, come.

MARCELLUS. How is't, my noble lord?

HORATIO.   What news, my lord?

HAMLET. O, wonderful!

HORATIO. Good my lord, tell it.

HAMLET.   No; you will reveal it.

HORATIO. Not I, my lord, by heaven.

MARCELLUS.   Nor I, my lord.

HAMLET. How say you, then; would heart of man once think
    it?
But you'll be secret?

HORATIO.   }
MARCELLUS. }   Aye, by heaven, my lord.

HAMLET. There's ne'er a villain dwelling in all Denmark
But he's an arrant knave.

HORATIO. There needs no ghost, my lord, come from the grave
To tell us this.

HAMLET.   Why, right; you are i' the right;
And so, without more circumstance at all,
I hold it fit that we shake hands and part:
You, as your business and desire shall point you;
For every man hath business and desire,
Such as it is; and for my own poor part,
Look you, I'll go pray.

HORATIO. These are but wild and whirling words, my lord.

HAMLET. I'm sorry they offend you, heartily;
Yes, faith, heartily.

HORATIO.   There's no offense, my lord.

HAMLET. Yes, by Saint Patrick, but there is, Horatio,
And much offense too. Touching this vision here,
It is an honest ghost, that let me tell you:
For your desire to know what is between us,
O'ermaster't as you may. And now, good friends,

As you are friends, scholars and soldiers,
Give me one poor request.

HORATIO.   What is't, my lord? we will.

HAMLET. Never make known what you have seen tonight.

MARCELLUS. }
HORATIO.   } My lord, we will not.

HAMLET.   Nay, but swear't.

HORATIO.   In faith,
My lord, not I.

MARCELLUS.   Nor I, my lord, in faith.

HAMLET. Upon my sword.

MARCELLUS.   We have sworn, my lord, already.

HAMLET. Indeed, upon my sword, indeed.

GHOST. [*Beneath*]   Swear.

HAMLET. Ah, ha, boy! say'st thou so? art thou there, true-
penny?
Come on: you hear this fellow in the cellarage:
Consent to swear.

HORATIO.   Propose the oath, my lord.

HAMLET. Never to speak of this that you have seen,
Swear by my sword.

GHOST. [*Beneath*] Swear.

HAMLET. Hic et ubique? then we'll shift our ground.
Come hither, gentlemen,
And lay your hands again upon my sword:
Never to speak of this that you have heard,
Swear by my sword.

GHOST. [*Beneath*] Swear.

HAMLET. Well said, old mole! canst work i' the earth so fast?
A worthy pioneer! Once more remove, good friends.

HORATIO. O day and night, but this is wondrous strange!

HAMLET. And therefore as a stranger give it welcome.
There are more things in heaven and earth, Horatio,
Than are dreamt of in your philosophy.
But come;
Here, as before, never, so help you mercy,
How strange or odd soe'er I bear myself,
As I perchance hereafter shall think meet
To put an antic disposition on,
That you, at such times seeing me, never shall,
With arms encumber'd thus, or this head-shake,
Or by pronouncing of some doubtful phrase,

As 'Well, well, we know,' or 'We could, an if we would,'
Or 'If we list to speak,' or 'There be, an if they might,'
Or such ambiguous giving out, to note
That you know aught to me: this not to do,
So grace and mercy at your most need help you,
Swear.

GHOST. [*Beneath*] Swear.

HAMLET. Rest, rest, perturbed spirit!   [*They swear.*]
So, gentlemen,
With all my love I do command me to you:
And what so poor a man as Hamlet is
May do, to express his love and friending to you,
God willing, shall not lack. Let us go in together;
And still your fingers on your lips, I pray.
The time is out of joint: O cursed spite,
That ever I was born to set it right!
Nay, come, let's go together.   [*Exeunt.*

ACT II

SCENE I — *A room in* POLONIUS' *house*.

Enter POLONIUS *and* REYNALDO.]

POLONIUS. Give him this money and these notes, Reynaldo.
REYNALDO. I will, my lord.
POLONIUS. You shall do marvelous wisely, good Reynaldo,
  Before you visit him, to make inquire
  Of his behavior.
REYNALDO.   My lord, I did intend it.
POLONIUS. Marry, well said, very well said. Look you, sir,
  Inquire me first what Danskers are in Paris,
  And how, and who, what means, and where they keep,
  What company, at what expense, and finding
  By this encompassment and drift of question
  That they do know my son, come you more nearer
  Than your particular demands will touch it:
  Take you, as 'twere, some distant knowledge of him,
  As thus, 'I know his father and his friends,
  And in part him:' do you mark this, Reynaldo?
REYNALDO. Aye, very well, my lord.
POLONIUS. 'And in part him; but,' you may say, 'not well:
  But if 't be he I mean, he's very wild,
  Addicted so and so;' and there put on him
  What forgeries you please; marry, none so rank
  As may dishonor him; take heed of that;
  But, sir, such wanton, wild and usual slips
  As are companions noted and most known
  To youth and liberty.
REYNALDO.   As gaming, my lord.
POLONIUS. Aye, or drinking, fencing, swearing, quarreling,
  Drabbing: you may go so far.
REYNALDO. My lord, that would dishonor him.
POLONIUS. Faith, no; as you may season it in the charge.
  You must not put another scandal on him,
  That he is open to incontinency;
  That's not my meaning: but breathe his faults so quaintly
  That they may seem the taints of liberty,
  The flash and outbreak of a fiery mind,

   A savageness in unreclaimed blood,
   Of general assault.

REYNALDO.   But, my good lord,—

POLONIUS. Wherefore should you do this?

REYNALDO.   Aye, my lord,
   I would know that.

POLONIUS.   Marry, sir, here's my drift,
   And I believe it is a fetch of warrant:
   You laying these slight sullies on my son,
   As 'twere a thing a little soil'd i' the working,
   Mark you,
   Your party in converse, him you would sound,
   Having ever seen in the prenominate crimes
   The youth you breathe of guilty, be assured
   He closes with you in this consequence;
   'Good sir,' or so, or 'friend,' or 'gentleman,'
   According to the phrase or the addition
   Of man and country.

REYNALDO.   Very good, my lord.

POLONIUS. And then, sir, does he this—he does—what was I
   about to say? By the mass, I was about to say something:
   where did I leave?

REYNALDO. At 'closes in the consequence,' at 'friend or so,'
   and 'gentleman.'

POLONIUS. At 'closes in the consequence,' aye, marry;
   He closes with you thus: 'I know the gentleman;
   I saw him yesterday, or t' other day,
   Or then, or then, with such, or such, and, as you say,
   There was a' gaming, there o'ertook in 's rouse,
   There falling out at tennis:' or perchance,
   'I saw him enter such a house of sale,'
   Videlicet, a brothel, or so forth.
   See you now;
   Your bait of falsehood takes this carp of truth:
   And thus do we of wisdom and of reach,
   With windlasses and with assays of bias,
   By indirections find directions out:
   So, by my former lecture and advice,
   Shall you my son. You have me, have you not?

REYNALDO. My lord, I have.

POLONIUS.   God be wi' ye; fare ye well.

REYNALDO. Good my lord!

POLONIUS. Observe his inclination in yourself.

REYNALDO. I shall, my lord.

POLONIUS. And let him ply his music.

REYNALDO.　　　　　　　　　　　　Well, my lord.

POLONIUS. Farewell!　　　　　　　　　　[Exit REYNALDO.

Enter OPHELIA.]

　　How now, Ophelia! what's the matter?

OPHELIA. O, my lord, I have been so affrighted!

POLONIUS. With what, i' the name of God?

OPHELIA. My lord, as I was sewing in my closet,
　　Lord Hamlet, with his doublet all unbraced,
　　No hat upon his head, his stockings foul'd,
　　Ungarter'd and down-gyved to his ankle;
　　Pale as his shirt, his knees knocking each other,
　　And with a look so piteous in purport
　　As if he had been loosed out of hell
　　To speak of horrors, he comes before me.

POLONIUS. Mad for thy love?

OPHELIA.　　　　　　　　My lord, I do not know,
　　But truly I do fear it.

POLONIUS.　　　　　What said he?

OPHELIA. He took me by the wrist and held me hard;
　　Then goes he to the length of all his arm,
　　And with his other hand thus o'er his brow,
　　He falls to such perusal of my face
　　As he would draw it. Long stay'd he so;
　　At last, a little shaking of mine arm,
　　And thrice his head thus waving up and down,
　　He raised a sigh so piteous and profound
　　As it did seem to shatter all his bulk
　　And end his being: that done, he lets me go:
　　And with his head over his shoulder turn'd,
　　He seem'd to find his way without his eyes,
　　For out o' doors he went without their help,
　　And to the last bended their light on me.

POLONIUS. Come, go with me: I will go seek the king,
　　This is the very ecstasy of love;
　　Whose violent property fordoes itself
　　And leads the will to desperate undertakings
　　As oft as any passion under heaven
　　That does afflict our natures. I am sorry.
　　What, have you given him any hard words of late?

OPHELIA. No, my good lord, but, as you did command,
 I did repel his letters and denied
 His access to me.
POLONIUS.   That hath made him mad.
 I am sorry that with better heed and judgment
 I had not quoted him: I fear'd he did but trifle
 And meant to wreck thee; but beshrew my jealousy!
 By heaven, it is as proper to our age
 To cast beyond ourselves in our opinions
 As it is common for the younger sort
 To lack discretion. Come, go we to the king:
 This must be known; which, being kept close, might move
 More grief to hide than hate to utter love.
 Come.   [*Exeunt.*

SCENE II — *A room in the castle.*

Flourish. Enter KING, QUEEN, ROSENCRANTZ,
   GUILDENSTERN, *and* ATTENDANTS.]
KING. Welcome, dear Rosencrantz and Guildenstern!
 Moreover that we much did long to see you,
 The need we have to use you did provoke
 Our hasty sending. Something have you heard
 Of Hamlet's transformation; so call it,
 Sith nor the exterior nor the inward man
 Resembles that it was. What it should be,
 More than his father's death, that thus hath put him
 So much from the understanding of himself,
 I cannot dream of: I entreat you both,
 That, being of so young days brought up with him
 And sith so neighbor'd to his youth and behavior,
 That you vouchsafe your rest here in our court
 Some little time: so by your companies
 To draw him on to pleasures, and to gather
 So much as from occasion you may glean,
 Whether aught to us unknown afflicts him thus,
 That open'd lies within our remedy.
QUEEN. Good gentlemen, he hath much talk'd of you,
 And sure I am two men there are not living
 To whom he more adheres. If it will please you
 To show us so much gentry and good will
 As to expend your time with us awhile

For the supply and profit of our hope,
Your visitation shall receive such thanks
As fits a king's remembrance.

ROSENCRANTZ.   Both your majesties
Might, by the sovereign power you have of us,
Put your dread pleasures more into command
Than to entreaty.

GUILDENSTERN.   But we both obey,
And here give up ourselves, in the full bent
To lay our service freely at your feet,
To be commanded.

KING. Thanks, Rosencrantz and gentle Guildenstern.

QUEEN. Thanks, Guildenstern and gentle Rosencrantz:
And I beseech you instantly to visit
My too much changed son. Go, some of you,
And bring these gentlemen where Hamlet is.

GUILDENSTERN. Heavens make our presence and our practices
Pleasant and helpful to him!

QUEEN.   Aye, amen!

[*Exeunt* ROSENCRANTZ, GUILDENSTERN,
and some ATTENDANTS.

Enter POLONIUS.]

POLONIUS. The ambassadors from Norway, my good lord,
Are joyfully return'd.

KING. Thou still hast been the father of good news.

POLONIUS. Have I, my lord? I assure my good liege,
I hold my duty as I hold my soul,
Both to my God and to my gracious king:
And I do think, or else this brain of mine
Hunts not the trail of policy so sure
As it hath used to do, that I have found
The very cause of Hamlet's lunacy.

KING. O, speak of that; that do I long to hear.

POLONIUS. Give first admittance to the ambassadors;
My news shall be the fruit to that great feast.

KING. Thyself do grace to them, and bring them in.

[*Exit* POLONIUS.

He tells me, my dear Gertrude, he hath found
The head and source of all your son's distemper.

QUEEN. I doubt it is no other but the main;
His father's death and our o'erhasty marriage.

KING. Well, we shall sift him.

Re-enter POLONIUS, *with* VOLTIMAND *and* CORNELIUS.]
                              Welcome, my good friends!
    Say, Voltimand, what from our brother Norway?
VOLTIMAND. Most fair return of greetings and desires.
    Upon our first, he sent out to suppress
    His nephew's levies, which to him appear'd
    To be a preparation 'gainst the Polack,
    But better look'd into, he truly found
    It was against your highness: whereat grieved,
    That so his sickness, age and impotence
    Was falsely borne in hand, sends out arrests
    On Fortinbras; which he, in brief, obeys,
    Receives rebuke from Norway, and in fine
    Makes vow before his uncle never more
    To give the assay of arms against your majesty.
    Whereon old Norway, overcome with joy,
    Gives him three thousand crowns in annual fee
    And his commission to employ those soldiers.
    So levied as before, against the Polack:
    With an entreaty, herein further shown,   [*Giving a paper.*
    That it might please you to give quiet pass
    Through your dominions for this enterprise,
    On such regards of safety and allowance
    As therein are set down.
KING.   It likes us well,
    And at our more consider'd time we'll read,
    Answer, and think upon this business.
    Meantime we thank you for your well-took labor:
    Go to your rest; at night we'll feast together:
    Most welcome home!   [*Exeunt* VOLTIMAND *and* CORNELIUS.
POLONIUS.   This business is well ended.
    My liege, and madam, to expostulate
    What majesty should be, what duty is,
    Why day is day, night night, and time is time,
    Were nothing but to waste night, day and time.
    Therefore, since brevity is the soul of wit
    And tediousness the limbs and outward flourishes,
    I will be brief. Your noble son is mad:
    Mad call I it; for, to define true madness,
    What is 't but to be nothing else but mad?
    But let that go.
QUEEN.   More matter, with less art.

POLONIUS. Madam, I swear I use no art at all.
That he is mad, 'tis true: 'tis true 'tis pity,
And pity 'tis 'tis true: a foolish figure;
But farewell it, for I will use no art.
Mad let us grant him then: and now remains
That we find out the cause of this effect,
Or rather say, the cause of this defect,
For this effect defective comes by cause:
Thus it remains and the remainder thus.
Perpend.
I have a daughter,—have while she is mine,—
Who in her duty and obedience, mark,
Hath given me this: now gather and surmise.   [*Reads.*
'To the celestial, and my soul's idol, the most beautified
    Ophelia,'—
That's an ill phrase, a vile phrase; 'beautified' is a vile
    phrase; but you shall hear.
Thus: [*Reads.*
'In her excellent white bosom, these,' &c.
QUEEN. Came this from Hamlet to her?
POLONIUS. Good madam, stay awhile; I will be faithful.
                                                     [*Reads.*

    'Doubt thou the stars are fire;
        Doubt that the sun doth move;
    Doubt truth to be a liar;
        But never doubt I love.
'O dear Ophelia, I am ill at these numbers;
I have not art to reckon my groans: but that
I love thee best, O most best, believe it.
Adieu. Thine evermore, most dear lady, whilst this ma-
    chine is to him,   HAMLET.'
This in obedience hath my daughter shown me;
And more above, hath his solicitings,
As they fell out by time, by means and place,
All given to mine ear.
KING.   But how hath she
Received his love?
POLONIUS.   What do you think of me?
KING. As of a man faithful and honorable.
POLONIUS. I would fain prove so. But what might you think,
When I had seen this hot love on the wing,—
As I perceived it, I must tell you that,

Before my daughter told me,—what might you,
Or my dear majesty your queen here, think,
If I had play'd the desk or table-book,
Or given my heart a winking, mute and dumb,
Or look'd upon this love with idle sight;
What might you think? No, I went round to work,
And my young mistress thus I did bespeak:
'Lord Hamlet is a prince, out of thy star;
This must not be:' and then I prescripts gave her,
That she should lock herself from his resort,
Admit no messengers, receive no tokens.
Which done, she took the fruits of my advice;
And he repulsed, a short tale to make,
Fell into a sadness, then into a fast,
Thence to a watch, thence into a weakness,
Thence to a lightness, and by this declension
Into the madness wherein now he raves
And all we mourn for.

KING. Do you think this?

QUEEN.   It may be, very like.

POLONIUS. Hath there been such a time, I 'ld fain know that,
That I have positively said ' 'tis so,'
When it proved otherwise?

KING.   Not that I know.

POLONIUS. [*Pointing to his head and shoulder*] Take this, from
this, if this be otherwise:
If circumstances lead me, I will find
Where truth is hid, though it were hid indeed
Within the center.

KING.   How may we try it further?

POLONIUS. You know, sometimes he walks for hours together
Here in the lobby.

QUEEN.   So he does, indeed.

POLONIUS. At such a time I'll loose my daughter to him:
Be you and I behind an arras then;
Mark the encounter: if he love her not,
And be not from his reason fall'n thereon,
Let me be no assistant for a state,
But keep a farm and carters.

KING.   We will try it.

QUEEN. But look where sadly the poor wretch comes reading.

POLONIUS. Away, I do beseech you, both away:
I'll board him presently.

[*Exeunt* KING, QUEEN, *and* ATTENDANTS.
Enter HAMLET, *reading*.]

O, give me leave: how does my good Lord Hamlet?

HAMLET. Well, God-a-mercy.

POLONIUS. Do you know me, my lord?

HAMLET. Excellent well; you are a fishmonger.

POLONIUS. Not I, my lord.

HAMLET. Then I would you were so honest a man.

POLONIUS. Honest, my lord!

HAMLET. Aye, sir; to be honest, as this world goes, is to be
one man picked out of ten thousand.

POLONIUS. That's very true, my lord.

HAMLET. For if the sun breed maggots in a dead dog, being a
good kissing carrion—Have you a daughter?

POLONIUS. I have, my lord.

HAMLET. Let her not walk i' the sun; conception is a blessing;
but as your daughter may conceive,—friend, look to 't.

POLONIUS. [*Aside*] How say you by that? Still harping on my
daughter: yet he knew me not at first; he said I was a fishmonger: he is far gone: and truly in my youth I suffered
much extremity for love; very near this. I'll speak to him
again.—What do you read, my lord?

HAMLET. Words, words, words.

POLONIUS. What is the matter, my lord?

HAMLET. Between who?

POLONIUS. I mean, the matter that you read, my lord.

HAMLET. Slanders, sir: for the satirical rogue says here that
old men have gray beards, that their faces are wrinkled,
their eyes purging thick amber and plum-tree gum, and
that they have a plentiful lack of wit, together with most
weak hams: all which, sir, though I most powerfully and
potently believe, yet I hold it not honesty to have it thus
set down; for yourself, sir, shall grow old as I am, if like a
crab you could go backward.

POLONIUS. [*Aside*] Though this be madness, yet there is
method in 't.—Will you walk out of the air, my lord?

HAMLET. Into my grave.

POLONIUS. Indeed, that's out of the air.   [*Aside*]
How pregnant sometimes his replies are! a happiness that
often madness hits on, which reason and sanity could not

so prosperously be delivered of. I will leave him, and suddenly contrive the means of meeting between him and my
daughter.—My honorable lord, I will most humbly take my
leave of you.

HAMLET. You cannot, sir, take from me anything that I will
more willingly part withal: except my life, except my life,
except my life.

POLONIUS. Fare you well, my lord.

HAMLET. These tedious old fools.

Re-enter ROSENCRANTZ *and* GUILDENSTERN.]

POLONIUS. You go to seek the Lord Hamlet; there he *is*.

ROSENCRANTZ. [*To* POLONIUS] God save you, sir!

             [*Exit* POLONIUS.

GUILDENSTERN. My honored lord!

ROSENCRANTZ. My most dear lord!

HAMLET. My excellent good friends! How dost thou, Guildenstern? Ah, Rosencrantz! Good lads, how do you both?

ROSENCRANTZ. As the indifferent children of the earth.

GUILDENSTERN. Happy, in that we are not over-happy;
On Fortune's cap we are not the very button.

HAMLET. Nor the soles of her shoe?

ROSENCRANTZ. Neither, my lord.

HAMLET. Then you live about her waist, or in the middle of
her favors?

GUILDENSTERN. Faith, her privates we.

HAMLET. In the secret parts of Fortune? Oh, most true; she is
a strumpet. What's the news?

ROSENCRANTZ. None, my lord, but that the world's grown
honest.

HAMLET. Then is doomsday near: but your news is not true.
Let me question more in particular: what have you, my
good friends, deserved at the hands of Fortune, that she
sends you to prison hither?

GUILDENSTERN. Prison, my lord!

HAMLET. Denmark's a prison.

ROSENCRANTZ. Then is the world one.

HAMLET. A goodly one; in which there are many confines,
wards and dungeons, Denmark being one o' the worst.

ROSENCRANTZ. We think not so, my lord.

HAMLET. Why, then, 'tis none to you; for there is nothing
either good or bad, but thinking makes it so: to me it is a
prison.

ROSENCRANTZ. Why, then your ambition makes it one; 'tis too narrow for your mind.

HAMLET. O God, I could be bounded in a nut-shell and count myself a king of infinite space, were it not that I have bad dreams.

GUILDENSTERN. Which dreams indeed are ambition; for the very substance of the ambitious is merely the shadow of a dream.

HAMLET. A dream itself is but a shadow.

ROSENCRANTZ. Truly, and I hold ambition of so airy and light a quality that it is but a shadow's shadow.

HAMLET. Then are our beggars bodies, and our monarchs and outstretched heroes the beggars' shadows. Shall we to the court? for, by my fay, I cannot reason.

ROSENCRANTZ. } We'll wait upon you.
GUILDENSTERN. }

HAMLET. No such matter: I will not sort you with the rest of my servants; for, to speak to you like an honest man, I am most dreadfully attended. But, in the beaten way of friendship, what make you at Elsinore?

ROSENCRANTZ. To visit you, my lord; no other occasion.

HAMLET. Beggar that I am, I am even poor in thanks; but I thank you: and sure, dear friends, my thanks are too dear a halfpenny. Were you not sent for? Is it your own inclining? Is it a free visitation? Come, deal justly with me: come, come; nay, speak.

GUILDENSTERN. What should we say, my lord?

HAMLET. Why, any thing, but to the purpose. You were sent for; and there is a kind of confession in your looks, which your modesties have not craft enough to color: I know the good king and queen have sent for you.

ROSENCRANTZ. To what end, my lord?

HAMLET. That you must teach me. But let me conjure you, by the rights of our fellowship, by the consonancy of our youth, by the obligation of our ever-preserved love, and by what more dear a better proposer could charge you withal, be even and direct with me, whether you were sent for, or no.

ROSENCRANTZ. [Aside to GUILDENSTERN] What say you?

HAMLET. [Aside] Nay then, I have an eye of you.— If you love me, hold not off.

GUILDENSTERN. My lord, we were sent for.

HAMLET. I will tell you why; so shall my anticipation prevent your discovery, and your secrecy to the king and queen moult no feather. I have of late—but wherefore I know not—lost all my mirth, forgone all custom of exercises; and indeed it goes so heavily with my disposition that this goodly frame, the earth, seems to me a sterile promontory; this most excellent canopy, the air, look you, this brave o'erhanging firmament, this majestical roof fretted with golden fire, why, it appears no other thing to me than a foul and pestilent congregation of vapors. What a piece of work is a man! how noble in reason! how infinite in faculty! in form and moving how express and admirable! in action how like an angel! in apprehension how like a god! the beauty of the world! the paragon of animals! And yet, to me, what is this quintessence of dust? man delights not me; no, nor woman neither, though by your smiling you seem to say so.

ROSENCRANTZ. My lord, there was no such stuff in my thoughts.

HAMLET. Why did you laugh then, when I said 'man delights not me'?

ROSENCRANTZ. To think, my lord, if you delight not in man, what lenten entertainment the players shall receive from you: we coted them on the way; and hither are they coming, to offer you service.

HAMLET. He that plays the king shall be welcome; his majesty shall have tribute of me; the adventurous knight shall use his foil and target; the lover shall not sigh gratis; the humorous man shall end his part in peace; the clown shall make those laugh whose lungs are tickle o' the sere, and the lady shall say her mind freely, or the blank verse shall halt for 't. What players are they?

ROSENCRANTZ. Even those you were wont to take such delight in, the tragedians of the city.

HAMLET. How chances it they travel? their residence, both in reputation and profit, was better both ways.

ROSENCRANTZ. I think their inhibition comes by the means of the late innovation.

HAMLET. Do they hold the same estimation they did when I was in the city? are they so followed?

ROSENCRANTZ. No, indeed, are they not.

HAMLET. How comes it? do they grow rusty?

ROSENCRANTZ. Nay, their endeavor keeps in the wonted pace:
but there is, sir, an eyrie of children, little eyases, that cry
out on the top of question and are most tyrannically
clapped for 't: these are now the fashion, and so berattle
the common stages—so they call them—that many wearing rapiers are afraid of goose-quills, and dare scarce come
thither.

HAMLET. What, are they children? who maintains 'em? how
are they escorted? Will they pursue the quality no longer
than they can sing? will they not say afterwards, if they
should grow themselves to common players,—as it is most
like, if their means are no better,—their writers do them
wrong, to make them exclaim against their own succession?

ROSENCRANTZ. Faith, there has been much to-do on both sides,
and the nation holds it no sin to tarre them to controversy:
there was for a while no money bid for argument unless the
poet and the player went to cuffs in the question.

HAMLET. Is 't possible?

GUILDENSTERN. O, there has been much throwing about of
brains.

HAMLET. Do the boys carry it away?

ROSENCRANTZ. Aye, that they do, my lord; Hercules and his
load too.

HAMLET. It is not very strange; for my uncle is king of Denmark, and those that would make mows at him while my
father lived, give twenty, forty, fifty, a hundred ducats
a-piece, for his picture in little. 'Sblood, there is something
in this more than natural, if philosophy could find it out.

[*Flourish of trumpets within.*

GUILDENSTERN. There are the players.

HAMLET. Gentlemen, you are welcome to Elsinore. Your
hands, come then: the appurtenance of welcome is fashion
and ceremony: let me comply with you in this garb, lest my
extent to the players, which, I tell you, must show fairly
outwards, should more appear like entertainment than
yours. You are welcome: but my uncle-father and aunt-
mother are deceived.

GUILDENSTERN. In what, my dear lord?

HAMLET. I am but mad north-north-west: when the wind is
southerly I know a hawk from a handsaw.

Re-enter POLONIUS.]

POLONIUS. Well be with you, gentlemen!

HAMLET. Hark you, Guildenstern; and you too: at each ear a
hearer: that great baby you see there is not yet out of his
swaddling clouts.

ROSENCRANTZ. Happily he's the second time come to them; for
they say an old man is twice a child.

HAMLET. I will prophesy he comes to tell me of the players;
mark it. You say right, sir: o' Monday morning; 'twas so,
indeed.

POLONIUS. My lord, I have news to tell you.

HAMLET. My lord, I have news to tell you. When Roscius was
an actor in Rome,——

POLONIUS. The actors are come hither, my lord.

HAMLET. Buz, buz!

POLONIUS. Upon my honor,——

HAMLET. Then came each actor on his ass,——

POLONIUS. The best actors in the world, either for tragedy,
comedy, history, pastoral, pastoral-comical, historical-pas-
toral, tragical-historical, tragical-comical-historical-pastoral,
scene individable, or poem unlimited: Seneca cannot be too
heavy, nor Plautus too light. For the law of writ and the
liberty, these are the only men.

HAMLET. O Jephthah, judge of Israel, what a treasure hadst
thou!

POLONIUS. What a treasure had he, my lord?

HAMLET. Why,

> 'One fair daughter, and no more,
>   The which he loved passing well.'

POLONIUS. [*Aside*] Still on my daughter.

HAMLET. Am I not i' the right, old Jephthah?

POLONIUS. If you call me Jephthah, my lord, I have a daughter that I love passing well.

HAMLET. Nay, that follows not.

POLONIUS. What follows, then, my lord?

HAMLET. Why,

> 'As by lot, God wot,'

and then you know,

> 'It came to pass, as most like it was,'—the first row of
the pious chanson will show you more; for look, where my
abridgment comes.

Enter four or five PLAYERS.]

You are welcome, masters; welcome, all. I am glad to see
thee well. Welcome, good friends. O, my old friend! Why

thy face is valanced since I saw thee last; comest thou to beard me in Denmark? What, my young lady and mistress! By'r lady, your ladyship is nearer to heaven than when I saw you last, by the altitude of a chopine. Pray God, your voice, like a piece of uncurrent gold, be not cracked within the ring. Masters, you are all welcome. We'll e'en to 't like French falconers, fly at any thing we see: we'll have a speech straight: come, give us a taste of your quality; come, a passionate speech.

FIRST PLAYER. What speech, my good lord?

HAMLET. I heard thee speak me a speech once, but it was never acted; or, if it was, not above once; for the play, I remember, pleased not the million; 'twas caviare to the general; but it was—as I received it, and others, whose judgments in such matters cried in the top of mine—an excellent play, well digested in the scenes, set down with as much modesty as cunning. I remember, one said there were no sallets in the lines to make the matter savory, nor no matter in the phrase that might indict the author to affection; but called it an honest method, as wholesome as sweet, and by very much more handsome than fine. One speech in it I chiefly loved: 'twas Æneas' tale to Dido; and thereabout of it especially, where he speaks of Priam's slaughter: if it live in your memory, begin at this line; let me see, let me see;

'The rugged Pyrrhus, like th' Hyrcanian beast,'—

It is not so: it begins with 'Pyrrhus.'

'The rugged Pyrrhus, he whose sable arms,
Black as his purpose, did the night resemble
When he lay couched in the ominous horse,
Hath now this dread and black complexion smear'd
With heraldry more dismal: head to foot
Now is he total gules; horribly trick'd
With the blood of fathers, mothers, daughters, sons,
Baked and impasted with the parching streets,
That lend a tyrannous and a damned light
To their lord's murder: roasted in wrath and fire,
And thus o'er-sized with coagulate gore,
With eyes like carbuncles, the hellish Pyrrhus
Old grandsire Priam seeks.'

So, proceed you.

POLONIUS. 'Fore God, my lord, well spoken, with good accent
   and good discretion.

FIRST PLAYER.   'Anon he finds him
   Striking too short at Greeks; his antique sword,
   Rebellious to his arm, lies where it falls,
   Repugnant to command; unequal match'd,
   Pyrrhus at Priam drives; in rage strikes wide;
   But with the whiff and wind of his fell sword
   The unnerved father falls. Then senseless Ilium,
   Seeming to feel this blow, with flaming top
   Stoops to his base, and with a hideous crash
   Takes prisoner Pyrrhus' ear: for, lo! his sword,
   Which was declining on the milky head
   Of reverend Priam, seem'd i' the air to stick:
   So, as a painted tyrant, Pyrrhus stood,
   And like a neutral to his will and matter,
   Did nothing.
   But as we often see, against some storm,
   A silence in the heavens, the rack stand still,
   The bold winds speechless and the orb below
   As hush as death, anon the dreadful thunder
   Doth rend the region, so after Pyrrhus' pause
   Aroused vengeance sets him new a-work;
   And never did the Cyclops' hammers fall
   On Mars's armor, forged for proof eterne,
   With less remorse than Pyrrhus' bleeding sword
   Now falls on Priam.
   Out, out, thou strumpet, Fortune! All you gods,
   In general synod take away her power,
   Break all the spokes and fellies from her wheel,
   And bowl the round nave down the hill of heaven
   As low as to the fiends!'

POLONIUS. This is too long.

HAMLET. It shall to the barber's, with your beard.
   Prithee, say on: he's for a jig or a tale of bawdry, or he
   sleeps: say on: come to Hecuba.

FIRST PLAYER. 'But who, O, who had seen the mobled queen—'

HAMLET. 'The mobled queen'?

POLONIUS. That's good; 'mobled queen' is good.

FIRST PLAYER. 'Run barefoot up and down, threatening the
   flames

With bisson rheum; a clout upon that head
Where late the diadem stood; and for a robe,
About her lank and all o'er-teemed loins,
A blanket, in the alarm of fear caught up:
Who this had seen, with tongue in venom steep'd
'Gainst Fortune's state would treason have pronounced:
But if the gods themselves did see her then,
When she saw Pyrrhus make malicious sport
In mincing with his sword her husband's limbs,
The instant burst of clamor that she made,
Unless things mortal move them not at all,
Would have made milch the burning eyes of heaven
And passion in the gods.'

POLONIUS. Look, whether he has not turned his color and has tears in 's eyes. Prithee, no more.

HAMLET. 'Tis well; I'll have thee speak out the rest of this soon. Good my lord, will you see the players well bestowed? Do you hear, let them be well used, for they are the abstracts and brief chronicles of the time: after your death you were better have a bad epitaph than their ill report while you live.

POLONIUS. My lord, I will use them according to their desert.

HAMLET. God's bodykins, man, much better: use every man after his desert, and who shall 'scape whipping? Use them after your own honor and dignity: the less they deserve, the more merit is in your bounty. Take them in.

POLONIUS. Come, sirs.

HAMLET. Follow him, friends: we'll hear a play to-morrow. [*Exit* POLONIUS *with all the* PLAYERS *but the first.*] Dost thou hear me, old friend; can you play the Murder of Gonzago?

FIRST PLAYER. Aye, my lord.

HAMLET. We'll ha 't to-morrow night. You could, for a need, study a speech of some dozen or sixteen lines, which I would set down and insert in 't, could you not?

FIRST PLAYER. Aye, my lord.

HAMLET. Very well. Follow that lord; and look you mock him not. [*Exit* FIRST PLAYER.] My good friends, I'll leave you till night: you are welcome to Elsinore.

ROSENCRANTZ. Good my lord!

HAMLET. Aye, so, God be wi' ye! [*Exeunt* ROSENCRANTZ *and* GUILDENSTERN.] Now I am alone.

O, what a rogue and peasant slave am I!
Is it not monstrous that this player here,
But in a fiction, in a dream of passion,
Could force his soul so to his own conceit
That from her working all his visage wann'd;
Tears in his eyes, distraction in 's aspect,
A broken voice, and his whole function suiting
With forms to his conceit? and all for nothing!
For Hecuba!
What's Hecuba to him, or he to Hecuba,
That he should weep for her? What would he do,
Had he the motive and the cue for passion
That I have? He would drown the stage with tears
And cleave the general air with horrid speech,
Make mad the guilty and appal the free,
Confound the ignorant, and amaze indeed
The very faculties of eyes and ears.
Yet I,
A dull and muddy-mettled rascal, peak,
Like John-a-dreams, unpregnant of my cause,
And can say nothing; no, not for a king,
Upon whose property and most dear life
A damn'd defeat was made. Am I a coward?
Who calls me villain? breaks my pate across?
Plucks off my beard, and blows it in my face?
Tweaks me by the nose? gives me the lie i' the throat,
As deep as to the lungs? who does me this?
Ha!
'Swounds, I should take it: for it cannot be
But I am pigeon-liver'd and lack gall
To make oppression bitter, or ere this
I should have fatted all the region kites
With this slave's offal: bloody, bawdy villain!
Remorseless, treacherous, lecherous, kindless villain!
O, vengeance!
Why, what an ass am I! This is most brave,
That I, the son of a dear father murder'd,
Prompted to my revenge by heaven and hell,
Must, like a whore, unpack my heart with words,
And fall a-cursing, like a very drab,
A scullion!
Fie upon 't! About, my brain! Hum, I have heard

That guilty creatures, sitting at a play,
Have by the very cunning of the scene
Been struck so to the soul that presently
They have proclaim'd their malefactions;
For murder, though it have no tongue, will speak
With most miraculous organ. I'll have these players
Play something like the murder of my father
Before mine uncle: I'll observe his looks;
I'll tent him to the quick: if he but blench,
I know my course. The spirit that I have seen
May be the devil; and the devil hath power
To assume a pleasing shape; yea, and perhaps
Out of my weakness and my melancholy,
As he is very potent with such spirits,
Abuses me to damn me. I'll have grounds
More relative than this. The play 's the thing
Wherein I'll catch the conscience of the king.   [*Exit.*

ACT III

S C E N E I — *A room in the castle.*

Enter KING, QUEEN, POLONIUS, OPHELIA, ROSENCRANTZ,
　　and GUILDENSTERN.]

KING. And can you, by no drift of circumstance,
　Get from him why he puts on this confusion,
　Grating so harshly all his days of quiet
　With turbulent and dangerous lunacy?

ROSENCRANTZ. He does confess he feels himself distracted,
　But from what cause he will by no means speak.

GUILDENSTERN. Nor do we find him forward to be sounded;
　But, with a crafty madness, keeps aloof,
　When we would bring him on to some confession
　Of his true state.

QUEEN.　　　　　　Did he receive you well?

ROSENCRANTZ. Most like a gentleman.

GUILDENSTERN. But with much forcing of his disposition.

ROSENCRANTZ. Niggard of question, but of our demands
　Most free in his reply.

QUEEN.　　　　　　　Did you assay him
　To any pastime?

ROSENCRANTZ. Madam, it so fell out that certain players
　We o'er-raught on the way: of these we told him,
　And there did seem in him a kind of joy
　To hear of it: they are about the court,
　And, as I think, they have already order
　This night to play before him.

POLONIUS.　　　　　　　　'Tis most true:
　And he beseech'd me to entreat your majesties
　To hear and see the matter.

KING. With all my heart; and it doth much content me
　To hear him so inclined.
　Good gentlemen, give him a further edge,
　And drive his purpose on to these delights.

ROSENCRANTZ. We shall, my lord.

　　　　　　　　[*Exeunt* ROSENCRANTZ *and* GUILDENSTERN.

KING.　　　　　　　　Sweet Gertrude, leave us too;
　For we have closely sent for Hamlet hither,

That he, as 'twere by accident, may here
Affront Ophelia:
Her father and myself, lawful espials,
Will so bestow ourselves that, seeing unseen,
We may of their encounter frankly judge,
And gather by him, as he is behaved,
If 't be the affliction of his love or no
That thus he suffers for.

QUEEN.   I shall obey you:
And for your part, Ophelia, I do wish
That your good beauties be the happy cause
Of Hamlet's wildness: so shall I hope your virtues
Will bring him to his wonted way again,
To both your honors.

OPHELIA.   Madam, I wish it may.   [*Exit* QUEEN.

POLONIUS. Ophelia, walk you here. Gracious, so please you,
We will bestow ourselves. [*To* OPHELIA.] Read on this
    book;
That show of such an exercise may color
Your loneliness. We are oft to blame in this,—
'Tis too much proved—that with devotion's visage
And pious action we do sugar o'er
The devil himself.

KING. [*Aside*]   O, 'tis too true!
How smart a lash that speech doth give my conscience!
The harlot's cheek, beautied with plastering art,
Is not more ugly to the thing that helps it
Than is my deed to my most painted word:
O heavy burthen!

POLONIUS. I hear him coming: let's withdraw, my lord.

                        [*Exeunt* KING *and* POLONIUS.

Enter HAMLET.]

HAMLET. To be, or not to be: that is the question:
Whether 'tis nobler in the mind to suffer
The slings and arrows of outrageous fortune,
Or to take arms against a sea of troubles,
And by opposing end them. To die: to sleep;
No more; and by a sleep to say we end
The heart-ache, and the thousand natural shocks
That flesh is heir to, 'tis a consummation
Devoutly to be wish'd. To die, to sleep;
To sleep: perchance to dream: aye, there's the rub;

For in that sleep of death what dreams may come,
When we have shuffled off this mortal coil,
Must give us pause: there's the respect
That makes calamity of so long life;
For who would bear the whips and scorns of time,
The oppressor's wrong, the proud man's contumely,
The pangs of despised love, the law's delay,
The insolence of office, and the spurns
That patient merit of the unworthy takes,
When he himself might his quietus make
With a bare bodkin? who would fardels bear,
To grunt and sweat under a weary life,
But that the dread of something after death,
The undiscover'd country from whose bourn
No traveler returns, puzzles the will,
And makes us rather bear those ills we have
Than fly to others that we know not of?
Thus conscience does make cowards of us all,
And thus the native hue of resolution
Is sicklied o'er with the pale cast of thought,
And enterprises of great pitch and moment
With this regard their currents turn awry
And lose the name of action. Soft you now!
The fair Ophelia! Nymph, in thy orisons
Be all my sins remember'd.

OPHELIA.　　　　　　　　Good my lord,
How does your honor for this many a day?

HAMLET. I humbly thank you: well, well, well.

OPHELIA. My lord, I have remembrances of yours,
That I have longed to re-deliver;
I pray you, now receive them.

HAMLET.　　　　　　　　No, not I;
I never gave you aught.

OPHELIA. My honor'd lord, you know right well you did;
And with them words of so sweet breath composed
As made the things more rich: their perfume lost,
Take these again; for to the noble mind
Rich gifts wax poor when givers prove unkind.
There, my lord.

HAMLET. Ha, ha! are you honest?

OPHELIA. My lord?

HAMLET. Are you fair?

OPHELIA. What means your lordship?

HAMLET. That if you be honest and fair, your honesty should admit no discourse to your beauty.

OPHELIA. Could beauty, my lord, have better commerce than with honesty?

HAMLET. Aye, truly; for the power of beauty will sooner transform honesty from what it is to a bawd than the force of honesty can translate beauty into his likeness: this was sometime a paradox, but now the time gives it proof. I did love you once.

OPHELIA. Indeed, my lord, you made me believe so.

HAMLET. You should not have believed me; for virtue cannot so inoculate our old stock, but we shall relish of it: I loved you not.

OPHELIA. I was the more deceived.

HAMLET. Get thee to a nunnery: why wouldst thou be a breeder of sinners? I am myself indifferent honest; but yet I could accuse me of such things that it were better my mother had not borne me: I am very proud, revengeful, ambitious; with more offenses at my beck than I have thoughts to put them in, imagination to give them shape, or time to act them in. What should such fellows as I do crawling between heaven and earth! We are arrant knaves all; believe none of us. Go thy ways to a nunnery. Where's your father?

OPHELIA. At home, my lord.

HAMLET. Let the doors be shut upon him, that he may play the fool no where but in 's own house. Farewell.

OPHELIA. O, help him, you sweet heavens!

HAMLET. If thou dost marry, I'll give thee this plague for thy dowry: be thou as chaste as ice, as pure as snow, thou shalt not escape calumny. Get thee to a nunnery, go: farewell. Or, if thou wilt needs marry, marry a fool; for wise men know well enough what monsters you make of them. To a nunnery, go; and quickly too. Farewell.

OPHELIA. O heavenly powers, restore him!

HAMLET. I have heard of your paintings too, well enough; God hath given you one face, and you make yourselves another: you jig, you amble, and you lisp, and nick-name God's creatures and make your wantonness your ignorance. Go to, I'll no more on 't; it hath made me mad. I say,

we will have no more marriages: those that are married already, all but one, shall live; the rest shall keep as they are.
To a nunnery, go. [*Exit.*

OPHELIA. O, what a noble mind is here o'erthrown!
The courtier's, soldier's, scholar's, eye, tongue, sword:
The expectancy and rose of the fair state,
The glass of fashion and the mold of form,
The observed of all observers, quite, quite down!
And I, of ladies most deject and wretched,
That suck'd the honey of his music vows,
Now see that noble and most sovereign reason,
Like sweet bells jangled, out of tune and harsh;
That unmatch'd form and feature of blown youth
Blasted with ecstasy: O, woe is me,
To have seen what I have seen, see what I see!

Re-enter KING *and* POLONIUS.]

KING. Love! his affections do not that way tend;
Nor what he spake, though it lack'd form a little,
Was not like madness. There's something in his soul
O'er which his melancholy sits on brood,
And I do doubt the hatch and the disclose
Will be some danger: which for to prevent,
I have in quick determination
Thus set it down:—he shall with speed to England,
For the demand of our neglected tribute:
Haply the seas and countries different
With variable objects shall expel
This something-settled matter in his heart,
Whereon his brains still beating puts him thus
From fashion of himself. What think you on 't?

POLONIUS. It shall do well: but yet do I believe
The origin and commencement of his grief
Sprung from neglected love. How now, Ophelia!
You need not tell us what Lord Hamlet said;
We heard it all. My lord, do as you please;
But, if you hold it fit, after the play,
Let his queen mother all alone entreat him
To show his grief: let her be round with him;
And I'll be placed, so please you, in the ear
Of all their conference. If she find him not,
To England send him, or confine him where

Your wisdom best shall think.

KING.　　　　　　　　　　　　It shall be so:
Madness in great ones must not unwatch'd go.　　　[*Exeunt.*

SCENE II — *A hall in the castle.*

Enter HAMLET *and* PLAYERS.]

HAMLET. Speak the speech, I pray you, as I pronounced it to
you, trippingly on the tongue: but if you mouth it, as many
of your players do, I had as lief the town-crier spoke my
lines. Nor do not saw the air too much with your hand,
thus; but use all gently: for in the very torrent, tempest,
and, as I may say, whirlwind of your passion, you must acquire and beget a temperance that may give it smoothness.
O, it offends me to the soul to hear a robustious periwig-
pated fellow tear a passion to tatters, to very rags, to split
the ears of the groundlings, who, for the most part, are
capable of nothing but inexplicable dumb-shows and noise:
I would have such a fellow whipped for o'er doing Termagant; it out-herods Herod: pray you, avoid it.

FIRST PLAYER. I warrant your honor.

HAMLET. Be not too tame neither, but let your own discretion
be your tutor: suit the action to the word, the word to the
action; with this special observance, that you o'erstep not
the modesty of nature: for anything so overdone is from the
purpose of playing, whose end, both at the first and now,
was and is, to hold, as 'twere, the mirror up to nature; to
show virtue her own feature, scorn her own image, and
the very age and body of the time his form and pressure.
Now this overdone or come tardy off, though it make the
unskillful laugh, cannot but make the judicious grieve; the
censure of the which one must in your allowance o'erweigh
a whole theater of others. O, there be players that I have
seen play, and heard others praise, and that highly, not to
speak it profanely, that neither having the accent of Christians nor the gait of Christians, pagan, nor man, have so
strutted and bellowed, that I have thought some of nature's
journeymen had made men, and not made them well, they
imitated humanity so abominably.

FIRST PLAYER. I hope we have reformed that indifferently
with us, sir.

HAMLET. O, reform it altogether. And let those that play your

clowns speak no more than is set down for them: for there
be of them that will themselves laugh, to set on some quantity of barren spectators to laugh too, though in the mean
time some necessary question of the play be then to be
considered: that's villainous, and shows a most pitiful ambition in the fool that uses it. Go, make you ready.

                         [*Exeunt* PLAYERS.

Enter POLONIUS, ROSENCRANTZ, *and* GUILDENSTERN.]

     How now, my lord! will the king hear this piece of work?
POLONIUS. And the queen too, and that presently.
HAMLET. Bid the players make haste.   [*Exit* POLONIUS.
     Will you two help to hasten them?
ROSENCRANTZ. ⎰
               ⎱ We will, my lord.
GUILDENSTERN. ⎰

             [*Exeunt* ROSENCRANTZ *and* GUILDENSTERN.
HAMLET. What ho! Horatio!
Enter HORATIO.]
HORATIO. Here, sweet lord, at your service.
HAMLET. Horatio, thou art e'en as just a man
     As e'er my conversation coped withal.
HORATIO. O, my dear lord,—
HAMLET.   Nay, do not think I flatter;
     For what advancement may I hope from thee,
     That no revenue hast but thy good spirits,
     To feed and clothe thee? Why should the poor be flatter'd?
     No, let the candied tongue lick absurd pomp,
     And crook the pregnant hinges of the knee
     Where thrift may follow fawning. Dost thou hear?
     Since my dear soul was mistress of her choice,
     And could of men distinguish, her election
     Hath seal'd thee for herself: for thou hast been
     As one, in suffering all, that suffers nothing;
     A man that fortune's buffets and rewards
     Hast ta'en with equal thanks: and blest are those
     Whose blood and judgment are so well commingled
     That they are not a pipe for fortune's finger
     To sound what stop she please. Give me that man
     That is not passion's slave, and I will wear him
     In my heart's core, aye, in my heart of heart,
     As I do thee. Something too much of this.
     There is a play to-night before the king;
     One scene of it comes near the circumstance

Which I have told thee of my father's death:
I prithee, when thou sees that act a-foot,
Even with the very comment of thy soul
Observe my uncle: if his occulted guilt
Do not itself unkennel in one speech
It is a damned ghost that we have seen,
And my imaginations are as foul
As Vulcan's stithy. Give him heedful note;
For I mine eyes will rivet to his face,
And after we will both our judgments join
In censure of his seeming.

HORATIO.   Well, my lord:
If he steal aught the whilst this play is playing,
And 'scape detecting, I will pay the theft.

HAMLET. They are coming to the play: I must be idle:
Get you a place.

Danish march. A flourish. Enter KING, QUEEN, POLO-
    NIUS, OPHELIA, ROSENCRANTZ, GUILDENSTERN,
    and other LORDS *attendant, with the* GUARD
    carrying torches.]

KING. How fares our cousin Hamlet?

HAMLET. Excellent, i' faith; of the chameleon's dish: I eat the
air, promise-crammed: you cannot feed capons so.

KING. I have nothing with this answer, Hamlet; these words
are not mine.

HAMLET. No, nor mine now. [*To* POLONIUS] My lord, you
played once i' the university, you say?

POLONIUS. That did I, my lord, and was accounted a good
actor.

HAMLET. What did you enact?

POLONIUS. I did enact Julius Cæsar: I was killed i' the Capitol; Brutus killed me.

HAMLET. It was a brute part of him to kill so capital a calf
there. Be the players ready?

ROSENCRANTZ. Aye, my lord; they stay upon your patience.

QUEEN. Come hither, my dear Hamlet, sit by me.

HAMLET. No, good mother, here's metal more attractive.

POLONIUS. [*To the* KING] O, ho! do you mark that?

HAMLET. Lady, shall I lie in your lap?
                          [*Lying down at* OPHELIA's *feet.*

OPHELIA. No, my lord.

HAMLET. I mean, my head upon your lap?

OPHELIA. Aye, my lord.

HAMLET. Do you think I meant country matters?

OPHELIA. I think nothing, my lord.

HAMLET. That's a fair thought to lie between maids' legs.

OPHELIA. What is, my lord.

HAMLET. Nothing.

OPHELIA. You are merry, my lord.

HAMLET. Who, I?

OPHELIA. Aye, my lord.

HAMLET. O God, your only jig-maker. What should a man do but be merry? for, look you, how cheerfully my mother looks, and my father died within 's two hours.

OPHELIA. Nay, 'tis twice two months, my lord.

HAMLET. So long? Nay then, let the devil wear black, for I'll have a suit of sables. O heavens! die two months ago, and not forgotten yet? Then there's hope a great man's memory may outlive his life half a year: but, by 'r lady, he must build churches then; or else shall he suffer not thinking on, with the hobby-horse, whose epitaph is, 'For, O, for, O, the hobby-horse is forgot.'

Hautboys play. The dumb-show enters.]

Enter a King and a Queen very lovingly; the Queen embracing him and he her. She kneels, and makes show of protestation unto him. He takes her up, and declines his head upon her neck; lays him down upon a bank of flowers: she, seeing him asleep, leaves him. Anon comes in a fellow, takes off his crown, kisses it, and pours poison in the King's ears, and exit. The Queen returns; finds the King dead, and makes passionate action. The Poisoner, with some two or three Mutes comes in again, seeming to lament with her. The dead body is carried away. The Poisoner woos the Queen with gifts: she seems loath and unwilling awhile, but in the end accepts his love.]

                                        [*Exeunt.*

OPHELIA. What means this, my lord?

HAMLET. Marry, this is miching mallecho; it means mischief.

OPHELIA. Belike this show imports the argument of the play.

Enter PROLOGUE.]

HAMLET. We shall know by this fellow: the players cannot keep counsel; they'll tell all.

OPHELIA. Will he tell us what this show means?

HAMLET. Aye, or any show that you'll show him: be not you ashamed to show, he'll not shame to tell you what it means.

OPHELIA. You are naught, you are naught: I'll mark the play.

PROLOGUE. For us, and for our tragedy,
   Here stooping to your clemency,
   We beg your hearing patiently.

HAMLET. Is this a prologue, or the posy of a ring?

OPHELIA. 'Tis brief, my lord.

HAMLET. As woman's love.

Enter two PLAYERS, KING *and* QUEEN.]

PLAYER KING. Full thirty times hath Phœbus' cart gone round
Neptune's salt wash and Tellus' orbed ground,
And thirty dozen moons with borrowed sheen
About the world have times twelve thirties been,
Since love our hearts and Hymen did our hands
Unite commutual in most sacred bands.

PLAYER QUEEN. So many journeys may the sun and moon
Make us again count o'er ere love be done!
But, woe is me, you are so sick of late,
So far from cheer and from your former state,
That I distrust you. Yet, though I distrust,
Discomfort you, my lord, it nothing must:
For women's fear and love holds quantity,
In neither aught, or in extremity.
Now, what my love is, proof hath made you know,
And as my love is sized, my fear is so:
Where love is great, the littlest doubts are fear,
Where little fears grow great, great love grows there.

PLAYER KING. Faith, I must leave thee, love, and shortly too;
My operant powers their functions leave to do:
And thou shalt live in this fair world behind,
Honor'd, beloved; and haply as one as kind
For husband shalt thou—

PLAYER QUEEN.   O, confound the rest!
Such love must needs be treason in my breast:
In second husband let me be accurst!
None wed the second but who kill'd the first.

HAMLET. [*Aside*] Wormwood, wormwood.

PLAYER QUEEN. The instances that second marriage move
Are base respects of thrift, but none of love:
A second time I kill my husband dead,

    When second husband kisses me in bed.

PLAYER KING. I do believe you think what now you speak,
    But what we do determine oft we break.
    Purpose is but the slave to memory,
    Of violent birth but poor validity:
    Which now, like fruit unripe, sticks on the tree,
    But fall unshaken when they mellow be.
    Most necessary 'tis that we forget
    To pay ourselves what to ourselves is debt:
    What to ourselves in passion we propose,
    The passion ending, doth the purpose lose.
    The violence of either grief or joy
    Their own enactures with themselves destroy:
    Where joy most revels, grief doth most lament;
    Grief joys, joy grieves, on slender accident.
    This world is not for aye, nor 'tis not strange
    That even our loves should with our fortunes change,
    For 'tis a question left us yet to prove,
    Whether love lead fortune or else fortune love.
    The great man down, you mark his favorite flies;
    The poor advanced makes friends of enemies:
    And hitherto doth love on fortune tend;
    For who not needs shall never lack a friend,
    And who in want a hollow friend doth try
    Directly seasons him his enemy.
    But, orderly to end where I begun,
    Our wills and fates do so contrary run,
    That our devices still are overthrown,
    Our thoughts are ours, their ends none of our own:
    So think thou wilt no second husband wed,
    But die thy thoughts when thy first lord is dead.

PLAYER QUEEN. Nor earth to me give food nor heaven light!
    Sport and repose lock from me day and night!
    To desperation turn my trust and hope!
    An anchor's cheer in prison be my scope!
    Each opposite, that blanks the face of joy,
    Meet what I would have well and it destroy!
    Both here and hence pursue me lasting strife,
    If, once a widow, ever I be wife!

HAMLET. If she should break it now!

PLAYER KING. 'Tis deeply sworn. Sweet, leave me here a while;
    My spirits grow dull, and fain I would beguile

The tedious day with sleep.   [*Sleeps.*

PLAYER QUEEN.   Sleep rock thy brain;
And never come mischance between us twain!   [*Exit.*

HAMLET. Madam, how like you this play?

QUEEN. The lady doth protest too much, methinks.

HAMLET. O, but she'll keep her word.

KING. Have you heard the argument? Is there no offense in 't?

HAMLET. No, no, they do but jest, poison in jest; no offense
i' the world.

KING. What do you call the play?

HAMLET. The Mouse-trap. Marry, how? Tropically. This play
is the image of a murder done in Vienna: Gonzago is the
duke's name; his wife, Baptista: you shall see anon; 'tis a
knavish piece of work; but what o' that? your majesty, and
we that have free souls, it touches us not: let the galled
jade wince, our withers are unwrung.

Enter LUCIANUS.]

This is one Lucianus, nephew to the king.

OPHELIA. You are as good as a chorus, my lord.

HAMLET. I could interpret between you and your love, if I
could see the puppets dallying.

OPHELIA. You are keen, my lord, you are keen.

HAMLET. It would cost you a groaning to take off my edge.

OPHELIA. Still better and worse.

HAMLET. So you must take your husbands. Begin, murderer;
pox, leave thy damnable faces, and begin. Come: the
croaking raven doth bellow for revenge.

LUCIANUS. Thoughts black, hands apt, drugs fit, and time
agreeing;
Confederate season, else no creature seeing;
Thou mixture rank, of midnight weeds collected,
With Hecate's ban thrice blasted, thrice infected,
Thy natural magic and dire property,
On wholesome life usurp immediately.

                        [*Pours the poison into the sleeper's ear.*

HAMLET. He poisons him i' the garden for his estate. His
name's Gonzago: the story is extant, and written in very
choice Italian: you shall see anon how the murderer gets
the love of Gonzago's wife.

OPHELIA. The king rises.

HAMLET. What! frighted with false fire!

QUEEN. How fares my lord?

POLONIUS. Give o'er the play.

KING. Give me some light. Away!

POLONIUS. Lights, lights, lights!

> [*Exeunt all but* HAMLET *and* HORATIO.

HAMLET. Why, let the stricken deer go weep,
    The hart ungalled play;
  For some must watch, while some must sleep:
    Thus runs the world away.
  Would not this, sir, and a forest of feathers—if the rest of
  my fortunes turn Turk with me—with two Provincial roses
  on my razed shoes, get me a fellowship in a cry of players,
  sir?

HORATIO. Half a share.

HAMLET. A whole one, I.
          For thou dost know, O Damon dear,
            This realm dismantled was
          Of Jove himself; and now reigns here
            A very, very—pajock.

HORATIO. You might have rhymed.

HAMLET. O good Horatio, I'll take the ghost's word for a
  thousand pounds. Didst perceive?

HORATIO. Very well, my lord.

HAMLET. Upon the talk of the poisoning?

HORATIO. I did very well note him.

HAMLET. Ah, ha! Come, some music! come, the recorders!
          For if the king like not the comedy,
          Why then, belike, he likes it not, perdy.
  Come, some music!

Re-enter ROSENCRANTZ *and* GUILDENSTERN.]

GUILDENSTERN. Good my lord, vouchsafe me a word with you.

HAMLET. Sir, a whole history.

GUILDENSTERN. The king, sir,—

HAMLET. Aye, sir, what of him?

GUILDENSTERN. Is in his retirement marvelous distempered.

HAMLET. With drink, sir?

GUILDENSTERN. No, my lord, rather with choler.

HAMLET. Your wisdom should show itself more richer to signify this to the doctor; for, for me to put him to his purgation would perhaps plunge him into far more choler.

GUILDENSTERN. Good my lord, put your discourse into some
  frame, and start not so wildly from my affair.

HAMLET. I am tame, sir: pronounce.

GUILDENSTERN. The queen, your mother, in most great affliction of spirit, hath sent me to you.

HAMLET. You are welcome.

GUILDENSTERN. Nay, good my lord, this courtesy is not of the
right breed. If it shall please you to make me a wholesome
answer, I will do your mother's commandment: if not, your
pardon and my return shall be the end of my business.

HAMLET. Sir, I cannot.

GUILDENSTERN. What, my lord?

HAMLET. Make you a wholesome answer; my wit's diseased:
but, sir, such answer as I can make, you shall command;
or rather, as you say, my mother: therefore no more, but
to the matter: my mother, you say,—

ROSENCRANTZ. Then thus she says; your behavior hath struck
her into amazement and admiration.

HAMLET. O wonderful son, that can so astonish a mother!
But is there no sequel at the heels of this mother's admiration? Impart.

ROSENCRANTZ. She desires to speak with you in her closet, ere
you go to bed.

HAMLET. We shall obey, were she ten times our mother.
Have you any further trade with us?

ROSENCRANTZ. My lord, you once did love me.

HAMLET. So I do still, by these pickers and stealers.

ROSENCRANTZ Good my lord, what is your cause of distemper?
you do surely bar the door upon your own liberty, if you
deny your griefs to your friend.

HAMLET. Sir, I lack advancement.

ROSENCRANTZ How can that be, when you have the voice of
the king himself for your succession in Denmark?

HAMLET. Aye sir, but 'while the grass grows,'—the proverb
is something musty.

Re-enter PLAYERS *with recorders.*]

O, the recorders! let me see one. To withdraw with you:
—why do you go about to recover the wind of me, as if
you would drive me into a toil?

GUILDENSTERN O, my lord, if my duty be too bold, my love
is too unmannerly.

HAMLET. I do not well understand that. Will you play upon
this pipe?

GUILDENSTERN. My lord, I cannot.

HAMLET. I pray you.

GUILDENSTERN. Believe me, I cannot.

HAMLET. I do beseech you.

GUILDENSTERN. I know no touch of it, my lord.

HAMLET. It is as easy as lying: govern these ventages with your fingers and thumb, give it breath with your mouth, and it will discourse most eloquent music. Look you, these are the stops.

GUILDENSTERN. But these cannot I command to any utterance of harmony; I have not the skill.

HAMLET. Why, look you now, how unworthy a thing you make of me! You would play upon me; you would seem to know my stops; you would pluck out the heart of my mystery; you would sound me from my lowest note to the top of my compass: and there is much music, excellent voice, in this little organ; yet cannot you make it speak. 'Sblood, do you think I am easier to be played on than a pipe? Call me what instrument you will, though you can fret me, yet you cannot play upon me.

Re-enter POLONIUS.]

God bless you, sir!

POLONIUS. My lord, the queen would speak with you, and presently.

HAMLET. Do you see yonder cloud that's almost in shape of a camel?

POLONIUS. By the mass, and 'tis like a camel, indeed.

HAMLET. Methinks it is like a weasel.

POLONIUS. It is backed like a weasel.

HAMLET. Or like a whale?

POLONIUS. Very like a whale.

HAMLET. Then I will come to my mother by and by. They fool me to the top of my bent. I will come by and by.

POLONIUS. I will say so.   [*Exit* POLONIUS.

HAMLET. 'By and by' is easily said. Leave me, friends.

         [*Exeunt all but* HAMLET.

'Tis now the very witching time of night,
When churchyards yawn, and hell itself breathes out
Contagion to this world: now could I drink hot blood,
And do such bitter business as the day
Would quake to look on. Soft! now to my mother.
O heart, lose not thy nature: let not ever
The soul of Nero enter this firm bosom:
Let me be cruel, not unnatural:

I will speak daggers to her, but use none;
My tongue and soul in this be hypocrites;
How in my words soever she be shent,
To give them seals never, my soul, consent!   [Exit.

SCENE III — A room in the castle.

Enter KING, ROSENCRANTZ, and GUILDENSTERN.]

KING. I like him not, nor stands it safe with us
    To let his madness range. Therefore prepare you;
    I your commission will forthwith dispatch,
    And he to England shall along with you:
    The terms of our estate may not endure
    Hazard so near us as doth hourly grow
    Out of his lunacies.

GUILDENSTERN.   We will ourselves provide:
    Most holy and religious fear it is
    To keep those many many bodies safe
    That live and feed upon your majesty.

ROSENCRANTZ. The single and peculiar life is bound
    With all the strength and armor of the mind
    To keep itself from noyance; but much more
    That spirit upon whose weal depends and rests
    The lives of many. The cease of majesty
    Dies not alone, but like a gulf doth draw
    What 's near it with it; it is a massy wheel,
    Fix'd on the summit of the highest mount,
    To whose huge spokes ten thousand lesser things
    Are mortised and adjoin'd; which, when it falls,
    Each small annexment, petty consequence,
    Attends the boisterous ruin. Never alone
    Did the king sigh, but with a general groan.

KING. Arm you, I pray you, to this speedy voyage,
    For we will fetters put about this fear,
    Which now goes too free-footed.

ROSENCRANTZ. }
GUILDENSTERN. }   We will haste us.

              [Exeunt ROSENCRANTZ and GUILDENSTERN.

Enter POLONIUS.]

POLONIUS. My lord, he's going to his mother's closet:
    Behind the arras I'll convey myself,
    To hear the process: I'll warrant she'll tax him home:

And, as you said, and wisely was it said,
'Tis meet that some more audience than a mother,
Since nature makes them partial, should o'erhear
The speech, of vantage. Fare you well, my liege:
I'll call upon you ere you go to bed,
And tell you what I know.

KING.　　　　　　　　　　Thanks, dear my lord.

[*Exit* POLONIUS.

O, my offense is rank, it smells to heaven;
It hath the primal eldest curse upon 't,
A brother's murder. Pray can I not,
Though inclination be as sharp as will:
My stronger guilt defeats my strong intent,
And like a man to double business bound,
I stand in pause where I shall first begin,
And both neglect. What if this cursed hand
Were thicker than itself with brother's blood,
Is there not rain enough in the sweet heavens
To wash it white as snow? Whereto serves mercy
But to confront the visage of offense?
And what's in prayer but this twofold force,
To be forestalled ere we come to fall,
Or pardon'd being down? Then I'll look up;
My fault is past. But O, what form of prayer
Can serve my turn? 'Forgive me my foul murder?'
That cannot be, since I am still possess'd
Of those effects for which I did the murder,
My crown, mine own ambition and my queen.
May one be pardon'd and retain the offense?
In the corrupted currents of this world
Offense's gilded hand may shove by justice,
And oft 'tis seen the wicked prize itself
Buys out the law: but 'tis not so above;
There is no shuffling, there the action lies
In his true nature, and we ourselves compell'd
Even to the teeth and forehead of our faults
To give in evidence. What then? what rests?
Try what repentance can: what can it not?
Yet what can it when one can not repent?
O wretched state! O bosom black as death!
O limed soul, that struggling to be free
Art more engaged! Help, angels! make assay!

Bow, stubborn knees, and, heart with strings of steel,
Be soft as sinews of the new-born babe!
All may be well.   [*Retires and kneels.*

Enter HAMLET.]

HAMLET. Now might I do it pat, now he is praying;
And now I'll do 't: and so he goes to heaven:
And so am I revenged. That would be scann'd;
A villain kills my father; and for that,
I, his sole son, do this same villain send
To heaven.
O, this is hire and salary, not revenge.
He took my father grossly, full of bread,
With all his crimes broad blown, as flush as May;
And how his audit stands who knows save heaven?
But in our circumstance and course of thought,
'Tis heavy with him: and am I then revenged,
To take him in the purging of his soul,
When he is fit and season'd for his passage?
No.
Up, sword, and know thou a more horrid hent:
When he is drunk asleep, or in his rage,
Or, in the incestuous pleasure of his bed;
At game, a-swearing, or about some act
That has no relish of salvation in 't;
Then trip him, that his heels may kick at heaven
And that his soul may be as damn'd and black
As hell, whereto it goes. My mother stays:
This physic but prolongs thy sickly days.   [*Exit.*
KING. [*Rising*] My words fly up, my thoughts remain below:
Words without thoughts never to heaven go.   [*Exit.*

SCENE IV — *The* QUEEN'S *closet.*

Enter QUEEN *and* POLONIUS.]

POLONIUS. He will come straight. Look you lay home to him:
Tell him his pranks have been too broad to bear with,
And that your grace hath screen'd and stood between
Much heat and him. I'll sconce me even here.
Pray you, be round with him.
HAMLET. [*Within*]   Mother, mother, mother!
QUEEN. I'll warrant you; fear me not. Withdraw,

I hear him coming. [POLONIUS *hides behind the arras.*
Enter HAMLET.]

HAMLET. Now, mother, what's the matter?

QUEEN. Hamlet, thou hast thy father much offended.

HAMLET. Mother, you have my father much offended.

QUEEN. Come, come, you answer with an idle tongue.

HAMLET. Go, go, you question with a wicked tongue.

QUEEN. Why, how now, Hamlet!

HAMLET.   What's the matter now?

QUEEN. Have you forgot me?

HAMLET.   No, by the rood, not so:
  You are the queen, your husband's brother's wife;
  And—would it were not so!—you are my mother.

QUEEN. Nay, then, I'll set those to you that can speak.

HAMLET. Come, come, and sit you down; you shall not budge;
  You go not till I set you up a glass
  Where you may see the inmost part of you.

QUEEN. What wilt thou do? thou wilt not murder me?
  Help, help, ho!

POLONIUS. [*Behind*] What, ho! help, help, help!

HAMLET. [*Drawing*] How now! a rat? Dead, for a ducat, dead!
                         [*Makes a pass through the arras.*

POLONIUS. [*Behind*] O, I am slain!   [*Falls and dies.*

QUEEN.   O me, what hast thou done?

HAMLET. Nay, I know not: is it the king?

QUEEN. O, what a rash and bloody deed is this!

HAMLET. A bloody deed! almost as bad, good mother,
  As kill a king and marry with his brother.

QUEEN. As kill a king!

HAMLET.   Aye, lady, 'twas my word.
                  [*Lifts up the arras and discovers* POLONIUS.
  Thou wretched, rash, intruding fool, farewell!
  I took thee for thy better: take thy fortune;
  Thou find'st to be too busy is some danger.
  Leave wringing of your hands: peace! sit you down,
  And let me wring your heart: for so I shall,
  If it be made of penetrable stuff;
  If damned custom have not brass'd it so,
  That it be proof and bulwark against sense.

QUEEN. What have I done, that thou darest wag thy tongue
  In noise so rude against me?

HAMLET.   Such an act

That blurs the grace and blush of modesty,
Calls virtue hypocrite, takes off the rose
From the fair forehead of an innocent love,
And sets a blister there; makes marriage vows
As false as dicers' oaths: O, such a deed
As from the body of contraction plucks
The very soul, and sweet religion makes
A rhapsody of words: heaven's face doth glow;
Yea, this solidity and compound mass,
With tristful visage, as against the doom,
Is thought-sick at the act.

QUEEN. Aye me, what act,
That roars so loud and thunders in the index?

HAMLET. Look here, upon this picture, and on this,
The counterfeit presentment of two brothers.
See what a grace was seated on this brow;
Hyperion's curls, the front of Jove himself,
An eye like Mars, to threaten and command;
A station like the herald Mercury
New-lighted on a heaven-kissing hill;
A combination and a form indeed,
Where every god did seem to set his seal
To give the world assurance of a man:
This was your husband. Look you now, what follows:
Here is your husband; like a mildew'd ear,
Blasting his wholesome brother. Have you eyes?
Could you on this fair mountain leave to feed,
And batten on this moor? Ha! have you eyes?
You cannot call it love, for at your age
The hey-day in the blood is tame, it's humble,
And waits upon the judgment: and what judgment
Would step from this to this? Sense sure you have,
Else could you not have motion: but sure that sense
Is apoplex'd: for madness would not err,
Nor sense to ecstasy was ne'er so thrall'd
But it reserved some quantity of choice,
To serve in such a difference. What devil was 't
That thus hath cozen'd you at hoodman-blind?
Eyes without feeling, feeling without sight,
Ears without hands or eyes, smelling sans all,
Or but a sickly part of one true sense
Could not so mope.

O shame! where is thy blush? Rebellious hell,
If thou canst mutine in a matron's bones,
To flaming youth let virtue be as wax
And melt in her own fire: proclaim no shame
When the compulsive ardor gives the charge,
Since frost itself as actively doth burn,
And reason panders will.

QUEEN.   O Hamlet, speak no more:
Thou turn'st mine eyes into my very soul,
And there I see such black and grained spots
As will not leave their tinct.

HAMLET.   Nay, but to live
In the rank sweat of an enseamed bed,
Stew'd in corruption, honeying and making love
Over the nasty sty,—

QUEEN.   O, speak to me no more;
These words like daggers enter in my ears;
No more, sweet Hamlet!

HAMLET.   A murderer and a villain;
A slave that is not twentieth part the tithe
Of your precedent lord; a vice of kings;
A cutpurse of the empire and the rule,
That from a shelf the precious diadem stole
And put it in his pocket!

QUEEN.   No more!

HAMLET. A king of shreds and patches—

Enter GHOST.]

Save me, and hover o'er me with your wings,
You heavenly guards! What would your gracious figure?

QUEEN. Alas, he's mad!

HAMLET. Do you not come your tardy son to chide,
That, lapsed in time and passion, lets go by
The important acting of your dread command?
O, say!

GHOST. Do not forget: this visitation
Is but to whet thy almost blunted purpose.
But look, amazement on thy mother sits:
O, step between her and her fighting soul:
Conceit in weakest bodies strongest works:
Speak to her, Hamlet.

HAMLET.   How is it with you, lady?

QUEEN. Alas, how is 't with you,
    That you do bend your eye on vacancy
    And with the incorporal air do hold discourse?
    Forth at your eyes your spirits wildly peep;
    And, as the sleeping soldiers in the alarm,
    Your bedded hairs, like life in excrements,
    Stand up and stand an end. O gentle son,
    Upon the heat and flame of thy distemper
    Sprinkle cool patience. Whereon do you look?
HAMLET. On him, on him! Look you how pale he glares!
    His form and cause conjoin'd, preaching to stones,
    Would make them capable. Do not look upon me,
    Lest with this piteous action you convert
    My stern effects: then what I have to do
    Will want true color; tears perchance for blood.
QUEEN. To whom do you speak this?
HAMLET.   Do you see nothing there?
QUEEN. Nothing at all; yet all that is I see.
HAMLET. Nor did you nothing hear?
QUEEN.   No, nothing but ourselves.
HAMLET. Why, look you there! look, how it steals away!
    My father, in his habit as he lived!
    Look, where he goes, even now, out at the portal!
                               [*Exit* GHOST.
QUEEN. This is the very coinage of your brain:
    This bodiless creation ecstasy
    Is very cunning in.
HAMLET.   Ecstasy!
    My pulse, as yours, doth temperately keep time,
    And makes as healthful music: it is not madness
    That I have utter'd: bring me to the test,
    And I the matter will re-word, which madness
    Would gambol from. Mother, for love of grace,
    Lay not that flattering unction to your soul,
    That not your trespass but my madness speaks:
    It will but skin and film the ulcerous place,
    Whiles rank corruption, mining all within,
    Infects unseen. Confess yourself to heaven;
    Repent what's past, avoid what is to come,
    And do not spread the compost on the weeds,
    To make them ranker. Forgive me this my virtue,
    For in the fatness of these pursy times

Virtue itself of vice must pardon beg,
Yea, curb and woo for leave to do him good.

QUEEN. O Hamlet, thou hast cleft my heart in twain.

HAMLET. O, throw away the worser part of it,
And live the purer with the other half.
Good night: but go not to my uncle's bed;
Assume a virtue, if you have it not.
That monster, custom, who all sense doth eat,
Of habits devil, is angel yet in this,
That to the use of actions fair and good
He likewise gives a frock or livery,
That aptly is put on. Refrain to-night,
And that shall lend a kind of easiness
To the next abstinence; the next more easy;
For use almost can change the stamp of nature,
And either curb the devil, or throw him out
With wondrous potency. Once more, good night:
And when you are desirous to be blest,
I'll blessing beg of you. For this same lord,

> [*Pointing to* POLONIUS.

I do repent: but heaven hath pleased it so,
To punish me with this, and this with me,
That I must be their scourge and minister.
I will bestow him, and will answer well
The death I gave him. So, again, good night.
I must be cruel, only to be kind:
Thus bad begins, and worse remains behind.
One word more, good lady.

QUEEN. What shall I do?

HAMLET. Not this, by no means, that I bid you do:
Let the bloat king tempt you again to bed;
Pinch wanton on your cheek, call you his mouse;
And let him, for a pair of reechy kisses,
Or paddling in your neck with his damn'd fingers,
Make you to ravel all this matter out,
That I essentially am not in madness,
But mad in craft. 'Twere good you let him know;
For who, that's but a queen, fair, sober, wise,
Would from a paddock, from a bat, a gib,
Such dear concernings hide? who would do so?
No, in despite of sense and secrecy,
Unpeg the basket on the house's top,

Let the birds fly, and like the famous ape,
To try conclusions, in the basket creep
And break your own neck down.

QUEEN. Be thou assured, if words be made of breath
And breath of life, I have no life to breathe
What thou hast said to me.

HAMLET. I must to England; you know that?

QUEEN.   Alack,
I had forgot: 'tis so concluded on.

HAMLET. There's letters seal'd: and my two schoolfellows,
Whom I will trust as I will adders fang'd,
They bear the mandate; they must sweep my way,
And marshal me to knavery. Let it work;
For 'tis the sport to have the enginer
Hoist with his own petar: and 't shall go hard
But I will delve one yard below their mines,
And blow them at the moon: O, 'tis most sweet
When in one line two crafts directly meet.
This man shall set me packing:
I'll lug the guts into the neighbor room.
Mother, good night. Indeed this counselor
Is now most still, most secret and most grave,
Who was in life a foolish prating knave.
Come, sir, to draw toward an end with you.
Good night, mother.

                    [*Exeunt severally;* HAMLET *dragging in* POLONIUS.

ACT IV

SCENE I — *A room in the castle.*

Enter KING, QUEEN, ROSENCRANTZ, *and* GUILDENSTERN.]

KING. There's matter in these sighs, these profound heaves:
　You must translate: 'tis fit we understand them.
　Where is your son?

QUEEN. Bestow this place on us a little while.
　　　　　　　　[*Exeunt* ROSENCRANTZ *and* GUILDENSTERN.
　Ah, mine own lord, what have I seen to-night!

KING. What, Gertrude? How does Hamlet?

QUEEN. Mad as the sea and wind, when both contend
　Which is the mightier: in his lawless fit,
　Behind the arras hearing something stir,
　Whips out his rapier, cries 'A rat, a rat!'
　And in this brainish apprehension kills
　The unseen good old man.

KING.　　　　　　　　O heavy deed!
　It had been so with us, had we been there:
　His liberty is full of threats to all,
　To you yourself, to us, to every one.
　Alas, how shall this bloody deed be answer'd?
　It will be laid to us, whose providence
　Should have kept short, restrain'd and out of haunt,
　This mad young man: but so much was our love,
　We would not understand what was most fit,
　But like the owner of a foul disease,
　To keep it from divulging, let it feed
　Even on the pith of life. Where is he gone?

QUEEN. To draw apart the body he hath kill'd:
　O'er whom his very madness, like some ore
　Among a mineral of metals base,
　Shows itself pure; he weeps for what is done.

KING. O Gertrude, come away!
　The sun no sooner shall the mountains touch,
　But we will ship him hence: and this vile deed
　We must, with all our majesty and skill,
　Both countenance and excuse. Ho, Guildenstern!

Re-enter ROSENCRANTZ *and* GUILDENSTERN.]

Friends both, go join you with some further aid:
Hamlet in madness hath Polonius slain,
And from his mother's closet he dragg'd him:
Go seek him out; speak fair, and bring the body
Into the chapel. I pray you, haste in this.

              [*Exeunt* ROSENCRANTZ *and* GUILDENSTERN.

Come, Gertrude, we'll call up our wisest friends;
And let them know, both what we mean to do,
And what's untimely done. . . .
Whose whisper o'er the world's diameter
As level as the cannon to his blank
Transports his poison'd shot, may miss our name
And hit the woundless air. O, come away!
My soul is full of discord and dismay.   [*Exeunt.*

S C E N E II — *Another room in the castle.*

Enter HAMLET.]

HAMLET. Safely stowed.

ROSENCRANTZ. ⎱ [*Within*] Hamlet! Lord Hamlet!
GUILDENSTERN. ⎰

HAMLET. But soft, what noise? who calls on Hamlet?
  O, here they come.

Enter ROSENCRANTZ *and* GUILDENSTERN.]

ROSENCRANTZ. What have you done, my lord, with the dead
  body?

HAMLET. Compounded it with dust, whereto 'tis kin.

ROSENCRANTZ. Tell us where 'tis, that we may take it thence
  And bear it to the chapel.

HAMLET. Do not believe it.

ROSENCRANTZ. Believe what?

HAMLET. That I can keep your counsel and not mine own.
  Besides, to be demanded of a sponge! what replication
  should be made by the son of a king?

ROSENCRANTZ. Take you me for a sponge, my lord?

HAMLET. Aye, sir; that soaks up the king's countenance, his
  rewards, his authorities. But such officers do the king best
  service in the end: he keeps them, like an ape, in the corner
  of his jaw; first mouthed, to be last swallowed: when he
  needs what you have gleaned, it is but squeezing you, and,
  sponge, you shall be dry again.

ROSENCRANTZ. I understand you not, my lord.

HAMLET. I am glad of it: a knavish speech sleeps in a foolish ear.

ROSENCRANTZ. My lord, you must tell us where the body is, and go with us to the king.

HAMLET. The body is with the king, but the king is not with the body. The king is a thing—

GUILDENSTERN. A thing, my lord?

HAMLET. Of nothing: bring me to him. Hide fox, and all after.

[*Exeunt.*

SCENE III — *Another room in the castle.*

Enter KING, *attended.*]

KING. I have sent to seek him, and to find the body.
How dangerous is it that this man goes loose!
Yet must not we put the strong law on him:
He's loved of the distracted multitude,
Who like not in their judgment, but their eyes;
And where 'tis so, the offender's scourge is weigh'd,
But never the offense. To bear all smooth and even,
This sudden sending away must seem
Deliberate pause: diseases desperate grown
By desperate appliance are relieved,
Or not at all.

Enter ROSENCRANTZ.]

　　　　　How now! what hath befall'n?

ROSENCRANTZ. Where the dead body is bestow'd, my lord,
We cannot get from him.

KING.　　　　　But where is he?

ROSENCRANTZ. Without, my lord; guarded, to know your pleasure.

KING. Bring him before us.

ROSENCRANTZ. Ho, Guildenstern! bring in my lord.

Enter HAMLET *and* GUILDENSTERN.]

KING. Now, Hamlet, where's Polonius?

HAMLET. At supper.

KING. At supper! where?

HAMLET. Not where he eats, but where he is eaten: a certain convocation of public worms are e'en at him. Your worm is your only emperor for diet: we fat all creatures else to fat us, and we fat ourselves for maggots: your fat king and

　　　your lean beggar is but variable service, two dishes, but to
　　　one table: that's the end.

KING. Alas, alas!

HAMLET. A man may fish with the worm that hath eat of a
　　　king, and eat of the fish that hath fed of that worm.

KING. What dost thou mean by this?

HAMLET. Nothing but to show you how a king may go a
　　　progress through the guts of a beggar.

KING. Where is Polonius?

HAMLET. In heaven; send thither to see: if your messenger
　　　find him not there, seek him i' the other place yourself. But
　　　indeed, if you find him not within this month, you shall
　　　nose him as you go up the stairs into the lobby.

KING. Go seek him there.　　　　　　　　[*To some* ATTENDANTS.

HAMLET. He will stay till you come.　　　[*Exeunt* ATTENDANTS.

KING. Hamlet this deed, for thine especial safety,
　　　Which we do tender, as we dearly grieve
　　　For that which thou hast done, must send thee hence
　　　With fiery quickness: therefore prepare thyself;
　　　The bark is ready and the wind at help,
　　　The associates tend, and every thing is bent
　　　For England.

HAMLET.　　　　　For England?

KING. ·　　　　　　　　　　　Aye, Hamlet.

HAMLET.　　　　　　　　　　　　　Good.

KING. So is it, if thou knew'st our purposes.

HAMLET. I see a cherub that sees them. But, come; for Eng-
　　　land! Farewell dear mother.

KING. Thy loving father, Hamlet.

HAMLET. My mother: father and mother is man and wife;
　　　man and wife is one flesh, and so, my mother. Come, for
　　　England!　　　　　　　　　　　　　　　　　　[*Exit*.

KING. Follow him at foot; tempt him with speed aboard;
　　　Delay it not I'll have him hence to-night:
　　　Away! for every thing is seal'd and done
　　　That else leans on the affair: pray you, make haste.

　　　　　　　　　　[*Exeunt* ROSENCRANTZ *and* GUILDENSTERN.

　　　And, England, if my love thou hold'st at aught—
　　　As my great power thereof may give thee sense,
　　　Since yet the cicatrice looks raw and red
　　　After the Danish sword, and thy free awe
　　　Pays homage to us—thou mayst not coldly set

Our sovereign process; which imports at full,
By letters conjuring to that effect,
The present death of Hamlet. Do it, England;
For like the hectic in my blood he rages,
And thou must cure me; till I know 'tis done,
Howe'er my haps, my joys were ne'er begun.   [*Exit.*

SCENE IV — *A plain in* DENMARK.

Enter FORTINBRAS, *a* CAPTAIN *and* SOLDIERS, *marching.*]

FORTINBRAS. Go, captain, from me greet the Danish king;
   Tell him that by his license Fortinbras
   Craves the conveyance of a promised march
   Over his kingdom. You know the rendezvous.
   If that his majesty would aught with us,
   We shall express our duty in his eye;
   And let him know so.
CAPTAIN.   I will do 't, my lord.
FORTINBRAS. Go softly on. [*Exeunt* FORTINBRAS *and* SOLDIERS.
Enter HAMLET, ROSENCRANTZ, GUILDENSTERN, *and others.*]
HAMLET. Good sir, whose powers are these?
CAPTAIN. They are of Norway, sir.
HAMLET. How purposed, sir, I pray you?
CAPTAIN. Against some part of Poland.
HAMLET. Who commands them, sir?
CAPTAIN. The nephew to Old Norway, Fortinbras.
HAMLET. Goes it against the main of Poland, sir,
   Or for some frontier?
CAPTAIN. Truly to speak, and with no addition,
   We go to gain a little patch of ground
   That hath in it no profit but the name.
   To pay five ducats, five, I would not farm it;
   Nor will it yield to Norway or the Pole
   A ranker rate, should it be sold in fee.
HAMLET. Why, then the Polack never will defend it.
CAPTAIN. Yes, it is already garrison'd.
HAMLET. Two thousand souls and twenty thousand ducats
   Will not debate the question of this straw:
   This is the imposthume of much wealth and peace,
   That inward breaks, and shows no cause without
   Why the man dies. I humbly thank you, sir.
CAPTAIN. God be wi' you, sir.   [*Exit.*

ROSENCRANTZ.   Will 't please you go, my lord?
HAMLET. I'll be with you straight. Go a little before.
                          [*Exeunt all but* HAMLET.

How all occasions do inform against me,
And spur my dull revenge! What is a man,
If his chief good and market of his time
Be but to sleep and feed? a beast, no more.
Sure, he that made us with such large discourse,
Looking before and after, gave us not
That capability and god-like reason
To fust in us unused. Now, whether it be
Bestial oblivion, or some craven scruple
Of thinking too precisely on the event,—
A thought which, quarter'd, hath but one part wisdom
And ever three parts coward,—I do not know
Why yet I live to say 'this thing's to do,'
Sith I have cause, and will, and strength, and means,
To do 't. Examples gross as earth exhort me:
Witness this army, of such mass and charge,
Led by a delicate and tender prince,
Whose spirit with divine ambition puff'd
Makes mouths at the invisible event,
Exposing what is mortal and unsure
To all that fortune, death and danger dare,
Even for an egg-shell. Rightly to be great
Is not to stir without great argument,
But greatly to find quarrel in a straw
When honor's at the stake. How stand I then,
That have a father kill'd, a mother stain'd,
Excitements of my reason and my blood,
And let all sleep, while to my shame I see
The imminent death of twenty thousand men,
That for a fantasy and trick of fame
Go to their graves like beds, fight for a plot
Whereon the numbers cannot try the cause,
Which is not tomb enough and continent
To hide the slain? O, from this time forth,
My thoughts be bloody, or be nothing worth!   [*Exit.*

S C E N E V — ELSINORE. *A room in the castle.*

Enter QUEEN, HORATIO, *and a* GENTLEMAN.]

QUEEN. I will not speak with her.

GENTLEMAN. She is importunate, indeed distract:
　Her mood will needs be pitied.

QUEEN.　　　　　　　　　　What would she have?

GENTLEMAN. She speaks much of her father, says she hears
　There's tricks i' the world, and hems and beats her heart,
　Spurns enviously at straws; speaks things in doubt,
　That carry but half sense: her speech is nothing,
　Yet the unshaped use of it doth move
　The hearers to collection; they aim at it,
　And botch the words up fit to their own thoughts;
　Which, as her winks and nods and gestures yield them,
　Indeed would make one think there might be thought,
　Though nothing sure, yet much unhappily.

HORATIO. 'Twere good she were spoken with, for she may
　　strew
　Dangerous conjectures in ill-breeding minds.

QUEEN. Let her come in.　　　　　　[*Exit* GENTLEMAN.
　[*Aside*] To my sick soul, as sin's true nature is,
　Each toy seems prologue to some great amiss:
　So full of artless jealousy is guilt,
　It spills itself in fearing to be spilt.

Re-enter GENTLEMAN, *with* OPHELIA.]

OPHELIA Where is the beauteous majesty of Denmark?

QUEEN How now Ophelia!

OPHELIA. [*Sings*] How should I your true love know
　　　　　　　　From another one?
　　　　　　　By his cockle hat and staff
　　　　　　　And his sandal shoon.

QUEEN. Alas, sweet lady, what imports this song?

OPHELIA. Say you? nay, pray you, mark.
　[*Sings*] He is dead and gone, lady,
　　　　　　He is dead and gone;
　　　　　　At his head a grass-green turf,
　　　　　　At his heels a stone.
　Oh, oh!

QUEEN.　Nay, but Ophelia,—

OPHELIA. Pray you, mark.

   [*Sings*] White his shroud as the mountain snow,—

Enter KING.]

QUEEN. Alas, look here, my lord.

OPHELIA. [*Sings*]   Larded with sweet flowers;

             Which bewept to the grave did go
               With true-love showers.

KING. How do you, pretty lady?

OPHELIA. Well, God 'ild you! They say the owl was a baker's
   daughter. Lord, we know what we are, but know not what
   we may be. God be at your table!

KING. Conceit upon her father.

OPHELIA. Pray you, let's have no words of this; but when they
   ask you what it means, say you this:

   [*Sings*]   To-morrow is Saint Valentine's day
           All in the morning betime,
      And I a maid at your window,
           To be your Valentine.
      Then up he rose, and donn'd his clothes,
           And dupp'd the chamber-door,
      Let in the maid, that out a maid
           Never departed more.

KING. Pretty Ophelia!

OPHELIA. Indeed, la, without an oath, I'll make an end on 't:

   [*Sings*]   By Gis and by Saint Charity,
           Alack, and fie for shame!
      Young men will do 't, if they come to 't;
           By cock, they are to blame.
      Quoth she, before you tumbled me,
           You promised me to wed.

   He answers:
           So would I ha' done, by yonder sun,
           An thou hadst not come to my bed.

KING. How long hath she been thus?

OPHELIA. I hope all will be well. We must be patient: but I
   cannot choose but weep, to think they should lay him i' the
   cold ground. My brother shall know of it: and so I thank
   you for your good counsel. Come, my coach! Good night,
   ladies; good night, sweet ladies; good night, good night.

                                            [*Exit.*

KING. Follow her close; give her good watch, I pray you.

                                    [*Exit* HORATIO.

O, this is the poison of deep grief; it springs
All from her father's death. O Gertrude, Gertrude,
When sorrows come, they come not single spies,
But in battalions! First, her father slain:
Next, your son gone; and he most violent author
Of his own just remove: the people muddied,
Thick and unwholesome in their thoughts and whispers,
For good Polonius' death; and we have done it greenly,
In hugger-mugger to inter him: poor Ophelia
Divided from herself and her fair judgment,
Without the which we are pictures, or mere beasts:
Last, and as much containing as all these,
Her brother is in secret come from France,
Feeds on his wonder, keeps himself in clouds,
And wants not buzzers to infect his ear
With pestilent speeches of his father's death;
Wherein necessity, of matter beggar'd,
Will nothing stick our person to arraign
In ear and ear. O my dear Gertrude, this,
Like to a murdering-piece, in many places
Gives me superfluous death.   [A noise within.

QUEEN.   Alack, what noise is this?
KING. Where are my Switzers? Let them guard the door.
Enter another GENTLEMAN.]
    What is the matter?

GENTLEMAN.   Save yourself, my lord:
    The ocean, overpeering of his list,
    Eats not the flats with more impetuous haste
    Than young Laertes, in a riotous head,
    O'erbears your officers. The rabble call him lord;
    And, as the world were now but to begin,
    Antiquity forgot, custom not known,
    The ratifiers and props of every word,
    They cry 'Choose we; Laertes shall be king!'
    Caps, hands and tongues applaud it to the clouds,
    'Laertes shall be king, Laertes king!'

QUEEN. How cheerfully on the false trail they cry!
    O, this is counter, you false Danish dogs!   [Noise within.
KING. The doors are broke.
Enter LAERTES, armed; DANES following.]
LAERTES. Where is this king? Sirs, stand you all without.
DANES. No, let's come in.

LAERTES.　　　　　　　　　　I pray you, give me leave.

DANES. We will, we will.　　　　　　[*They retire within the door.*

LAERTES. I thank you: keep the door. O thou vile king,
　Give me my father!

QUEEN.　　　　　　　　Calmly, good Laertes.

LAERTES. That drop of blood that's calm proclaims me bastard;
　Cries cuckold to my father; brands the harlot
　Even here, between the chaste unsmirched brows
　Of my true mother.

KING.　　　　　　　　What is the cause, Laertes,
　That thy rebellion looks so giant-like?
　Let him go, Gertrude; do not fear our person:
　There's such divinity doth hedge a king,
　That treason can but peep to what it would,
　Acts little of his will. Tell me, Laertes,
　Why thou art thus incensed: let him go, Gertrude:
　Speak, man.

LAERTES. Where is my father?

KING.　　　　　　　　　　　　Dead.

QUEEN.　　　　　　　　　　　　But not by him.

KING. Let him demand his fill.

LAERTES. How came he dead? I'll not be juggled with:
　To hell, allegiance! vows, to the blackest devil!
　Conscience and grace, to the profoundest pit!
　I dare damnation: to this point I stand,
　That both the worlds I give to negligence,
　Let come what comes; only I'll be revenged
　Most throughly for my father.

KING.　　　　　　　　　　Who shall stay you?

LAERTES. My will, not all the world:
　And for my means, I'll husband them so well,
　They shall go far with little.

KING.　　　　　　　　Good Laertes,
　If you desire to know the certainty
　Of your dear father's death, is 't writ in your revenge
　That, swoopstake, you will draw both friend and foe,
　Winner and loser?

LAERTES. None but his enemies.

KING.　　　　　　　　　　Will you know them then?

LAERTES. To his good friends thus wide I'll ope my arms;
　And, like the kind life-rendering pelican,
　Repast them with my blood.

KING.   Why, now you speak
  Like a good child and a true gentleman.
  That I am guiltless of your father's death,
  And am most sensibly in grief for it,
  It shall as level to your judgment pierce
  As day does to your eye.
DANES. [*Within*]   Let her come in.
LAERTES. How now! what noise is that?
Re-enter OPHELIA.]
  O heat, dry up my brains! tears seven times salt,
  Burn out the sense and virtue of mine eye!
  By heaven, thy madness shall be paid with weight,
  Till our scale turn the beam. O rose of May!
  Dear maid, kind sister, sweet Ophelia!
  O heavens! is 't possible a young maid's wits
  Should be as mortal as an old man's life?
  Nature is fine in love, and where 'tis fine
  It sends some precious instance of itself
  After the thing it loves.
OPHELIA. [*Sings*] They bore him barefaced on the bier:
               Hey non nonny, nonny, hey nonny:
               And in his grave rain'd many a tear,—
  Fare you well, my dove!
LAERTES. Hadst thou thy wits, and didst persuade revenge,
  It could not move thus.
OPHELIA. [*Sings*] You must sing down a-down,
               An you call him a-down-a.
  O, how the wheel becomes it! It is the false steward, that
  stole his master's daughter.
LAERTES. This nothing's more than matter.
OPHELIA. There's rosemary, that's for remembrance: pray you,
  love, remember: and there is pansies, that's for thoughts.
LAERTES. A document in madness; thoughts and remembrance
  fitted.
OPHELIA. There's fennel for you, and columbines: there's rue
  for you: and here's some for me: we may call it herb of
  grace o' Sundays: O, you must wear your rue with a difference. There's a daisy: I would give you some violets, but
  they withered all when my father died: they say he made a
  good end,—
  [*Sings*] For bonnie sweet Robin is all my joy.

LAERTES. Thought and affliction, passion, hell itself,
　　She turns to favor and to prettiness.
OPHELIA. [*Sings*]　　And will he not come again?
　　　　　　　　　And will he not come again?
　　　　　　　　　　No, no, he is dead,
　　　　　　　　　　Go to thy death-bed,
　　　　　　　　He never will come again.
　　　　　　　　His beard was as white as snow,
　　　　　　　　All flaxen was his poll:
　　　　　　　　　He is gone, he is gone,
　　　　　　　　　And we cast away moan:
　　　　　　　　God ha' mercy on his soul!
　　And of all Christian souls, I pray God. God be wi' you.
　　　　　　　　　　　　　　　　　　　　[*Exit.*

LAERTES. Do you see this, O God?
KING. Laertes, I must commune with your grief,
　　Or you deny me right. Go but apart,
　　Make choice of whom your wisest friends you will.
　　And they shall hear and judge 'twixt you and me:
　　If by direct or by collateral hand
　　They find us touched, we will our kingdom give,
　　Our crown, our life, and all that we call ours,
　　To you in satisfaction; but if not,
　　Be you content to lend your patience to us,
　　And we shall jointly labor with your soul
　　To give it due content.
LAERTES.　　　　　　　Let this be so;
　　His means of death, his obscure funeral,
　　No trophy, sword, nor hatchment o'er his bones,
　　No noble rite nor formal ostentation,
　　Cry to be heard, as 'twere from heaven to earth,
　　That I must call 't in question.
KING.　　　　　　　So you shall;
　　And where the offense is let the great axe fall.
　　I pray you, go with me.　　　　　　　[*Exeunt.*

SCENE VI — *Another room in the castle.*

Enter HORATIO *and a* SERVANT.]
HORATIO. What are they that would speak with me?
SERVANT. Sea-faring men, sir: they say they have letters for
　　you.

HORATIO. Let them come in.　　　　　　　[*Exit* SERVANT.

　I do not know from what part of the world

　I should be greeted, if not from Lord Hamlet.

Enter SAILORS.]

FIRST SAILOR. God bless you, sir.

HORATIO. Let him bless thee too.

FIRST SAILOR. He shall, sir, an 't please him.

　There's a letter for you, sir; it comes from the ambassador
that was bound for England; if your name be Horatio, as
I am let to know it is.

HORATIO. [*Reads*] 'Horatio, when thou shalt have overlooked
this, give these fellows some means to the king: they have
letters for him. Ere we were two days old at sea, a pirate of
very warlike appointment gave us chase. Finding ourselves
too slow of sail, we put on a compelled valor, and in the
grapple I boarded them: on the instant they got clear of our
ship; so I alone became their prisoner. They have dealt
with me like thieves of mercy: but they knew what they
did; I am to do a good turn for them. Let the king have the
letters I have sent; and repair thou to me with as much
speed as thou wouldst fly death. I have words to speak in
thine ear will make thee dumb; yet are they much too light
for the bore of the matter. These good fellows will bring
thee where I am. Rosencrantz and Guildenstern hold their
course for England: of them I have much to tell thee. Farewell.

　　　　　　　'He that thou knowest thine, HAMLET.'

Come, I will make you way for these your letters;

And do 't the speedier, that you may direct me

To him from whom you brought them.　　　　　[*Exeunt.*

SCENE VII — *Another room in the castle.*

Enter KING *and* LAERTES.]

KING. Now must your conscience my acquittance seal,

　And you must put me in your heart for friend,

　Sith you have heard, and with a knowing ear,

　That he which hath your noble father slain

　Pursued my life.

LAERTES.　　　　　It well appears: but tell me

　Why you proceeded not against these feats,

　So crimeful and so capital in nature,

As by your safety, wisdom, all things else,
You mainly were stirr'd up.

KING.   O, for two special reasons,
Which may to you perhaps seem much unsinew'd,
But yet to me they're strong. The queen his mother
Lives almost by his looks; and for myself—
My virtue or my plague, be it either which—
She's so conjunctive to my life and soul,
That, as the star moves not but in his sphere,
I could not but by her. The other motive,
Why to a public count I might not go,
Is the great love the general gender bear him;
Who, dipping all his faults in their affection,
Would, like the spring that turneth wood to stone,
Convert his gyves to graces; so that my arrows,
Too slightly timber'd for so loud a wind,
Would have reverted to my bow again
And not where I had aim'd them.

LAERTES. And so have I a noble father lost;
A sister driven into desperate terms,
Whose worth, if praises may go back again,
Stood challenger on mount of all the age
For her perfections: but my revenge will come.

KING. Break not your sleeps for that: you must not think
That we are made of stuff so flat and dull
That we can let our beard be shook with danger
And think it pastime. You shortly shall hear more:
I loved your father, and we love ourself;
And that, I hope, will teach you to imagine—

Enter a MESSENGER, *with letters.*]

How now! what news?

MESSENGER.   Letters, my lord, from Hamlet:
This to your majesty; this to the queen.

KING. From Hamlet! who brought them?

MESSENGER. Sailors, my lord, they say; I saw them not:
They were given me by Claudio; he received them
Of him that brought them.

KING.   Laertes, you shall hear them.
Leave us.   [*Exit* MESSENGER.

[*Reads*] 'High and mighty, you shall know I am set naked on
your kingdom. To-morrow shall I beg leave to see your
kingly eyes: when I shall, first asking your pardon there-

unto, recount the occasion of my sudden and more strange
return.　　　　　　　　　　　　　　　　　　　HAMLET.'
　What should this mean? Are all the rest come back?
　Or is it some abuse, and no such thing?

LAERTES. Know you the hand?

KING. 'Tis Hamlet's character. 'Naked'!
　And in a postscript here, he says 'alone.'
　Can you advise me?

LAERTES. I'm lost in it, my lord. But let him come;
　It warms the very sickness in my heart,
　That I shall live and tell him to his teeth,
　"Thus diddest thou.'

KING.　　　　　　　　If it be so, Laertes,—
　As how should it be so? how otherwise?—
　Will you be ruled by me?

LAERTES.　　　　　　　Aye, my lord;
　So you will not o'errule me to a peace.

KING. To thine own peace. If he be now return'd,
　As checking at his voyage, and that he means
　No more to undertake it, I will work him
　To an exploit now ripe in my device,
　Under the which he shall not choose but fall:
　And for his death no wind of blame shall breathe,
　But even his mother shall uncharge the practice,
　And call it accident.

LAERTES.　　　　　　My lord, I will be ruled;
　The rather, if you could devise it so
　That I might be the organ.

KING.　　　　　　　　It falls right.
　You have been talk'd of since your travel much,
　And that in Hamlet's hearing, for a quality
　Wherein, they say, you shine; your sum of parts
　Did not together pluck such envy from him,
　As did that one, and that in my regard
　Of the unworthiest siege.

LAERTES.　　　　　　What part is that, my lord?

KING. A very riband in the cap of youth,
　Yet needful too; for youth no less becomes
　The light and careless livery that it wears
　Than settled age his sables and his weeds,
　Importing health and graveness. Two months since,
　Here was a gentleman of Normandy:—

I've seen myself, and served against, the French,
And they can well on horseback: but this gallant
Had witchcraft in 't; he grew unto his seat,
And to such wondrous doing brought this horse
As had he been incorpsed and demi-natured
With the brave beast: so far he topp'd my thought
That I, in forgery of shapes and tricks,
Come short of what he did.

LAERTES.   A Norman was 't?

KING. A Norman.

LAERTES. Upon my life, Lamord.

KING.   The very same.

LAERTES. I know him well: he is the brooch indeed
And gem of all the nation.

KING. He made confession of you,
And gave you such a masterly report,
For art and exercise in your defense,
And for your rapier most especial,
That he cried out, 'twould be a sight indeed
If one could match you: the scrimers of their nation,
He swore, had neither motion, guard, nor eye,
If you opposed them. Sir, this report of his
Did Hamlet so unvenom with his envy
That he could nothing do but wish and beg
Your sudden coming o'er, to play with him.
Now, out of this—

LAERTES.   What out of this, my lord?

KING. Laertes, was your father dear to you?
Or are you like the painting of a sorrow,
A face without a heart?

LAERTES.   Why ask you this?

KING. Not that I think you did not love your father,
But that I know love is begun by time,
And that I see, in passages of proof,
Time qualifies the spark and fire of it.
There lives within the very flame of love
A kind of wick or snuff that will abate it;
And nothing is at a like goodness still,
For goodness, growing to a plurisy,
Dies in his own too much: that we would do
We should do when we would; for this 'would' changes
And hath abatements and delays as many

As there are tongues, are hands, are accidents,
And then this 'should' is like a spendthrift sigh,
That hurts by easing. But, to the quick o' the ulcer:
Hamlet comes back: what would you undertake,
To show yourself your father's son in deed
More than in words?

LAERTES.   To cut his throat i' the church.

KING. No place indeed should murder sanctuarize;
Revenge should have no bounds. But, good Laertes,
Will you do this, keep close within your chamber.
Hamlet return'd shall know you are come home:
We'll put on those shall praise your excellence
And set a double varnish on the fame
The Frenchman gave you; bring you in fine together
And wager on your heads: he, being remiss,
Most generous and free from all contriving,
Will not peruse the foils, so that with ease,
Or with a little shuffling, you may choose
A sword unbated, and in a pass of practice
Requite him for your father.

LAERTES.   I will do 't.
And for that purpose I'll anoint my sword.
I bought an unction of a mountebank,
So mortal that but dip a knife in it,
Where it draws blood no cataplasm so rare,
Collected from all simples that have virtue
Under the moon, can save the thing from death
That is but scratch'd withal: I'll touch my point
With this contagion, that, if I gall him slightly,
It may be death.

KING.   Let's further think of this,
Weigh what convenience both of time and means
May fit us to our shape: if this should fail,
And that our drift look through our bad performance,
'Twere better not assay'd: therefore this project
Should have a back or second, that might hold
If this did blast in proof. Soft! let me see:
We'll make a solemn wager on your cunnings:
I ha 't:
When in your motion you are hot and dry—
As make your bouts more violent to that end—
And that he calls for drink, I'll have prepared him

    A chalice for the nonce; whereon but sipping,
    If he by chance escape your venom'd stuck,
    Our purpose may hold there. But stay, what noise?
Enter QUEEN.]
    How now, sweet queen!
QUEEN. One woe doth tread upon another's heel,
    So fast they follow: your sister's drown'd, Laertes.
LAERTES. Drown'd! O, where?
QUEEN. There is a willow grows aslant a brook,
    That shows his hoar leaves in the glassy stream;
    There with fantastic garlands did she come
    Of crow-flowers, nettles, daisies, and long purples,
    That liberal shepherds give a grosser name,
    But our cold maids do dead men's fingers call them:
    There, on the pendent boughs her coronet weeds
    Clambering to hang, an envious sliver broke;
    When down her weedy trophies and herself
    Fell in the weeping brook. Her clothes spread wide,
    And mermaid-like a while they bore her up,
    Which time she chanted snatches of old tunes,
    As one incapable of her own distress,
    Or like a creature native and indued
    Unto that element: but long it could not be
    Till that her garments, heavy with their drink,
    Pull'd the poor wretch from her melodious lay
    To muddy death.
LAERTES.   Alas, then she is drown'd!
QUEEN. Drown'd, drown'd.
LAERTES. Too much of water hast thou, poor Ophelia,
    And therefore I forbid my tears: but yet
    It is our trick; nature her custom holds,
    Let shame say what it will: when these are gone,
    The woman will be out. Adieu, my lord:
    I have a speech of fire that fain would blaze,
    But that this folly douts it.   *[Exit.*
KING.   Let's follow, Gertrude:
    How much I had to do to calm his rage!
    Now fear I this will give it start again;
    Therefore let's follow.   *[Exeunt.*

ACT V

S C E N E I — *A churchyard.*

Enter two CLOWNS, *with spades, &c.*]

FIRST CLOWN. Is she to be buried in Christian burial that willfully seeks her own salvation?

SECOND CLOWN. I tell thee she is; and therefore make her
grave straight: the crowner hath sat on her, and finds it
Christian burial.

FIRST CLOWN. How can that be, unless she drowned herself
in her own defense?

SECOND CLOWN. Why, 'tis found so.

FIRST CLOWN. It must be 'se offendendo;' it cannot be else.
For here lies the point: if I drown myself wittingly, it argues an act: and an act hath three branches; it is, to act, to
do, to perform: argal, she drowned herself wittingly.

SECOND CLOWN. Nay, but hear you, goodman delver.

FIRST CLOWN. Give me leave. Here lies the water; good: here
stands the man; good: if the man go to this water and
drown himself, it is, will he, nill he, he goes; mark you that;
but if the water come to him and drown him, he drowns
not himself: argal, he that is not guilty of his own death
shortens not his own life.

SECOND CLOWN. But is this law?

FIRST CLOWN. Aye, marry, is 't; crowner's quest law.

SECOND CLOWN. Will you ha' the truth on 't? If this had not
been a gentlewoman, she should have been buried out o'
Christian burial.

FIRST CLOWN. Why, there thou say'st: and the more pity that
great folk should have countenance in this world to drown
or hang themselves, more than their even Christian. Come,
my spade. There is no ancient gentlemen but gardeners,
ditchers and grave-makers: they hold up Adam's profession.

SECOND CLOWN. Was he a gentleman?

FIRST CLOWN. A' was the first that ever bore arms.

SECOND CLOWN. Why, he had none.

FIRST CLOWN. What, art a heathen? How dost thou understand the Scripture? The Scripture says Adam digged:

could he dig without arms? I'll put another question to
thee: if thou answerest me not to the purpose, confess thyself—·

SECOND CLOWN. Go to.

FIRST CLOWN. What is he that builds stronger than either the
mason, the shipwright, or the carpenter?

SECOND CLOWN. The gallows-maker; for that frame outlives a
thousand tenants.

FIRST CLOWN. I like thy wit well, in good faith: the gallows
does well; but how does it well? it does well to those that
do ill: now, thou dost ill to say the gallows is built stronger
than the church: argal, the gallows may do well to thee.
To 't again, come.

SECOND CLOWN. 'Who builds stronger than a mason, a shipwright, or a carpenter?'

FIRST CLOWN. Aye, tell me that, and unyoke.

SECOND CLOWN. Marry, now I can tell.

FIRST CLOWN. To 't.

SECOND CLOWN. Mass, I cannot tell.

Enter HAMLET *and* HORATIO, *afar off.*]

FIRST CLOWN. Cudgel thy brains no more about it, for your
dull ass will not mend his pace with beating, and when
you are asked this question next, say 'a grave-maker:' the
houses that he makes last till doomsday. Go, get thee to
Yaughan; fetch me a stoup of liquor.

[*Exit* SECOND CLOWN.

[FIRST CLOWN *digs and sings.*

> In youth, when I did love, did love,
>   Methought it was very sweet,
> To contract, O, the time, for-a my behove,
>   O, methought, there-a was nothing-a meet.

HAMLET. Has this fellow no feeling of his business that he
sings at grave-making?

HORATIO. Custom hath made it in him a property of easiness.

HAMLET. 'Tis e'en so: the hand of little employment hath he
daintier sense.

FIRST CLOWN.   [*Sings*] But age, with his stealing steps,
>   Hath claw'd me in his clutch,
>   And hath shipped me intil the land,
>   As if I had never been such.

[*Throws up a skull.*

HAMLET. That skull had a tongue in it, and could sing once:
how the knave jowls it to the ground, as if it were Cain's
jaw-bone, that did the first murder! It might be the pate
of a politician, which this ass now o'er-reaches; one that
would circumvent God, might it not?

HORATIO. It might, my lord.

HAMLET. Or of a courtier, which could say, 'Good morrow,
sweet lord! How dost thou, sweet lord?' This might be my
lord such-a-one, that praised my lord such-a-one's horse,
when he meant to beg it; might it not?

HORATIO. Aye, my lord.

HAMLET. Why, e'en so: and now my Lady Worm's; chapless,
and knocked about the mazzard with a sexton's spade:
here's fine revolution, an we had the trick to see 't. Did
these bones cost no more the breeding, but to play at loggats with 'em? mine ache to think on 't.

FIRST CLOWN. [*Sings*] A pick-axe, and a spade, a spade,
　　　　　　For a shrouding sheet:
　　　　　O, a pit of clay for to be made
　　　　　For such a guest is meet.
　　　　　　　　　　　　[*Throws up another skull.*

HAMLET. There's another: why may not that be the skull of a
lawyer? Where be his quiddities now, his quillets, his cases,
his tenures, and his tricks? why does he suffer this rude
knave now to knock him about the sconce with a dirty
shovel, and will not tell him of his action of battery? Hum!
This fellow might be in 's time a great buyer of land, with
his statutes, his recognizances, his fines, his double vouchers, his recoveries: is this the fine of his fines and the recovery of his recoveries, to have his fine pate full of fine
dirt? will his vouchers vouch him no more of his purchases,
and double ones too, than the length and breadth of a pair
of indentures? The very conveyances of his lands will
hardly lie in this box; and must the inheritor himself have
no more, ha?

HORATIO. Not a jot more, my lord.

HAMLET. Is not parchment made of sheep-skins?

HORATIO. Aye, my lord, and of calf-skins too.

HAMLET. They are sheep and calves which seek our assurance
in that. I will speak to this fellow. Whose grave's this, sirrah?

FIRST CLOWN. Mine, sir.

[*Sings*] O, a pit of clay for to be made
            For such a guest is meet.

HAMLET. I think it be thine indeed, for thou liest in 't.

FIRST CLOWN. You lie out on 't, sir, and therefore 'tis not
    yours: for my part, I do not lie in 't, and yet it is mine.

HAMLET. Thou dost lie in 't, to be in 't and say it is thine; 'tis
    for the dead, not for the quick; therefore thou liest.

FIRST CLOWN. 'Tis a quick lie, sir; 'twill away again, from me
    to you.

HAMLET. What man dost thou dig it for?

FIRST CLOWN. For no man, sir.

HAMLET. What woman then?

FIRST CLOWN. For none neither.

HAMLET. Who is to be buried in 't?

FIRST CLOWN. One that was a woman, sir; but, rest her soul,
    she's dead.

HAMLET. How absolute the knave is! we must speak by the
    card, or equivocation will undo us. By the Lord, Horatio,
    these three years I have taken note of it; the age is grown so
    picked that the toe of the peasant comes so near the heel
    of the courtier, he galls his kibe. How long hast thou been
    a grave-maker?

FIRST CLOWN. Of all the days i' the year, I came to 't that day
    that our last King Hamlet o'ercame Fortinbras.

HAMLET. How long is that since?

FIRST CLOWN. Cannot you tell that? every fool can tell that:
    it was that very day that young Hamlet was born: he that
    is mad, and sent into England.

HAMLET. Aye, marry, why was he sent into England?

FIRST CLOWN. Why, because a' was mad; a' shall recover his
    wits there: or, if a' do not, 'tis no great matter there.

HAMLET. Why?

FIRST CLOWN. 'Twill not be seen in him there; there the men
    are as mad as he.

HAMLET. How came he mad?

FIRST CLOWN. Very strangely, they say.

HAMLET. How 'strangely'?

FIRST CLOWN. Faith, e'en with losing his wits.

HAMLET. Upon what ground?

FIRST CLOWN. Why, here in Denmark: I have been sexton
    here, man and boy, thirty years.

HAMLET. How long will a man lie i' the earth ere he rot?

FIRST CLOWN. I' faith, if a' be not rotten before a' die—as we have many pocky corses now-a-days, that will scarce hold the laying in—a' will last you some eight year or nine year: a tanner will last you nine year.

HAMLET. Why he more than another?

FIRST CLOWN. Why, sir, his hide is so tanned with his trade that a' will keep out water a great while; and your water is a sore decayer of your whoreson dead body. Here's a skull now: this skull has lain in the earth three and twenty years.

HAMLET. Whose was it?

FIRST CLOWN. A whoreson mad fellow's it was: whose do you think it was?

HAMLET. Nay, I know not.

FIRST CLOWN. A pestilence on him for a mad rogue! a' poured a flagon of Rhenish on my head once. This same skull, sir, was Yorick's skull, the king's jester.

HAMLET. This?

FIRST CLOWN. E'en that.

HAMLET. Let me see. [*Takes the skull.*] Alas, poor Yorick! I knew him, Horatio: a fellow of infinite jest, of most excellent fancy: he hath borne me on his back a thousand times; and now how abhorred in my imagination it is! my gorge rises at it. Here hung those lips that I have kissed I know not how oft. Where be your gibes now? your gambols? your songs? your flashes of merriment, that were wont to set the table on a roar? Not one now, to mock your own grinning? quite chop-fallen? Now get you to my lady's chamber and tell her, let her paint an inch thick, to this favor she must come; make her laugh at that. Prithee, Horatio tell me one thing.

HORATIO. What's that, my lord?

HAMLET. Dost thou think Alexander looked o' this fashion i' the earth?

HORATIO. E'en so.

HAMLET. And smelt so? pah! 　　　　　　[*Puts down the skull.*

HORATIO. E'en so, my lord.

HAMLET. To what base uses we may return, Horatio! Why may not imagination trace the noble dust of Alexander, till he find it stopping a bung-hole?

HORATIO. 'Twere to consider too curiously, to consider so.

HAMLET. No, faith, not a jot; but to follow him thither with
modesty enough and likelihood to lead it: as thus: Alexander died, Alexander was buried, Alexander returneth into
dust; the dust is earth; of earth we make loam; and why of
that loam, whereto he was converted, might they not stop
a beer-barrel?

Imperious Cæsar, dead and turn'd to clay,
Might stop a hole to keep the wind away:
O, that that earth, which kept the world in awe,
Should patch a wall to expel the winter's flaw!

But soft! but soft! aside: here comes the king.
Enter PRIESTS &c, *in procession; the Corpse of
Ophelia,* LAERTES *and* MOURNERS *following;*
KING, QUEEN, *their trains, & c.*]
The queen, the courtiers: who is this they follow?
And with such maimed rites? This doth betoken
The corse they follow did with desperate hand
Fordo its own life: 'twas of some estate.
Couch we awhile, and mark.   [*Retiring with* HORATIO.
LAERTES. What ceremony else?
HAMLET. That is Laertes, a very noble youth: mark.
LAERTES. What ceremony else?
FIRST PRIEST. Her obsequies have been as far enlarged
As we have warranty: her death was doubtful;
And, but that great command o'ersways the order
She should in ground unsanctified have lodged
Till the last trumpet; for charitable prayers,
Shards, flints and pebbles should be thrown on her:
Yet here she is allow'd her virgin crants,
Her maiden strewments and the bringing home
Of bell and burial.
LAERTES. Must there no more be done?
FIRST PRIEST.   No more be done:
We should profane the service of the dead
To sing a requiem and such rest to her
As to peace-parted souls.
LAERTES.   Lay her i' the earth:
And from her fair and unpolluted flesh
May violets spring! I tell thee, churlish priest,

A ministering angel shall my sister be,
When thou liest howling.

HAMLET.　　　　　　　What, the fair Ophelia!

QUEEN. [*Scattering flowers*] Sweet to the sweet: farewell!
I hoped thou shouldst have been my Hamlet's wife;
I thought thy bride-bed to have deck'd, sweet maid,
And not have strew'd thy grave.

LAERTES.　　　　　　　O, treble woe
Fall ten times treble on that cursed head
Whose wicked deed thy most ingenious sense
Deprived thee of! Hold off the earth a while,
Till I have caught her once more in mine arms.

　　　　　　　　　　　[*Leaps into the grave.*

Now pile your dust upon the quick and dead,
Till of this flat a mountain you have made
To o'ertop old Pelion or the skyish head
Of blue Olympus.

HAMLET. [*Advancing*] What is he whose grief
Bears such an emphasis? whose phrase of sorrow
Conjures the wandering stars and makes them stand
Like wonder-wounded hearers? This is I,
Hamlet the Dane.　　　　　　[*Leaps into the grave.*

LAERTES. The devil take thy soul!　　　[*Grappling with him.*

HAMLET.　　　　　　　Thou pray'st not well.
I prithee, take thy fingers from my throat;
For, though I am not splenitive and rash,
Yet have I in me something dangerous,
Which let thy wisdom fear. Hold off thy hand.

KING. Pluck them asunder.

QUEEN.　　　　　　　Hamlet, Hamlet!

ALL.　　　　　　　　　　Gentlemen,—

HORATIO. Good my lord, be quiet.

　　　　　　　[*The* ATTENDANTS *part them, and they
　　　　　　　　　　come out of the grave.*

HAMLET. Why, I will fight with him upon this theme
Until my eyelids will no longer wag.

QUEEN. O my son, what theme?

HAMLET I loved Ophelia: forty thousand brothers
Could not, with all their quantity of love,
Make up my sum. What wilt thou do for her?

KING. O, he is mad, Laertes.

QUEEN. For love of God, forbear him.

HAMLET. 'Swounds, show me what thou 'lt do:
   Woo't weep? woo't fight? woo't fast? woo't tear thyself?
   Woo't drink up eisel? eat a crocodile?
   I'll do't. Dost thou come here to whine?
   To outface me with leaping in her grave?
   Be buried quick with her, and so will I:
   And, if thou prate of mountains, let them throw
   Millions of acres on us, till our ground,
   Singeing his pate against the burning zone,
   Make Ossa like a wart! Nay, an thou 'lt mouth,
   I'll rant as well as thou.

QUEEN.   This is mere madness:
   And thus a while the fit will work on him;
   Anon, as patient as the female dove
   When that her golden couplets are disclosed,
   His silence will sit drooping.

HAMLET.   Hear you, sir;
   What is the reason that you use me thus?
   I loved you ever: but it is no matter;
   Let Hercules himself do what he may,
   The cat will mew, and dog will have his day.   [Exit.

KING. I pray thee, good Horatio, wait upon him.

                        [Exit HORATIO.

   [To LAERTES] Strengthen your patience in our last night's
      speech;
   We'll put the matter to the present push.
   Good Gertrude, set some watch over your son.
   This grave shall have a living monument:
   An hour of quiet shortly shall we see;
   Till then, in patience our proceeding be.   [Exeunt.

SCENE II — A hall in the castle.

Enter HAMLET and HORATIO.]

HAMLET. So much for this, sir: now shall you see the other;
   You do remember all the circumstance?

HORATIO. Remember it, my lord?

HAMLET. Sir, in my heart there was a kind of fighting,
   That would not let me sleep: methought I lay
   Worse than the mutines in the bilboes. Rashly,
   And praised be rashness for it, let us know,

Our indiscretion sometime serves us well
When our deep plots do pall; and that should learn us
There's a divinity that shapes our ends,
Rough-hew them how we will.

HORATIO.   That is most certain.

HAMLET. Up from my cabin.
My sea-gown scarf'd about me, in the dark
Groped I to find out them; had my desire,
Finger'd their packet, and in fine withdrew
To mine own room again; making so bold,
My fears forgetting manners, to unseal
Their grand commission; where I found, Horatio,—
O royal knavery!—an exact command,
Larded with many several sorts of reasons,
Importing Denmark's health and England's too,
With, ho! such bugs and goblins in my life,
That, on the supervise, no leisure bated,
No, not to stay the grinding of the axe,
My head should be struck off.

HORATIO.   Is't possible?

HAMLET. Here's the commission: read it at more leisure,
But wilt thou hear now how I did proceed?

HORATIO. I beseech you.

HAMLET. Being thus be-netted round with villainies,—
Ere I could make a prologue to my brains,
They had begun the play,—I sat me down;
Devised a new commission; wrote it fair:
I once did hold it, as our statists do,
A baseness to write fair, and labor'd much
How to forget that learning; but, sir, now
It did me yeoman's service: wilt thou know
The effect of what I wrote?

HORATIO.   Aye, good my lord.

HAMLET. An earnest conjuration from the king,
As England was his faithful tributary,
As love between them like the palm might flourish,
As peace should still her wheaten garland wear
And stand a comma 'tween their amities,
And many such-like 'As'es of great charge,
That, on the view and knowing of these contents,
Without debatement further, more or less,

He should the bearers put to sudden death,
Not shriving-time allow'd.

HORATIO.   How was this seal'd?

HAMLET. Why, even in that was heaven ordinant.
I had my father's signet in my purse,
Which was the model of that Danish seal:
Folded the writ up in the form of the other;
Subscribed it; gave 't the impression; placed it safely,
The changeling never known. Now, the next day
Was our sea-fight; and what to this was sequent
Thou know'st already.

HORATIO. So Guildenstern and Rosencrantz go to 't.

HAMLET. Why, man, they did make love to this employment;
They are not near my conscience; their defeat
Does by their own insinuation grow:
'Tis dangerous when the baser nature comes
Between the pass and fell-incensed points
Of mighty opposites.

HORATIO.   Why, what a king is this!

HAMLET. Does it not, think'st thee, stand me now upon—
He that hath kill'd my king, and whored my mother;
Popp'd in between the election and my hopes;
Thrown out his angle for my proper life,
And with such cozenage—is't not perfect conscience,
To quit him with this arm? and is't not to be damn'd,
To let this canker of our nature come
In further evil?

HORATIO. It must be shortly known to him from England
What is the issue of the business there.

HAMLET. It will be short: the interim is mine;
And a man's life's no more than to say 'One.'
But I am very sorry, good Horatio,
That to Laertes I forgot myself;
For, by the image of my cause, I see
The portraiture of his: I'll court his favors:
But, sure, the bravery of his grief did put me
Into a towering passion.

HORATIO.   Peace! who comes here?

Enter OSRIC.]

OSRIC. Your lordship is right welcome back to Denmark.

HAMLET. I humbly thank you, sir. Dost know this waterfly?

HORATIO. No, my good lord.

HAMLET. Thy state is the more gracious, for 'tis a vice to know him. He hath much land, and fertile: let a beast be lord of beasts, and his crib shall stand at the king's mess: 'tis a clough, but, as I say, spacious in the possession of dirt.

OSRIC. Sweet lord, if your lordship were at leisure, I should impart a thing to you from his majesty.

HAMLET. I will receive it, sir, with all diligence of spirit. Put your bonnet to his right use; 'tis for the head.

OSRIC. I thank your lordship, it is very hot.

HAMLET. No, believe me, 'tis very cold; the wind is northerly.

OSRIC. It is indifferent cold, my lord, indeed.

HAMLET. But yet methinks it is very sultry and hot, or my complexion—

OSRIC. Exceedingly, my lord; it is very sultry, as 'twere,—I cannot tell how. But, my lord, his majesty bade me signify to you that he has laid a great wager on your head: sir, this is the matter—

HAMLET. I beseech you, remember—

[HAMLET *moves him to put on his hat.*

OSRIC. Nay, good my lord; for mine ease, in good faith. Sir, here is newly come to court Laertes; believe me, an absolute gentleman, full of most excellent differences, of very soft society and great showing: indeed, to speak feelingly of him, he is the card or calendar of gentry, for you shall find in him the continent of what part a gentleman would see.

HAMLET. Sir, his definement suffers no perdition in you; though, I know, to divide him inventorially would dizzy the arithmetic of memory, and yet but yaw neither, in respect of his quick sail. But in the verity of extolment, I take him to be a soul of great article, and his infusion of such dearth and rareness, as, to make true diction of him, his semblable is his mirror, and who else would trace him, his umbrage, nothing more.

OSRIC. Your lordship speaks most infallibly of him.

HAMLET. The concernancy, sir? why do we wrap the gentleman in our more rawer breath?

OSRIC. Sir?

HORATIO. Is 't not possible to understand in another tongue? You will do 't, sir, really.

HAMLET. What imports the nomination of this gentleman?

OSRIC. Of Laertes?

HORATIO. His purse is empty already; all's golden words are
spent.

HAMLET. Of him, sir.

OSRIC. I know you are not ignorant—

HAMLET. I would you did, sir; yet, in faith, if you did, it
would not much approve me. Well, sir?

OSRIC. You are not ignorant of what excellence Laertes is—

HAMLET. I dare not confess that, lest I should compare with
him in excellence; but, to know a man well, were to know
himself.

OSRIC. I mean, sir, for his weapon; but in the imputation laid
on him by them, in his meed he's unfellowed.

HAMLET. What's his weapon?

OSRIC. Rapier and dagger.

HAMLET. That's two of his weapons: but, well.

OSRIC. The king, sir, hath wagered with him six Barbary
horses: against the which he has imponed, as I take it, six
French rapiers and poniards, with their assigns, as girdle,
hanger, and so: three of the carriages, in faith, are very
dear to fancy, very responsive to the hilts, most delicate
carriages, and of very liberal conceit.

HAMLET. What call you the carriages?

HORATIO. I knew you must be edified by the margent ere you
had done.

OSRIC. The carriages, sir, are the hangers.

HAMLET. The phrase would be more germane to the matter
if we could carry a cannon by our sides: I would it might
be hangers till then. But, on: six Barbary horses against
six French swords, their assigns, and three liberal-conceited
carriages; that's the French bet against the Danish. Why is
this 'imponed,' as you call it?

OSRIC. The king, sir, hath laid, sir, that in a dozen passes between yourself and him, he shall not exceed you three hits:
he hath laid on twelve for nine; and it would come to immediate trial, if your lordship would vouchsafe the answer.

HAMLET. How if I answer 'no'?

OSRIC. I mean, my lord, the opposition of your person in trial.

HAMLET. Sir, I will walk here in the hall: if it please his
majesty, it is the breathing time of day with me; let the
foils be brought, the gentleman willing, and the king hold
his purpose, I will win for him an I can; if not, I will gain
nothing but my shame and the odd hits.

OSRIC. Shall I redeliver you e'en so?

HAMLET. To this effect, sir, after what flourish your nature will.

OSRIC. I commend my duty to your lordship.

HAMLET. Yours, yours. [*Exit* OSRIC.] He does well to commend it himself; there are no tongues else for's turn.

HORATIO. This lapwing runs away with the shell on his head.

HAMLET. He did comply with his dug before he sucked it. Thus has he—and many more of the same breed that I know the drossy age dotes on—only got the tune of the time and outward habit of encounter; a kind of yesty collection, which carries them through and through the most fond and winnowed opinions; and do but blow them to their trial, the bubbles are out.

Enter a LORD.]

LORD. My lord, his majesty commended him to you by young Osric, who brings back to him, that you attend him in the hall: he sends to know if your pleasure hold to play with Laertes, or that you will take longer time.

HAMLET. I am constant to my purposes; they follow the king's pleasure: if his fitness speaks, mine is ready; now or whensoever, provided I be so able as now.

LORD. The king and queen and all are coming down.

HAMLET. In happy time.

LORD. The queen desires you to use some gentle entertainment to Laertes before you fall to play.

HAMLET. She well instructs me.　　　　　　　　　　[*Exit* LORD.

HORATIO. You will lose this wager, my lord.

HAMLET. I do not think so; since he went into France, I have been in continual practice; I shall win at the odds. But thou wouldst not think how ill all's·here about my heart: but it is no matter.

HORATIO. Nay, good my lord,—

HAMLET. It is but foolery; but it is such a kind of gaingiving as would perhaps trouble a woman.

HORATIO. If your mind dislike anything, obey it. I will forestall their repair hither, and say you are not fit.

HAMLET. Not a whit; we defy augury: there is special providence in the fall of a sparrow. If it be now, 'tis not to come; if it be not to come, it will be now; if it be not now, yet it will come: the readiness is all; since no man has aught of what he leaves, what is't to leave betimes? Let be.

Enter KING, QUEEN, LAERTES, *and* LORDS, OSRIC *and*
    other ATTENDANTS *with foils and gauntlets; a*
    table and flagons of wine on it.]

KING. Come, Hamlet, come, and take this hand from me.
              [*The* KING *puts* LAERTES' *hand into* HAMLET'S.

HAMLET. Give me your pardon, sir: I've done you wrong;
  But pardon't, as you are a gentleman.
  This presence knows,
  And you must needs have heard, how I am punish'd
  With sore distraction. What I have done,
  That might your nature, honor and exception
  Roughly awake, I here proclaim was madness.
  Was't Hamlet wrong'd Laertes? Never Hamlet:
  If Hamlet from himself be ta'en away,
  And when he's not himself does wrong Laertes,
  Then Hamlet does it not, Hamlet denies it.
  Who does it then? His madness: if't be so,
  Hamlet is of the faction that is wrong'd;
  His madness is poor Hamlet's enemy.
  Sir, in this audience,
  Let my disclaiming from a purposed evil
  Free me so far in your most generous thoughts,
  That I have shot mine arrow o'er the house,
  And hurt my brother.

LAERTES.   I am satisfied in nature,
  Whose motive, in this case, should stir me most
  To my revenge: but in my terms of honor
  I stand aloof, and will no reconcilement,
  Till by some elder masters of known honor
  I have a voice and precedent of peace,
  To keep my name ungored. But till that time
  I do receive your offer'd love like love
  And will not wrong it.

HAMLET.   I embrace it freely,
  And will this brother's wager frankly play.
  Give us the foils. Come on.

LAERTES.   Come, one for me.

HAMLET. I'll be your foil, Laertes: in mine ignorance
  Your skill shall, like a star i' the darkest night,
  Stick fiery off indeed.

LAERTES.   You mock me, sir.

HAMLET. No, by this hand.

KING. Give them the foils, young Osric. Cousin Hamlet,
  You know the wager?

HAMLET.   Very well, my lord;
  Your grace has laid the odds o' the weaker side.

KING. I do not fear it; I have seen you both:
  But since he is better'd, we have therefore odds.

LAERTES. This is too heavy; let me see another.

HAMLET. This likes me well. These foils have all a length?
                                        [*They prepare to play.*

OSRIC. Aye, my good lord.

KING. Set me the stoups of wine upon that table.
  If Hamlet give the first or second hit,
  Or quit in answer to the third exchange,
  Let all the battlements their ordnance fire;
  The king shall drink to Hamlet's better breath;
  And in the cup an union shall he throw,
  Richer than that which four successive kings
  In Denmark's crown have worn. Give me the cups;
  And let the kettle to the trumpet speak,
  The trumpet to the cannoneer without,
  The cannons to the heavens, the heaven to earth,
  'Now the king drinks to Hamlet.' Come, begin;
  And you, the judges, bear a wary eye.

HAMLET. Come on, sir.

LAERTES.   Come, my lord.   [*They play.*

HAMLET.   One.

LAERTES.   No.

HAMLET.   Judgment.

OSRIC. A hit, a very palpable hit.

LAERTES.   Well; again.

KING. Stay; give me drink. Hamlet, this pearl is thine;
  Here's to thy health.
              [*Trumpets sound, and cannon shot off within.*
              Give him the cup.

HAMLET. I'll play this bout first; set it by awhile.
  Come. [*They play.*] Another hit; what say you?

LAERTES. A touch, a touch, I do confess.

KING. Our son shall win.

QUEEN.   He's fat and scant of breath.
  Here, Hamlet, take my napkin, rub thy brows:
  The queen carouses to thy fortune, Hamlet.

HAMLET. Good madam!

KING.   Gertrude, do not drink.

QUEEN. I will, my lord; I pray you, pardon me.

KING. [Aside] It is the poison'd cup; it is too late.

QUEEN. Come, let me wipe thy face.

LAERTES. My lord, I'll hit him now.

KING.   I do not think't.

LAERTES. [Aside] And yet it is almost against my conscience.

HAMLET. Come, for the third, Laertes: you but dally;
  I pray you, pass with your best violence;
  I am afeard you make a wanton of me.

LAERTES. Say you so? come on.   [They play.

OSRIC. Nothing, neither way.

LAERTES. Have at you now!

            [LAERTES wounds HAMLET; then, in scuffling, they
              change rapiers, and HAMLET wounds LAERTES.

KING.   Part them; they are incensed.

HAMLET. Nay, come, again.   [The QUEEN falls.

OSRIC.   Look to the queen there, ho!

HORATIO. They bleed on both sides. How is it, my lord?

OSRIC. How is't, Laertes?

LAERTES. Why, as a woodcock to mine own spring, Osric;
  I am justly kill'd with mine own treachery.

HAMLET. How does the queen?

KING.   She swounds to see them bleed.

QUEEN. No, no, the drink, the drink,—O my dear Hamlet,—
  The drink, the drink! I am poison'd.   [Dies.

HAMLET. O villainy! Ho! let the door be lock'd:
  Treachery! seek it out.   [LAERTES falls.

LAERTES. It is here, Hamlet: Hamlet, thou art slain;
  No medicine in the world can do thee good,
  In thee there is not half an hour of life;
  The treacherous instrument is in thy hand,
  Unbated and envenom'd: the foul practice
  Hath turn'd itself on me; lo, here I lie,
  Never to rise again: thy mother's poison'd:
  I can no more: the king, the king's to blame.

HAMLET. The point envenom'd too!
  Then, venom, to thy work.   [Stabs the KING.

ALL. Treason! treason!

KING. O, yet defend me, friends; I am but hurt.

HAMLET. Here, thou incestuous, murderous, damned Dane,

　　Drink off this potion: is thy union here?
　　Follow my mother.　　　　　　　　　　*[King dies.*
LAERTES.　　　　　　　He is justly served;
　　It is a poison temper'd by himself.
　　Exchange forgiveness with me, noble Hamlet:
　　Mine and my father's death come not upon thee,
　　Nor thine on me!　　　　　　　　　　*[Dies.*
HAMLET. Heaven make thee free of it! I follow thee.
　　I am dead, Horatio. Wretched queen, adieu!
　　You that look pale and tremble at this chance,
　　That are but mutes or audience to this act,
　　Had I but time—as this fell sergeant, death,
　　Is strict in his arrest—O, I could tell you—
　　But let it be. Horatio, I am dead;
　　Thou livest; report me and my cause aright
　　To the unsatisfied.
HORATIO　　　　　　　Never believe it:
　　I am more an antique Roman than a Dane:
　　Here's yet some liquor left.
HAMLET.　　　　　　　　　As thou'rt a man,
　　Give me the cup: let go; by heaven, I'll have 't.
　　O good Horatio, what a wounded name,
　　Things standing thus unknown, shall live behind me!
　　If thou didst ever hold me in thy heart,
　　Absent thee from felicity a while,
　　And in this harsh world draw thy breath in pain,
　　To tell my story.　　　　*[March afar off, shot within.*
　　　　　　　What warlike noise is this?
OSRIC. Young Fortinbras, with conquest come from Poland,
　　To the ambassadors of England gives
　　This warlike volley.
HAMLET.　　　　　　O, I die, Horatio;
　　The potent poison quite o'er-crows my spirit:
　　I cannot live to hear the news from England;
　　But I do prophesy the election lights
　　On Fortinbras: he has my dying voice;
　　So tell him, with the occurrents, more and less,
　　Which have solicited. The rest is silence.　　*[Dies.*
HORATIO. Now cracks a noble heart. Good night sweet prince,
　　And flights of angels sing thee to thy rest!　*[March within.*
　　Why does the drum come hither?

Enter FORTINBRAS, *and the* ENGLISH AMBASSADORS,
　　with drum, colors, and ATTENDANTS.]

FORTINBRAS. Where is this sight?

HORATIO.　　　　　　　　　　What is it you would see?
　If aught of woe or wonder, cease your search.

FORTINBRAS. This quarry cries on havoc. O proud death,
　What feast is toward in thine eternal cell,
　That thou so many princes at a shot
　So bloodily hast struck?

FIRST AMBASSADOR.　　　　The sight is dismal;
　And our affairs from England come too late:
　The ears are senseless that should give us hearing,
　To tell him his commandment is fulfill'd,
　That Rosencrantz and Guildenstern are dead:
　Where should we have our thanks?

HORATIO.　　　　　　　　　　Not from his mouth
　Had it the ability of life to thank you:
　He never gave commandment for their death.
　But since so jump upon this bloody question,
　You from the Polack wars, and you from England,
　Are here arrived, give order that these bodies
　High on a stage be placed to the view;
　And let me speak to the yet unknowing world
　How these things came about: so shall you hear
　Of carnal bloody and unnatural acts,
　Of accidental judgments, casual slaughters,
　Of deaths put on by cunning and forced cause,
　And, in this upshot, purposes mistook
　Fall'n on the inventors' heads: all this can I
　Truly deliver.

FORTINBRAS.　　　Let us haste to hear it,
　And call the noblest to the audience.
　For me with sorrow I embrace my fortune:
　I have some rights of memory in this kingdom,
　Which now to claim my vantage doth invite me.

HORATIO. Of that I shall have also cause to speak,
　And from his mouth whose voice will draw on more:
　But let this same be presently perform'd,
　Even while men's minds are wild; lest more mischance
　On plots and errors happen.

FORTINBRAS.　　　　　　Let four captains
　Bear Hamlet, like a soldier, to the stage;

For he was likely, had he been put on,
To have proved most royally: and, for his passage,
The soldiers' music and the rites of war
Speak loudly for him.
Take up the bodies: such a sight as this
Becomes the field, but here shows much amiss.
Go, bid the soldiers shoot.

> [*A dead march. Exeunt, bearing off the bodies:
> after which a peal of ordnance is shot off.*

MACBETH

Macbeth

BY

MARK VAN DOREN

THE brevity of *Macbeth* is so much a function of its brilliance that we might lose rather than gain by turning up the lost scenes of legend. This brilliance gives us in the end somewhat less than the utmost that tragedy can give. The hero, for instance, is less valuable as a person than Hamlet, Othello, or Lear; or Antony, or Coriolanus, or Timon. We may not rejoice in his fall as Dr. Johnson says we must, yet we have known too little about him and have found too little virtue in him to experience at his death the sense of an unutterable and tragic loss made necessary by ironies beyond our understanding He commits murder in violation of a nature which we can assume to have been noble, but we can only assume this Macbeth has surrendered his soul before the play begins When we first see him he is already invaded by those fears which are to render him vicious and which are finally to make him abominable. They will also reveal him as a great poet. But his poetry, like the poetry of the play, is to be concerned wholly with sensation and catastrophe. *Macbeth* like *Lear* is all end; the difference appearing in the speed with which doom rushes down, so that this rapidest of tragedies suggests whirlwinds rather than glaciers, and in the fact that terror rather than pity is the mode of the accompanying music. *Macbeth*, then, is not in the fullest known sense a tragedy. But we do not need to suppose that this is because important parts of it have been lost. More of it would have had to be more of the same. And the truth is that no significant scene seems to be missing *Macbeth* is incomparably brilliant as it stands and within its limits perfect. What it does it does with flawless force It hurls a universe against a man, and if the universe that strikes is more impressive than the man who is stricken, great as his size and gaunt as his soul may be, there is no good reason for doubting that this is what Shakespeare intended. The triumph of *Macbeth* is the construction of a world, and nothing like it has ever been constructed in twenty-one hundred lines.

This world, which is at once without and within Macbeth, can be most easily described as "strange." The word, like the witches, is always somewhere doing its work. Even in the battle which precedes the play the Thane of Glamis has made "strange images of death" (I, iii), and when he comes home to his lady his face is "as a book where men may read strange matters" (I, v). Duncan's horses after his murder turn wild in nature and devour each other—"a thing most strange and certain" (II, iv). Nothing is as it should be in such a world. "Who would have thought the old man to have had so much blood in him?" There is a drift of disorder in all events, and the air is murky with unwelcome miracles.

It is a dark world too, inhabited from the beginning by witches who meet on a blasted heath in thunder and lightning, and who hover through fog and filthy air as they leave on unspeakable errands. It is a world wherein "men must not walk too late" (III, vi), for the night that was so pretty in *Romeo and Juliet, A Midsummer Night's Dream,* and *The Merchant of Venice* has grown terrible with ill-smelling mists and the stench of blood. The time that was once a playground for free and loving spirits has closed like a trap, or yawned like a bottomless pit. The "dark hour" that Banquo borrows from the night is his last hour on earth which has lost the distinction between sun and gloom.

> Darkness does the face of earth entomb,
> When living light should kiss it.   [II, iv]

The second of these lines makes a sound that is notable in the play for its rarity: the sound of life in its normal ease and lightness. Darkness prevails because the witches, whom Banquo calls its instruments, have willed to produce it. But Macbeth is its instrument too, as well as its victim. And the weird sisters no less than he are expressions of an evil that employs them both and has roots running farther into darkness than the mind can guess.

It is furthermore a world in which nothing is certain to

keep its shape. Forms shift and consistencies alter, so that what was solid may flow and what was fluid may congeal to stone.

> The earth hath bubbles, as the water has,
> And these are of them, [I, iii]

says Banquo of the vanished witches. Macbeth addresses the "sure and firm set earth" (II, i), but nothing could be less firm than the whole marble and the founded rock he has fancied his life to be. At the very moment he speaks he has seen a dagger which is not there, and the "strange infirmity" he confesses at the banquet will consist of seeing things that cannot be. His first apostrophe to the witches had been to creatures

> That look not like the inhabitants o' the earth,
> And yet are on 't. [I, iii]

So now a dead man lives; Banquo's brains are out but he rises again, and "this is more strange than such a murder is."

> Take any shape but that, and my firm nerves
> Shall never tremble. [III, iv]

But the shape of everything is wrong, and the nerves of Macbeth are never proof against trembling. The cardinal instance of transformation is himself. Bellona's bridegroom has been turned to jelly.

The current of change pouring forever through this universe has, as a last effect, dissolved it. And the dissolution of so much that was solid has liberated deadly fumes, has thickened the air until it suffocates all breathers. If the footing under men is less substantial than it was, the atmosphere they must push through is almost too heavy for life. It is confining, swarming, swelling; it is viscous, it is sticky; and it threatens strangulation. All of the speakers in the play conspire to create the impression that this is so. Not only do the witches in their opening scene wail "Fair is foul, and foul is fair," but the military men who enter after them anticipate in their talk of recent battle the imagery of entanglement to come.

> Doubtful it stood,
> As two spent swimmers that do cling together
> And choke their art. . . .
> The multiplying villainies of nature
> Do swarm upon him. . . .
> So from that spring whence comfort seem'd to come
> Discomfort swells.   [I, ii]

Macbeth's sword is reported to have "smok'd with bloody execution," and he and Banquo were "as cannons overcharg'd with double cracks;" they

> Doubly redoubled strokes upon the foe.

The hyperbole is ominous, the excess is sinister. In the third scene, after what seemed corporal in the witches has melted into the wind, Ross and Angus join Banquo and Macbeth to report the praises of Macbeth that had poured in on Duncan "as thick as hail," and to salute the new thane of Cawdor. The witches then have been right in two respects, and Macbeth says in an aside:

> Two truths are told,
> As happy prologues to the swelling act
> Of the imperial theme.   [I, iii]

But the imagined act of murder swells in his mind until it is too big for its place, and his heart beats as if it were choking in its chamber.

> Why do I yield to that suggestion
> Whose horrid image doth unfix my hair
> And make my seated heart knock at my ribs,
> Against the use of nature? Present fears
> Are less than horrible imaginings.
> My thought, whose murder yet is but fantastical,
> Shakes so my single state of man that function
> Is smother'd in surmise, and nothing is
> But what is not.   [I, iii]

Meanwhile Lady Macbeth at home is visited by no such fears. When the crisis comes she will break sooner than her husband does, but her brittleness then will mean the same thing that her melodrama means now: she is a slighter person than Macbeth, has a poorer imagination, and holds in her mind

less of that power which enables it to stand up under torture.
The news that Duncan is coming to her house inspires her to
pray that her blood be made thick; for the theme of thickness
is so far not terrible in her thought.

> Come, thick night,
> And pall thee in the dunnest smoke of hell,
> That my keen knife see not the wound it makes,
> Nor heaven peep through the blanket of the dark
> To cry, "Hold, hold!"   [I, v]

The blanket of the dark—it seems to her an agreeable image,
and by no means suggests an element that can enwrap or
smother. With Macbeth it is different; his soliloquy in the
seventh scene shows him occupied with images of nets and
tangles: the consequences of Duncan's death may coil about
him like an endless rope.

> If it were done when 't is done, then 't were well
> It were done quickly. If the assassination
> Could trammel up the consequence, and catch
> With his surcease success; that but this blow
> Might be the be-all and the end-all here,
> But here, upon this bank and shoal of time,
> We'd jump the life to come. But in these cases
> We still have judgement here, that we but teach
> Bloody instructions, which, being taught, return
> To plague the inventor.   [I, vii]

And his voice rises to shrillness as he broods in terror upon
the endless echo which such a death may make in the world.

> His virtues
> Will plead like angels, trumpet-tongu'd, against
> The deep damnation of his taking-off;
> And pity, like a naked new-born babe
> Striding the blast, or heaven's cherubin hors'd
> Upon the sightless couriers of the air,
> Shall blow the horrid deed in every eye,
> That tears shall drown the wind.   [I, vii]

It is terror such as this that Lady Macbeth must endeavor to
allay in what is after all a great mind. Her scolding cannot
do so. She has commanded him to screw his courage to the
sticking-point, but what is the question that haunts him when

he comes from Duncan's bloody bed, with hands that can
never be washed white again?

> Wherefore could not I pronounce "Amen"?
> I had most need of blessing, and "Amen"
> Stuck in my throat.   [II, ii]

He must not consider such things so deeply, his lady warns
him. But he does, and in good time she will follow suit. That
same night the Scottish earth, shaking in a convincing sympathy as the Roman earth in *Julius Caesar* never shook, con-
siders the grievous state of a universe that suffocates in the
breath of its own history. Lamentings are heard in the air,
strange screams of death, and prophecies of dire combustion
and confused events (II, iii). And the next morning, says Ross
to an old man he meets,

> By the clock 't is day,
> And yet dark night strangles the travelling lamp.
>   [II, iv]

Macbeth is now king, but his fears "stick deep" in Banquo
(III, i). The thought of one more murder that will give him
perhaps the "clearness" he requires (III, i) seems for a moment to free his mind from its old obsessive horror of dusk
and thickness, and he can actually invoke these conditions—
in the only verse he ever uses with conscious literary intention.

> Come, seeling night,
> Scarf up the tender eye of pitiful day,
> And with thy bloody and invisible hand
> Cancel and tear to pieces that great bond
> Which keeps me pale! Light thickens, and the crow
> Makes wing to the rooky wood;
> Good things of day begin to droop and drowse,
> While night's black agents to their preys do rouse.
>   [III, ii]

The melodrama of this, and its inferiority of effect, may warn
us that Macbeth is only pretending to hope. The news of
Fleance's escape brings him at any rate his fit again, and he
never more ceases to be "cabin'd, cribb'd, confin'd" (III, iv).
He is caught in the net for good, his feet have sunk into
quicksands from which they cannot be freed, his bosom like

Lady Macbeth's is "stuff'd" with "perilous stuff which weighs
upon the heart" (v, iii)—the figure varies, but the theme
does not. A strange world not wholly of his own making has
closed around him and rendered him motionless. His gestures
are spasmodic at the end, like those of one who knows he is
hopelessly engulfed. And every metaphor he uses betrays his
belief that the universal congestion is past cure:

> What rhubarb, senna, or what purgative drug,
> Would scour these English hence?   [v, iii]

The answer is none.

The theme never varies, however rich the range of symbols
employed to suggest it. One of these symbols is of course the
fear that shakes Macbeth as if he were an object not human;
that makes him start when the witches call him "King hereafter," that sets his heart knocking as his ribs, that wrings
from him unsafe extremities of rhetoric, that reduces him to
a maniac when Banquo walks again, that spreads from him
to all of Scotland until its inhabitants "float upon a wild and
violent sea" of terror (IV, ii), and that in the end, when he
has lost the capacity to feel anything any longer, drains from
him so that he almost forgets its taste (v, v). Another symbol,
and one that presents itself to several of our senses at once, is
blood. Never in a play has there been so much of this substance, and never has it been so sickening. "What bloody man
is that?" The second scene opens with a messenger running
in to Duncan red with wounds. And blood darkens every
scene thereafter. It is not bright red, nor does it run freely
and wash away. Nor is it a metaphor as it was in *Julius
Caesar*. It is so real that we see, feel, and smell it on everything. And it sticks. "This is a sorry sight," says Macbeth as he
comes from Duncan's murder, staring at his hands. He had
not thought there would be so much blood on them, or that
it would stay there like that. Lady Macbeth is for washing the
"filthy witness" off, but Macbeth knows that all great Neptune's ocean will not make him clean; rather his hand,
plunged into the green, will make it all one red. The blood of
the play is everywhere physical in its looks and gross in its
quantity. Lady Macbeth "smears" the grooms with it, so that
when they are found they seem "badg'd" and "unmannerly
breech'd" with gore, and "steep'd" in the colors of their trade.

The murderer who comes to report Banquo's death has blood on his face, and the "blood-bolter'd Banquo" when he appears shakes "gory locks" at Macbeth, who in deciding upon the assassination has reflected that

> I am in blood
> Stepp'd in so far that, should I wade no more,
> Returning were as tedious as go o'er.   [III, iv]

Richard III had said a similar thing, but he suggested no veritable pool or swamp of blood as this man does; and his victims, wailing over their calamities, did not mean the concrete thing Macduff means when he cries, "Bleed, bleed, poor country!" (IV, iii). The world of the play quite literally bleeds. And Lady Macbeth, walking in her sleep, has definite stains upon the palms she rubs and rubs. "Yet here's a spot. . . . What, will these hands ne'er be clean? . . . Here's the smell of the blood still; all the perfumes of Arabia will not sweeten this little hand."

A third symbol, of greater potency than either fear or blood, is sleeplessness. Just as there are more terrors in the night than day has ever taught us, and more blood in a man than there should be, so there is less sleep in this disordered world than the minimum which once had been required for health and life. One of the final signs of that disorder is indeed the death of sleep.

> Methought I heard a voice cry, "Sleep no more!
> Macbeth does murder sleep. . . .
> Glamis hath murder'd sleep, and therefore Cawdor
> Shall sleep no more; Macbeth shall sleep no more."
> [II, ii]

Nothing that Macbeth says is more terrible than this, and no dissolution suffered by his world is more ominous. For sleep in Shakespeare is ever the privilege of the good and the reward of the innocent. If it has been put to death there is no goodness left. One of the witches knows how to torture sailors by keeping sleep from their pent-house lids (I, iii), but only Macbeth can murder sleep itself. The result in the play is an ultimate weariness. The "restless ecstasy" with which Macbeth's bed is made miserable, and

> the affliction of these terrible dreams
> That shake us nightly   [III, ii]

—such things are dreadful, but his final fatigue is more dreadful still, for it is the fatigue of a soul that has worn itself out with watching fears, wading in blood, and waking to the necessity of new murders for which the hand has no relish. Macbeth's hope that when Macduff is dead he can "sleep in spite of thunder" (IV, i) is after all no hope. For there is no sleep in Scotland (III, vi), and least of all in a man whose lids have lost the art of closing. And whose heart has lost the power of trembling like a guilty thing.

> The time has been, my senses would have cool'd
> To hear a night-shriek, and my fell of hair
> Would at a dismal treatise rouse and stir
> As life were in 't. I have supp'd full with horrors;
> Direness, familiar to my slaughterous thoughts,
> Cannot once start me.   [V, v]

Terror has degenerated into tedium, and only death can follow, either for Macbeth who lacks the season of all natures or for his lady who not only walks but talks when she should sleep, and who will not die holily in her bed.

Meanwhile, however, another element has gone awry, and it is one so fundamental to man's experience that Shakespeare has given it a central position among those symbols which express the disintegration of the hero's world. Time is out of joint, inoperative, dissolved. "The time has been," says Macbeth, when he could fear; and "the time has been" that when the brains were out a man would die, and there an end (III, iv). The repetition reveals that Macbeth is haunted by a sense that time has slipped its grooves; it flows wild and formless through his world, and is the deep cause of all the anomalies that terrify him. Certain of these anomalies are local or specific: the bell that rings on the night of the murder, the knocking at the gate, the flight of Macduff into England at the very moment Macbeth plans his death, and the disclosure that Macduff was from his mother's womb untimely ripp'd. Many things happen too soon, so that tidings are like serpents that strike without warning. "The King comes here tonight," says a messenger, and Lady Macbeth is startled out of all composure: "Thou 'rt mad to say it!" (I, v). But other anom-

alies are general, and these are the worst. The words of
Banquo to the witches:

> If you can look into the seeds of time,
> And say which grain will grow and which will not,   [I, iii]

plant early in the play a conception of time as something
which fulfills itself by growing—and which, the season being
wrong, can swell to monstrous shape. Or it can find crannies
in the mold and extend secret, sinister roots into dark soil that
never has known them. Or it can have no growth at all; it can
rot and fester in its place, and die. The conception wavers,
like the courage of Macbeth, but it will not away. Duncan
welcomes Macbeth to Forres with the words:

> I have begun to plant thee, and will labour
> To make thee full of growing.   [I, iv]

But Macbeth, like time itself, will burgeon beyond bounds.
"Nature's germens" will

> > tumble all together,
> Even till destruction sicken.   [IV, i]

When Lady Macbeth, greeting her husband, says with ex-
cited assurance:

> Thy letters have transported me beyond
> This ignorant present, and I feel now
> The future in the instant,   [I, v]

she cannot suspect, nor can he, how sadly the relation between present and future will maintain itself. If the present
is the womb or seed-bed of the future, if time is a succession
of growths each one of which lives cleanly and freely after
the death of the one before it, then what is to prevail will
scarcely be recognizable as time. The seed will not grow; the
future will not be born out of the present; the plant will not
disentangle itself from its bed, but will stick there in still-
birth.

> Thou sure and firm set earth,
> Hear not my steps, which way they walk, for fear
> Thy very stones prate of my whereabout,
> And take the present horror from the time,
> Which now suits with it,   [II, i]

prays Macbeth on the eve of Duncan's death. But time and
horror will not suit so neatly through the nights to come; the
present moment will look like all eternity, and horror will be
smeared on every hour. Macbeth's speech when he comes
back from viewing Duncan's body may have been rehearsed
and is certainly delivered for effect; yet he best knows what
the terms signify:

> Had I but died an hour before this chance,
> I had liv'd a blessed time; for, from this instant,
> There's nothing serious in mortality.   [II, iii]

He has a premonition even now of time's disorders; of his
own premature descent into the sear, the yellow leaf (v, iii);
of his failure like any other man to

> pay his breath
> To time and mortal custom.   [IV, i]

"What, will the line stretch out to the crack of doom?" he
cries when Banquo's eight sons appear to him in the witches'
cavern (IV, i). Time makes sense no longer; its proportions
are strange, its content meaningless. For Lady Macbeth in her
mind's disease the minutes have ceased to march in their true
file and order; her sleep-walking soliloquy (v, i) recapitulates
the play, but there is no temporal design among the fragments
of the past—the blood, the body of Duncan, the fears of her
husband, the ghost of Banquo, the slaughter of Lady Macduff, the ringing of the bell, and again the blood—which float
detached from one another in her memory. And for Macbeth
time has become

> a tale
> Told by an idiot, full of sound and fury,
> Signifying nothing.   [v, v]

Death is dusty, and the future is a limitless desert of tomor-
rows. His reception of the news that Lady Macbeth has died
is like nothing else of a similar sort in Shakespeare. When
Northumberland was told of Hotspur's death he asked his
grief to wait upon his revenge:

> For this I shall have time enough to mourn.
> [*Henry IV*, 2-1, i]

And when Brutus was told of Portia's death he knew how to play the stoic:

> With meditating that she must die once,
> I have the patience to endure it now.
>
> [*Julius Caesar*, IV, iii]

But Macbeth, drugged beyond feeling, supped full with horrors, and tired of nothing so much as of coincidence in calamity, can only say in a voice devoid of tone:

> She should have died hereafter;
> There would have been a time for such a word.   [v, v]

There would, that is, if there were such a thing as time. Then such words as "died" and "hereafter" would have their meaning. Not now, however, for time itself has died.

Duncan was everything that Macbeth is not. We saw him briefly, but the brilliance of his contrast with the thane he trusted has kept his memory beautiful throughout a play whose every other feature has been hideous. He was "meek" and "clear" (I, vii), and his mind was incapable of suspicion. The treachery of Cawdor bewildered him:

> There's no art
> To find the mind's construction in the face.
> He was a gentleman on whom I built
> An absolute trust   [I, iv]

—this at the very moment when Macbeth was being brought in for showers of praise and tears of plenteous joy! For Duncan was a free spirit and could weep, a thing impossible to his murderer's stopped heart. The word "love" was native to his tongue; he used it four times within the twenty lines of his conversation with Lady Macbeth, and its clear beauty as he spoke it was reflected that night in the diamond he sent her by Banquo (II, i). As he approached Macbeth's castle in the late afternoon the building had known its only moment of serenity and fairness. It was because Duncan could look at it and say:

> This castle hath a pleasant seat; the air
> Nimbly and sweetly recommends itself
> Unto our gentle senses.   [I, vi]

The speech itself was nimble, sweet, and gentle; and Banquo's explanation was in tone:

> This guest of summer,
> The temple-haunting martlet, does approve,
> By his loved masonry, that the heaven's breath
> Smells wooingly here; no jutty, frieze,
> Buttress, nor coign of vantage, but this bird
> Hath made his pendent bed and procreant cradle.
> Where they most breed and haunt, I have observ'd
> The air is delicate.

Summer, heaven, wooing, and procreation in the delicate air —such words suited the presence of a king who when later on he was found stabbed in his bed would actually offer a fair sight to guilty eyes. His blood was not like the other blood in the play, thick and fearfully discolored. It was bright and beautiful, as no one better than Macbeth could appreciate:

> Here lay Duncan,
> His silver skin lac'd with his golden blood   [II, iii]

—the silver and the gold went with the diamond, and with Duncan's gentle senses that could smell no treachery though a whole house reeked with it. And Duncan of course could sleep. After life's fitful fever he had been laid where nothing could touch him further (III, ii). No terrible dreams to shake him nightly, and no fears of things lest they come stalking through the world before their time in borrowed shapes.

Our memory of this contrast, much as the doings of the middle play work to muffle it, is what gives power to Malcolm and Macduff at the end.

> Angels are bright still, though the brightest fell.   [IV, iii]

Scotland may seem to have become the grave of men and not their mother (IV, iii); death and danger may claim the whole of that bleeding country; but there is another country to the south where a good king works miracles with his touch. The rest of the world is what it always was; time goes on; events stretch out through space in their proper forms. Shakespeare again has enclosed his evil within a universe of good, his storm center within wide areas of peace. And from this outer

world Malcolm and Macduff will return to heal Scotland of
its ills. Their conversation in London before the pious Edward's palace (iv, iii) is not an interruption of the play; it is
one of its essential parts, glancing forward as it does to a conclusion wherein Macduff can say, "The time is free" (v, viii),
and wherein Malcolm can promise that deeds of justice,
"planted newly with the time," will be performed "in measure, time, and place" (v, viii). Malcolm speaks the language
of the play, but he has recovered its lost idiom. Blood will
cease to flow, movement will recommence, fear will be forgotten, sleep will season every life, and the seeds of time will
blossom in due order. The circle of safety which Shakespeare
has drawn around his central horror is thinly drawn, but it is
finely drawn and it holds.

The Story of the Play

ACT I

MACBETH and Banquo, two commanding generals under King Duncan of Scotland, achieve a signal victory over a rebel army, although the latter is supported by Norwegian troops. On their return from battle the two Scottish generals are accosted by three witches, who hail Macbeth as Thane of Glamis, Thane of Cawdor, and future King of Scotland. Afterwards they promise Banquo that his sons shall sit upon the throne. Macbeth is already Thane of Glamis, but nothing more. While the witches' announcement is yet sounding in his ears, messengers from the King arrive and confer upon him, in Duncan's name, and because of his victory, the title of Thane of Cawdor. This verification of two terms of the witches' greeting leads Macbeth secretly to hope for the third —the throne itself. He communicates this wish to his wife, a cruel, unscrupulous woman, and their joint desire develops into a plot against the King. The monarch, suspecting nothing, seeks to do Macbeth still further honor by visiting him.

ACT II

DURING the visit the King is murdered by Macbeth, aided by his wife. Malcolm and Donalbain, the King's sons, flee the country in terror; and Macbeth seeks to divert suspicion concerning the deed from himself to them. Since the sons have fled, Macbeth, as next heir, is crowned King of Scotland. The third prediction of the witches is accomplished, though at a price of blood.

ACT III

MACBETH, however, is unsatisfied. He bethinks himself that Banquo also was promised something by the Weird Sisters— namely that his children shall one day mount the throne. The thought is galling to Macbeth, who wishes to make the crown secure for his own posterity. He plots to kill Banquo and his only son, Fleance. To further the plot he makes a great feast and invites Banquo and Fleance particularly. On their way thither they are waylaid and Banquo is slain by murderers in Macbeth's employ, but Fleance escapes.

While the slain Banquo's blood is yet warm and flowing, Macbeth's feast is spread. It is indeed a regal repast, and King Macbeth himself says that but one feature is lacking—the presence of his chief guest, Banquo. This he says to divert suspicion, for he has already received news of Banquo's violent end. But scarcely has he uttered the words when the ghost of Banquo appears at Macbeth's seat. No one sees him save Macbeth, but his alarm causes the banquet to break up in confusion.

ACT IV

MACBETH, harried by doubts and fears, resolves upon and obtains another interview with the witches. He is warned to beware of Macduff; he is promised that "none of woman born shall harm Macbeth"; he is advised to fear naught till Birnam wood shall come against him. Still unsatisfied, he demands again to know if Banquo's issue shall reign in the kingdom, and from what the witches show he becomes convinced that the crown is assigned to them. The first news that greets him upon leaving the witches is that Macduff has escaped to England to join forces with Malcolm, the late king's eldest son. Enraged, Macbeth storms Macduff's castle and puts Lady Macduff and her children to the sword.

ACT V

THE QUEEN meanwhile is almost insane over the thought of her own share in Macbeth's crimes. She walks in her sleep and endeavors to wash imaginary bloodstains from her hands. Finally she expires, "as 'tis thought, by self and violent hands."

Macbeth also is growing tired of life, but the hags' last prophecies spur him to renewed effort. He is almost unmanned, therefore, when word is brought that Birnam wood is moving against him; for this was one of the apparently impossible threats of the witches. The moving woods were really branches of the trees of Birnam lopped off and carried by the invading troops of Malcolm and Macduff to protect their advance against him. Still Macbeth believes himself invulnerable, and fearing none save one "that was not born of woman," he rushes forth to battle. He fights with almost superhuman strength and valor till he meets Macduff, against whom he remembers that he has been warned by the witches. At first he shrinks from fighting Macduff, but when brought to bay, exclaims: "I bear a charmed life, which must not yield to one of woman born." "Despair thy charm," retorts his foe, "Macduff was from his mother's womb untimely ripp'd." And in the ensuing duel Macbeth is slain. Malcolm is hailed King of Scotland.

J. WALKER McSPADDEN

List of Characters

DUNCAN, *king of Scotland*

MALCOLM,
DONALBAIN, } *his sons*

MACBETH,
BANQUO, } *generals of the King's army*

MACDUFF,
LENNOX,
ROSS,
MENTEITH,
ANGUS,
CAITHNESS, } *noblemen of Scotland*

FLEANCE, *son to* BANQUO

SIWARD, *earl of Northumberland, general of the English forces*

Young SIWARD, *his son*

SEYTON, *an officer attending on* MACBETH

Boy, *son to* MACDUFF

An English Doctor

A Scotch Doctor

A Sergeant

A Porter

An Old Man

Lady MACBETH

Lady MACDUFF

Gentlewoman attending on Lady MACBETH

HECATE

Three Witches

Apparitions

Lords, Gentlemen, Officers, Soldiers, Murderers, Attendants, and Messengers

THE THREE WITCHES

MACBETH

Lady MACBETH

MALCOLM

Macbeth

SCENE — SCOTLAND; ENGLAND.

ACT I

SCENE I — *A deserted place.*

Thunder and lightning. Enter three WITCHES.]

FIRST WITCH. When shall we three meet again
  In thunder, lightning, or in rain?

SECOND WITCH. When the hurlyburly's done,
  When the battle's lost and won.

THIRD WITCH. That will be ere the set of sun.

FIRST WITCH. Where the place?

SECOND WITCH.　　　　　　　　Upon the heath.

THIRD WITCH. There to meet with Macbeth.

FIRST WITCH. I come, Graymalkin.

ALL. Paddock calls:—anon!
  Fair is foul, and foul is fair.
  Hover through the fog and filthy air.　　　　　　　*[Exeunt.*

SCENE II — *A camp near* FORRES.

Alarum within. Enter DUNCAN, MALCOLM, DONALBAIN,
  LENNOX, *with* ATTENDANTS, *meeting a bleeding*
  SERGEANT.]

DUNCAN. What bloody man is that? He can report,
  As seemeth by his plight, of the revolt of
  The newest state.

MALCOLM.　　　　　This is the sergeant
  Who like a good and hardy soldier fought
  'Gainst my captivity. Hail, brave friend!
  Say to the king the knowledge of the broil
  As thou didst leave it.

SERGEANT.　　　　　Doubtful it stood;
  As two spent swimmers, that do cling together

And choke their art. The merciless Macdonwald—
Worthy to be a rebel, for to that
The multiplying villainies of nature
Do swarm upon him—from the western isles
Of kerns and gallowglasses is supplied;
And fortune, on his damned quarrel smiling,
Show'd like a rebel's whore: but all's too weak:
For brave Macbeth—well he deserves that name—
Disdaining fortune, with his brandish'd steel,
Which smoked with bloody execution,
Like valor's minion carved out his passage
Till he faced the slave;
Which ne'er shook hands, nor bade farewell to him,
Till he unseam'd him from the nave to the chaps,
And fix'd his head upon our battlements.

DUNCAN. O valiant cousin! worthy gentleman!

SERGEANT. As whence the sun 'gins his reflection
Shipwrecking storms and direful thunders break,
So from that spring whence comfort seem'd to come
Discomfort swells. Mark, king of Scotland, mark:
No sooner justice had, with valor arm'd,
Compell'd these skipping kerns to trust their heels,
But the Norweyan lord, surveying vantage,
With furbish'd arms and new supplies of men,
Began a fresh assault.

DUNCAN.   Dismay'd not this
Our captains, Macbeth and Banquo?

SERGEANT.   Yes;
As sparrows eagles, or the hare the lion.
If I say sooth, I must report they were
As cannons overcharged with double cracks; so they
Doubly redoubled strokes upon the foe:
Except they meant to bathe in reeking wounds,
Or memorize another Golgotha,
I cannot tell—
But I am faint; my gashes cry for help.

DUNCAN. So well thy words become thee as thy wounds;
They smack of honor both. Go get him surgeons.

                              [*Exit* SERGEANT, *attended.*

Who comes here?

Enter ROSS.]

MALCOLM.   The worthy thane of Ross.
LENNOX. What a haste looks through his eyes! So should he
    look
  That seems to speak things strange.
ROSS.   God save the king!
DUNCAN. Whence camest thou, worthy thane?
ROSS.   From Fife, great king;
  Where the Norweyan banners flout the sky
  And fan our people cold. Norway himself
  With terrible numbers,
  Assisted by that most disloyal traitor
  The thane of Cawdor, began a dismal conflict;
  Till that Bellona's bridegroom, lapp'd in proof,
  Confronted him with self-comparisons,
  Point against point rebellious, arm 'gainst arm,
  Curbing his lavish spirit: and, to conclude,
  The victory fell on us.
DUNCAN.   Great happiness!
ROSS. That now
  Sweno, the Norway's-king, craves composition;
  Nor would we deign him burial of his men
  Till he disbursed, at Saint Colme's inch,
  Ten thousand dollars to our general use.
DUNCAN. No more that thane of Cawdor shall deceive
  Our bosom interest: go pronounce his present death,
  And with his former title greet Macbeth.
ROSS. I'll see it done.
DUNCAN. What he hath lost, noble Macbeth hath won.
                                              [*Exeunt.*

SCENE III — *A heath.*

Thunder. Enter the three WITCHES.]
FIRST WITCH. Where hast thou been, sister?
SECOND WITCH. Killing swine.
THIRD WITCH. Sister, where thou?
FIRST WITCH. A sailor's wife had chestnuts in her lap,
  And mounch'd, and mounch'd, and mounch'd.
  'Give me,' quoth I:
  'Aroint thee, witch!' the rump-fed ronyon cries.
  Her husband's to Aleppo gone, master o' the Tiger;

But in a sieve I'll thither sail,
And, like a rat without a tail,
I'll do, I'll do, and I'll do.
SECOND WITCH. I'll give thee a wind.
FIRST WITCH. Thou'rt kind.
THIRD WITCH. And I another.
FIRST WITCH. I myself have all the other;
And the very ports they blow,
All the quarters that they know
I' the shipman's card.
I will drain him dry as hay:
Sleep shall neither night nor day
Hang upon his pent-house lid;
He shall live a man forbid:
Weary se'nnights nine times nine
Shall he dwindle, peak, and pine:
Though his bark cannot be lost,
Yet it shall be tempest-tost.
Look what I have.
SECOND WITCH. Show me, show me.
FIRST WITCH. Here I have a pilot's thumb,
Wreck'd as homeward he did come.   [*Drum within.*
THIRD WITCH. A drum, a drum!
Macbeth doth come.
ALL. The weird sisters, hand in hand,
Posters of the sea and land,
Thus do go about, about:
Thrice to thine, and thrice to mine,
And thrice again, to make up nine.
Peace! the charm's wound up.
Enter MACBETH *and* BANQUO.]
MACBETH. So foul and fair a day I have not seen.
BANQUO. How far is't call'd to Forres? What are these
So wither'd, and so wild in their attire,
That look not like the inhabitants o' the earth,
And yet are on't? Live you? or are you aught
That man may question? You seem to understand me,
By each at once her choppy finger laying
Upon her skinny lips: you should be women,
And yet your beards forbid me to interpret
That you are so.
MACBETH.   Speak, if you can: what are you?

FIRST WITCH. All hail, Macbeth! hail to thee, thane of Glamis!

SECOND WITCH. All hail, Macbeth! hail to thee, thane of Cawdor!

THIRD WITCH. All hail, Macbeth, thou shalt be king hereafter!

BANQUO. Good sir, why do you start, and seem to fear
    Things that do sound so fair? I' the name of truth,
    Are ye fantastical, or that indeed
    Which outwardly ye show? My noble partner
    You greet with present grace and great prediction
    Of noble having and of royal hope,
    That he seems rapt withal: to me you speak not:
    If you can look into the seeds of time,
    And say which grain will grow and which will not,
    Speak then to me, who neither beg nor fear
    Your favors nor your hate.

FIRST WITCH. Hail!

SECOND WITCH. Hail!

THIRD WITCH. Hail!

FIRST WITCH. Lesser than Macbeth, and greater.

SECOND WITCH. Not so happy, yet much happier.

THIRD WITCH. Thou shalt get kings, though thou be none:
    So all hail, Macbeth and Banquo!

FIRST WITCH. Banquo and Macbeth, all hail!

MACBETH. Stay, you imperfect speakers, tell me more:
    By Sinel's death I know I am thane of Glamis;
    But how of Cawdor? the thane of Cawdor lives,
    A prosperous gentleman; and to be king
    Stands not within the prospect of belief,
    No more than to be Cawdor. Say from whence
    You owe this strange intelligence? or why
    Upon this blasted heath you stop our way
    With such prophetic greeting? Speak, I charge you.
                            [WITCHES *vanish.*

BANQUO. The earth hath bubbles as the water has,
    And these are of them: whither are they vanish'd?

MACBETH. Into the air, and what seem'd corporal melted
    As breath into the wind. Would they had stay'd!

BANQUO. Were such things here as we do speak about?
    Or have we eaten on the insane root
    That takes the reason prisoner?

MACBETH. Your children shall be kings.

BANQUO.   You shall be king.

MACBETH. And thane of Cawdor too: were it not so?

BANQUO. To the selfsame tune and words. Who's here?

Enter ROSS *and* ANGUS.]

ROSS. The king hath happily received, Macbeth,
    The news of thy success: and when he reads
    Thy personal venture in the rebels' fight,
    His wonders and his praises do contend
    Which should be thine or his: silenced with that,
    In viewing o'er the rest o' the selfsame day,
    He finds thee in the stout Norweyan ranks,
    Nothing afeard of what thyself did'st make,
    Strange images of death. As thick as hail
    Came post with post, and every one did bear
    Thy praises in his kingdom's great defense,
    And pour'd them down before him.

ANGUS.   We are sent
    To give thee, from our royal master, thanks;
    Only to herald thee into his sight,
    Not pay thee.

ROSS. And for an earnest of a greater honor,
    He bade me, from him, call thee thane of Cawdor:
    In which addition, hail, most worthy thane!
    For it is thine.

BANQUO.   What, can the devil speak true?

MACBETH. The thane of Cawdor lives: why do you dress me
    In borrow'd robes?

ANGUS.   Who was the thane lives yet,
    But under heavy judgment bears that life
    Which he deserves to lose. Whether he was combined
    With those of Norway, or did line the rebel
    With hidden help and vantage, or that with both
    He labor'd in his country's wreck, I know not;
    But treasons capital, confess'd and proved,
    Have overthrown him.

MACBETH. [*Aside*]   Glamis, and thane of Cawdor:
    The greatest is behind.—Thanks for your pains.—
    Do you not hope your children shall be kings,
    When those that gave the thane of Cawdor to me
    Promised no less to them?

BANQUO.   That, trusted home,
    Might yet enkindle you unto the crown,

Besides the thane of Cawdor. But 'tis strange:
And oftentimes, to win us to our harm,
The instruments of darkness tell us truths,
Win us with honest trifles, to betray 's
In deepest consequence.
Cousins, a word, I pray you.

MACBETH. [*Aside*]   Two truths are told,
As happy prologues to the swelling act
Of the imperial theme.—I thank you, gentlemen.—
[*Aside*] This supernatural soliciting
Cannot be ill; cannot be good: if ill,
Why hath it given me earnest of success,
Commencing in a truth? I am thane of Cawdor:
If good, why do I yield to that suggestion
Whose horrid image doth unfix my hair
And make my seated heart knock at my ribs,
Against the use of nature? Present fears
Are less than horrible imaginings:
My thought, whose murder yet is but fantastical,
Shakes so my single state of man that function
Is smother'd in surmise, and nothing is
But what is not.

BANQUO.   Look, how our partner's rapt.

MACBETH. [*Aside*] If chance will have me king, why, chance
  may crown me,
Without my stir.

BANQUO.   New honors come upon him,
Like our strange garments, cleave not to their mold
But with the aid of use.

MACBETH. [*Aside*]   Come what come may,
Time and the hour runs through the roughest day.

BANQUO. Worthy Macbeth, we stay upon your leisure.

MACBETH. Give me your favor: my dull brain was wrought
With things forgotten. Kind gentlemen, your pains
Are register'd where every day I turn
The leaf to read them. Let us toward the king.
Think upon what hath chanced, and at more time,
The interim having weigh'd it, let us speak
Our free hearts each to other.

BANQUO.   Very gladly.

MACBETH. Till then, enough. Come, friends.   [*Exeunt.*

SCENE IV — FORRES. *The palace.*

Flourish. Enter DUNCAN, MALCOLM, DONALBAIN,
    LENNOX, *and* ATTENDANTS.]

DUNCAN. Is execution done on Cawdor? Are not
    Those in commission yet return'd?

MALCOLM.   My liege,
    They are not yet come back. But I have spoke
    With one that saw him die, who did report
    That very frankly he confess'd his treasons,
    Implored your highness' pardon and set forth
    A deep repentance: nothing in his life
    Became him like the leaving it; he died
    As one that had been studied in his death,
    To throw away the dearest thing he owed
    As 'twere a careless trifle.

DUNCAN.   There's no art
    To find the mind's construction in the face:
    He was a gentleman on whom I built
    An absolute trust.

Enter MACBETH, BANQUO, ROSS, *and* ANGUS.]
                O worthiest cousin!
    The sin of my ingratitude even now
    Was heavy on me: thou art so far before,
    That swiftest wing of recompense is slow
    To overtake thee. Would thou hadst less deserved,
    That the proportion both of thanks and payment
    Might have been mine! only I have left to say,
    More is thy due than more than all can pay.

MACBETH. The service and the loyalty I owe,
    In doing it, pays itself. Your highness' part
    Is to receive our duties; and our duties
    Are to your throne and state children and servants;
    Which do but what they should, by doing every thing
    Safe toward your love and honor.

DUNCAN.   Welcome hither:
    I have begun to plant thee, and will labor
    To make thee full of growing. Noble Banquo,
    That hast no less deserved, nor must be known
    No less to have done so: let me infold thee
    And hold thee to my heart.

BANQUO.   There if I grow,
  The harvest is your own.
DUNCAN.   My plenteous joys,
  Wanton in fullness, seek to hide themselves
  In drops of sorrow. Sons, kinsmen, thanes,
  And you whose places are the nearest, know,
  We will establish our estate upon
  Our eldest, Malcolm, whom we name hereafter
  The Prince of Cumberland: which honor must
  Not unaccompanied invest him only,
  But signs of nobleness, like stars, shall shine
  On all deservers. From hence to Inverness,
  And bind us further to you.
MACBETH. The rest is labor, which is not used for you:
  I'll be myself the harbinger, and make joyful
  The hearing of my wife with your approach;
  So humbly take my leave.
DUNCAN.   My worthy Cawdor!
MACBETH. [*Aside*] The Prince of Cumberland! that is a step
  On which I must fall down, or else o'erleap,
  For in my way it lies. Stars, hide your fires;
  Let not light see my black and deep desires:
  The eye wink at the hand; yet let that be
  Which the eye fears, when it is done, to see.   [*Exit.*
DUNCAN. True, worthy Banquo; he is full so valiant,
  And in his commendations I am fed;
  It is a banquet to me. Let's after him,
  Whose care is gone before to bid us welcome:
  It is a peerless kinsman.   [*Flourish. Exeunt.*

SCENE V — INVERNESS. MACBETH's *castle.*

Enter LADY MACBETH, *reading a letter.*]

LADY MACBETH. 'They met me in the day of success; and I
  have learned by the perfectest report, they have more in
  them than mortal knowledge. When I burned in desire
  to question them further, they made themselves air, into
  which they vanished. Whiles I stood rapt in the wonder of
  it, came missives from the king, who all-hailed me "Thane
  of Cawdor;" by which title, before, these weird sisters
  saluted me, and referred me to the coming on of time, with
  "Hail, king that shalt be!" This have I thought good to

deliver thee, my dearest partner of greatness, that thou
mightst not lose the dues of rejoicing, by being ignorant
of what greatness is promised thee. Lay it to thy heart, and
farewell.'
Glamis thou art, and Cawdor, and shalt be
What thou art promised: yet do I fear thy nature;
It is too full o' the milk of human kindness
To catch the nearest way: thou wouldst be great;
Are not without ambition, but without
The illness should attend it: what thou wouldst highly,
That wouldst thou holily; wouldst not play false,
And yet wouldst wrongly win; thou 'ldst have, great Glamis,
That which cries 'Thus thou must do, if thou have it;
And that which rather thou dost fear to do
Than wishest should be undone.' Hie thee hither,
That I may pour my spirits in thine ear,
And chastise with the valor of my tongue
All that impedes thee from the golden round,
Which fate and metaphysical aid doth seem
To have thee crown'd withal.

Enter a MESSENGER.]

                                        What is your tidings?
MESSENGER. The king comes here to-night.
LADY MACBETH.   Thou 'rt mad to say it:
Is not thy master with him? who, were 't so,
Would have inform'd for preparation.
MESSENGER. So please you, it is true: our thane is coming:
One of my fellows had the speed of him,
Who, almost dead for breath, had scarcely more
Than would make up his message.
LADY MACBETH.   Give him tending;
He brings great news.   [*Exit* MESSENGER.
                          The raven himself is hoarse
That croaks the fatal entrance of Duncan
Under my battlements. Come, you spirits
That tend on mortal thoughts, unsex me here,
And fill me, from the crown to the toe, top-full
Of direst cruelty! make thick my blood,
Stop up the access and passage to remorse,
That no compunctious visitings of nature
Shake my fell purpose, nor keep peace between
The effect and it! Come to my woman's breasts,

And take my milk for gall, you murdering ministers,
Wherever in your sightless substances
You wait on nature's mischief! Come, thick night,
And pall thee in the dunnest smoke of hell,
That my keen knife see not the wound it makes,
Nor heaven peep through the blanket of the dark,
To cry 'Hold, hold!'

Enter MACBETH.]

                          Great Glamis! worthy Cawdor!
Greater than both, by the all-hail hereafter!
Thy letters have transported me beyond
This ignorant present, and I feel now
The future in the instant.

MACBETH.   My dearest love,
Duncan comes here to-night.

LADY MACBETH.   And when goes hence?

MACBETH. To-morrow, as he purposes.

LADY MACBETH.   O, never
Shall sun that morrow see!
Your face, my thane, is as a book where men
May read strange matters. To beguile the time,
Look like the time; bear welcome in your eye,
Your hand, your tongue: look like the innocent flower,
But be the serpent under 't. He that's coming
Must be provided for: and you shall put
This night's great business into my dispatch;
Which shall to all our nights and days to come
Give solely sovereign sway and masterdom.

MACBETH. We will speak further.

LADY MACBETH.   Only look up clear;
To alter favor ever is to fear:
Leave all the rest to me.   [*Exeunt.*

S C E N E VI — *Before* MACBETH's *castle.*

Hautboys and torches. Enter DUNCAN, MALCOLM,
        DONALBAIN, BANQUO, LENNOX, MACDUFF,
        ROSS, ANGUS, *and* ATTENDANTS.]

DUNCAN. This castle hath a pleasant seat; the air
Nimbly and sweetly recommends itself
Unto our gentle senses.

BANQUO.   This guest of summer,

The temple-haunting martlet, does approve
By his loved mansionry that the heaven's breath
Smells wooingly here: no jutty, frieze,
Buttress, nor coign of vantage, but this bird
Hath made his pendant bed and procreant cradle:
Where they most breed and haunt, I have observed
The air is delicate.

Enter LADY MACBETH.]

DUNCAN.   See, see, our honor'd hostess!
The love that follows us sometime is our trouble,
Which still we thank as love. Herein I teach you
How you shall bid God 'ild us for your pains,
And thank us for your trouble.

LADY MACBETH.   All our service
In every point twice done, and then done double,
Were poor and single business to contend
Against those honors deep and broad wherewith
Your majesty loads our house: for those of old,
And the late dignities heap'd up to them,
We rest your hermits.

DUNCAN.   Where's the thane of Cawdor?
We coursed him at the heels, and had a purpose
To be his purveyor: but he rides well,
And his great love, sharp as his spur, hath holp him
To his home before us. Fair and noble hostess,
We are your guest to-night.

LADY MACBETH.   Your servants ever
Have theirs, themselves, and what is theirs, in compt,
To make their audit at your highness' pleasure,
Still to return your own.

DUNCAN.   Give me your hand;
Conduct me to mine host: we love him highly,
And shall continue our graces towards him.
By your leave, hostess.   [*Exeunt.*

S C E N E VII — MACBETH'S *castle.*

Hautboys and torches. Enter a SEWER, *and divers*
    SERVANTS *with dishes and service, and pass*
     over the stage. Then enter MACBETH.]

MACBETH. If it were done when 'tis done, then 'twere well
It were done quickly: if the assassination

Could trammel up the consequence, and catch,
With his surcease, success; that but this blow
Might be the be-all and the end-all here,
But here, upon this bank and shoal of time,
We 'ld jump the life to come. But in these cases
We still have judgment here; that we but teach
Bloody instructions, which being taught return
To plague the inventor: this even-handed justice
Commends the ingredients of our poison'd chalice
To our own lips. He's here in double trust:
First, as I am his kinsman and his subject,
Strong both against the deed; then, as his host,
Who should against his murderer shut the door,
Not bear the knife myself. Besides, this Duncan
Hath borne his faculties so meek, hath been
So clear in his great office, that his virtues
Will plead like angels trumpet-tongued against
The deep damnation of his taking-off:
And pity, like a naked new-born babe,
Striding the blast, or heaven's cherubin horsed
Upon the sightless couriers of the air,
Shall blow the horrid deed in every eye,
That tears shall drown the wind. I have no spur
To prick the sides of my intent, but only
Vaulting ambition, which o'erleaps itself
And falls on the other.

Enter LADY MACBETH.]

                  How now! what news?

LADY MACBETH. He has almost supp'd: why have you left the
    chamber?

MACBETH. Hath he ask'd for me?

LADY MACBETH.   Know you not he has?

MACBETH. We will proceed no further in this business:
    He hath honor'd me of late; and I have bought
    Golden opinions from all sorts of people,
    Which would be worn now in their newest gloss,
    Not cast aside so soon.

LADY MACBETH.   Was the hope drunk
    Wherein you dress'd yourself? hath it slept since?
    And wakes it now, to look so green and pale
    At what it did so freely? From this time
    Such I account thy love. Art thou afeard

    To be the same in thine own act and valor
As thou art in desire? Would'st thou have that
Which thou esteem'st the ornament of life,
And live a coward in thine own esteem,
Letting 'I dare not' wait upon 'I would,'
Like the poor cat i' the adage?

MACBETH.   Prithee, peace:
I dare do all that may become a man;
Who dares do more is none.

LADY MACBETH.   What beast was 't then
That made you break this enterprise to me?
When you durst do it, then you were a man;
And, to be more than what you were, you would
Be so much more the man. Nor time nor place
Did then adhere. and yet you would make both:
They have made themselves, and that their fitness now
Does unmake you. I have given suck, and know
How tender 'tis to love the babe that milks me:
I would, while it was smiling in my face,
Have pluck'd my nipple from his boneless gums,
And dash'd the brains out, had I so sworn as you
Have done to this.

MACBETH.   If we should fail?

LADY MACBETH.   We fail!
But screw your courage to the sticking-place,
And we'll not fail. When Duncan is asleep—
Whereto the rather shall his day's hard journey
Soundly invite him—his two chamberlains
Will I with wine and wassail so convince,
That memory, the warder of the brain,
Shall be a fume, and the receipt of reason
A limbec only: when in swinish sleep
Their drenched natures lie as in a death,
What cannot you and I perform upon
The unguarded Duncan? what not put upon
His spongy officers, who shall bear the guilt
Of our great quell?

MACBETH.   Bring forth men-children only;
For thy undaunted mettle should compose
Nothing but males. Will it not be received,
When we have mark'd with blood those sleepy two

Of his own chamber, and used their very daggers,
That they have done 't?

LADY MACBETH.   Who dares receive it other,
As we shall make our griefs and clamor roar
Upon his death?

MACBETH.   I am settled, and bend up
Each corporal agent to this terrible feat.
Away, and mock the time with fairest show:
False face must hide what the false heart doth know.

                                        [*Exeunt.*

ACT II

SCENE I—INVERNESS. *Court of* MACBETH'S *castle.*

Enter BANQUO, *and* FLEANCE *bearing a torch before him.*]

BANQUO. How goes the night, boy?

FLEANCE. The moon is down; I have not heard the clock.

BANQUO. And she goes down at twelve.

FLEANCE.　　　　　　　　　　　I take 't, 'tis later, sir.

BANQUO. Hold, take my sword. There's husbandry in heaven,
　Their candles are all out. Take thee that too.
　A heavy summons lies like lead upon me,
　And yet I would not sleep. Merciful powers,
　Restrain in me the cursed thoughts that nature
　Gives way to in repose!

Enter MACBETH, *and a* SERVANT *with a torch.*]

　　　　　　　　　　　　Give me my sword.
　Who's there?

MACBETH. A friend.

BANQUO. What, sir, not yet at rest? The king's a-bed:
　He hath been in unusual pleasure, and
　Sent forth great largess to your offices:
　This diamond he greets your wife withal,
　By the name of most kind hostess; and shut up
　In measureless content.

MACBETH.　　　　　　　　　　Being unprepared,
　Our will became the servant to defect,
　Which else should free have wrought.

BANQUO.　　　　　　　　　　　　　　All's well.
　I dreamt last night of the three weird sisters:
　To you they have show'd some truth.

MACBETH.　　　　　　　　　　　　I think not of them:
　Yet, when we can entreat an hour to serve,
　We would spend it in some words upon that business,
　If you would grant the time.

BANQUO.　　　　　　　　　　At your kind'st leisure.

MACBETH. If you shall cleave to my consent, when 'tis,
　It shall make honor for you.

BANQUO.　　　　　　　　　So I lose none

In seeking to augment it, but still keep
My bosom franchised and allegiance clear,
I shall be counsel'd.

MACBETH.   Good repose the while!

BANQUO. Thanks, sir: the like to you!

                    [*Exeunt* BANQUO *and* FLEANCE.

MACBETH. Go bid thy mistress, when my drink is ready,
    She strike upon the bell. Get thee to bed.   [*Exit* SERVANT.
    Is this a dagger which I see before me,
    The handle toward my hand? Come, let me clutch thee.
    I have thee not, and yet I see thee still.
    Art thou not, fatal vision, sensible
    To feeling as to sight? or art thou but
    A dagger of the mind, a false creation,
    Proceeding from the heat-oppressed brain?
    I see thee yet, in form as palpable
    As this which now I draw.
    Thou marshal'st me the way that I was going;
    And such an instrument I was to use.
    Mine eyes are made the fools o' the other senses,
    Or else worth all the rest: I see thee still;
    And on thy blade and dudgeon gouts of blood,
    Which was not so before. There's no such thing:
    It is the bloody business which informs
    Thus to mine eyes. Now o'er the one half-world
    Nature seems dead, and wicked dreams abuse
    The curtain'd sleep; witchcraft celebrates
    Pale Hecate's offerings; and wither'd murder,
    Alarum'd by his sentinel, the wolf,
    Whose howl's his watch, thus with his stealthy pace,
    With Tarquin's ravishing strides, towards his design
    Moves like a ghost. Thou sure and firm-set earth,
    Hear not my steps, which way they walk, for fear
    Thy very stones prate of my whereabout,
    And take the present horror from the time,
    Which now suits with it. Whiles I threat, he lives:
    Words to the heat of deeds too cold breath gives.

                    [*A bell rings.*

    I go, and it is done: the bell invites me.
    Hear it not, Duncan, for it is a knell
    That summons thee to heaven, or to hell.   [*Exit.*

SCENE II — *The same.*

Enter LADY MACBETH.]

LADY MACBETH. That which hath made them drunk hath made
　　me bold;
　　What hath quench'd them hath given me fire. Hark! Peace!
　　It was the owl that shriek'd, the fatal bellman,
　　Which gives the stern'st good-night. He is about it:
　　The doors are open, and the surfeited grooms
　　Do mock their charge with snores. I have drugg'd their
　　　possets,
　　That death and nature do contend about them,
　　Whether they live or die.

MACBETH. [*Within*]　　　Who's there? what, ho!

LADY MACBETH. Alack, I am afraid they have awaked
　　And 'tis not done: the attempt and not the deed
　　Confounds us. Hark! I laid their daggers ready;
　　He could not miss 'em. Had he not resembled
　　My father as he slept, I had done 't.

Enter MACBETH.]

　　　　　　　　　　　My husband!

MACBETH. I have done the deed. Didst thou not hear a noise?

LADY MACBETH. I heard the owl scream and the crickets cry.
　　Did not you speak?

MACBETH.　　　　　When?

LADY MACBETH.　　　　Now.

MACBETH.　　　　　　As I descended?

LADY MACBETH. Aye.

MACBETH. Hark!
　　Who lies i' the second chamber?

LADY MACBETH.　　　　　　Donalbain.

MACBETH. This is a sorry sight.　　　[*Looking on his hands.*

LADY MACBETH. A foolish thought, to say a sorry sight.

MACBETH. There's one did laugh in 's sleep, and one cried
　　'Murder!'
　　That they did wake each other: I stood and heard them:
　　But they did say their prayers, and address'd them
　　Again to sleep.

LADY MACBETH. There are two lodged together.

MACBETH. One cried 'God bless us!' and 'Amen' the other,
　　As they had seen me with these hangman's hands:

Listening their fear, I could not say 'Amen,'
When they did say 'God bless us!'

LADY MACBETH. Consider it not so deeply.

MACBETH. But wherefore could not I pronounce 'Amen'?
I had most need of blessing, and 'Amen'
Stuck in my throat.

LADY MACBETH.　　　　　　These deeds must not be thought
After these ways; so, it will make us mad.

MACBETH. Methought I heard a voice cry 'Sleep no more!
Macbeth does murder sleep'—the innocent sleep,
Sleep that knits up the ravel'd sleave of care,
The death of each day's life, sore labor's bath,
Balm of hurt minds, great nature's second course,
Chief nourisher in life's feast,—

LADY MACBETH.　　　　　　　　What do you mean?

MACBETH. Still it cried 'Sleep no more!' to all the house:
'Glamis hath murder'd sleep, and therefore Cawdor
Shall sleep no more: Macbeth shall sleep no more.'

LADY MACBETH. Who was it that thus cried? Why, worthy
　　thane,
You do unbend your noble strength, to think
So brainsickly of things. Go get some water,
And wash this filthy witness from your hand.
Why did you bring these daggers from the place?
They must lie there: go carry them, and smear
The sleepy grooms with blood.

MACBETH.　　　　　　　　　　　I'll go no more:
I am afraid to think what I have done;
Look on 't again I dare not.

LADY MACBETH.　　　　　　　Infirm of purpose!
Give me the daggers: the sleeping and the dead
Are but as pictures: 'tis the eye of childhood
That fears a painted devil. If he do bleed,
I'll gild the faces of the grooms withal,
For it must seem their quilt.　　　　[*Exit. Knocking within.*

MACBETH.　　　　　　　　　Whence is that knocking?
How is 't with me, when every noise appals me?
What hands are here? ha! they pluck out mine eyes!
Will all great Neptune's ocean wash this blood
Clean from my hand? No; this my hand will rather
The multitudinous seas incarnadine,
Making the green one red.

Re-enter LADY MACBETH.]

LADY MACBETH. My hands are of your color, but I shame
 To wear a heart so white. [*Knocking within.*] I hear a
  knocking
 At the south entry: retire we to our chamber:
 A little water clears us of this deed:
 How easy it is then! Your constancy
 Hath left you unattended. [*Knocking within.*] Hark! more
  knocking:
 Get on your nightgown, lest occasion call us
 And show us to be watchers: be not lost
 So poorly in your thoughts.

MACBETH. To know my deed, 'twere best not know myself.
           [*Knocking within.*]
 Wake Duncan with thy knocking! I would thou could'st!
             [*Exeunt.*

SCENE III — *The same.*

Enter a PORTER. *Knocking within.*]

PORTER. Here's a knocking indeed! If a man were porter of
hell-gate, he should have old turning the key. [*Knocking
within.*] Knock, knock, knock! Who's there, i' the name of
Beelzebub? Here's a farmer, that hanged himself on th'
expectation of plenty: come in time; have napkins enow
about you; here you'll sweat for 't. [*Knocking within.*]
Knock, knock! Who's there, in th' other devil's name?
Faith, here's an equivocator, that could swear in both the
scales against either scale; who committed treason enough
for God's sake, yet could not equivocate to heaven: O, come
in, equivocator. [*Knocking within.*] Knock, knock, knock!
Who's there? Faith, here's an English tailor come hither, for
stealing out of a French hose: come in, tailor; here you may
roast your goose. [*Knocking within.*] Knock, knock; never
at quiet! What are you? But this place is too cold for hell.
I'll devil-porter it no further: I had thought to have let in
some of all professions, that go the primrose way to the
everlasting bonfire. [*Knocking within.*] Anon, anon! I pray
you, remember the porter.   [*Opens the gate.*

Enter MACDUFF *and* LENNOX.]

MACDUFF. Was it so late, friend, ere you went to bed,
 That you do lie so late?

PORTER. Faith, sir, we were carousing till the second cock:
and drink, sir, is a great provoker of three things.

MACDUFF. What three things does drink especially provoke?

PORTER. Marry, sir, nose-painting, sleep and urine. Lechery,
sir, it provokes and unprovokes; it provokes the desire, but
it takes away the performance: therefore much drink may
be said to be an equivocator with lechery; it makes him and
it mars him; it sets him on and it takes him off; it persuades
him and disheartens him; makes him stand to and not stand
to; in conclusion, equivocates him in a sleep, and giving him
the lie, leaves him.

MACDUFF. I believe drink gave thee the lie last night.

PORTER. That it did, sir, i' the very throat on me: but I re-
quited him for his lie, and, I think, being too strong for
him, though he took up my leg sometime, yet I made a
shift to cast him.

MACDUFF. Is thy master stirring?

Enter MACBETH.]

    Our knocking has awaked him; here he comes.

LENNOX. Good morrow, noble sir.

MACBETH.   Good morrow, both.

MACDUFF. Is the king stirring, worthy thane?

MACBETH.   Not yet.

MACDUFF. He did command me to call timely on him: I had
almost slipp'd the hour.

MACBETH.   I'll bring you to him.

MACDUFF. I know this is a joyful trouble to you;
But yet 'tis one.

MACBETH. The labor we delight in physics pain.
This is the door.

MACDUFF.   I'll make so bold to call,
For 'tis my limited service.   [*Exit.*

LENNOX. Goes to the king hence to-day?

MACBETH.   He does; he did appoint so.

LENNOX. The night has been unruly: where we lay,
Our chimneys were blown down, and, as they say,
Lamentings heard i' the air, strange screams of death,
And prophesying with accents terrible
Of dire combustion and confused events
New hatch'd to the woeful time: the obscure bird

Clamor'd the livelong night: some say, the earth
Was feverous and did shake.

MACBETH.　　　　　　　　'Twas a rough night.

LENNOX. My young remembrance cannot parallel
A fellow to it.

Re-enter MACDUFF.]

MACDUFF. O horror, horror, horror! Tongue nor heart
Cannot conceive nor name thee.

MACBETH.⎱
LENNOX. ⎰　　　　　　　What's the matter?

MACDUFF. Confusion now hath made his masterpiece.
Most sacrilegious murder hath broke ope
The Lord's anointed temple, and stole thence
The life o' the building.

MACBETH.　　　　　What is 't you say? the life?

LENNOX. Mean you his majesty?

MACDUFF. Approach the chamber, and destroy your sight
With a new Gorgon: do not bid me speak;
See, and then speak yourselves.

　　　　　　　　　　　[*Exeunt* MACBETH *and* LENNOX.
　　　　　　　　　Awake, awake!

Ring the alarum-bell. Murder and treason!
Banquo and Donalbain! Malcolm! awake!
Shake off this downy sleep, death's counterfeit,
And look on death itself! up, up, and see
The great doom's image! Malcolm! Banquo!
As from your graves rise up, and walk like sprites,
To countenance this horror. Ring the bell.　　[*Bell rings.*

Enter LADY MACBETH.]

LADY MACBETH. What's the business,
That such a hideous trumpet calls to parley
The sleepers of the house? speak, speak!

MACDUFF.　　　　　　　　O gentle lady,
'Tis not for you to hear what I can speak:
The repetition, in a woman's ear,
Would murder as it fell.

Enter BANQUO.]

　　　　　　　O Banquo, Banquo!
Our royal master's murder'd.

LADY MACBETH.　　　　　Woe, alas!
What, in our house?

BANQUO.　　　　　Too cruel any where.

    Dear Duff, I prithee, contradict thyself,
    And say it is not so.

Re-enter MACBETH *and* LENNOX, *with* ROSS.]

MACBETH. Had I but died an hour before this chance,
    I had lived a blessed time; for from this instant
    There's nothing serious in mortality:
    All is but toys: renown and grace is dead;
    The wine of life is drawn, and the mere lees
    Is left this vault to brag of.

Enter MALCOLM *and* DONALBAIN.]

DONALBAIN. What is amiss?

MACBETH.   You are, and do not know 't:
    The spring, the head, the fountain of your blood
    Is stopp'd; the very source of it is stopp'd.

MACDUFF. Your royal father's murder'd.

MALCOLM.   O, by whom?

LENNOX. Those of his chamber, as it seem'd, had done 't:
    Their hands and faces were all badged with blood;
    So were their daggers, which unwiped we found
    Upon their pillows:
    They stared, and were distracted; no man's life
    Was to be trusted with them.

MACBETH. O, yet I do repent me of my fury,
    That I did kill them.

MACDUFF.   Wherefore did you so?

MACBETH. Who can be wise, amazed, temperate and furious,
    Loyal and neutral, in a moment? No man:
    The expedition of my violent love
    Outrun the pauser reason. Here lay Duncan,
    His silver skin laced with his golden blood,
    And his gash'd stabs look'd like a breach in nature
    For ruin's wasteful entrance; there, the murderers,
    Steep'd in the colors of their trade, their daggers
    Unmannerly breech'd with gore: who could refrain,
    That had a heart to love, and in that heart
    Courage to make 's love known?

LADY MACBETH.   Help me hence, ho!

MACDUFF. Look to the lady.

MALCOLM. [*Aside to* DONALBAIN] Why do we hold our
    tongues,
    That most may claim this argument for ours?

DONALBAIN. [*Aside to* MALCOLM] What should be spoken here,
    where our fate,
    Hid in an auger-hole, may rush, and seize us?
    Let's away;
    Our tears are not yet brew'd.
MALCOLM. [*Aside to* DONALBAIN] Nor our strong sorrow
    Upon the foot of motion.
BANQUO.   Look to the lady:
                      [LADY MACBETH *is carried out.*
    And when we have our naked frailties hid,
    That suffer in exposure, let us meet,
    And question this most bloody piece of work,
    To know it further. Fears and scruples shake us:
    In the great hand of God I stand, and thence
    Against the undivulged pretense I fight
    Of treasonous malice.
MACDUFF.   And so do I.
ALL.   So all.
MACBETH. Let's briefly put on manly readiness,
    And meet i' the hall together.
ALL.   Well contented.
        [*Exeunt all but* MALCOLM *and* DONALBAIN.
MALCOLM. What will you do? Let's not consort with them:
    To show an unfelt sorrow is an office
    Which the false man does easy. I'll to England.
DONALBAIN. To Ireland, I; our separated fortune
    Shall keep us both the safer: here we are
    There's daggers in men's smiles: the near in blood,
    The nearer bloody.
MALCOLM.   This murderous shaft that's shot
    Hath not yet lighted, and our safest way
    Is to avoid the aim. Therefore to horse;
    And let us not be dainty of leave-taking,
    But shift away: there's warrant in that theft
    Which steals itself when there's no mercy left.   [*Exeunt.*

SCENE IV — *Outside* MACBETH'S *castle.*

Enter ROSS *with an* OLD MAN.]
OLD MAN. Threescore and ten I can remember well:
    Within the volume of which time I have seen

Hours dreadful and things strange, but this sore night
Hath trifled former knowings.

ROSS.   Ah, good father,
Thou seest, the heavens, as troubled with man's act,
Threaten his bloody stage: by the clock 'tis day,
And yet dark night strangles the traveling lamp:
Is 't night's predominance, or the day's shame,
That darkness does the face of earth entomb,
When living light should kiss it?

OLD MAN.   'Tis unnatural,
Even like the deed that's done. On Tuesday last
A falcon towering in her pride of place
Was by a mousing owl hawk'd at and kill'd.

ROSS. And Duncan's horses—a thing most strange and cer-
    tain—
Beauteous and swift, the minions of their race,
Turn'd wild in nature, broke their stalls, flung out,
Contending 'gainst obedience, as they would make
War with mankind.

OLD MAN.   'Tis said they eat each other.

ROSS. They did so, to the amazement of mine eyes,
That look'd upon 't.

Enter MACDUFF.]
                     Here comes the good Macduff.
How goes the world, sir, now?

MACDUFF.   Why, see you not?

ROSS. Is 't known who did this more than bloody deed?

MACDUFF. Those that Macbeth hath slain.

ROSS.   Alas, the day!
What good could they pretend?

MACDUFF.   They were suborn'd:
Malcolm and Donalbain, the king's two sons,
Are stol'n away and fled, which puts upon them
Suspicion of the deed.

ROSS.   'Gainst nature still:
Thriftless ambition, that wilt ravin up
Thine own life's means! Then 'tis most like
The sovereignty will fall upon Macbeth.

MACDUFF. He is already named, and gone to Scone
To be invested.

ROSS.   Where is Duncan's body?

MACDUFF. Carried to Colme-kill.
  The sacred storehouse of his predecessors
  And guardian of their bones.
ROSS.   Will you to Scone?
MACDUFF. No, cousin, I'll to Fife.
ROSS.   Well, I will thither.
MACDUFF. Well, may you see things well done there: adieu!
  Lest our old robes sit easier than our new!
ROSS. Farewell, father.
OLD MAN. God's benison go with you, and with those
  That would make good of bad and friends of foes!

                                              [*Exeunt.*

ACT III

SCENE I — FORRES. *The palace.*

Enter BANQUO.]

BANQUO. Thou hast it now: king, Cawdor, Glamis, all,
   As the weird women promised, and I fear
   Thou play'dst most foully for 't: yet it was said
   It should not stand in thy posterity,
   But that myself should be the root and father
   Of many kings. If there come truth from them—
   As upon thee, Macbeth, their speeches shine—
   Why, by the verities on thee made good,
   May they not be my oracles as well
   And set me up in hope? But hush, no more.

Sennet sounded. Enter MACBETH, *as king;* LADY
     MACBETH *as queen;* LENNOX, ROSS, LORDS,
     LADIES, *and* ATTENDANTS.]

MACBETH. Here's our chief guest.

LADY MACBETH.   If he had been forgotten,
   It had been as a gap in our great feast,
   And all-thing unbecoming.

MACBETH. To-night we hold a solemn supper, sir,
   And I'll request your presence.

BANQUO.   Let your highness
   Command upon me, to the which my duties
   Are with a most indissoluble tie
   For ever knit.

MACBETH. Ride you this afternoon?

BANQUO. Aye, my good lord.

MACBETH. We should have else desired your good advice,
   Which still hath been both grave and prosperous,
   In this day's council; but we'll take to-morrow.
   Is 't far you ride?

BANQUO. As far, my lord, as will fill up the time
   'Twixt this and supper: go not my horse the better,
   I must become a borrower of the night
   For a dark hour or twain.

MACBETH.   Fail not our feast.

BANQUO. My lord, I will not.

MACBETH. We hear our bloody cousins are bestow'd
　　In England and in Ireland, not confessing
　　Their cruel parricide, filling their hearers
　　With strange invention: but of that to-morrow,
　　When therewithal we shall have cause of state
　　Craving us jointly. Hie you to horse: adieu,
　　Till you return at night. Goes Fleance with you?
BANQUO. Aye, my good lord: our time does call upon 's.
MACBETH. I wish your horses swift and sure of foot,
　　And so I do commend you to their backs.
　　Farewell.　　　　　　　　　　　　[*Exit* BANQUO.
　　Let every man be master of his time
　　Till seven at night; to make society
　　The sweeter welcome, we will keep ourself
　　Till supper-time alone: while then, God be with you!
　　　　　　[*Exeunt all but* MACBETH *and an* ATTENDANT.
　　Sirrah, a word with you: attend those men
　　Our pleasure?
ATTENDANT. They are, my lord, without the palace gate.
MACBETH. Bring them before us.　　　[*Exit* ATTENDANT.
　　　　　　　　　　To be thus is nothing;
　　But to be safely thus: our fears in Banquo
　　Stick deep: and in his royalty of nature
　　Reigns that which would be fear'd: 'tis much he dares,
　　And, to that dauntless temper of his mind,
　　He hath a wisdom that doth guide his valor
　　To act in safety There is none but he
　　Whose being I do fear: and under him
　　My Genius is rebuked, as it is said
　　Mark Antony's was by Cæsar. He chid the sisters,
　　When first they put the name of king upon me,
　　And bade them speak to him; then prophet-like
　　They hail'd him father to a line of kings:
　　Upon my head they placed a fruitless crown
　　And put a barren scepter in my gripe,
　　Thence to be wrench'd with an unlineal hand,
　　No son of mine succeeding. If 't be so,
　　For Banquo's issue have I filed my mind;
　　For them the gracious Duncan have I murder'd;
　　Put rancors in the vessel of my peace
　　Only for them, and mine eternal jewel
　　Given to the common enemy of man,

To make them kings, the seed of Banquo kings!
Rather than so, come, fate, into the list,
And champion me to the utterance! Who's there?
Re-enter ATTENDANT, *with two* MURDERERS.]
Now go to the door, and stay there till we call.

[*Exit* ATTENDANT.

Was it not yesterday we spoke together?
FIRST MURDERER. It was, so please your highness.
MACBETH.   Well then, now
Have you consider'd of my speeches? Know
That it was he in the times past which held you
So under fortune, which you thought had been
Our innocent self: this I made good to you
In our last conference; pass'd in probation with you,
How you were borne in hand, how cross'd, the instruments,
Who wrought with them, and all things else that might
To half a soul and to a notion crazed
Say 'Thus did Banquo.'
FIRST MURDERER.   You made it known to us.
MACBETH. I did so; and went further, which is now
Our point of second meeting. Do you find
Your patience so predominant in your nature,
That you can let this go? Are you so gospell'd,
To pray for this good man and for his issue,
Whose heavy hand hath bow'd you to the grave
And beggar'd yours for ever?
FIRST MURDERER.   We are men, my liege.
MACBETH. Aye, in the catalogue ye go for men;
As hounds and greyhounds, mongrels, spaniels, curs,
Shoughs, water-rugs and demi-wolves, are clept
All by the name of dogs: the valued file
Distinguishes the swift, the slow, the subtle,
The housekeeper, the hunter, every one
According to the gift which bounteous nature
Hath in him closed, whereby he does receive
Particular addition, from the bill
That writes them all alike: and so of men.
Now if you have a station in the file,
Not i' the worst rank of manhood, say it,
And I will put that business in your bosoms
Whose execution takes your enemy off,
Grapples you to the heart and love of us,

Who wear our health but sickly in his life,
Which in his death were perfect.

SECOND MURDERER.   I am one, my liege,
  Whom the vile blows and buffets of the world
  Have so incensed that I am reckless what
  I do to spite the world.

FIRST MURDERER.   And I another
  So weary with disasters, tugg'd with fortune,
  That I would set my life on any chance,
  To mend it or be rid on 't.

MACBETH.   Both of you
  Know Banquo was your enemy.

BOTH MURDERERS.   True, my lord.

MACBETH. So is he mine, and in such bloody distance
  That every minute of his being thrusts
  Against my near'st of life: and though I could
  With barefaced power sweep him from my sight
  And bid my will avouch it, yet I must not,
  For certain friends that are both his and mine,
  Whose loves I may not drop, but wail his fall
  Who I myself struck down: and thence it is
  That I to your assistance do make love,
  Masking the business from the common eye
  For sundry weighty reasons.

SECOND MURDERER.   We shall, my lord,
  Perform what you command us.

FIRST MURDERER.   Though our lives—

MACBETH. Your spirits shine through you. Within this hour at
    most
  I will advise you where to plant yourselves,
  Acquaint you with the perfect spy o' the time,
  The moment on 't; for 't must be done to-night,
  And something from the palace; always thought
  That I require a clearness: and with him—
  To leave no rubs nor botches in the work—
  Fleance his son, that keeps him company,
  Whose absence is no less material to me
  Than is his father's, must embrace the fate
  Of that dark hour. Resolve yourselves apart:
  I'll come to you anon.

BOTH MURDERERS.   We are resolved, my lord.

MACBETH. I'll call upon you straight: abide within.

          [Exeunt MURDERERS.

 It is concluded: Banquo thy soul's flight,
 If it find heaven, must find it out to-night.   *[Exit.*

Scene II — *The palace.*

Enter LADY MACBETH *and a* SERVANT.]

LADY MACBETH. Is Banquo gone from court?

SERVANT. Aye, madam, but returns again to-night.

LADY MACBETH. Say to the king, I would attend his leisure
 For a few words.

SERVANT.   Madam, I will.   *[Exit.*

LADY MACBETH.   Naught 's had, all 's spent,
 Where our desire is got without content:
 'Tis safer to be that which we destroy
 Than by destruction dwell in doubtful joy.

Enter MACBETH.]
 How now, my lord! why do you keep alone,
 Of sorriest fancies your companions making;
 Using those thoughts which should indeed have died
 With them they think on? Things without all remedy
 Should be without regard: what's done is done.

MACBETH. We have scotch'd the snake, not kill'd it:
 She 'll close and be herself, whilst our poor malice
 Remains in danger of her former tooth.
 But let the frame of things disjoint, both the worlds suffer,
 Ere we will eat our meal in fear, and sleep
 In the affliction of these terrible dreams
 That shake us nightly: better be with the dead,
 Whom we, to gain our peace, have sent to peace,
 Than on the torture of the mind to lie
 In restless ecstasy. Duncan is in his grave;
 After life's fitful fever he sleeps well;
 Treason has done his worst: nor steel, nor poison,
 Malice domestic, foreign levy, nothing,
 Can touch him further.

LADY MACBETH.   Come on;
 Gentle mv lord, sleek o'er your rugged looks;
 Be bright and jovial among your guests to-night.

MACBETH. So shall I, love; and so, I pray, be you:
 Let your remembrance apply to Banquo;

Present him eminence, both with eye and tongue:
Unsafe the while, that we
Must lave our honors in these flattering streams,
And make our faces visards to our hearts,
Disguising what they are.

LADY MACBETH.   You must leave this.

MACBETH. O, full of scorpions is my mind, dear wife!
Thou know'st that Banquo, and his Fleance, lives.

LADY MACBETH. But in them nature's copy's not eterne.

MACBETH. There's comfort yet; they are assailable;
Then be thou jocund: ere the bat hath flown
His cloister'd flight: ere to black Hecate's summons
The shard-borne beetle with his drowsy hums
Hath rung night's yawning peal, there shall be done
A deed of dreadful note.

LADY MACBETH.   What's to be done?

MACBETH. Be innocent of the knowledge, dearest chuck,
Till thou applaud the deed. Come, seeling night,
Scarf up the tender eye of pitiful day.
And with thy bloody and invisible hand
Cancel and tear to pieces that great bond
Which keeps me pale! Light thickens, and the crow
Makes wing to the rooky wood:
Good things of day begin to droop and drowse,
Whiles night's black agents to their preys do rouse.
Thou marvel'st at my words: but hold thee still;
Things bad begun make strong themselves by ill:
So, prithee, go with me.   [*Exeunt.*

S C E N E III — *A park near the palace.*

Enter three MURDERERS.]

FIRST MURDERER. But who did bid thee join with us?

THIRD MURDERER.   Macbeth.

SECOND MURDERER. He needs not our mistrust; since he de-
livers
Our offices, and what we have to do,
To the direction just.

FIRST MURDERER.   Then stand with us.
The west yet glimmers with some streaks of day:
Now spurs the lated traveler apace

To gain the timely inn, and near approaches
The subject of our watch.

THIRD MURDERER.   Hark! I hear horses.

BANQUO. [*Within*] Give us a light there, ho!

SECOND MURDERER.   Then 'tis he: the rest
That are within the note of expectation
Already are i' the court.

FIRST MURDERER.   His horses go about.

THIRD MURDERER. Almost a mile: but he does usually—
So all men do—from hence to the palace gate
Make it their walk.

SECOND MURDERER.   A light, a light!

Enter BANQUO, *and* FLEANCE *with a torch.*]

THIRD MURDERER.   'Tis he.

FIRST MURDERER. Stand to 't.

BANQUO. It will be rain to-night.

FIRST MURDERER.   Let it come down.

[*They set upon* BANQUO.

BANQUO. O, treachery! Fly, good Fleance, fly, fly, fly!
Thou mayst revenge. O slave.   [*Dies.* FLEANCE *escapes.*

THIRD MURDERER. Who did strike out the light?

FIRST MURDERER.   Was 't not the way?

THIRD MURDERER. There's but one down; the son is fled.

SECOND MURDERER.   We have lost
Best half of our affair.

FIRST MURDERER. Well, let 's away and say how much is done.

[*Exeunt.*

SCENE IV — *Hall in the palace.*

A banquet prepared. Enter MACBETH, LADY MACBETH,
ROSS, LENNOX, LORDS, *and* ATTENDANTS.]

MACBETH. You know your own degrees; sit down: at first
And last a hearty welcome.

LORDS.   Thanks to your majesty.

MACBETH. Ourself will mingle with society
And play the humble host.
Our hostess keeps her state, but in best time
We will require her welcome.

LADY MACBETH. Pronounce it for me, sir, to all our friends,
For my heart speaks they are welcome.

Enter first MURDERER *to the door.*]

MACBETH. See, they encounter thee with their heart's thanks.
  Both sides are even: here I'll sit 'i the midst:
  Be large in mirth; anon we'll drink a measure
  The table round. [*Approaching the door*] There's blood
    upon thy face.

MURDERER 'Tis Banquo's then.

MACBETH 'Tis better thee without than he within.
  Is he dispatch'd?

MURDERER My lord, his throat is cut; that I did for him.

MACBETH Thou art the best o' the cut-throats: yet he's good
  That did the like for Fleance: if thou didst it,
  Thou art the nonpareil.

MURDERER.   Most royal sir,
  Fleance is 'scaped.

MACBETH. [*Aside*] Then comes my fit again: I had else been
    perfect,
  Whole as the marble, founded as the rock,
  As broad and general as the casing air:
  But now I am cabin'd, cribb'd, confined, bound in
  To saucy doubts and fears.—But Banquo's safe?

MURDERER Aye, my good lord: safe in a ditch he bides,
  With twenty trenched gashes on his head;
  The least a death to nature.

MACBETH.   Thanks for that.
  [*Aside*] There the grown serpent lies; the worm that's fled
  Hath nature that in time will venom breed,
  No teeth for the present. Get thee gone: to-morrow
  We'll hear ourselves again.   [*Exit* MURDERER.

LADY MACBETH.   My royal lord,
  You do not give the cheer: the feast is sold
  That is not often vouch'd, while 'tis a making,
  'Tis given with welcome: to feed were best at home;
  From thence the sauce to meat is ceremony;
  Meeting were bare without it.

MACBETH.   Sweet remembrancer!
  Now good digestion wait on appetite,
  And health on both!

LENNOX.   May 't please your highness sit.

The GHOST *of* BANQUO *enters and sits in* MACBETH's *place*.]

MACBETH. Here had we now our country's honor roof'd,
  Were the graced person of our Banquo present;

Who may I rather challenge for unkindness
Than pity for mischance!

ROSS. His absence, sir,
Lays blame upon his promise. Please 't your highness
To grace us with your royal company.

MACBETH. The table's full.

LENNOX. Here is a place reserved, sir.

MACBETH. Where?

LENNOX. Here, my good lord. What is 't that moves your highness?

MACBETH. Which of you have done this?

LORDS. What, my good lord?

MACBETH. Thou canst not say I did it: never shake
Thy gory locks at me.

ROSS. Gentlemen, rise: his highness is not well.

LADY MACBETH. Sit, worthy friends: my lord is often thus,
And hath been from his youth: pray you, keep seat;
The fit is momentary; upon a thought
He will again be well: if much you note him,
You shall offend him and extend his passion:
Feed, and regard him not. Are you a man?

MACBETH. Aye, and a bold one, that dare look on that
Which might appal the devil.

LADY MACBETH. O proper stuff!
This is the very painting of your fear:
This is the air-drawn dagger which, you said,
Let you to Duncan. O, these flaws and starts,
Impostors to true fear, would well become
A woman's story at a winter's fire,
Authorized by her grandam. Shame itself!
Why do you make such faces? When all 's done,
You look but on a stool.

MACBETH. Prithee, see there! behold! look! lo! how say you?
Why, what care I? If thou canst nod, speak too.
If charnel-houses and our graves must end.
Those that we bury back, our monuments
Shall be the maws of kites.   [*Exit* GHOST.

LADY MACBETH. What, quite unmann'd in folly?

MACBETH. If I stand here, I saw him.

LADY MACBETH. Fie, for shame!

MACBETH. Blood hath been shed ere now, i' the olden time,
Ere humane statute purged the gentle weal;

Aye, and since too, murders have been perform'd
Too terrible for the ear: the time has been,
That, when the brains were out, the man would die,
And there an end; but now they rise again,
With twenty mortal murders on their crowns,
And push us from our stools: this is more strange
Than such a murder is.

LADY MACBETH.   My worthy lord,
Your noble friends do lack you.

MACBETH.   I do forget.
Do not muse at me, my most worthy friends;
I have a strange infirmity, which is nothing
To those that know me. Come, love and health to all;
Then I'll sit down. Give me some wine, fill full.
I drink to the general joy o' the whole table,
And to our dear friend Banquo, whom we miss;
Would he were here! to all and him we thirst,
And all to all.

LORDS.   Our duties, and the pledge.

Re-enter GHOST.]

MACBETH. Avaunt! and quit my sight! let the earth hide thee!
Thy bones are marrowless, thy blood is cold;
Thou hast no speculation in those eyes
Which thou dost glare with.

LADY MACBETH.   Think of this, good peers,
But as a thing of custom: 'tis no other;
Only it spoils the pleasure of the time.

MACBETH. What man dare, I dare:
Approach thou like the rugged Russian bear,
The arm'd rhinoceros, or the Hyrcan tiger;
Take any shape but that, and my firm nerves
Shall never tremble: or be alive again,
And dare me to the desert with thy sword;
If trembling I inhabit then, protest me
The baby of a girl. Hence, horrible shadow!
Unreal mockery, hence!   [*Exit* GHOST.
                    Why, so: being gone,
I am a man again. Pray you, sit still.

LADY MACBETH. You have displaced the mirth, broke the good
    meeting,
With most admired disorder.

MACBETH.   Can such things be,
And overcome us like a summer's cloud,
Without our special wonder? You make me strange
Even to the disposition that I owe,
When now I think you can behold such sight,
And keep the natural ruby of your cheeks,
When mine is blanch'd with fear.

ROSS.   What sights, my lord?

LADY MACBETH. I pray you, speak not; he grows worse and
    worse;
Question enrages him: at once, good night:
Stand not upon the order of your going,
But go at once.

LENNOX.   Good night; and better health
Attend his majesty!

LADY MACBETH.   A kind good night to all!
                [Exeunt all but MACBETH *and* LADY MACBETH.

MACBETH. It will have blood: they say blood with have blood:
Stones have been known to move and trees to speak;
Augurs and understood relations have
By maggot-pies and choughs and rooks brought forth
The secret'st man of blood. What is the night?

LADY MACBETH. Almost at odds with morning, which is which.

MACBETH. How say'st thou, that Macduff denies his person
At our great bidding?

LADY MACBETH.   Did you send to him, sir?

MACBETH. I hear it by the way, but I will send:
There's not a one of them but in his house
I keep a servant fee'd. I will to-morrow,
And betimes I will, to the weird sisters:
More shall they speak, for now I am bent to know,
By the worst means, the worst. For mine own good
All causes shall give way: I am in blood
Stepp'd in so far that, should I wade no more,
Returning were as tedious as go o'er:
Strange things I have in head that will to hand,
Which must be acted ere they may be scann'd.

LADY MACBETH. You lack the season of all natures, sleep.

MACBETH. Come, we'll to sleep. My strange and self-abuse
Is the initiate fear that wants hard use:
We are yet but young in deed.   [*Exeunt.*

Scene V — *A heath.*

Thunder. Enter the three Witches, *meeting* Hecate.]

FIRST WITCH. Why, how now, Hecate! you look angerly.

HECATE. Have I not reason, beldams as you are,
    Saucy and over-bold? How did you dare
    To trade and traffic with Macbeth
    In riddles and affairs of death;
    And I, the mistress of your charms,
    The close contriver of all harms,
    Was never call'd to bear my part,
    Or show the glory of our art?
    And, which is worse, all you have done
    Hath been but for a wayward son,
    Spiteful and wrathful; who, as others do,
    Loves for his own ends, not for you.
    But make amends now: get you gone,
    And at the pit of Acheron
    Meet me i' the morning: thither he
    Will come to know his destiny:
    Your vessels and your spells provide,
    Your charms and every thing beside.
    I am for the air; this night I'll spend
    Unto a dismal and a fatal end:
    Great business must be wrought ere noon:
    Upon the corner of the moon
    There hangs a vaporous drop profound;
    I'll catch it ere it comes to ground:
    And that distill'd by magic sleights
    Shall raise such artificial sprights
    As by the strength of their illusion
    Shall draw him on to his confusion:
    He shall spurn fate, scorn death, and bear
    His hopes 'bove wisdom, grace and fear:
    And you all know security
    Is mortals' chiefest enemy.
        [*Music and a song within:* 'Come away, come away,' *&c.*
    Hark! I am call'd; my little spirit, see,
    Sits in a foggy cloud, and stays for me.   [*Exit.*

FIRST WITCH. Come, let 's make haste; she'll soon be back
    again.   [*Exeunt.*

SCENE VI — FORRES. *The palace.*

Enter LENNOX *and another* LORD.]

LENNOX. My former speeches have but hit your thoughts,
Which can interpret farther: only I say
Things have been strangely borne. The gracious Duncan
Was pitied of Macbeth: marry, he was dead:
And the right-valiant Banquo walk'd too late;
Whom, you may say, if 't please you, Fleance kill'd,
For Fleance fled: men must not walk too late.
Who cannot want the thought, how monstrous
It was for Malcolm and for Donalbain
To kill their gracious father? damned fact!
How it did grieve Macbeth! did he not straight,
In pious rage, the two delinquents tear,
That were the slaves of drink and thralls of sleep?
Was not that nobly done? Aye, and wisely too;
For 'twould have anger'd any heart alive
To hear the men deny 't. So that, I say,
He has borne all things well: and I do think
That, had he Duncan's sons under his key—
As, an 't please heaven, he shall not—they should find
What 'twere to kill a father; so should Fleance.
But, peace! for from broad words, and 'cause he fail'd
His presence at the tyrant's feast, I hear,
Macduff lives in disgrace: sir, can you tell
Where he bestows himself?

LORD.   The son of Duncan,
From whom this tyrant holds the due of birth,
Lives in the English court, and is received
Of the most pious Edward with such grace
That the malevolence of fortune nothing
Takes from his high respect. Thither Macduff
Is gone to pray the holy king, upon his aid
To wake Northumberland and warlike Siward:
That by the help of these, with Him above
To ratify the work, we may again
Give to our tables meat, sleep to our nights,
Free from our feasts and banquets bloody knives,
Do faithful homage and receive free honors:
All which we pine for now: and this report

Hath so exasperated the king that he
Prepares for some attempt of war.

LENNOX.   Sent he to Macduff?

LORD. He did: and with an absolute 'Sir not I,'
The cloudy messenger turns me his back,
And hums, as who would say 'You'll rue the time
That clogs me with this answer.'

LENNOX.   And that well might
Advise him to a caution, to hold what distance
His wisdom can provide. Some holy angel
Fly to the court of England and unfold
His message ere he come, that a swift blessing
May soon return to this our suffering country
Under a hand accursed!

LORD.   I'll send my prayers with him.

[*Exeunt.*

ACT IV

Scene I — *A cavern. In the middle, a boiling cauldron.*

Thunder. Enter the three Witches.]
FIRST WITCH. Thrice the brinded cat hath mew'd.
SECOND WITCH. Thrice and once the hedge-pig whined.
THIRD WITCH. Harpier cries ' 'Tis time, 'tis time.'
FIRST WITCH. Round about the cauldron go:
   In the poison'd entrails throw.
   Toad, that under cold stone
   Days and nights has thirty one
   Swelter'd venom sleeping got,
   Boil thou first i' the charmed pot.
ALL. Double, double toil and trouble;
   Fire burn and cauldron bubble.
SECOND WITCH. Fillet of a fenny snake,
   In the cauldron boil and bake;
   Eye of newt and toe of frog,
   Wool of bat and tongue of dog,
   Adder's fork and blind-worm's sting,
   Lizard's leg and howlet's wing,
   For a charm of powerful trouble,
   Like a hell-broth boil and bubble.
ALL. Double, double toil and trouble;
   Fire burn and cauldron bubble.
THIRD WITCH. Scale of dragon, tooth of wolf,
   Witches' mummy, maw and gulf
   Of the ravin'd salt-sea shark,
   Root of hemlock digged i' the dark,
   Liver of blaspheming Jew,
   Gall of goat and slips of yew
   Silver'd in the moon's eclipse,
   Nose of Turk and Tartar's lips,
   Finger of birth-strangled babe
   Ditch-deliver'd by a drab,
   Make the gruel thick and slab:
   Add thereto a tiger's chaudron,
   For the ingredients of our cauldron.

ALL. Double, double toil and trouble;
　Fire burn and cauldron bubble.
SECOND WITCH. Cool it with a baboon's blood,
　Then the charm is firm and good.
Enter HECATE *to the other three* WITCHES.]
HECATE. O, well done! I commend your pains;
　And every one shall share i' the gains:
　And now about the cauldron sing,
　Like elves and fairies in a ring,
　Enchanting all that you put in.
　　　　[*Music and a song: 'Black spirits,' &c.* HECATE *retires.*
SECOND WITCH. By the pricking of my thumbs,
　Something wicked this way comes:
　Open, locks,
　Whoever knocks!
Enter MACBETH.]
MACBETH. How now, you secret, black, and midnight hags!
　What is 't you do?
ALL.　　　　　　　A deed without a name.
MACBETH. I conjure you, by that which you profess,
　Howe'er you come to know it, answer me:
　Though you untie the winds and let them fight
　Against the churches! though the yesty waves
　Confound and swallow navigation up;
　Though bladed corn be lodged and trees blown down;
　Though castles topple on their warders' heads;
　Though palaces and pyramids do slope
　Their heads to their foundations; though the treasure
　Of nature's germins tumble all together,
　Even till destruction sickens; answer me
　To what I ask you.
FIRST WITCH.　　　　Speak.
SECOND WITCH.　　　　　Demand.
THIRD WITCH.　　　　　　　　We'll answer.
FIRST WITCH. Say, if thou 'dst rather hear it from our mouths,
　Or from our masters?
MACBETH.　　　　　Call 'em, let me see 'em.
FIRST WITCH. Pour in sow's blood, that hath eaten
　Her nine farrow; grease that's sweaten
　From the murderer's gibbet throw
　Into the flame.

ALL.   Come, high or low;
  Thyself and office deftly show!

Thunder. FIRST APPARITION: *an armed Head*.]

MACBETH. Tell me, thou unknown power,—

FIRST WITCH.   He knows thy thought:
  Hear his speech, but say thou nought.

FIRST APPARITION. Macbeth! Macbeth! Macbeth! beware Macduff;
  Beware the thane of Fife. Dismiss me: enough.

                                        [*Descends.*

MACBETH. Whate'er thou art, for thy good caution thanks;
  Thou hast harp'd my fear aright: but one word more,—

FIRST WITCH. He will not be commanded: here's another,
  More potent than the first.

Thunder. SECOND APPARITION: *a bloody Child*.]

SECOND APPARITION. Macbeth! Macbeth! Macbeth!

MACBETH. Had I three ears, I 'ld hear thee.

SECOND APPARITION. Be bloody, bold and resolute; laugh to
    scorn
  The power of man, for none of woman born
  Shall harm Macbeth.   [*Descends.*

MACBETH. Then live, Macduff: what need I fear of thee?
  But yet I'll make assurance doubly sure,
  And take a bond of fate: thou shalt not live;
  That I may tell pale-hearted fear it lies,
  And sleep in spite of thunder.

Thunder. THIRD APPARITION: *a Child crowned, with a
    tree in his hand.*]

                                     What is this,
  That rises like the issue of a king,
  And wears upon his baby-brow the round
  And top of sovereignty?

ALL.   Listen, but speak not to 't.

THIRD APPARITION. Be lion-mettled, proud, and take no care
  Who chafes, who frets, or where conspirers are:
  Macbeth shall never vanquish'd be until
  Great Birnam wood to high Dunsinane hill
  Shall come against him.   [*Descends.*

MACBETH.   That will never be:
  Who can impress the forest, bid the tree
  Unfix his earth-bound root? Sweet bodements! good!
  Rebellion's head, rise never, till the wood

Of Birnam rise, and our high-placed Macbeth
Shall live the lease of nature, pay his breath
To time and mortal custom. Yet my heart
Throbs to know one thing: tell me, if your art
Can tell so much: shall Banquo's issue ever
Reign in this kingdom?   [*Hautboys.*

ALL.   Seek to know no more.

MACBETH. I will be satisfied: deny me this,
  And an eternal curse fall on you! Let me know:
  Why sinks that cauldron? and what noise is this?

FIRST WITCH. Show!

THIRD WITCH. Show!

ALL. Show his eyes, and grieve his heart;
  Come like shadows, so depart!

A show of eight Kings, the last with a glass in his hand;
      BANQUO's *Ghost following.*]

MACBETH. Thou art too like the spirit of Banquo: down!
  Thy crown does sear mine eye-balls. And thy hair,
  Thou other gold-bound brow, is like the first.
  A third is like the former. Filthy hags!
  Why do you show me this? A fourth! Start, eyes!
  What, will the line stretch out to the crack of doom?
  Another yet! A seventh! I'll see no more:
  And yet the eighth appears, who bears a glass
  Which shows me many more; and some I see
  That two-fold balls and treble scepters carry:
  Horrible sight! Now I see 'tis true;
  For the blood-bolter'd Banquo smiles upon me,
  And points at them for his. What, is this so?

FIRST WITCH. Aye, sir, all this is so: but why
  Stands Macbeth thus amazedly?
  Come, sisters, cheer we up his spirits,
  And show the best of our delights:
  I'll charm the air to give a sound,
  While you perform your antic round,
  That this great king may kindly say
  Our duties did his welcome pay.

                    [*Music. The* WITCHES *dance, and then
                              vanish, with* HECATE.

MACBETH. Where are they? Gone? Let this pernicious hour
  Stand aye accursed in the calendar!
  Come in, without there!

Enter LENNOX.]

LENNOX. What's your grace's will?

MACBETH. Saw you the weird sisters?

LENNOX. No, my lord.

MACBETH. Came they not by you?

LENNOX. No indeed, my lord.

MACBETH. Infected be the air whereon they ride,
And damn'd all those that trust them! I did hear
The galloping of horse: who was 't came by?

LENNOX. 'Tis two or three, my lord, that bring you word
Macduff is fled to England.

MACBETH. Fled to England!

LENNOX. Aye, my good lord.

MACBETH. [*Aside*] Time, thou anticipatest my dread exploits:
The flighty purpose never is o'ertook
Unless the deed go with it: from this moment
The very firstlings of my heart shall be
The firstlings of my hand. And even now,
To crown my thoughts with acts, be it thought and done:
The castle of Macduff I will surprise;
Seize upon Fife; give to the edge o' the sword
His wife, his babes, and all unfortunate souls
That trace him in his line. No boasting like a fool;
This deed I'll do before this purpose cool:
But no more sights!—Where are these gentlemen?
Come, bring me where they are. [*Exeunt.*

SCENE II — FIFE. MACDUFF'S *castle*.

Enter LADY MACDUFF, *her* SON, *and* ROSS.]

LADY MACDUFF. What had he done, to make him fly the land?

ROSS. You must have patience, madam.

LADY MACDUFF. He had none:
His flight was madness: when our actions do not,
Our fears do make us traitors.

ROSS. You know not
Whether it was his wisdom or his fear.

LADY MACDUFF. Wisdom! to leave his wife, to leave his babes,
His mansion and his titles in a place
From whence himself does fly? He loves us not;
He wants the natural touch: for the poor wren,
The most diminutive of birds, will fight,

Her young ones in her nest, against the owl.
All is the fear and nothing is the love;
As little is the wisdom, where the flight
So runs against all reason.

ROSS.　　　　　　　　　My dearest coz,
I pray you, school yourself: but, for your husband,
He is noble, wise, judicious, and best knows
The fits o' the season. I dare not speak much further:
But cruel are the times, when we are traitors
And do not know ourselves; when we hold rumor
From what we fear, yet know not what we fear,
But float upon a wild and violent sea
Each way and move. I take my leave of you:
Shall not be long but I'll be here again:
Things at the worst will cease, or else climb upward
To what they were before. My pretty cousin,
Blessing upon you!

LADY MACDUFF. Father'd he is, and yet he's fatherless.

ROSS. I am so much a fool, should I stay longer,
It would be my disgrace and your discomfort:
I take my leave at once.　　　　　　　　　　[*Exit.*

LADY MACDUFF.　　　　　　Sirrah, your father's dead:
And what will you do now? How will you live?

SON. As birds do, mother.

LADY MACDUFF.　　　　　What, with worms and flies?

SON. With what I get, I mean; and so do they.

LADY MACDUFF. Poor bird! thou 'ldst never fear the net nor
　　lime,
The pitfall nor the gin.

SON. Why should I, mother? Poor birds they are not set for.
My father is not dead, for all your saying.

LADY MACDUFF. Yes, he is dead: how wilt thou do for a father?

SON. Nay, how will you do for a husband?

LADY MACDUFF. Why, I can buy me twenty at any market.

SON. Then you'll buy 'em to sell again.

LADY MACDUFF. Thou speak'st with all thy wit, and yet, i'
　　faith,
With wit enough for thee.

SON. Was my father a traitor, mother?

LADY MACDUFF. Aye, that he was.

SON. What is a traitor?

LADY MACDUFF. Why, one that swears and lies.

SON. And be all traitors that do so?

LADY MACDUFF. Every one that does so is a traitor, and must
    be hanged.

SON. And must they all be hanged that swear and lie?

LADY MACDUFF. Every one.

SON. Who must hang them?

LADY MACDUFF. Why, the honest men.

SON. Then the liars and swearers are fools; for there are liars
    and swearers enow to beat the honest men and hang up
    them.

LADY MACDUFF. Now, God help thee, poor monkey!
    But how wilt thou do for a father?

SON. If he were dead, you 'ld weep for him: if you would not,
    it were a good sign that I should quickly have a new father.

LADY MACDUFF. Poor prattler, how thou talk'st!

Enter a MESSENGER.]

MESSENGER. Bless you, fair dame! I am not to you known,
    Though in your state of honor I am perfect.
    I doubt some danger does approach you nearly:
    If you will take a homely man's advice,
    Be not found here; hence, with your little ones.
    To fright you thus, methinks I am too savage;
    To do worse to you were fell cruelty,
    Which is too nigh your person. Heaven preserve you!
    I dare abide no longer.   [*Exit.*

LADY MACDUFF.   Whither should I fly?
    I have done no harm. But I remember now
    I am in this earthly world, where to do harm
    Is often laudable, to do good sometime
    Accounted dangerous folly: why then, alas,
    Do I put up that womanly defense,
    To say I have done no harm?—What are these faces?

Enter MURDERERS.]

FIRST MURDERER. Where is your husband?

LADY MACDUFF. I hope, in no place so unsanctified
    Where such as thou mayst find him.

FIRST MURDERER.   He's a traitor.

SON. Thou liest, thou shag-ear'd villain!

FIRST MURDERER.   What, you egg!
                                   [*Stabbing him.*

Young fry of treachery!

SON.   He has kill'd me, mother:
Run away, I pray you!   [*Dies.*
                    [*Exit* LADY MACDUFF, *crying 'Murderer!'*
                    [*Exeunt* MURDERERS, *following her.*

SCENE III — ENGLAND. *Before the* KING'S *palace.*

Enter MALCOLM *and* MACDUFF.]

MALCOLM. Let us seek out some desolate shade, and there
    Weep our sad bosoms empty.

MACDUFF.   Let us rather
    Hold fast the mortal sword, and like good men
    Bestride our down-fall'n birthdom: each new morn
    New widows howl, new orphans cry, new sorrows
    Strike heaven on the face, that it resounds
    As if it felt with Scotland and yell'd out
    Like syllable of dolor.

MALCOLM.   What I believe, I'll wail;
    What know, believe; and what I can redress,
    As I shall find the time to friend, I will.
    What you have spoke, it may be so perchance.
    This tyrant, whose sole name blisters our tongues,
    Was once thought honest: you have loved him well;
    He hath not touch'd you yet. I am young; but something
    You may deserve of him through me; and wisdom
    To offer up a weak, poor, innocent lamb
    To appease an angry god.

MACDUFF. I am not treacherous.

MALCOLM.   But Macbeth is.
    A good and virtuous nature may recoil
    In an imperial charge. But I shall crave your pardon;
    That which you are, my thoughts cannot transpose:
    Angels are bright still, though the brightest fell:
    Though all things foul would wear the brows of grace,
    Yet grace must still look so.

MACDUFF.   I have lost my hopes.

MALCOLM. Perchance even there where I did find my doubts.
    Why in that rawness left you wife and child,
    Those precious motives, those strong knots of love,
    Without leave-taking? I pray you,
    Let not my jealousies be your dishonors,

But mine own safeties. You may be rightly just,
Whatever I shall think.

MACDUFF.   Bleed, bleed, poor country:
Great tyranny, lay thou thy basis sure,
For goodness dare not check thee: wear thou thy wrongs;
The title is affeer'd. Fare thee well, lord:
I would not be the villain that thou think'st
For the whole space that's in the tyrant's grasp
And the rich East to boot.

MALCOLM.   Be not offended:
I speak not as in absolute fear of you.
I think our country sinks beneath the yoke;
It weeps, it bleeds, and each new day a gash
Is added to her wounds: I think withal
There would be hands uplifted in my right;
And here from gracious England have I offer
Of goodly thousands: but for all this,
When I shall tread upon the tyrant's head,
Or wear it on my sword, yet my poor country
Shall have more vices than it had before,
More suffer and more sundry ways than ever,
By him that shall succeed.

MACDUFF.   What should he be?

MALCOLM. It is myself I mean: in whom I know
All the particulars of vice so grafted
That, when they shall be open'd, black Macbeth
Will seem as pure as snow, and the poor state
Esteem him as a lamb, being compared
With my confineless harms.

MACDUFF.   Not in the legions
Of horrid hell can come a devil more damn'd
In evils to top Macbeth.

MALCOLM.   I grant him bloody,
Luxurious, avaricious, false, deceitful,
Sudden, malicious, smacking of every sin
That has a name: but there's no bottom, none,
In my voluptuousness: your wives, your daughters,
Your matrons, and your maids, could not fill up
The cistern of my lust, and my desire
All continent impediments would o'erbear,
That did oppose my will: better Macbeth
Than such an one to reign.

MACDUFF. Boundless intemperance
In nature is a tyranny; it hath been
The untimely emptying of the happy throne,
And fall of many kings. But fear not yet
To take upon you what is yours: you may
Convey your pleasures in a spacious plenty,
And yet seem cold, the time you may so hoodwink:
We have willing dames enough; there cannot be
That vulture in you, to devour so many
As will to greatness dedicate themselves,
Finding it so inclined.

MALCOLM. With this there grows
In my most ill-composed affection such
A stanchless avarice that, were I king,
I should cut off the nobles for their lands,
Desire his jewels and this other's house:
And my more-having would be as a sauce
To make me hunger more, that I should forge
Quarrels unjust against the good and loyal,
Destroying them for wealth.

MACDUFF. This avarice
Sticks deeper, grows with more pernicious root
Than summer-seeming lust, and it hath been
The sword of our slain kings: yet do not fear;
Scotland hath foisons to fill up your will
Of your mere own: all these are portable,
With other graces weigh'd.

MALCOLM. But I have none: the king-becoming graces,
As justice, verity, temperance, stableness,
Bounty, perseverance, mercy, lowliness,
Devotion, patience, courage, fortitude,
I have no relish for them, but abound
In the division of each several crime,
Acting in many ways. Nay, had I power, I should
Pour the sweet milk of concord into hell,
Uproar the universal peace, confound
All unity on earth.

MACDUFF. O Scotland, Scotland!

MALCOLM. If such a one be fit to govern, speak:
I am as I have spoken.

MACDUFF. Fit to govern!
No, not to live. O nation miserable!

With an untitled tyrant bloody-scepter'd,
When shalt thou see thy wholesome days again,
Since that the truest issue of thy throne
By his own interdiction stands accursed,
And does blaspheme his breed? Thy royal father
Was a most sainted king: the queen that bore thee,
Oftener upon her knees than on her feet,
Died every day she lived. Fare thee well!
These evils thou repeat'st upon thyself
Have banish'd me from Scotland. O my breast,
Thy hope ends here!

MALCOLM.   Macduff, this noble passion,
Child of integrity, hath from my soul
Wiped the black scruples, reconciled my thoughts
To thy good truth and honor. Devilish Macbeth
By many of these trains hath sought to win me
Into his power; and modest wisdom plucks me
From over-credulous haste: but God above
Deal between thee and me! for even now
I put myself to thy direction, and
Unspeak mine own detraction; here abjure
The taints and blames I laid upon myself,
For strangers to my nature. I am yet
Unknown to woman, never was forsworn,
Scarcely have coveted what was mine own,
At no time broke my faith, would not betray
The devil to his fellow, and delight
No less in truth than life: my first false speaking
Was this upon myself: what I am truly,
Is thine and my poor country's to command:
Whither indeed, before thy here-approach,
Old Siward, with ten thousand warlike men,
Already at a point, was setting forth.
Now we'll together, and the chance of goodness
Be like our warranted quarrel! Why are you silent?

MACDUFF. Such welcome and unwelcome things at once
'Tis hard to reconcile.

Enter a DOCTOR.]

MALCOLM. Well, more anon. Comes the king forth, I pray you?

DOCTOR. Aye, sir; there are a crew of wretched souls
That stay his cure: their malady convinces
The great assay of art; but at his touch,

Such sanctity hath heaven given his hand,
They presently amend.

MALCOLM.   I thank you, doctor.   [*Exit* DOCTOR.

MACDUFF. What's the disease he means?

MALCOLM.   'Tis call'd the evil:
A most miraculous work in this good king;
Which often, since my here-remain in England,
I have seen him do. How he solicits heaven,
Himself best knows: but strangely-visited people,
All swoln and ulcerous, pitiful to the eye,
The mere despair of surgery, he cures,
Hanging a golden stamp about their necks,
Put on with holy prayers: and 'tis spoken,
To the succeeding royalty he leaves
The healing benediction. With this strange virtue
He hath a heavenly gift of prophecy,
And sundry blessings hang about his throne
That speak him full of grace.

Enter ROSS.]

MACDUFF.   See, who comes here?

MALCOLM. My countryman; but yet I know him not.

MACDUFF. My ever gentle cousin, welcome hither.

MALCOLM. I know him now: good God, betimes remove
The means that makes us strangers!

ROSS.   Sir, amen.

MACDUFF. Stands Scotland where it did?

ROSS.   Alas, poor country!
Almost afraid to know itself! It cannot
Be call'd our mother, but our grave: where nothing,
But who knows nothing, is once seen to smile;
Where sighs and groans and shrieks that rend the air,
Are made, not mark'd; where violent sorrow seems
A modern ecstasy: the dead man's knell
Is there scarce ask'd for who; and good men's lives
Expire before the flowers in their caps,
Dying or ere they sicken.

MACDUFF.   O, relation
Too nice, and yet too true!

MALCOLM.   What's the newest grief?

ROSS. That of an hour's age doth hiss the speaker;
Each minute teems a new one.

MACDUFF.   How does my wife?

ROSS. Why, well.

MACDUFF.   And all my children?

ROSS.   Well too.

MACDUFF. The tyrant has not batter'd at their peace?

ROSS. No; they were well at peace when I did leave 'em.

MACDUFF. Be not a niggard of your speech: how goes 't?

ROSS. When I came hither to transport the tidings,
　　Which I have heavily borne, there ran a rumor
　　Of many worthy fellows that were out;
　　Which was to my belief witness'd the rather,
　　For that I saw the tyrant's power a-foot:
　　Now is the time of help; your eye in Scotland
　　Would create soldiers, make our women fight,
　　To doff their dire distresses.

MALCOLM.   Be 't their comfort
　　We are coming thither: gracious England hath
　　Lent us good Siward and ten thousand men;
　　An older and a better soldier none
　　That Christendom gives out.

ROSS.   Would I could answer
　　This comfort with the like! But I have words
　　That would be howl'd out in the desert air,
　　Where hearing should not latch them.

MACDUFF.   What concern they?
　　The general cause? or is it a fee-grief
　　Due to some single breast?

ROSS.   No mind that's honest
　　But in it shares some woe, though the main part
　　Pertains to you alone.

MACDUFF.   If it be mine,
　　Keep it not from me, quickly let me have it.

ROSS. Let not your ears despise my tongue for ever,
　　Which shall possess them with the heaviest sound
　　That ever yet they heard.

MACDUFF.   Hum! I guess at it.

ROSS. Your castle is surprised; your wife and babes
　　Savagely slaughter'd: to relate the manner,
　　Were, on the quarry of these murder'd deer,
　　To add the death of you.

MALCOLM.   Merciful heaven!
　　What, man! ne'er pull your hat upon your brows;
　　Give sorrow words: the grief that does not speak

Whispers the o'erfraught heart, and bids it break.
MACDUFF. My children too?
ROSS.   Wife, children, servants, all
  That could be found.
MACDUFF.   And I must be from thence!
  My wife kill'd too?
ROSS.   I have said.
MALCOLM.   Be comforted:
  Let's make us medicines of our great revenge,
  To cure this deadly grief.
MACDUFF. He has no children. All my pretty ones?
  Did you say all? O hell-kite! All?
  What, all my pretty chickens and their dam
  At one fell swoop?
MALCOLM. Dispute it like a man.
MACDUFF.   I shall do so;
  But I must also feel it as a man:
  I cannot but remember such things were,
  That were most precious to me. Did heaven look on,
  And would not take their part? Sinful Macduff,
  They were all struck for thee! naught that I am,
  Not for their own demerits, but for mine,
  Fell slaughter on their souls: heaven rest them now!
MALCOLM. Be this the whetstone of your sword: let grief
  Convert to anger; blunt not the heart, enrage it.
MACDUFF. O, I could play the woman with mine eyes,
  And braggart with my tongue! But, gentle heavens,
  Cut short all intermission; front to front
  Bring thou this fiend of Scotland and myself;
  Within my sword's length set him; if he 'scape,
  Heaven forgive him too!
MALCOLM.   This tune goes manly.
  Come, go we to the king; our power is ready;
  Our lack is nothing but our leave. Macbeth
  Is ripe for shaking, and the powers above
  Put on their instruments. Receive what cheer you may;
  The night is long that never finds the day.   [*Exeunt.*

ACT V

Scene I — Dunsinane. *Ante-room in the castle.*

Enter a Doctor of Physic *and a* Waiting-Gentlewoman.]
DOCTOR. I have two nights watched with you, but can perceive no truth in your report. When was it she last walked?
GENTLEWOMAN. Since his majesty went into the field, I have
seen her rise from her bed, throw her nightgown upon her,
unlock her closet, take forth paper, fold it, write upon 't,
read it, afterwards seal it, and again return to bed; yet all
this while in a most fast sleep.
DOCTOR. A great perturbation in nature, to receive at once the
benefit of sleep and do the effects of watching! In this
slumbery agitation, besides her walking and other actual
performances, what, at any time, have you heard her say?
GENTLEWOMAN That sir, which I will not report after her.
DOCTOR. You may to me, and 'tis most meet you should.
GENTLEWOMAN Neither to you nor any one, having no wit-
ness to confirm my speech.
Enter LADY MACBETH, *with a taper.*]
Lo you, here she comes! This is her very guise, and, upon
my life, fast asleep Observe her; stand close.
DOCTOR. How come she by that light?
GENTLEWOMAN. Why, it stood by her: she has light by her
continually; 'tis her command.
DOCTOR. You see, her eyes are open.
GENTLEWOMAN Aye, but their sense is shut.
DOCTOR. What is it she does now? Look, how she rubs her
hands.
GENTLEWOMAN. It is an accustomed action with her, to seem
thus washing her hands: I have known her continue in this
a quarter of an hour.
LADY MACBETH Yet here's a spot.
DOCTOR Hark! she speaks: I will set down what comes from
her, to satisfy my remembrance the more strongly.
LADY MACBETH Out, damned spot! out, I say! One: two:
why, then 'tis time to do 't. Hell is murky. Fie, my lord,
fie! a soldier, and afeard? What need we fear who knows
it, when none can call our power to account? Yet who

would have thought the old man to have had so much
blood in him?

DOCTOR. Do you mark that?

LADY MACBETH. The thane of Fife had a wife; where is she
now? What, will these hands ne'er be clean? No more o'
that, my lord, no more o' that: you mar all with this start-
ing.

DOCTOR. Go to, go to; you have known what you should not.

GENTLEWOMAN. She has spoke what she should not, I am sure
of that: heaven knows what she has known.

LADY MACBETH. Here's the smell of the blood still: all the perfumes of Arabia will not sweeten this little hand. Oh, oh,
oh!

DOCTOR. What a sigh is there! the heart is sorely charged.

GENTLEWOMAN. I would not have such a heart in my bosom
for the dignity of the whole body.

DOCTOR. Well, well, well,—

GENTLEWOMAN. Pray God it be, sir.

DOCTOR. This disease is beyond my practice: yet I have
known those which have walked in their sleep who have
died holily in their beds.

LADY MACBETH. Wash your hands; put on your nightgown;
look not so pale: I tell you yet again, Banquo's buried; he
cannot come out on 's grave.

DOCTOR. Even so?

LADY MACBETH. To bed, to bed; there's knocking at the gate:
come, come, come, come, give me your hand: what's done
cannot be undone: to bed, to bed, to bed.　　　　[*Exit.*

DOCTOR. Will she go now to bed?

GENTLEWOMAN. Directly.

DOCTOR. Foul whisperings are abroad: unnatural deeds
Do breed unnatural troubles: infected minds
To their deaf pillows will discharge their secrets:
More needs she the divine than the physician.
God, God forgive us all! Look after her;
Remove from her the means of all annoyance,
And still keep eyes upon her. So good night:
My mind she has mated and amazed my sight:
I think, but dare not speak.

GENTLEWOMAN.　　　　　　　Good night, good doctor.

　　　　　　　　　　　　　　　　　　[*Exeunt.*

Scene II — *The country near* Dunsinane.

Drum and colors. Enter Menteith, Caithness,
      Angus, Lennox, *and* Soldiers.]

MENTEITH. The English power is near, led on by Malcolm,
    His uncle Siward and the good Macduff:
    Revenges burn in them; for their dear causes
    Would to the bleeding and the grim alarm
    Excite the mortified man.

ANGUS.   Near Birnam wood
    Shall we well meet them; that way are they coming.

CAITHNESS. Who knows if Donalbain be with his brother?

LENNOX. For certain, sir, he is not: I have a file
    Of all the gentry: there is Siward's son,
    And many unrough youths, that even now
    Protest their first of manhood.

MENTEITH.   What does the tyrant?

CAITHNESS. Great Dunsinane he strongly fortifies:
    Some say he's mad; others, that lesser hate him,
    Do call it valiant fury: but, for certain,
    He cannot buckle his distemper'd cause
    Within the belt of rule.

ANGUS.   Now does he feel
    His secret murders sticking on his hands;
    Now minutely revolts upbraid his faith-breach;
    Those he commands move only in command,
    Nothing in love: now does he feel his title
    Hang loose about him, like a giant's robe
    Upon a dwarfish thief.

MENTEITH.   Who then shall blame
    His pester'd senses to recoil and start,
    When all that is within him does condemn
    Itself for being there?

CAITHNESS.   Well, march we on,
    To give obedience where 'tis truly owed:
    Meet we the medicine of the sickly weal,
    And with him pour we, in our country's purge,
    Each drop of us.   [*Exeunt, marching.*

LENNOX.   Or so much as it needs
    To dew the sovereign flower and drown the weeds.
    Make we our march towards Birnam.

Scene III — Dunsinane. *A room in the castle.*

Enter Macbeth, Doctor, *and* Attendants.]

MACBETH. Bring me no more reports; let them fly all:
Till Birnam wood remove to Dunsinane
I cannot taint with fear. What's the boy Malcolm?
Was he not born of woman? The spirits that know
All mortal consequences have pronounced me thus:
'Fear not, Macbeth; no man that's born of woman
Shall e'er have power upon thee.' They fly, false thanes,
And mingle with the English epicures:
The mind I sway by and the heart I bear
Shall never sag with doubt nor shake with fear.

Enter a SERVANT.]

The devil damn thee black, thou cream-faced loon!
Where got'st thou that goose look?

SERVANT. There is ten thousand—

MACBETH.   Geese, villain?

SERVANT.   Soldiers, sir.

MACBETH. Go prick thy face and over-red thy fear,
Thou lily-liver'd boy. What soldiers, patch!
Death of my soul! those linen cheeks of thine
Are counselors to fear. What soldiers, whey-face!

SERVANT. The English force, so please you.

MACBETH. Take thy face hence.   [*Exit* SERVANT.
Seyton!—I am sick at heart,
When I behold—Seyton, I say!—This push
Will cheer me ever, or disseat me now.
I have lived long enough: my way of life
Is fall'n into the sear, the yellow leaf,
And that which should accompany old age,
As honor, love, obedience, troops of friends,
I must not look to have; but, in their stead,
Curses, not loud but deep, mouth-honor, breath,
Which the poor heart would fain deny, and dare not.
Seyton!

Enter SEYTON.]

SEYTON. What's your gracious pleasure?

MACBETH.   What news more?

SEYTON. All is confirm'd, my lord, which was reported.

MACBETH. I'll fight, till from my bones my flesh be hacked.
　　Give me my armor.
SEYTON. 　　　　　　　　　　'Tis not needed yet.
MACBETH. I'll put it on.
　　Send out more horses, skirr the country round;
　　Hang those that talk of fear. Give me mine armor.
　　How does your patient, doctor?
DOCTOR. 　　　　　　　　　　　Not so sick, my lord,
　　As she is troubled with thick-coming fancies,
　　That keep her from her rest.
MACBETH. 　　　　　　　　　　Cure her of that.
　　Canst thou not minister to a mind diseased,
　　Pluck from the memory a rooted sorrow,
　　Raze out the written troubles of the brain,
　　And with some sweet oblivious antidote
　　Cleanse the stuff'd bosom of that perilous stuff
　　Which weighs upon the heart?
DOCTOR. 　　　　　　　　　　　Therein the patient
　　Must minister to himself.
MACBETH. Throw physic to the dogs, I'll none of it.
　　Come, put mine armor on; give me my staff.
　　Seyton, send out Doctor, the thanes fly from me.
　　Come, sir, dispatch. If thou couldst, doctor, cast
　　The water of my land, find her disease
　　And purge it to a sound and pristine health,
　　I would applaud thee to the very echo,
　　That should applaud again. Pull 't off, I say.
　　What rhubarb, senna, or what purgative drug,
　　Would scour these English hence? Hear'st thou of them?
DOCTOR. Aye, my good lord; your royal preparation
　　Makes us hear something.
MACBETH. 　　　　　　　　　Bring it after me.
　　I will not be afraid of death and bane
　　Till Birnam forest come to Dunsinane.
DOCTOR. [*Aside*] Were I from Dunsinane away and clear,
　　Profit again should hardly draw me here. 　　　　　[*Exeunt.*

SCENE IV — *Country near* BIRNAM *wood.*

Drum and colors. Enter MALCOLM, *old* SIWARD *and his* SON, MACDUFF, MENTEITH, CAITHNESS, ANGUS, LENNOX, ROSS, *and* SOLDIERS, *marching.*]

MALCOLM. Cousins, I hope the days are near at hand
   That chambers will be safe.

MENTEITH.   We doubt it nothing.

SIWARD. What wood is this before us?

MENTEITH.   The wood of Birnam.

MALCOLM. Let every soldier hew him down a bough,
   And bear 't before him: thereby shall we shadow
   The numbers of our host, and make discovery
   Err in report of us.

SOLDIERS.   It shall be done.

SIWARD. We learn no other but the confident tyrant
   Keeps still in Dunsinane, and will endure
   Our setting down before 't.

MALCOLM.   'Tis his main hope:
   For where there is advantage to be given,
   Both more and less have given him the revolt,
   And none serve with him but constrained things
   Whose hearts are absent too.

MACDUFF.   Let our just censures
   Attend the true event, and put we on
   Industrious soldiership.

SIWARD.   The time approaches,
   That will with due decision make us know
   What we shall say we have and what we owe.
   Thoughts speculative their unsure hopes relate,
   But certain issue strokes must arbitrate:
   Towards which advance the war.   [*Exeunt, marching.*

SCENE V — DUNSINANE. *Within the castle.*

Enter MACBETH, SEYTON, *and* SOLDIERS, *with drum and colors.*]

MACBETH. Hang out our banners on the outward walls;
   The cry is still 'They come;' our castle's strength
   Will laugh a siege to scorn: here let them lie
   Till famine and the ague eat them up:

Were they not forced with those that should be ours,
We might have met them dareful, beard to beard,
And beat them backward home.   [*A cry of women within.*
                                    What is that noise?

SEYTON. It is the cry of women, my good lord.   [*Exit.*

MACBETH. I have almost forgot the taste of fears:
    The time has been, my senses would have cool'd
    To hear a night-shriek, and my fell of hair
    Would at a dismal treatise rouse and stir
    As life were in 't: I have supp'd full with horrors;
    Direness, familiar to my slaughterous thoughts,
    Cannot once start me.

Re-enter SEYTON.]
                                    Wherefore was that cry?

SEYTON. The queen, my lord, is dead.

MACBETH. She should have died hereafter;
    There would have been a time for such a word.
    To-morrow, and to-morrow, and to-morrow,
    Creeps in this petty pace from day to day,
    To the last syllable of recorded time;
    And all our yesterdays have lighted fools
    The way to dusty death. Out, out, brief candle!
    Life's but a walking shadow, a poor player
    That struts and frets his hour upon the stage
    And then is heard no more: it is a tale
    Told by an idiot, full of sound and fury,
    Signifying nothing.

Enter a MESSENGER.]
    Thou comest to use thy tongue; thy story quickly.

MESSENGER. Gracious my lord,
    I should report that which I say I saw,
    But know not how to do it.

MACBETH.   Well, say, sir.

MESSENGER. As I did stand my watch upon the hill,
    I look'd toward Birnam, and anon, methought,
    The wood began to move.

MACBETH.   Liar and slave!

MESSENGER. Let me endure your wrath, if 't be not so:
    Within this three mile may you see it coming;
    I say, a moving grove.

MACBETH.   If thou speak'st false,
    Upon the next tree shalt thou hang alive,

Till famine cling thee: if thy speech be sooth,
I care not if thou dost for me as much.
I pull in resolution, and begin
To doubt the equivocation of the fiend
That lies like truth: 'Fear not, till Birnam wood
Do come to Dunsinane:' and now a wood
Comes toward Dunsinane, Arm, arm, and out!
If this which he avouches does appear,
There is nor flying hence nor tarrying here.
I 'gin to be a-weary of the sun,
And wish the estate o' the world were now undone.
Ring the alarum-bell! Blow, wind! come, wrack!
At least we'll die with harness on our back.   [*Exeunt.*

S C E N E VI — DUNSINANE. *Before the castle.*

Drum and colors. Enter MALCOLM, *old* SIWARD,
    MACDUFF, *and their Army, with boughs.*]

MALCOLM. Now near enough; your leavy screens throw down,
    And show like those you are. You, worthy uncle,
    Shall, with my cousin, your right noble son,
    Lead our first battle: worthy Macduff and we
    Shall take upon 's what else remains to do,
    According to our order.
SIWARD.   Fare you well.
    Do we but find the tyrant's power to-night,
    Let us be beaten, if we cannot fight.
MACDUFF. Make all our trumpets speak; give them all breath,
    Those clamorous harbingers of blood and death.   [*Exeunt.*

S C E N E VII — *Another part of the field.*

Alarums. Enter MACBETH.]

MACBETH. They have tied me to a stake; I cannot fly,
    But bear-like I must fight the course. What's he
    That was not born of woman? Such a one
    Am I to fear, or none.
Enter young SIWARD.]
YOUNG SIWARD. What is thy name?
MACBETH.   Thou 'lt be afraid to hear it.
YOUNG SIWARD. No; though thou call'st thyself a hotter name
    Than any is in hell.

MACBETH. My name's Macbeth.

YOUNG SIWARD. The devil himself could not pronounce a title
  More hateful to mine ear.

MACBETH. No, nor more fearful.

YOUNG SIWARD. Thou liest, abhorred tyrant; with my sword
  I'll prove the lie thou speak'st.
                    [*They fight, and young* SIWARD *is slain.*

MACBETH. Thou wast born of woman.
  But swords I smile at, weapons laugh to scorn,
  Brandish'd by man that's of a woman born. [*Exit.*
Alarums. Enter MACDUFF.]

MACDUFF. That way the noise is. Tyrant, show thy face!
  If thou be'st slain and with no stroke of mine,
  My wife and children's ghosts will haunt me still.
  I cannot strike at wretched kerns, whose arms
  Are hired to bear their staves: either thou, Macbeth,
  Or else my sword, with an unbatter'd edge,
  I sheathe again undeeded. There thou shouldst be;
  By this great clatter, one of greatest note
  Seems bruited: let me find him, fortune!
  And more I beg not. [*Exit Alarums.*
Enter MALCOLM *and old* SIWARD.]

SIWARD. This way, my lord; the castle's gently render'd:
  The tyrant's people on both sides do fight;
  The noble thanes do bravely in the war;
  The day almost itself professes yours,
  And little is to do.

MALCOLM. We have met with foes
  That strike beside us.

SIWARD. Enter, sir, the castle. [*Exit. Alarum.*

SCENE VIII — *Another part of the field.*

Enter MACBETH.]

MACBETH. Why should I play the Roman fool, and die
  On mine own sword? whiles I see lives, the gashes
  Do better upon them.

Enter MACDUFF.]

MACDUFF. Turn, hell-hound, turn!

MACBETH. Of all men else I have avoided thee:
  But get thee back; my soul is too much charged
  With blood of thine already.

MACDUFF.   I have no words:
  My voice is in my sword, thou bloodier villain
  Than terms can give thee out!   [*They fight.*
MACBETH.   Thou losest labor:
  As easy mayst thou the intrenchant air
  With thy keen sword impress as make me bleed:
  Let fall thy blade on vulnerable crests;
  I bear a charmed life, which must not yield
  To one of woman born.
MACDUFF.   Despair thy charm,
  And let the angel whom thou still hast served
  Tell thee, Macduff was from his mother's womb
  Untimely ripp'd.
MACBETH. Accursed be that tongue that tells me so,
  For it hath cow'd my better part of man!
  And be these juggling fiends no more believed,
  That palter with us in a double sense;
  That keep the word of promise to our ear,
  And break it to our hope. I'll not fight with thee.
MACDUFF. Then yield thee, coward,
  And live to be the show and gaze o' the time:
  We'll have thee, as our rarer monsters are,
  Painted upon a pole, and underwrit,
  'Here may you see the tyrant.'
MACBETH.   I will not yield,
  To kiss the ground before young Malcolm's feet,
  And so be baited with the rabble's curse.
  Though Birnam wood be come to Dunsinane,
  And thou opposed, being of no woman born,
  Yet I will try the last: before my body
  I throw my warlike shield: lay on, Macduff;
  And damn'd be him that first cries 'Hold enough!'
                    [*Exeunt, fighting. Alarums.*

Retreat. Flourish. Enter, with drum and colors,
    MALCOLM, *old* SIWARD, ROSS, *the other*
    THANES, *and* SOLDIERS.]

MALCOLM. I would the friends we miss were safe arrived.
SIWARD. Some must go off: and yet, by these I see,
  So great a day as this is cheaply bought.
MALCOLM. Macduff is missing, and your noble son.
ROSS. Your son, my lord, has paid a soldier's debt:

He only lived but till he was a man;
The which no sooner had his prowess confirm'd
In the unshrinking station where he fought,
But like a man he died.

SIWARD.   Then he is dead?

ROSS. Aye, and brought off the field: your cause of sorrow
Must not be measured by his worth, for then
It hath no end.

SIWARD.   Had he his hurts before?

ROSS. Aye, on the front.

SIWARD.   Why then, God's soldier be he!
Had I as many sons as I have hairs,
I would not wish them to a fairer death:
And so his knell is knoll'd.

MALCOLM.   He's worth more sorrow,
And that I'll spend for him.

SIWARD.   He's worth no more:
They say he parted well and paid his score:
And so God be with him! Here comes newer comfort.

Re-enter MACDUFF, *with* MACBETH's *head*.]

MACDUFF. Hail, king! for so thou art: behold, where stands
The usurper's cursed head: the time is free:
I see thee compass'd with thy kingdom's pearl,
That speak my salutation in their minds;
Whose voices I desire aloud with mine:
Hail, King of Scotland!

ALL.   Hail, King of Scotland!   [*Flourish.*

MALCOLM. We shall not spend a large expense of time
Before we reckon with your several loves,
And make us even wtih you. My thanes and kinsmen,
Henceforth be earls, the first that ever Scotland
In such an honor named. What's more to do,
Which would be planted newly with the time,
As calling home our exiled friends abroad
That fled the snares of watchful tyranny,
Producing forth the cruel ministers
Of this dead butcher and his fiend-like queen,
Who, as 'tis thought, by self and violent hands
Took off her life; this, and what needful else
That calls upon us, by the grace of Grace
We will perform in measure, time and place:

So thanks to all at once and tc each one,
Whom we invite to see us crown'd at Scone.

[*Flourish. Exeunt.*

GLOSSARIES

GLOSSARY

FOR

Romeo and Juliet

A, one, the same; II. iv.

A', he; I. iii.

ABUSED, disfigured; IV. i.

ADVANCED, raised; V. iii.

ADVENTURE, venture, II. ii.

ADVISE, think over it; III. v.

AFEARD, afraid; II. ii.

AFFECTING, affected; II. iv.

AFFECTIONS, inclinations; I. i.

AFFRAY, frighten; III. v.

AFORE, before; II. iv.

AFORE ME, "by my life"; III. iv.

AGAINST, in preparation of; III. iv.

AGATE-STONE, figures cut in the agate-stone, much worn in rings; I. iv.

ALL ALONG, at your full length; V. iii.

ALL SO SOON, as soon; I. i.

AMBLING, moving in an affected manner; I. iv.

AMBUSCADOES, ambuscades; I. iv.

AMERCE, punish; III. i.

AN, if; I. i.

AN IF, if; V. i.

ANCIENT, old, aged; II. iii.

ANTIC FACE, quaint mask; I. v.

APACE, quickly; II. iv.

APE, a term of endearment; II. i.

APPERTAINING RAGE TO, rage belonging to; III. i.

APT TO, ready for; III. i.

APT UNTO, ready for; III. iii.

AS, as if; II. v.

——, namely; IV. iii.

ASCEND, ascend to; III. iii.

ASPIRED, mounted to; III. i.

ASSOCIATE, accompany; V. ii.

AS THAT, as to that heart; II. ii.

ATHWART, across, over; (so); I. iv.

ATOMIES = atoms, little creatures as tiny as atoms; I. iv.

ATTACH, arrest; V. iii.

ATTENDING, attentive; II. ii.

BAKED MEATS, pastry; IV. iv.

BANDY, beat to and fro, hurry; II. v.

BANDYING, quarreling; III. i.

BANQUET, dessert; I. v.

BARE, lean, poor; V. i.

——, did bear; V. ii.

BATING, to flap or flutter the wings; a term of falconry; III. ii.

BEAR A BRAIN, have a good memory; I. iii.

BECOMED, becoming; IV. ii.

BEHOVEFUL, befitting; IV. iii.

BENT, inclination, disposition; II. ii.

BEPAINT, paint, II. ii.

BESCREEN'D, screened, hidden; II. ii.

BETOSSED, deeply agitated; V. iii.

BETTER TEMPER'D, of better quality; III. iii.

BILL, a kind of pike or halberdt, carried by watchmen; I. i.

BLAZE, make known; III. iii.

BLAZON, trumpet forth; II. vi.

BRACE, couple; V. iii.

BRIEF, briefly; III. iii.

BROAD GOOSE, "far and wide a b.g."; prob. = far and wide abroad, a goose; II. iv.

BROKEN, cracked; I. ii.

Brow, face, countenance; III. v.

Burn daylight, waste time; I. iv.

Butt-shaft, a kind of arrow; II. iv.

By and by, directly; II. ii.

By my fay, a slight oath; I. v.

By my troth, on my word; II. iv.

By the rood, a slight oath; I. iii.

Caitiff, wretched, miserable; V. i.

Canker, canker-worm; II. iii.

Captain of compliments, "complete master of all the laws of ceremony"; II. iv.

Carry coals, endure affronts; I. i.

Chapless, without jaws; IV. i.

Charge, weight; V. ii.

Cheerly, cheerily; I. v.

Cheveril, the skin of the kid; II. iv.

Chinks, a popular term for money; I. v.

Chop-logic, sophist; III. v.

Circumstance, details; II. v.

Civil, sober, grave; III. ii.

Close, closely, very near; III. i.

Closed, enclosed; I. iv.

Closely, secretly; V. iii.

Closet, chamber; IV. ii.

Cockatrice, the fabulous serpent, said to kill by a look; III. ii.

Cock-a-hoop, "set c.-a-h.", i.e. "pick a quarrel"; I. v.

Cockerel, young cock; I. iii.

Coil, ado, confusion; II. v.

Coldly, coolly, calmly; III. i.

Come near ye, hit it; I. v.

Comfortable, helpful; V. iii.

Commission, warrant; IV. i.

Concealed, "secretly married"; III. iii.

Conceit, imagination; II. vi.

Concludes, ends; III. i.

Conduct, conductor; V. iii.

Conduit, the human figures on wells which spouted water; III. v.

Confounds, destroys; II. vi.

Conjurations, entreaties; V. iii.

Consort, used with play on the two meanings of the word; (i.) a company of musicians, (ii.) associate, keep company; III. i.

Consorted, associated; II. i.

Content thee, keep your temper; I. v.

Contrary, contradict, oppose; I. v.

Convey, conveyance; II. iv.

Corse, corpse; III. ii.

Cot-quean, a man who busies himself with women's business; IV. iv.

Counterfeit, "gave the c.", played the trick; II. iv.

Countervail, balance; II. vi.

County, count; I. iii.

Court-cupboard, side-board for setting out plate; I. v.

Courtship, courtliness; III. iii.

Cousin, kinsman; I. v.

Cover, book cover; used with a quibble on the law phrase for a married woman, who is styled a *femme couverte;* I. iii.

Cross, perverse; IV. iii.

——, thwart, hinder; V. iii.

Crotchets, used with play upon both senses of the word (i.) whims, fancies; (ii.) notes in music; IV. v.

Crow, crow-bar; V. ii.

Crow-keeper, scarecrow; I. iv.

Crush a cup, I. ii.

Cunning, skill, art; II. ii.

Cures with, is cured by; I. ii.

Cynthia, the moon; III. v.

Damnation, "ancient d.", "old sinner"; III. v.

Dared, challenged; used with play upon the two senses of the word; II. iv.

Dares, ventures; II. iv.

Date, time, duration; I. iv.

Date is out, is out of fashion; I. iv.

Dateless, without limit; V. iii.

DEAR, true; III. iii.
——, important; V. ii.
DEATH, to death; III. i.
DEFENCE, defensive weapons; III. iii.
DEMESNES, landed estates; III. v.
DENY, refuse; I. v.
DEPART, go away, part; III. i.
DEPEND, impend; III. i.
DESPERATE, reckless; III. iv.
DESPITE, defiance; V. iii.
DETERMINE OF, decide; III. ii.
DEW-DROPPING SOUTH, rainy south; I. iv.
DIGRESSING, deviating; III. iii.
DISCOVER, reveal; III. i.
DISCOVERED, betrayed; II. ii.
DISLIKE, displease; II. ii.
DISPARAGEMENT, injury, harm; I. v.
DISPLANT, transplant; III. iii.
DISPUTE, argue, reason; III. iii.
DISTEMPERATURE, disease; II. iii.
DISTEMPER'D, diseased; II. iii.
DISTRAUGHT, distracted; IV. iii.
DIVISION, variation; III. v.
DOCTRINE, instruction; I. i.
DOFF, put off; II. ii.
DOUBT, fear, distrust; V. iii.
DRAVE, did drive, urged; I. i.
DRIFT, plan, scheme; IV. i.
DRY-BEAT, thrash; III. i.
DUMP, a melancholy strain in music; IV. v.
DUN'S THE MOUSE, keep still; I. iv.

ELF-LOCKS, hair matted together by the elves; I. iv.
EMPTY, hungry; V. iii.
ENCOUNTER, meeting; II. vi.
ENDART, dart; I. iii.
ENFORCE, force; V. iii.
ENPIERCED, pierced through; I. iv.
ENVIOUS, malignant; III. ii.
ETHIOP, a native of Ethiopia; I. v.
EVENING MASS, the practice of saying mass in the afternoon lingered on for some time; IV. i.

EXPIRE, end; I. iv.
EXTREMES, sufferings; IV. i.
EXTREMITY, "everything in e.", i.e. at a desperate pass; I. iii.

FAIN, gladly; II. ii.
FAIR, fair one, beautiful woman; Prol. II.
FANTASTICOES, coxcombs; II. iv.
FAREWELL COMPLIMENT, away with ceremony; II. ii.
FEARFUL, full of fear; III. iii.
FEELING, heartfelt; III. v.
FEE-SIMPLE, hereditary and unconditional property; III. i.
FESTERING, rotting; IV. iii.
FETTLE, prepare; III. v.
FINE, penalty; I. v.
FIRST HOUSE, "of the best school of fencing"; II. iv.
FITS, "it fits," it is becoming; I. v.
FLECKED, spotted; II. iii.
FLEER, sneer; I. v.
FLIRT-GILLS, flirting women; II. iv.
FLOWERED, alluding probably to the shoes punched with holes; II. iv.
FOND, foolish; III. iii.
FOOLISH, trifling; I. v.
FORBEAR, abstain from; III. i.
FORM, used with play upon both senses of the word; II. iv.
FORSWORN, "be f.", commit perjury; III. v.
FORTH, from out of; I. i.
FORTUNE'S FOOL, the sport of fortune; III. i.
FRANK, liberal; II. i.
FREE-TOWN, Villafranca; I. i.
FRIEND, lover; III. v.
FRIGHTENED, terrified; I. iv.
FROM, away from, to avoid; III. i.
FURNISH, deck; IV. ii.

GEAR, matter; II. iv.
GHOSTLY, spiritual; II. ii.
GIVE LEAVE, leave us; a courteous form of dismissal; I. iii.
GIVE YOU, i.e. retort by calling you; IV. v.
GLEEK, scoff; IV. v.
GLOOMING, gloomy; V. iii.

God-den, good evening; I. ii.

God gi' god-den, God give you a good evening; I. ii.

God save the mark, God have mercy; III. ii.

God ye good den, God give you good evening; II. iv.

God ye good morrow, God give you good morning; II. iv.

Good goose, bite not, a proverbial expression; II. iv.

Goodman boy, a familiar appellation; I. v.

Gore, "gore blood" = clotted blood; III. ii.

Grace, virtue, potency; II. iii.

Grievance, grief, sorrow; I. i.

Gyves, fetters; II. ii.

Hai, a home-thrust in fencing; II. iv.

Hall, "a hall, a hall," make room; I. v.

Hap, "dear h.", good fortune; II. ii.

Harlotry, a term of contempt for a silly wench; IV. ii.

Have at thee, take care; I. i.

Havior, behavior; II. ii.

He, man; V. i.

Healthsome, wholesome; IV. iii.

Heartless, spiritless, cowardly; I. i.

"Heart's ease," a popular tune of the time; IV. v.

Heaviness, sorrow; III. iv.

Heavy, sad, troubled; I. i.

Hie you, hasten; II. v.

High-lone, without help; I. iii.

Highmost, highest; II. v.

Hilding, base wretch; III. v.

Hinds, serfs, menials; I. i.

His, its; II. vi.; V. iii.

Hoar, hoary, moldy; II. iv.

Holidame, salvation; I. iii.

Holp, helped; I. ii.

Homely, plain, simple; II. iii.

Honey nurse, a term of endearment; II. v.

Hood, cover with a hood, (as the hawk was hooded till let fly at the game); III. ii.

Humorous, moist, capricious; II. i.

Humor, inclination, bent; I. i.

Hunts-up, "the tune played to wake the hunters"; III. v.

I'll be a candle-holder, I'll be an idle spectator; I. iv.

Ill-divining, misgiving; III. v.

Impeach, accuse; V. iii.

In, into; V. i.

Inconstant, capricious, fickle; IV. i.

Inherit, possess; I. ii.

Indite, (?) insist on inviting, II. iv.

In happy time, à propos; III. v.

It, its; I. iii.

Jack, a term of contempt for a silly fellow; III. i.

Jaunce, jaunt; II. v.

Jealous, in any way suspicious; V. iii.

Jealous-hood, jealousy; IV. iv.

Joint-stools, folding chairs; I. v.

Joy, rejoice; II. ii.

Keep, make; III. iv.

Kindly, exactly, aptly; II. iv.

Label, a seal appended to a deed; IV. i.

"Lady, lady, lady," a phrase quoted from an old ballad; II. iv.

Lammas-eve, the day before Lammas-tide, i.e. July 31st; I. iii.

Lantern, a turret full of windows; V. iii.

Late, lately; III. i.

Lay, wager, stake; I. iii.

Learn, teach; III. ii.

Learn'd me, taught myself; IV. ii.

Let, hindrance; II. ii.

Level, aim; III. iii.

Lieve, lief, gladly; II. iv.

Like, likely; IV. iii.

Like of, like; I. iii.

List, choose; I. i.

LOGGER-HEAD, blockhead; IV. iv.

LONG, "l. to speak," long in speaking, slow to speak; IV. i.

LONG SPINNERS' LEGS, long-legged spiders; I. iv.

LOVE, *i.e.* Venus; II. v.

MAB, the queen of the fairies; I. iv.

MADE, was doing; V. iii.

MAMMET, puppet; III. v.

MANAGE, course; III. i.

MANAGE, handle, use; I. i.

MANDRAKE, a plant, the root of which was supposed to resemble the human figure, and when torn from the earth to cause madness and even death; IV. iii.

MAR, elect; I. iii.

MARCHPANE, marzipan, a kind of almond paste; I. v.

MARGENT, margin; I. iii.

MARK-MAN, marksman; I. i.

MARRIED, harmonious; I. iii.

MEAN, means, instrument; III. iii.

MEASURE, a stately dance; I. iv.

MEDICINE, medicinal; II. iii.

MERCHANT, used contemptuously; II. iv.

MEW'D UP, shut up; III. iii.

MICKLE, great; II. iii.

MINION, saucy person; III. v.

MINSTREL, "give you the m.", *i.e.* call you a minstrel; IV. v.

MINUTE, minutes; V. iii.

MISADVENTURE, misfortune; V. i.

MISTEMPER'D, "compounded and hardened to an ill end"; I. i.

MODERN, commonplace, trite; III. ii.

MOODY, peevish, angry; III. i.

MORROW, morning; II. ii.

MOUSE-HUNT, a woman hunter; IV. iv.

MOVED, exasperated; I. i.

MUCH UPON THESE YEARS, about the same age; I. iii.

MUFFLE, hide; V. iii.

"MY HEART IS FULL OF WOE," a line of a popular ballad; IV. v.

NATURAL, idiot; II. iv.

NAUGHT, bad; III. ii.

NEEDLY WILL, of necessity must; III. ii.

NEEDY, joyless; III. v.

NEIGHBOR-STAINED, stained with the blood of countrymen; I. i.

NEW, just; I. i.

——, afresh, anew; I. i.

NICE, trifling; III. i.

NONE, "she will n.", she will have nothing to do with it; III. v.

NOTED, noticed, observed; V. i.

NOTHING, not at all; I. i.

O, grief, lamentation; III. iii.

O', on; III. i.

ODDS, "at o.", at variance; I. ii.

O'ER-PERCH, leap over; II. ii.

OLD, accustomed, practised; III. iii.

ON, of; I. iv.

ONCE, only; I. iii.

OPERATION, effect; III. i.

ORCHARD, garden; II. i.

OSIER CAGE, basket made of the water willow; II. iii.

OUTRAGE, outcry; V. iii.

OVERWHELMING, over-hanging; V. i.

OWES, owns; II. ii.

PALY, pale; IV. i.

PART, side; I. i.

PARTISAN, a kind of pike; I. i.

PARTS, natural gifts; III. iii.

PASSADO, a thrust in fencing; II. iv; III. i.

PASSING, surpassingly; I. i.

PAST COMPARE, past comparison; II. v.

PASTRY, the room in which pies were made; IV. iv.

PAY, give; I. i.

PEEVISH, silly, childish; IV. ii.

PERFORCE, compulsory; I. v.

PERDONA-MI'S, people who are continually saying pardon me; II. iv.

PERUSE, examine; V. iii.

PHAETHON, the son of Helios, the Sun god; III. ii.

PILCHER, scabbard; (used contemptuously); III. i.

PIN, the center of the butt in archery; II. iv.

PLANTAIN-LEAF, (supposed to be efficacious in healing wounds); I. ii.

PLATS, plaits, braids; I. iv.

PLUCKS, pulls; II. ii.

POOR JOHN, a coarse kind of fish, salted and dried; I. i.

POPERIN PEAR, a kind of pear; II. i.

PORTLY, well-bred; I. v.

POST, "in p.", in haste; V. iii.

PRESENCE, state room; V. iii.

PRESENT, immediate, instant; IV. i.

PRETTY FOOL, a term of endearment; I. iii.

PREVAILS, avails; III. iii.

PRICK, point; II. iv.

PRICK-SONG, music sung from notes; II. iv.

PRINCE OF CATS, (used with reference to *Tybalt,* the name of the cat in *Reynard the Fox*); II. iv.

PRINCOX, pert boy, saucy boy; I. v.

PROCURES, causes her to come; III. v.

PRODIGIOUS, monstrous; I. v.

PROOF, experience; I. i.

PROPERER, handsomer; II. iv.

PROROGUE, delay; IV. i.

PROROGUED, put off, delayed; II. ii.

PUMP, low shoe; II. iv.

PUNTO REVERSO, a back-handed stroke in fencing; II. iv.

PURGE, clear from suspicion; V. iii.

PURGED, cleared from smoke; I. i.

QUIT, reward; II. iv.

QUOTE, take note of; I. iv.

RAPIER, a small sword used in thrusting; I. v.

REASON, speak, talk; III. i.

RECKONING, estimation; I. ii.

REEKY, squalid, foul; IV. i.

REMEDIES, "both our r.", the healing of both of us; II. iii.

RESPECTIVE, regardful; II. i.

REST YOU MERRY, God keep you merry; I. ii.

RETORTS, throws back; III. i.

ROPERY, roguery, tricks; II. iv.

ROSEMARY, an herb used at bridals and burials; IV. v.

ROTE, "did read by rote and could not spell," (Schmidt); II. iii.

RUNAGATE, vagabond; III. v.

RUSH'D, "with partial eagerness eluded the law"; III. iii.

RUSHES, covering of floors; I. iv.

SACK, destroy; III. iii.

SADLY, seriously; I. i.

SADNESS, seriousness; I. i.

SCANT, scarcely; I. ii.

SCATHE, harm; I. v.

SET ABROACH, incited, caused; I. i.

SET UP MY REST, make up my mind; V. iii.

SHIELD, "God s.", God forbid; IV. i.

SHIFT, change; I. v.

SHRIFT, confession and consequent absolution; IV. ii.

SHRIVED, given absolution; II iv.

SIMPLENESS, folly; III. iii.

SIMPLES, medicinal herbs; V. i.

SINGLE-SOLED, contemptible; II. iv.

SIRRAH, a term of address to an inferior; IV. ii.

SIR-REVERENCE, used apologetically, when referring to something improper; I. iv.

SKAINS-MATES, (?) scapegraces; II. iv.

SLIP, used with a play upon slip = a counterfeit coin; II. iv.

SLOP, large loose breeches; II. iv.

SOBER-SUITED, quietly clad; III. ii.

So HO! a sporting term; II. iv.

SOLEMNITY, celebration of nuptials; IV. v.

SOME OTHER WHERE = somewhere else, elsewhere; I. i.

SOMETIME, sometimes; I. iv.

SOON-SPEDING, quickly acting, quickly despatching; V. i.

SORT, choose, select; IV. ii.

SORTED OUT, discovered; III. v.

SPED, despatched, undone; III. i.

SPITE, vexation; II. i.

——, "in s. of me," in defiance, to my mortification; I. i.

SPLEEN, heat, impetuosity; III. i.

SPOKE HIM FAIR, spoke to him with gentle words; III. i.

STARVETH, "looks out hungrily"; V. i.

STATE, "the whole of your fortune depends on this"; III. iii.

STAY, detain; V. iii.

——, linger; III. iii.

——, wait for; II. v.

STAY'D, delayed; V. iii.

STEADS, helps; II. iii.

STILL, always; I. i.

STINT, cease; I. iii.

STOCCATA, a thrust in fencing; III. i.

STRAIGHT, straightway; I. iii.

STRAIN'D, forced; II. iii.

STRAINS, constrains, wrenches; IV. i.

STRANGE, reserved, distant; II. i.

——, retiring, unfamiliar; III. ii.

STRATAGEMS, amazing deeds; III. v.

STRUCKEN, struck; I. i.

SURCEASE, cease to beat; IV. i.

SWASHING, dashing; I. i.

SWEETING, a sweet apple; II. iv.

SWEET WATER, perfumed waters; V. iii.

SWOUNDED, swooned; III. ii.

TACKLED STAIR, rope ladder; II. iv.

TAKE ME WITH YOU, let me understand aright; III. v.

TAKE THE WALL, get the better of (used quibblingly); I. i.

TASSEL-GENTLE, male hawk; II. ii.

TEEN, sorrow; I. iii.

TEMPER, mix; III. v.

TENDER, bid, offer; III. iv.

——, hold, regard; III. i.

TETCHY, fretful, peevish; I. iii.

THEE, thyself; V. iii.

THEREWITHAL, with it; V. iii.

THOROUGH, through; II. iv.

THOUGHT, hoped; IV. v.

THOU's, thou shalt; I. iii.

TIMELESS, untimely; V. iii.

TITAN, the sun-god; II. iii.

To, as to; II. iii.

TO-NIGHT, last night; I. iv.; II. iv.

TOWARDS, at hand; I. v.

TOY, folly, idle fancy; IV. i.

TRENCHER, plate; I. v.

TRIED, proved; IV. iii.

TRUCKLE-BED, a bed to be pushed under another; II. i.

TUTOR, teach; III. i.

UNATTAINED, sound, impartial; I. ii.

UNBRUISED, unhurt; II. iii.

UNCOMFORTABLE, cheerless, joyless; IV. v.

UNFURNISH'D, unprovided; IV. ii.

UNMANN'D, untrained; III. ii.

UNSTUFF'D, not overcharged; II. iii.

UTTERS THEM, causes them to pass from one to another; V. i.

VALIDITY, value; III. iii.

VANISH'D, issued; II. iii.

VANITY, trivial pursuit, vain delight; II. vi.

VERSAL, universal; II. iv.

VIEW, outward appearance; I. i.

——, sight; I. i.

VISOR, mask; I. v.

WARE, aware; I. i.

WAX. "a man of w.", as pretty as if modelled in wax; I. ii.

WAXES, grows; I. v.

WEEDS, garments; V. i.

WELL SAID, well done; I. v.

WHAT, who; I. v.

——, "what dares," how dare; I. v.

WHO, which; I. i.; I. iv.

——, he who; I. i.

WIT, wisdom; I. iv.

——, "sentiments"; I. i.

WITH, by; I. iv.

——, through; V. iii.

WITHAL, with, by it; I. i.

WITHOUT, outside of; III. iii.

WOT, know; III. ii.

WRIT, written; I. iii.

WROUGHT, brought about; III. v.

YET NOT, not yet; II. ii.

YOND, yonder; I. v.

'ZOUNDS, a contraction of "God's wounds"; an oath, III. i.

GLOSSARY

FOR

Julius Caesar

ABIDE, answer for, suffer for: III. i.

ABJECTS, things cast away; IV. i.

ABOUT, go about; I. i.

——!, set to work; III. ii.

ABROAD, about in; III. ii.

ACROSS, crossed, folded; II. i.

ADDRESS'D, ready; III. i.

ADVANTAGE, profit us; III. i.

AFTER, afterwards; I. ii.

AGAINST, over against, near; I. iii.

ALL OVER, one after the other; II. i.

ALONE, only; IV. iii.

AN, if; I. ii.

ANCHISES, the father of Æneas; when Troy was sacked he bore him on his shoulders from the burning town; I. ii.

ANGEL, darling, favorite; III. ii.

ANNOY, injure, harm; II. i.

ANSWER, be ready for combat; V. i.

ANSWER'D, atoned for; III. ii.

ANSWERED, faced; IV. i.

APACE, quickly; V. iii.

APPARENT, manifest; II. i.

APPOINT, settle upon; IV. i.

APPREHENSIVE, endowed with intelligence; III. i.

APT, suitable, likely, II. ii.

——, ready, fit; III. i.

——, impressionable; V. iii.

ARRIVE, reach; I. ii.

ASTONISH, stun with terror; I. iii.

ATE, the goddess of Mischief and Revenge; III. i.

AT HAND, in hand; IV. ii.

AUGHT, anything; I. ii.

AUGURERS, professional interpreters of omens; II. i.

BAIT, hunt, chase; IV. iii.

BANG, blow; III. iii.

BARREN-SPIRITED, dull; IV. i.

BASE, low; II. i.

BASTARDY, act of baseness; II. i.

BATTLES, forces; V. i.

BAY, bark at; IV. iii.

BAY'D, driven to bay; III. i.

BEAR A HAND OVER, hold in check (as a rider); I. ii.

BEAR HARD, bear ill-will against; I. ii.; II. i.

BEAR ME, receive from me; III. iii.

BEARS (BETRAYED) WITH GLASSES, alluding to the stories that bears were surprised by means of mirrors, which they would gaze into, affording an opportunity of taking a surer aim; II. i.

BEAT, beaten; V. v.

BEHAVIORS, conduct; I. ii.

BEHOLDING, beholden; II. ii.

BELIKE, perhaps; III. ii.

BEND, look; I. ii.

BENDING, pressing on; IV. iii.

BEST, "you were b.," it were best for you; III. iii.

BESTOW, spend; V. v.

BETIMES, in good time, early; II. i.

BILLS, billets, written documents; V. ii.

BIRD OF NIGHT, *i.e.* the owl; I. iii.

BLOOD, "Pompey's b."; Gnæus, Pompey's son, had been killed at Munda, and Cæsar's triumph was in honor of the victory; I. i.

BLOODS, "young b.," young people; IV. iii.

BONDMAN, used with a play upon "bond," i.e. document; I. iii.

BONES, body, corpse; V. v.

BOOTLESS, without avail; III. i.

BOSOMS, "in their b.", in their confidence; V. i.

BREAK WITH, broach the subject to; II. i.

BRING, take; III. ii.

BROTHER, i.e. brother-in-law (Cassius having married a sister of Brutus); II. i.

BROUGHT, accompanied; I. iii.

BRUTUS, "old B.", i.e. Lucius Junius Brutus, who expelled the Tarquins; I. iii.

——, "Decius B.", i.e. Decimus B who was placed next after Octavius in Cæsar's will; I. iii.

BUDGE, give way; IV. iii.

BUSTLING RUMOR, noise of tumult; II. iv.

BY, near, close to; III. i.

CALCULATE, speculate upon future events; I. iii.

CALPURNIA, Cæsar's fourth wife; I. ii.

CARRIONS, worthless beings; II. i.

CAST, "c. yourself in wonder," i.e. throw yourself into wonder; I. iii.

CAUTELOUS, crafty; II. i.

CENSURE, judge; III. ii.

CEREMONIES, festal ornaments; I. i.

——, religious observances; II. i.

——, omens; II. ii.

CHAFING WITH, fretting against; I. ii.

CHANCE, happen; II. iv.

CHANCED, happened; I. ii.

CHANGE, exchange; V. iii.

——, "in his own c." by some change of disposition towards me; IV. ii.

——, change countenance; III. i.

CHARACTERY, writing; II. i.

CHARGE, weight upon; III. iii.

CHARGES, troops; IV. ii.

CHARM, conjure; II. i.

CHECK'D, reproved; IV. iii.

CHEW UPON, ponder; I. ii.

CHOLER, anger; IV. iii.

CHOPPED, chapped; I. ii.

CHOSE, chosen; II. i.

CLEAN, entirely; I. iii.

CLIMATE, region; I. iii.

CLOSE, hidden; I. iii.

——, come to terms; III. i.

CLOSET, room; III. ii.

COBBLER, botcher (used quibblingly); I. i.

COGNIZANCE, badges of honors; II. ii.

COLOSSUS, a gigantic statue said to have stood astride at the entrance of the harbor at Rhodes; I. ii.

COLOUR, pretext; II. i.

COME BY, get possession; II. i.

COMPANION, fellows (used contemptuously); IV. iii.

COMPARE, let us compare, we will compare; III. ii.

COMPASS, circle, course; V. iii.

COMPLEXION, appearance; I. iii.

CONCEIT, think of; III. i.

CONCEITED, conceived; I. iii.

CONCEPTIONS, ideas; I. ii.

CONCLUDED, decided; II. ii.

CONDITION, disposition; II. i.

CONFINES, boundaries; III. i.

CONN'D BY ROTE, learnt by heart; IV. iii.

CONSORTED, escorted; V. i.

CONSTANCY, firmness; II. iv.

CONSTANT, firm; III. i.

CONSTANTLY, firmly; V. i.

CONSTRUE, explain; II. i.

CONTENT, easy; I. iii.

——, calm; IV. ii.

——, glad; V. i.

CONTRIVE, conspire, plot; II. iii.

CONTRIVER, schemer, plotter; II. i.

CONTROVERSY, "hearts of c.", spirits eager for resistance; I. ii.

CORSE, corpse; III. i.

COUCHING, stoopings; III. i.

COUNTERS, round pieces of metal used in calculations; IV. iii.

COURSE, "run his c.", alluding to the course of the Luperci round the city wall; I. i.

COURTESIES, bowings, bendings of the knee; III. i.

CROSS LIGHTNING, forked lightning; I. iii.

CULL OUT, pick out; I. i.

CYNIC, rude man; IV. iii.

DAMN, condemn; IV. i.

DEARER, more bitterly, more intensely; III. i.

DEGREES, steps; II. i.

DELIVER, relate to; III. i.

DINT, impression; III. ii.

DIRECTLY, plainly; I. i.; III. iii

——, straight; I. ii.; IV. i.

DISCOMFORT, discourse; V. iii.

DISCOVER, show; I. ii.

DISHONOR, insult; IV. iii.

DISROBE, strip of their decorations; I. i.

DISTRACTED, distracted; IV. iii.

DOUBLET, the inner garment of a man; II. i.

DOUBTED, suspected; IV. ii.

DRACHMA, a Greek coin worth about 18¢.; III. ii.

DRAWN, assembled; I. iii.

ELEMENT, sky; I. iii.

ELEPHANTS BETRAYED WITH HOLES, "elephants were seduced into pitfalls"; II. i.

EMULATION, jealousy, envy; II. iii.

ENFORCED, exaggerated; III. ii.

——, struck hard; IV. iii.

ENFRANCHISEMENT, liberty, freedom; III. i.

ENLARGE, give vent to; IV. ii.

ENROLLED, recorded; III. ii.

ENSIGN, standard; V. i.

——, standard-bearer; V. iii.

ENTERTAIN, take into service; V. v.

ENVIOUS, spiteful, malicious; II. i.; III. ii.

ENVY, hatred, malice; II. i.

EPICURUS, "I held E. strong." i.e. I followed the Epicurean school, which held the belief in omens as mere superstition; V. iii.

EREBUS, the region of utter darkness between Earth and Hades; II. i.

ETERNAL, damned; I. ii.

EVEN, "e. field," i.e. level ground; V. i.

——, pure, unblemished; II. i.

E'ER, always; V. iii.

EVILS, evil things; II. i.

EXHALATIONS, meteors; II. i.

EXIGENT, exigency, crisis; V. i.

EXORCIST, one who raises spirits; II. i.

EXPEDITION, march; IV. iii.

EXTENUATED, undervalued, detracted from; III. ii.

EXTREMITIES, extremes; II. i.

FACE, boldness; V. i.

——, "f. of men", sense of danger depicted on men's faces; II. i.

FACTION, body of conspirators; II. i.

FACTIOUS, active; I. iii.

FAIN, gladly; I. ii.

FALL, happen; III. i.

——, let fall; IV. ii.

FALLING SICKNESS, epilepsy; I. ii.

FALLS, turns out, is; III. i.

FAMED WITH, made famous by; I. ii.

FAMILIAR INSTANCE, marks of familiarity; IV. ii.

FANTASIES, imaginings; II. i.

FASHION, shape, form; II. i.

FASHION, "begins his f.", begin to be fashionable with him; IV. i.

——, work upon, shape; II. i.

FAVOR, appearance; I. ii.

——, countenance; II. i.

FAVOR'S, appearance is; I. iii.

HONORABLE, honorably; V. i.

HOOTED, shouted with wonder; I. ii.

HOOTING, crying; I. iii.

HORSE, cavalry; IV. ii.

HOWEVER, although; I. ii.

HUMOR, distemper, caprice; II. i.

——, distempered humour, passing caprice; IV. iii.

HUMOURS, damp airs; II. i.

HURTLED, clashed; II. ii.

HYBLA, a town in Sicily famous for its honey; V. i.

IDES OF MARCH, *i.e.* fifteenth of March; I. ii.

IDLE BED, bed of idleness; II. i.

ILLUMINATE, illumine; I. iii.

IMAGES, statues of Cæsar; I. i.

IN, on; IV. i.

——, into; V. iii.

INCERTAIN, uncertain; V. i.

INCORPORATE, closely united; I. iii.

INDIFFERENTLY, impartially; I. ii.

INDIRECTION, dishonest practice; IV. iii.

INSUPPRESSIVE, not to be suppressed, II. i.

INTERMIT, delay; I. i.

JADE, a worthless horse; IV. ii.

JEALOUS ON, suspicious about; I. ii.

JIGGING, rhyming; IV. iii.

JOY, rejoice; V. v.

KERCHIEF, a covering for the head (a sign of illness); II. i.

KIND, nature; I. iii.

——, species; II. i.

KNAVE, boy; IV. iii.

LAUGHTER, jester; I. ii.

LAY OFF, take away from; I. ii.

LEFT, left off; IV. iii.

LEGIONS, bodies of infantry; IV. iii.

LET BLOOD, used equivocally with a play upon the surgical operation of "blood-letting"; III. i.

LETHE, death; III. i.

LIABLE, subject; II. ii.

LIES, halts; III. i.

LIGHT, alight; V. iii.

LIKE, "every l. is not the same," *i.e.* "to be like a thing is not to be that same thing"; II. ii.

——, same; IV. ii.

——, likely; I. ii.

LISTEN, listen to; IV. i.

LIVE, if I live; III. i.

LOOK, be sure, see; I. iii.

LOOK FOR, expect; IV. iii.

LOVER, friend; II. iii.

LOW-CROOKED, lowly bendings of the knee, III. i.

LUPERCAL, "the feast of L.", *i.e.* the Lupercalia; a feast of purification; I. i.

LUSTY, strong; III. ii.

MAIN, confident, firm; II. i.

MAKE FORTH, go on, forward; V. i.

MAKES TO, presses towards; III. i.

MAKE TO, advance; V. iii.

MARK, notice, observe; I. ii.

MARR'D, disfigured; III. ii.

MART, traffic; IV. iii.

MAY BUT, only may; I. iii.

ME, "plucked me ope"; I. ii.

MEAN, means; III. i.

MECHANICAL, belonging to the working-classes, mechanics; I. i.

METAL, mettle, temper; I. i.

METTLE, "quick m.", full of spirit; I. ii.

MIND, presentiment; III. i.

MISGIVING, presentiment, foreboding of ill; III. i.

MISTOOK, mistaken; I. ii.

MOCK, taunt; II. ii.

MODESTY, moderation; III. i.

MOE, more; II. i.

MONSTROUS, unnatural; I. iii.

MORTAL INSTRUMENTS, bodily powers; II. i.

MORTIFIED, deadened; II. i.

MOTION, impulse; II. i.

NAPKINS, handkerchiefs; III. ii.

NEATS-LEATHER, ox-hide; I. i.

PUBLIC CHAIR, the pulpit; III. ii.

PUISSANT, powerful; III. i.

PULPITS, *rostra,* platform; III. i.

PURGER, healers; II. i.

PURPOSE, "to the p.", to hit the purpose; III. i.

PUT ON, betray; II. i.

PUTS ON, assumes; I. ii.

QUALITY, natural disposition; I. iii.

QUESTION, subject; III. ii.

QUESTION, "call in q.", discuss, consider; IV. iii.

RAISE, rouse; IV. iii.

RANGE, roam; II. i.

RANK, too full of blood; III. i.

REARS, raises; III. i.

REGARD, consideration; III. i.

REMORSE, pity; II. i.

RENDER'D, given in reply; II. ii.

REPLICATION, echo; I. i.

RESOLVED, satisfied; III. i.

RESPECT, "of the best r.", held in the greatest respect; I. ii.

——, take notice of; IV. iii.

——, "in r. of," *i.e.* in comparison with; I. i.

REST, remain; V. i.

RESTING, not subject to motion; III. i.

RETENTIVE, restraining; I. iii.

RHEUMY, moist; II. i.

RIVED, split, torn; I. iii.; IV. iii.

ROME, used quibblingly with a play upon "room"; the pronunciation of the words was almost identical; I. ii.

ROUND, rung, step; II. i.

ROUT, disorderly company, mob; I. ii.

RUDE, brutal; III. ii.

SAD, serious; I. ii.

SATISFIED, given satisfaction, convinced; III. i.

SAVE ONLY, except; V. v.

SCHEDULE, paper written on; III. i.

SCOPE, full play; IV. iii.

SEARCH, pierce; V. iii.

SECURITY, over-confidence; II. iii.

SENNET, a set of notes on the cornet, or trumpet; I. ii.

SERVED, attended to; III. i.

SET ON, proceed; I. ii.

——, set forward; IV. iii.

SEVERAL, different; I. ii.

——, special; II. i.

——, separate; III. ii.

SHADOW, reflected image; I. ii.

SHALLOWS, sandbanks; IV. iii.

SHOW, demonstration; I. ii.

SHREWD, mischievous; II. i.

SHREWDLY, close enough; III. i.

SIGN'D, stamped, stained; III. i.

SIRRAH, a form of address to inferiors; IV. iii.

SLAUGHTER, "have added s.", have added another victim; V. i.

SLIGHT, worthless; IV. i.

SLIGHTED OFF, treated with contempt; IV. iii.

SLIP, "let s.", unleash; III. i.

SMATCH, snack, taste; V. v.

So, if only; I. ii.

SOFTLY, slowly; V. i.

SOIL, blemish; I. ii.

SOMETIME, sometimes; II. i.

SOOTH, in sooth, in truth; II. iv.

So PLEASE HIM, if it please him to; III. i.

SORT, rank; I. i.

——, way; I. ii.

——, "in s.", in a manner, after a fashion; II. i.

SPARE, lean; I. ii.

SPEAK TO ME, tell me; IV. iii.

SPEED, prosper; I. ii.

SPLEEN, passion; IV. iii.

SPOIL, "sign'd in thy spoil", *i.e.* having the stains of thy blood as their badges; III. i.

STALE, make common; I. ii.

STALED, make stale or common; IV. i.

STAND UPON, trouble about; III. i.

STARE, stand on end; IV. iii.

STARS, fortunes, fates; I. ii.

STATE, court; I. ii.

——, state of things; I. iii.

STAY, wait; I. iii.

——, await; V. i.

STERILE CURSE, the curse of being barren; I. ii.

STILL, always; I. ii.

STOLE, stolen; II. i.

STOMACHS, inclination; V. i.

STOOD ON, regarded, attached any importance to; II. ii.

STRAIN, race; V. i.

STRANGE-DISPOSED, strangely disposed; I. iii.

STRENGTH OF MALICE, III. i.

STRICKEN, struck II. i.

STRUCKEN, struck; III. i.

SUBURBS, outskirts; II. i.

SUCCESS, good fortune; II. ii.

——, issue; V. iii.

SUDDEN, quick; III. i.

SUFFERANCE, patience; I. iii.

——, suffering; II. i.

SUREST, most safely; IV. i.

SURLY, sullenly; I. iii.

SWAY, "the s. of the earth", equilibrium; I. iii.

SWEAR, let swear; II. i.

SWORE, caused to take an oath; V. iii.

SWOUND, swoon; I. ii.

TAG-RAG PEOPLE, the common people, rabble; I. ii.

TAKE THOUGHT, give way to melancholy; II. i.

TARDY, slow, laggard; I. ii.

TASTE, sort, way; IV. i.

TEMPER, constitution; I. ii.

TENOR, contents, IV. iii.

THASOS, an island in the Ægean, off the coast of Thrace; V. iii.

THAT, suppose that done; II. i.

THEN, in that case; V. i.

THESE AND THESE, such and such; II. i.

THEWS, muscles, strength; I. iii.

THICK, dim, short-sighted; V. iii.

THIS, "by this", i.e. by this time, now; I. iii.

THREAT, threaten; V. i.

THUNDER-STONE, thunderbolt; I. iii.

TIBER BANKS, the banks of the Tiber; I. i.

TIDE OF TIMES, course of times; III. i.

TIME OF LIFE, full period of life; V. i.

TIME'S ABUSE, abuses of the time; II. i.

TINCTURES, memorial bloodstains; II. ii.

'TIS JUST, just so, exactly; I. ii.

TO FRIEND, as our friend; III. i.

TOILS, snares; nets; II. i.

TO-NIGHT, last night; II. ii.

TOOK, taken; II. i.

TRASH, rubbish; I. iii.

TROPHIES, tokens of victory; I. i.

TRUE, honest; I. ii.

TURN HIM GOING, send him off; III. iii.

UNBRACED, unbuttoned; I. iii.; II. i.

UNDERGO, undertake; I. iii.

UNDERLINGS, mean fellows; I. ii.

UNFIRM, not fixed, not firm; I. iii.

UNGENTLY, unkindly; II. i.

UNICORNS, "u. may be betrayed with trees"; alluding to the belief that unicorns were captured by the huntsmen standing against a tree, and stepping aside when the animal charged; its horn spent its force on the trunk and stuck fast; II. i.

UNLUCKILY, foreshowing misfortune ominously; III. iii.

UNMERITABLE, undeserving; IV. i.

UNPURGED, "u. air," i.e. unpurged by the sun; II. i.

UNSHAKED OF, "u. o. motion," i.e. undisturbed by any motion; III. i.

UNTROD, "this u. state," i.e. this new state of affairs; III. i.

UPMOST, uppermost, topmost; II. i.

UPON, "u. a heap," in a heap, crowded all together; I. iii.

——, in intruding upon; II. i.

——, conditionally upon; III. i.

——, "u. a wish," as soon as wished for; III. ii.

——, in consequence of; IV. iii.

USE, custom; II. i.

——, "did u.", were accustomed; I. ii.

VAUNTING, boasting; IV. iii.

VENTURES, what we have ventured, risked; IV. iii.

VESTURE, garment; III. ii.

VOICE, vote; III. i.

VOID, open; II. iv.

VOUCHSAFE, vouchsafe to accept; II. i.

VULGAR, common herd; I. i.

WAFTURE, waving; II. i.

WARN, summon; V. i.

WASPISH, petulant; IV. iii.

WEEP, shed; I. i.

WEIGHING, taking into consideration; II. i.

WELL, in a friendly way; IV. ii.

WELL GIVEN, well disposed; I. ii.

WHAT, "what night," *i.e.* what a night; I. iii.

——!, an exclamation of impatience; II. i.

WHEN, an exclamation of impatience; II. i.

WHERE, when; I. ii.

WHET, instigate, II. i.

WHO, the man who; I. iii.

——, which; V. i.

WHOLE, well, healthy; II. i.

WIND, turn, wheel; IV. i.

WIT, intelligence, III. ii.

WITH, by; I. iii.; III. i.; III. ii.

WITH A THOUGHT, quick as thought; V. iii.

WIVES, women; III. i.

WOE THE WHILE!, alas the time!; I. iii.

WORD, "at a w.", at his word; I. ii.

WORLD, condition of affairs; I. ii.

WORTHLESS, unworthy; V. i.

YEARNS, grieves; II. ii.

YET, still; II. i.

GLOSSARY

FOR

Hamlet

A', he; (Ff. *"he"*); II. i.

ABOUT, get to your work! II. ii.

ABOVE, "more a.", moreover; II. ii.

ABSOLUTE, positive; V. i.; perfect, faultless (used by Osric), V. ii.

ABSTRACT, summary; II. ii.

ABUSE, delusion; IV. vii.

ABUSES, deceives; II. ii.

ACQUITTANCE, acquittal; IV. vii.

ACT, operation; I. ii.

ADDITION, title; I. iv.

ADDRESS, prepare; I. ii.

ADMIRATION, wonder; I. ii.

ADULTERATE, adulterous; I. v.

AFEARD, afraid; V. ii.

AFFECTION, affectation; II. ii.

AFFRONT, confront, encounter; III. i.

A-FOOT, in progress, III. ii.

AFTER, according to; II. ii.

AGAINST, in anticipation of; III. iv.

AIM, guess; IV. v.

ALLOWANCE, permission; II. ii.

AMAZE, confound, bewilder; II. ii.

AMAZEMENT, astonishment; III. ii.

AMBITION, attainment of ambition; III. iii.

AMBLE, move in an affected manner; III. i.

AMISS, misfortune; IV. v.

ANCHOR'S, hermit's; III. ii.

"AND WILL HE NOT COME AGAIN," etc., a well-known song; IV. v.

AN END, on end; I. v.

ANGEL, angling-line; V. ii.

AN IF, if; I. v.

ANNEXMENT, appendage; III. iii.

ANON, soon, presently; II. ii.

ANSWER, reply to a challenge; V. ii.

ANSWER'D, explained; IV. i.

ANTIC, disguised, fantastic; I. v.

ANTIQUE, ancient; V. ii.

APART, aside, away; IV. i.

APE, "the famous ape," etc., reference to an old fable which has not yet been identified; III. iv.

APOPLEX'D, affected with apoplexy; III. iv.

APPOINTMENT, equipment; IV. vi.

APPREHENSION, conception; II. ii.

APPROVE, affirm, confirm, I. i.

—— credit, make approved, V. ii.

APPURTENANCE, proper accompaniment; II. ii.

ARGAL, Clown's blunder for *ergo;* V. i.

ARGUMENT, plot of a play; II. ii.

——, subject in dispute, IV. iv.

ARM YOU, prepare yourselves; III. iii.

ARRAS, tapestry; II. ii.

ARTICLE, clause in an agreement, I. i.; "a soul of great a." *i.e.,* a soul with so many qualities that its inventory would be very large; V. ii.

AS, as if; II. i.

414

——, as if, as though, IV. v.; so, IV. vii.; namely, I. iv.

As'es, used quibblingly; V. ii.

Aslant, across; IV. vii.

Assault, "of general a.", "incident to all men"; II. i.

Assay, trial, test; II. ii.

——, try; III. i.

——, "make a.", "throng to the rescue"; III. iii.

Assays of bias, indirect aims; II. i.

Assigns, appendages; V. ii.

Assistant, helpful; I. iii.

Assurance, security; with play upon the legal sense of the word; V. i.

Attent, attentive; I. ii.

Attribute, reputation; I. iv.

Aught, "hold'st at a.", holds of any value, values at all; IV. iii.

Authorities, offices of authority, attributes of power; IV. ii.

Avouch, declaration; I. i.

A-work, at work; II. ii.

Back, "support in reverse"; IV. vii.

Baked-meats, pastry; "funeral b.", cold entertainment prepared for the mourners at a funeral; I. ii.

Ban, curse; III. ii.

Bare, mere; III. i.

Bark'd about, grew like bark around; I. v.

Barren, foolish; III. ii.

Barr'd, debarred, excluded; I. ii.

Batten, grow fat; III. iv.

Beaten, well-worn, familiar; II. ii.

Beating, striking; I. i.

Beautied, beautified; III. i.

Beautified, beautiful; II. ii.

Beaver, visor; I. ii.

Bedded, lying flat; III. iv.

Beetles, projects, juts over; I. iv.

Behove, behoof, profit; V. i.

Bent, straining, tension; II. ii.

——, "to the top of my b.", to the utmost; III. ii.

Beshrew, a mild oath; II. i.

Besmirch, soil, sully; I. iii.

Bespeak, address; speak to; II. ii.

Best, "in all my b.", to the utmost of my power; I. ii.

Bestowed, placed, lodged; II. ii.

Beteem, allow, permit; I. ii.

Bethought, thought of; I. iii.

Bilboes, stocks or fetters used for prisoners on board ship; V. ii.

Bisson, 'b. rheum,' *i.e.* blinding tears; II. ii.

Blank, "the *white* mark at which arrows were aimed"; IV. i.

Blanks, makes pale; III. ii.

Blast in proof, "a metaphor taken from the trying or proving of firearms or cannon, which blast or burst in the proof"; IV. vii.

Blastments, blighting influences; I. iii.

Blazon, "eternal b.", publication of eternal mysteries; I. v.

Blench, start aside; II. ii.

Blood, passion, IV. iv.; "b. and judgment," passion and reason, III. ii.

Blown, in its bloom; III. i.

Board, address; II. ii.

Bodes, forbodes, portends; I. i.

Bodkin, the old word for dagger; III. i.

Bodykins, diminutive of body; II. ii.

"Bonnie Sweet Robin," the first words of a well-known song of the period; IV. v.

Bore, caliber, importance of a question; IV. vi.

Borne in hand, deceived with false hopes; II. ii.

Bound, ready, prepared; I. v.

——, was bound; I. ii.

Bourn, limit, boundary; III. i.

Brainish, imaginary; IV. i.

Brave, glorious; II. ii.

Bravery, bravado; V. ii.

BREATHE, whisper; II. i.

BREATHING, whispering; I. iii.

BREATHING TIME, time for exercise; V. ii.

BRINGING HOME, strictly, the bridal procession from church; applied to a maid's funeral; V. i.

BROAD, unrestrained; III. iv.

BROKE, broken; IV. v.

BROKERS, go betweens; I. iii.

BROOCH, an ornament worn in the hat; IV. vii.

BROOD, "on b.", brooding; III. i.

BRUIT, proclaim abroad; I. ii.

BUDGE, stir, move; III. iv.

BUGS, bugbears; V. ii.

BULK, body; II. i.

BUSINESS, do business; I. ii.

BUTTONS, buds; I. iii.

BUZ, BUZ! an interjection used to interrupt the teller of a story already well known; II. ii.

BUZZERS, whisperers; IV. v.

BY AND BY, immediately; III. ii.

BY'R LADY, a slight oath; III. ii.

CAN, can do; III. iii.

CANDIED, sugared, flattering; III. ii.

CANKER, canker worm; I. iii.

CANON, divine law; I. ii.

CAPABLE, capable of feeling; III. iv.

CAP-A-PE, from head to foot; I. ii.

CARD, "by the c.", with precision (alluding probably to the shipman's card); V. i.

CARNAL, sensual· V. ii.

CAROUSES, drinks· V. ii.

CARRIAGE, tenor, import; I. i.

CARRY IT AWAY, gain the victory; II. ii.

CART, car, chariot; III. ii.

CARVE FOR, choose for, please; I. iii.

CAST, casting, moulding; I. i.

——, contrive; "c. beyond ourselves," to be oversuspicious; II. i.

CATAPLASM, plaster; IV. vii.

CAUTEL, deceit, falseness; I. iii.

CAVIARE, "at that time a new and fashionable delicacy not relished by the vulgar, and therefore used by Shakespeare to signify anything above their comprehension" (Nares); II. ii.

CEASE, extinction; III. iii.

CENSURE, opinion; I. iii.

CENTER, i.e., of the Earth; II. ii.

CEREMENTS, cloths used as shrouds for dead bodies; I. iv.

CHAMELEON, an animal supposed to feed on air; III. ii.

CHANGE, exchange; I. ii.

CHANSON, song; II. ii.

CHARACTER, hand-writing; IV. vii.

——, write, imprint; I. iii.

CHARGE, expense; IV. iv.; load, weight; V. ii.

CHARIEST, most scrupulous, I. iii.

CHECKING AT, "to check at," a term in falconry, applied to a hawk when she forsakes her proper game and follows some other; IV. vii.

CHEER, fare; III. ii.

CHIEF, chiefly, especially; I. iii.

CHOPINE, a high cork shoe; II. ii.

CHORUS, interpreter of the action of a play; III. ii.

CHOUGH, a sordid and wealthy boor; V. ii.

CICATRICE, scar; IV. iii.

CIRCUMSTANCE, circumlocution; I. v.

——, "c. of thought", details of thought which lead to a conclusion; III. iii.

CLAPPED, applauded; II. ii.

CLEPE, call; I. iv.

CLIMATURES, regions; I. i.

CLOSELY, secretly; III. i.

CLOSES WITH, agrees with: II. i.

COAGULATE, clotted; II. ii.

COCKLE HAT, a mussel-shell in the hat was a badge of pilgrims bound for places of devotion beyond sea; IV. v.

COIL, "mortal c.", mortal life, turmoil of mortality: III. i.

COLD, chaste; IV. vii.

COLDLY, lightly; IV. iii.

COLLATERAL, indirect; IV. v.

COLLEAGUED, leagued; I. ii.

COLLECTION, an attempt to collect some meaning from it; IV. v.

COLUMBINES, flowers emblematic of faithlessness; IV, v.

COMBAT, duel; I. i.

COMMA, "a c. 'tween their amities"; the smallest break; V. ii.

COMMANDMENT, command; III. ii.

COMMENT, "the very c. of thy soul", "all thy powers of observation"; (Ff. "my soul"); III. ii.

COMMERCE, intercourse; III. i.

COMPELLED, enforced; IV. vi.

COMPLETE STEEL, full armor; I. iv.

COMPLEXION, temperament; I. iv.

COMPLY, use ceremony; II. ii.

COMPULSATORY, compelling; I. i.

COMPULSIVE, compelling; III. iv.

CONCEIT, imagination; III. iv.

——, design; "liberal c.", tasteful, elaborate design; V. ii.

CONCERNANCY, meaning; V. ii.

CONCLUSIONS, experiments; III. iv.

CONDOLEMENT, sorrow; I. ii.

CONFEDERATE, favoring; III. ii.

CONFINE, boundary, territory; I. i.

CONFINES, prisons; II. ii.

CONFRONT, outface; III. iii.

CONFUSION, confusion of mind; III. i.

CONGREGATION, collection; II. ii.

CONGRUING, agreeing; IV. iii.

CONJUNCTIVE, closely joined; IV. vii.

CONSEQUENCE, "in this c."; in the following way; II. i.

CONSIDER'D, "at our more c. time," when we have more time for consideration: II. ii.

CONSONANCY, friendship; II. ii.

CONSTANTLY, fixedly; I. ii.

CONTAGION, contagious thing; IV. vii.

CONTENT, please, gratify; III. i.

CONTINENT, that which contains, IV. iv.; inventory; V. ii.

CONTRACTION, the making of the marriage contract; III. iv.

CONTRIVING, plotting; IV. vii.

CONVERSATION, intercourse; III. ii.

CONVERSE, conversation; II. i.

CONVOY, conveyance; I. iii.

COPED WITHAL, met with; III. ii.

CORSE, corpse; I. iv.

COTED, overtook, passed by; II. ii.

COUCHED, concealed: II. ii.

COUCH WE, let us lie down, conceal ourselves; V. i.

COUNT, account, trial; IV. vii.

COUNTENANCE, favor; IV. iv.

COUNTER, hounds "run counter" when they follow the scent in the wrong direction; IV. v.

COUNTERFEIT PRESENTMENT, portrait; III. iv.

COUPLE, join, add; I. v.

COUPLETS, "golden c.", "the pigeon lays only two eggs, at a time, and the newly hatched birds are covered with yellow down"; V. i.

COUSIN, used of a nephew; I. ii.

COZENAGE, deceit, trickery; V. ii.

COZEN'D, cheated; III. iv.

CRACKED WITHIN THE RING, "there was formerly a ring on the coin, within which the sovereign's head was placed; if the crack extended from the edge beyond this ring, the coin was rendered unfit for currency"; II. ii.

CRANTS, garland, used for the chaplet carried before a maiden's coffin; V. i.

CREDENT, credulous; I. iii.

CREW, did crow; I. i.

CRIED, "c. in the top of mine", were higher than mine; II. ii.

CRIES ON, cries out; V. ii.

CRIMEFUL, criminal; IV. vii.

CROCODILE, "woo't eat a c.", referring probably to the toughness of its skin; V. i.

CROOK, make to bend; III. ii.

CROSS, go across its way; (to cross the path of a ghost was to come under its evil influence); I. i.

CROW-FLOWERS, (probably) buttercups; IV. vii.

CROWNER, coroner; V. i.

CRY, company; III. ii.

CUFFS, fisticuffs, blows; II. ii.

CUNNINGS, respective skill; IV. vii.

CURB, cringe; "c. and woo", "bend and truckle"; III. iv.

CURIOUSLY, fancifully; V. i.

CURRENTS, courses; III. iii.

DAINTIER, more delicate; V. i.

DAISY, emblem of faithlessness; IV, v.

DANE, King of Denmark; I. i.

DANSKER, Danes; II. i.

DAY AND NIGHT, an exclamation; I. v.

DEAREST, heartily, earnestly; IV. iii.

DEARTH, high value; V. ii.

DECLINE UPON, sink down to; I. v.

DECLINING, falling, going from bad to worse; II. ii.

DEFEAT, destruction; II. ii.

DEFEATED, disfigured, marred; I. ii.

DEFENCE, skill in weapons; IV. vii.

DEFINEMENT, definition; V. ii.

DEJECT, dejected; III. i.

DELATED, set forth in detail; I. ii.

DELIVER, relate; I. ii.

DELVER, digger; V. i.

DEMANDED OF, questioned by; IV. ii.

DENOTE, mark, portray; I. ii.

DESIRES, good wishes; II. ii.

DEXTERITY, nimbleness, celerity; I. ii.

DIET, "your worm is your only emperor for d.", a grim play of words upon "the Diet of Worms"; IV. iii.

DIFFERENCES, "excellent d.", distinguishing qualities; V. ii.

DISAPPOINTED, (?) unappointed, unprepared; I. v.

DISCLOSE, hatching; III. i.

DISCLOSED, hatched; V. i.

DISCOURSE, conversation; III. i.

———, "d. of reason," i.e. the reasoning faculty; I. ii.

DISCOVERY, confession; II. ii.

DISJOINT, disjointed; I. ii.

DISPATCH, hasten to get ready, III. iii.

DISPATCH'D, deprived; I. v.

DISPOSITION, nature; I. iv.

DISTEMPER, "your cause of d.", the cause of your disorder; III. ii.

DISTEMPERED, disturbed; III. ii.

DISTILL'D, dissolved, melted; I. ii.

DISTRACT, distracted; IV. v.

DISTRUST, "I d. you," i.e. I am anxious about you; III. ii.

DIVULGING, being divulged; IV. i.

DO, "to do," to be done; IV. iv.

DOCUMENT, instruction; IV. v.

DOLE, grief; I. ii.

DOOM, Doomsday; III. iv.

DOUBT, suspect, fear; I. ii.

DOUTS, extinguishes; IV. vii.

DOWN-GYVED, pulled down like gyves or fetters; II. i.

DRAB, strumpet; II. ii.

DREADFUL, full of dread; I. ii.

DRIFT, "d. of circumstance," roundabout methods; III. i.

DRIVES AT, rushes upon; II. ii.

DUCATS, gold coins; II. ii.

DULL THY PALM, i.e. "make callous thy palm by shaking every man by the hand" (Johnson); I. iii.

DUMB SHOW, a show unaccompanied by words, preceding the dialogue and foreshadow-

ing the action of a play; III.
ii.

DUPP'D, opened; IV. v.

DYE, tinge; I. iii.

EAGER, sharp, sour; I. v.

EALE, ? = e'ile (*i.e.* "evil"); I.
iv.

EAR, "in the e.", within hearing;
III. i.

EASINESS, unconcernedness; V.
i.

EAT, eaten; IV. iii.

ECSTASY, madness; II. i.

EDGE, incitement; III. i.

EFFECTS, purposes; III. iv.

EISEL, vinegar; the terms usually
employed by older English
writers for the bitter drink
given to Christ; V. i.

ELSINORE, the residence of the
Danish kings; II. ii.

EMULATE, emulous; I. i.

ENACT, act; III. ii.

ENACTURES, actions; III. ii.

ENCOMPASSMENT, circumven-
tion; II. i.

ENCUMBER'D, folded; I. v.

ENGAGED, entangled; III. iii.

ENGINER, engineer; I. iv.

ENSEAMED, defiled, filthy; III.
iv.

ENTERTAINMENT, "gentle e.",
show of kindness; V. ii.

ENTREATMENTS, solicitations; I.
iii.

ENVIOUSLY, angrily; IV. v.

ERRING, wandering, roaming; I.
i.

ESCOTED, maintained; II. ii.

ESPIALS, spies; III. i.

ESTATE, rank; V. i.

ETERNAL, ? = infernal; V. ii.

EVEN, straightforward; II. ii.

EVEN CHRISTIAN, fellow-Chris-
tian; V. i.

EVENT, result, issue; IV. iv.

EXCEPTION, objection; V. ii.

EXCREMENTS, outgrowth (used
of hair and nails); III. iv.

EXPECTANCY, hope; III. i.

EXPOSTULATE, discuss; II. ii.

EXPRESS, expressive, perfect; II.
ii.

EXTENT, behavior; II. ii.

EXTOLMENT, praise; V. ii.

EXTRAVAGANT, vagrant, wandering beyond its limit or confine; I. i.

EXTREMITY, "in ex.", going to
extremes; III. ii.

EYASES, unfledged birds; II. ii.

EYE, presence; IV. iv.

EYRIE, a brood of nestlings; II.
ii.

FACULTIES, peculiar nature; II.
ii.

FACULTY, ability, II. ii.

FAIR, gently; IV. i.

FALLS, falls out, happens; IV.
vii.

FANCY, "express'd in f.", gaudy;
I. iii.

FANG'D, having fangs; III. iv.

FANTASY, imagination, I. i.;
whim, caprice, IV. iv.

FARDELS, packs, burdens; III. i.

FARM, take the lease of it; IV.
iv.

FASHION, a mere temporary
mood; I. iii.; "f. of himself,"
i.e. his usual demeanor; III.
i.

FAT; fatten; IV. iii.

FAT, "f. and scant of breath", ?
= out of training; V. ii.

FAVOR, charm, IV. v.; appearance, V. i.

FAWNING, cringing; III. ii.

FAY, faith; II. ii.

FEAR, object of fear; III. iii.

——, fear for, I. iii.; IV. v.

FEATURE, figure, form; III. i.

FEE, payment, value, I. iv.; fee-
simple, IV. iv.

FELLIES, the outside of wheels;
II. ii.

FELLOWSHIP, partnership; III.
ii.

FENNEL, symbol of flattery; IV.
v.

FETCH, artifice; "fetch of warrant," justifiable stratagem;
II. i.

FEW, "in f.", in brief; I. iii.

FIERCE, wild, terrible; I. i.

FIERY QUICKNESS, hot haste; IV. iii.

FIGURE, figure of speech; II. ii.

FIND, find out, detect; III. i.

FINE OF HIS FINES, end of his fines; with a play upon the other sense of the word; V. i.

FIRST, *i.e.* first request; II. ii.

FIT, prepared, ready; V. ii.

FITNESS, convenience; V. ii.

FITS, befits; I. ii.

FLAW, gust of wind; V. i.

FLUSH, in full vigor; III. iii.

FLUSHING, redness; "had left the f." *i.e.* had ceased to produce redness; I. ii.

FOIL, used with play upon its two senses, (i.) blunted rapier, (ii.) gold-leaf used to set off a jewel; V. ii.

FOND, foolish; I. v.

FOND AND WINNOWED, foolish and over-refined; V. ii.

FOOLS OF NATURE, made fools of by nature; I. iv.

FOOT, "at f.", at his heels; IV. iii.

FOR, as for, I. iii.; in place of, instead, V. i.; "for all," once for all, I. iii.; "for and" and also V. i.

FORDO, destroy; V. i.

FOREKNOWING, foreknowledge, prescience; I. i.

FORESTALLED, prevented; III. iii.

FORGED PROCESS, false statement of facts; I. v.

FORGERY, invention, imagination; IV. vii.

FORGONE, given up; II. ii.

FORTUNE'S STAR, an accidental mark or defect; I. iv.

FORWARD, disposed; III. i.

FOUR, "f. hours", probably used for indefinite time; II. ii.

FRAME, order, sense; III. ii.

FREE, willing, not enforced, IV. iii.; innocent, II. ii.; III. ii.

FRET, vex, annoy; with a play upon "*fret* = 'small lengths of wire on which the fingers press the strings in playing the guitar' "; III. ii.

FRETTED, carved, adorned; II. ii.

FRIENDING, friendliness; I. v.

FRIGHTED, frightened; III. ii.

FROM, away from, contrary to; III. ii.

FRONT, forehead; III. iv.

FRUIT, dessert, II. ii.

FRUITS, consequences; II. ii.

FUNCTION, the whole action of the body; II. ii.

FUST, become moldy; IV. iv.

GAGED, pledged; I. i.

GAIN-GIVING, misgiving; V. ii.

GAIT, proceeding; I. ii.

GALLED, wounded, injured; III. i.

GALLS, hurts, injuries; I. iii.

GARB, fashion, manners; II. ii.

GENDER, "general g.", common race of men; IV. vii.

GENERAL, general public; II. ii.

GENTRY, courtesy; II. ii., V. ii.

GERMANE, akin; V. ii.

GIB, a tom-cat; III. iv.

GIBBER, gabble; I. i.

GIBES, jeers; V. i.

GIS, a corruption of Jesus; IV. v.

GIVING OUT, indication; I. v.

GLIMPSES, glimmering light; I. iv.

GLOBE, head; I. v.

GO ABOUT, attempt; II. ii.

GO BACK AGAIN, *i.e.*, refer to what one was, but is no more; IV. vii.

GOD-A-MERCY, God have mercy; II. ii.

GOD BE WI' YE, good bye; II. i.

GOD 'ILD YOU, God yield, reward you; IV. v.

GOD KISSING CARRION, said of "the sun breeding maggots in a dead dog": II. ii.

GOOD, good sirs· I. i.

GOOD MY BROTHER, my good brother; I. iii.

GOOSE-QUILLS, "afraid of g.", *i.e.* afraid of being satirized; II. ii.

GO TO, an exclamation of impatience; I. iii.

GRACE, honour; I. ii.

GRACIOUS, *i.e.* Gracious king; III. i.

——, benign, full of blessing; I. i.

GRAINED, dyed in grain; III. iv.

GRATING, offending, vexing; III. i.

GREEN, inexperienced; I. iii.

GREENLY, foolishly; IV. v.

GROSS, great, palpable; IV. iv.

——, "in the g.", *i.e.* in a general way; I. i.

GROUNDLINGS, rabble who stood in the *pit* of the theater; III. ii.

GRUNT, groan; III. i.

GULES, red, a term of heraldry; II. ii.

GULF, whirlpool; III. iii.

HABIT, "outward h.", external politeness; V. ii.

HANDSAW, heron; II. ii.

HANDSOME, "more h. than fine"; "*handsome* denotes genuine natural beauty; *fine* artificial laboured beauty" (Delius); II. ii.

HAP, happen; I. ii.

HAPLY, perchance, perhaps; III. i.

HAPPILY, perchance; I. i.

HAPPY, "in h. time", in good time (*à la bonne heure*); V. ii.

HAPS, fortune; IV. iii.

HATCHMENT, an armorial escutcheon used at a funeral; IV. v.

HAUNT, "out of h.", from the haunts of men; IV. i.

HAVE, "you h. me," you understand me; II. i.

HAVE AFTER, let us follow; I. iv.

HAVE AT YOU, I'll hit you; V. ii.

HAVIOR, deportment; I. ii.

HEAD, armed force; IV. v.

HEALTH, "spirit of health", "healed or saved spirit"; I. iv.

HEARSED, coffined; I. iv.

HEAT, anger; III. iv.

HEAVY, "'tis h.", it goes hard; III. iii.

HEBENON, hen bane; I. v.

HECATE, the goddess of mischief and revenge; III. ii.

HECTIC, continual fever; IV. iii.

HEDGE, encompass; IV. v.

HEIGHT, "at h.", to the utmost; I. iv.

HENT, hold, seizure; III. iii.

HERALDRY, "law and h.", *i.e.* heraldic law; I. i.

HERB OF GRACE, rue, IV. v.

HEROD, a common character in the mystery plays, represented as a furious tyrant; III. ii.

HEY-DAY, frolicsome wildness; III. iv.

HEY NON NONNY, meaningless refrain common in old songs; IV. v.

HIC ET UBIQUE, here and everywhere; I. v.

HIDE FOX, AND ALL AFTER, a children's hide-and-seek game; IV. ii.

HIES, hastens; I. i.

HILLO, a falconer's cry to recall his hawk; I. v.

HIM, he whom; II. i.

HIS, its; I. iii.

HOAR LEAVES, the silvery-grey underside of willow leaves; IV. vii.

HOBBY-HORSE, a principal figure in the old morris dances; III. ii.

HOIST, *i.e.* hoised, hoisted; III. iv.

HOLDS QUANTITY, keep their relative proportion; III. ii.

HOLD UP, continue; V. i.

HOME, thoroughly; III. iii.

HONEST, virtuous; III. i.

HONESTY, virtue; III. i.

HOODMAN-BLIND, blind man's buff; III. iv.

HOOPS, bands; I. iii.

HUGGER-MUGGER, "in h.", *i.e.* in secrecy and in haste; IV. v.

HUMOROUS, full of humors or caprices; "the h. man", a standing character of many plays of the period; II. ii.

HUSBAND, manage; IV. v.

HUSBANDRY, thrift, economy; I. iii.

HUSH (used as adjective); II. ii.

HYPERION, Phœbus Apollo; I. ii.

HYRCANIAN BEAST, *i.e.* the tiger; II. ii.

I, = (?) "aye"; III. ii.

IDLE, unoccupied; III. ii.

ILIUM, the palace in Troy; II. ii.

ILL-BREEDING, hatching mischief; IV. v.

ILLUME, illumine; I. i.

IMAGE, representation; III. ii.

IMMEDIATE, "most i.", nearest; I. ii.

IMPART, (?) bestow myself, give all I can bestow; I. ii.

IMPASTED, made into paste; II. ii.

IMPERIOUS, imperial; V. i.

IMPLORATORS, implorers; I. iii.

IMPONED, staked; V. ii.

IMPORTANT, momentous; III. iv.

IMPORTING, having for import; I. ii.

——, concerning; V. ii.

IMPOSTHUME, abscess; IV. iv.

IMPRESS, impressment; I. i.

IMPUTATION, reputation; V. ii.

IN, into; III. iv.

INCAPABLE, insensible to; IV. vii.

INCORPORAL, immaterial; III. iv.

INCORPSED, incorporate; IV. vii.

INCORRECT, not subdued; I. ii.

INDENTURES, "a pair of i.", "agreements were usually made in duplicate, both being written on the same sheet, which was cut in a crooked or *indented* line, so that the parts would tally with each other"; V. i.

INDEX, prologue, prefare; III. iv.

INDICT, accuse; II. ii.

INDIFFERENT, ordinary; II. ii.

——, indifferently, fairly; III. i.

INDIFFERENTLY, pretty well; III. ii.

INDIRECTIONS, indirect means; II. i.

INDIVIDABLE, "scene ind.", probably a play in which the unity of place is preserved; II. ii.

INDUED, suited· IV. vii.

INEXPLICABLE, senseless; III. ii.

INFUSION, qualities; V. ii.

INGENIOUS, conscious; V. i.

INHERITOR, possessor; V. i.

INHIBITION, prohibition; II. ii.

INNOVATION, change (for the worse); II. ii.

INQUIRE, enquiry II. i.

INSINUATION, meddling; V. ii.

INSTANCE, example; IV. v.

INSTANCES, motives; III. ii.

INSTANT, immediate; I. v.

INTENTS, purposes; I. iv.

IN THAT, inasmuch as; I. ii.

INURN'D, entombed, interred; I. iv.

INVESTMENTS, vestures; I. iii.

IT, its; I. ii.

JEALOUSY, suspicion; II. i.

"JEPHTHAH, JUDGE OF ISRAEL," *etc.*, a quotation from an old ballad; II. ii.

JIG, a ludicrous ballad; II. ii.

——, walk as if dancing a jig; III. i.

JOHN-A-DREAMS, John of Dreams, John the Dreamer II. ii.

JOINTRESS, dowager; I. ii.

JOWLS, knocks; V. i.

JOYS, gladdens; III. ii.

JUMP, just; I. i.

KEEP, dwell; II. i.

KETTLE, kettle-drum; V. ii.

KIBE, chilblain on the heel; V. i.

KIND, "more than kin, and less than k."; used equivocally for (i.) natural, and (ii.) affectionate, with a play upon "kin"; I. ii.

KINDLESS, unnatural; II. ii.

KNOTTED, interwoven; I. v.

KNOW, acknowledge; V. ii.

LABORSOME, laborious; I. ii.

LACK, be wanting; I. v.

LAPSED, "l. in time and passion"; having let time slip by indulging in mere passion; III. iv.

LAPWING, the symbol of a forward fellow; V. ii.

LARDED, garnished; IV. v.

LAWLESS, unruly (Ff., *"Landlesse"*); I. i.

LAZAR-LIKE, like a leper; I. v.

LEANS ON, depends on; IV. iii.

LEARN, teach; V. ii.

LEAVE, permission, I. ii.

——, leave off, II. i.; give up, III. iv.

LENDS, gives; I. iii.

LENTEN, meager; II. ii.

LETHE, the river of oblivion ("Lethe wharf" = Lethe's bank); I. v.

LETS, hinders; I. iv.

LET TO KNOW, informed; IV. vi.

LIBERAL, free-spoken; IV. vii.

LIEF, gladly, willingly; III. ii.

LIFE, "the single and peculiar l.", the private individual; III. iii.

——, "in my l.", *i.e.* in my continuing to live; V. ii.

LIGHTNESS, lightheadedness; II. ii.

LIKE, likely; I. ii.

LIKES, pleases; II. ii.

LIMED, caught as with birdlime; III. iii.

LIST, muster-roll; I. i.

——, boundary; IV. v.

——, listen to; I. iii.

LIVING, lasting; V. i.

LOAM, clay; V. i.

LOGGATS, a game somewhat resembling bowls; V. i.

LONG PURPLES, "the early *purple orchis* which blossoms in April and May"; IV. vii.

LOOK THROUGH, show itself; IV. vii.

LOSE, waste, throw away; I. ii.

LUXURY, lust; I. v.

MACHINE, body; II. ii.

MAIMED, imperfect; V. i.

MAIN, main point; II. ii.

——, the country as a whole; IV. iv.

MAKE, brings; II. ii.

MANNER, fashion, custom; I. iv.

MARGENT, margin; it was a common practice to write comment or gloss in the margins of old books; V. ii.

MARK, watch; III. ii.

MARKET OF HIS TIME, "that for which he sells his time"; IV. iv.

MART, marketing, traffic; I. i.

MARVELOUS, marvelously; II. i.

MASSY, massive; III. iii.

MATIN, morning; I. v.

MATTER, sense; IV. v.

——, subject (misunderstood willfully by Hamlet to mean "cause of dispute"); II. ii.

MAZZARD, skull; V. i.

MEANS, means of access; IV. vi.

MEED, merit; V. ii.

MEET, proper; I. v.

MERELY, absolutely; I. ii.

METAL, mettle; I. i.

MICHING MALLECHO, mouching (*i.e.* skulking) mischief; III. ii.

MIGHT, could; I. i.

MIGHTIEST, very mighty; I. i.

MILCH, milk-giving = moist = tearful (Pope *"melt"*); II. ii.

MILKY, white; II. ii.

MINCING, cutting in pieces; II. ii.

MINERAL, mine; IV. i.

MINING, undermining; III. iv.

MISTOOK, mistaken; V. ii.

MOBLED, muffled; II. ii.

MODEL, exact copy; V. ii.

MOIETY, portion; I. i.

MOIST, "the moist star," *i.e.* the moon; I. i.

MOLE OF NATURE, natural defect, blemish; I. iv.

MOPE, be stupid; III. iv.

MORTAL, deadly; IV. vii.

MORTISED, joined with a mortise; III. iii.

MOST, greatest; I. v.

ORDER, prescribed rule; V. i.

ORDINANT, ordaining; V. ii.

ORDNANCE, cannon; V. ii.

ORE, gold; IV. i.

OR ERE, before; I. ii.

ORGAN, instrument; IV. vii.

ORISONS, prayers; III. i.

OSSA, reference to story of the giants, who piled Olympus, Pelion, and Ossa, three mountains in Thessaly, upon each other, in their attempt to scale heaven; V. i.

OSTENTATION, funeral pomp; IV. v.

OUTSTRETCHED, puffed up; II. ii.

OVERLOOKED, perused; IV. vi.

OVERPEERING, overflowing, rising above; IV. v.

OWL WAS A BAKER'S DAUGHTER, alluding to a story current among the folk telling how Christ went into a baker's shop, and asked for bread, but was refused by the baker's daughter, in return for which He transformed her into an owl; IV. v.

PACKING, contriving; III. iv.

PADDOCK, toad; III. iv.

PAINTED, "p. tyrant," i.e. tyrant in a picture, II. ii.; unreal, fictitious, III. i.

PAJOCK, = peacock = a turkey; III. ii.

PALL, become useless; V. ii.

PANSIES, "love-in-idleness," the symbol of thought; IV. v.

PARDON, permission to take leave; I. ii.

PARLE, parley; I. i.

PART, quality, gift; IV. vii.

PARTISAN, a kind of halberd; I. i.

PARTS, gifts, endowments; IV. vii.

PARTY, person, companion; II. i.

PASS, passage; II. ii.

——, "p. of practice," treacherous thrust; IV. vii.

PASSAGE, "for his p.", to accom-

pany his departure, in place of the passingbell; V. ii.

PASSETH, surpasseth; I. ii.

PASSION, violent sorrow; II. ii.

PASSIONATE, full of feeling; II. ii.

PATE, a contemptuous word for head; V. i.

PATIENCE, permission; III. ii.

PAUSE, time for reflection; III. i.

——, "deliberate p.", a matter for deliberate arrangement; IV. iii.

——, "in p.", in doubt; III. iii.

PEACE-PARTED, having departed in peace; V. i.

PEAK, sneak, play a contemptible part; II. ii.

PELICAN, a bird which is supposed to feed its young with its own blood; IV. v.

PERDY, a corruption of par Dieu; III .ii.

PERIWIG-PATED, wearing a wig; III. ii.

PERPEND, consider; II. ii.

PERUSAL, study, examination; II. i.

PERUSE, examine closely; IV. vii.

PETAR, petard, "an Engine wherewith strong gates are burst open"; III. iv.

PICKED, refined, fastidious; V. i.

PICKERS AND STEALERS, i.e., hands; III. ii.

PICTURE IN LITTLE, miniature; II. ii.

PIGEON-LIVER'D, too mild tempered; II. ii.

PIONER, pioneer; I. v.

PITCH, height, importance; III. i.

PITEOUS, pitiful; II. i.

PITH AND MARROW, the most valuable part; I. iv.

PLAUSIVE, plausible, pleasing; I. iv.

PLAUTUS, "P. too light," alluding to the fact that Plautus was taken as the word for comedy by the Academic playwrights; II. ii.

PLAYED I' THE UNIVERSITY, alluding to the old academic practice of acting Latin or English plays at Christmastide, or in honor of distinguished visitors; III. ii.

PLAYED, "p. the desk or tablebook", *i.e.* been the agent of their corespondence; II. ii.

PLOT, piece of ground; IV. iv.

PLURISY, plethora, a fullness of blood; IV. vii.

POINT, "at p." completely; I. ii.

POLACK, Pole; II. ii.

——, Polish; V. ii.

POLACKS, Poles; I. i.

POLE, pole-star; I. i.

POLITICIAN, plotter, schemer; V. i.

PORPENTINE, porcupine; I. v.

POSSET, curdle; I. v.

POSY, motto, verse on a ring; III. ii.

POWERS, armed force; IV. iv.

PRACTICE, artifice, plot; IV. vii.

PRECEDENT, former; III. iv.

PRECURSE, forerunning; I. i.

PREGNANT, yielding, ready; III. ii.

PRENOMINATE, aforesaid; II. i.

PRESCRIPTS, orders; II. i.

PRESENTLY, immediately; II. ii.

PRESENT PUSH, immediate proof; V. i.

PRESSURE, impress, imprint; III. ii.

PRESSURES, impressions; I. v.

PREVENT, anticipate; II. ii.

PRICK'D ON, incited; I. i.

PRIMAL, first; III. iii.

PRIMY, spring-like; I. iii.

PRIVATES, common soldiers; II. ii.

PROBATION, proof; I. i.

PROCESS, decree; IV. iii.

PRODIGAL, prodigally; I. iii.

PROFIT, advantage; II. ii.

PROGRESS, journey made by a sovereign through his own country; IV. iii.

PRONOUNCE, speak on; III. ii.

PROOF, trial of strength; II. ii.

PROPER, appropriate; II. i.

——, own, very; V. ii.

PROPERTY, kingly right; II. ii.

PROPOSER, orator; II. ii.

PROVIDENCE IN THE FALL OF A SPARROW, alluding to *Matthew* x. 29, "Are not two sparrows sold for a farthing? and one of them shall not fall on the ground without your Father"; V. i.

PROVINCIAL ROSES, rosettes of ribbon worn on shoes; III. ii.

PUFF'D, bloated; I. iii.

PURGATION, "put him to his p.", "a play upon the legal and medical senses of the word"; III. ii.

PURSY, fat with pampering; III. iv.

PUT ON, incite, instigate, IV. vii.; tried, V. ii.; assume, I. v.

PUT ON ME, impressed upon me; I. iii.

QUAINTLY, artfully, skillfully; II. i.

QUALITY, profession; II. ii.

QUANTITY, measure, portion; III. iv.

QUARRY, heap of dead; V. ii.

QUESTION, talk; III. i.

——, "cry out on the top of q.", *i.e.* speak in a high key, or in a high childish treble; II. ii.

QUESTIONABLE, inviting question; I. iv.

QUEST LAW, inquest law; V. i.

QUICK, alive; IV. i.

QUIDDITIES, subleties; V. i.

QUIETUS, a law term for the official settlement of an account; III. i.

QUILLETS, subtle arguments; V. i.

QUINTESSENCE, the highest or fifth essence; II. ii.

QUIT, requite; V. ii.

QUOTED, observed, noted; II. i.

RACK, mass of clouds in motion; II. ii.

RANGE, roam at large; III. iii.

RANKER, richer, greater; IV. iv.

RANKLY, grossly; I. v.

RAPIER, a small sword; V. ii.

RASHLY, hastily; V. ii.

RAVEL OUT, unravel; III. iv.

RAZED, slashed; III. ii.

REACH, capacity; II. i.

RECKS, cares, minds; I. iii.

RECOGNIZANCES, "a recognizance is a bond or obligation of record testifying the recogniser to owe to the recognisee a certain sum of money" (Cowell); V. i.

RECORDERS, kind of flageolet; III. ii.

RECOVERIES, a law term; (v. "Vouchers"); V. i.

REDE, counsel, advice; I. iii.

REDELIVER, report; V. ii.

REELS, dances wildly; I. iv.

REGARDS, conditions; II. ii.

REGION, air; II. ii.

RELATIVE, to the purpose; II. ii.

RELISH OF, have a flavor; III. i.

REMEMBRANCES, mementos; III. i.

REMISS, careless; IV. vii.

REMORSE, pity; II. ii.

REMOVE, removal; IV. v.

REMOVED, retired, secluded; I. iv.

REPAST, feed; IV. v.

REPLICATION, reply, answer; IV. ii.

REQUITE, repay; I. ii.

RESIDENCE, a fixed abode as opposed to strolling; used technically of theatrical companies; II. ii.

RESOLUTES, desperadoes; I. i.

RESOLVE, dissolve, melt; I. ii.

RE-SPEAKING, re-echoing; I. ii.

RESPECT, consideration; III. i.

REST, stay, abode; II. ii.

RESTS, remains; III. iii.

RETROGRADE, contrary; I. ii.

RETURN'D, "had r.", would have returned; I. i.

REVEREND, venerable; II. ii.

REVOLUTION, change; V. i.

RE-WORD, repeat in the very words; III. iv.

RHAPSODY, a collection of meaningless words; III. iv.

RHENISH, Rhenish wine; I. iv.

RIBAND, ribbon, ornament; IV. vii.

RIGHTS OF MEMORY, rights remembered; V. ii.

RITES, funeral service; V. i.

RIVALS, partners, sharers; I. i.

ROBUSTIOUS, sturdy; III. ii.

ROMAGE, bustle, turmoil; I. i.

ROOD, cross; "by the rood," an oath; III. iv.

ROOTS ITSELF, takes root; I. v.

ROSCIUS, the most celebrated actor of ancient Rome; II. ii.

ROSE, charm, grace; III. iv.

ROSEMARY, an herb; the symbol of remembrance, particularly used at weddings and funerals; IV. v.

ROUGH-HEW, make the rough, or first form; a technical term in carpentering; V. ii.

ROUND, in a straightforward manner; III. ii.

ROUSE, bumper, revel; I. ii.

ROW, stanza; II. ii.

RUB, impediment; a term in the game of bowls; III. i.

RUE, called also "herb of grace"; emblematic of repentance (Ophelia is probably playing on *rue* = repentance, and *"rue even for ruth"* = pity; the former signification for the queen, the latter for herself); IV. v.

SABLES, fur used for the trimming of rich robes; perhaps with a play on *"sable"* = black; III. ii.

SALLETS, salads; used metaphorically for "relish"; II. ii.

SANDAL SHOON, shoes consisting of soles tied to the feet; IV. v.

SANS, without; III. iv.

SATE, satiate; I. v.

SATYR, taken as a type of deformity; I. ii.

SAWS, maxims; I. v.

SAY'ST, say'st well; V. i.

'SBLOOD, a corruption of *"God's blood"*; an oath; II. ii.

SCANN'D, carefully considered; III. iii.

'SCAPES, escapes; I. iii.

SCARF'D, put on loosely like a scarf; V. ii.

SCHOLAR, a man of learning, and hence versed in Latin, the language of exorcists; I. i.

SCHOOL, university; I. ii.

SCONCE, colloquial term for head; V. i.

——, esconce; III. iv.

SCOPE, utmost aim; III. ii.

SCOURGE, punishment; IV. iii.

SCRIMERS, fencers; IV. vii.

SCULLION, the lowest servant; used as a term of contempt; II. ii.

SEALS, "to give them s.", to ratify by action; III. ii.

SEASON, temper, restrain; I. ii.

——, ripen; I. iii.

——, qualify; II. i.

SEASONS, matures, seasons; III. ii.

SECURE, careless, unsuspicious; (Johnson, "secret"); I. v.

SEEMING, appearance; III. ii.

SEIZED OF, possessed of; I. i.

SEMBLANCE, equal, like; V. ii.

SENECA, "S. cannot be too heavy," alluding to the rhetorical Senecan plays taken as models for tragedy by the Academic playwrights; II. ii.

SENSE, feeling; sensibility; III. iv.

SENSIBLY, feelingly; IV. v.

SE OFFENDENDO, Clown's blunder for se defendendo; V. i.

SEQUENT, following; V. ii.

SERGEANT, sheriff's officer; V. ii.

SET, regard, esteem; IV. iii.

SEVERAL, different; V. ii.

SHALL, will; III. i.

SHALL ALONG, shall go along; III. iii.

SHAPE, "to our s.", to act our part; IV. vii.

SHARDS, fragments of poetry; V. i.

SHARK'D UP, picked up without selection; I. i.

SHEEN, brightness, luster; III. ii.

SHEETED, enveloped in shrouds; I. i.

SHENT, reproached; III. ii.

SHORT, "kept s.", kept, as it were, tethered, under control; IV. i.

SHOULD, would; III. ii.

SHREDS AND PATCHES, alluding to the motley dress worn by the clown; III. iv.

SHREWDLY, keenly, piercingly; I. iv.

SHRIVING-TIME, time for confession and absolution; V. ii.

SIEGE, rank; IV. vii.

SIMPLE, silly, weak; I. ii.

SIMPLES, herbs; IV. vii.

SITH, since; III. iv.

SKIRTS, outskirts, borders; I. i.

SLANDER, abuse; I. iii.

SLEDDED, traveling in sledges; I. i.

SLIPS, faults, offences; II. i.

SLIVER, a small branch of a tree; IV. vii.

SO, such; III. i.; provided that; IV. vii.

SOFTLY, slowly; IV. iv.

SOFT YOU NOW, hush; III. i.

SOIL, stain; I. iv.

SOLE, only; III. iii.

SOLICITED, urged, moved; V. ii.

SOMETHING, somewhat; I. iii.

SOMETIMES, formerly; I. i.

SORT, associate; II. ii.

——, turn out; I. i.

SOVEREIGNTY, "your s. of reason", the command of your reason; I. iv.

SPLENTIVE, passionate; V. i.

SPRINGES, snares; I. iii.

SPURNS, kicks; IV. v.

STAND ME UPON, be incumbent on me; V. ii.

STAR, sphere; II. ii.

STATION, attitude in standing; III. iv.

STATISTS, statesmen; V. ii.

STAY, wait for; V. ii.

STAY'D, waited; I. iii.

STAYS, waits for me; III. iii.

STAY UPON, await; III. ii.

STICK FIERY OFF, "stand in brilliant relief"; V. ii.

STIFFLY, strongly; I. v.

STILL, always; I. i.

STITHY, smithy; III. ii.

STOMACH, courage; I. i.

STOUP, drinking cup; V. i.

STRAIGHT, straightaway; II. ii.

STRANGER, "as a s.", *i.e.* without doubt or question; I. v.

STREWMENTS, strewing of flowers over the corpse and grave; V. i.

STRIKE, blast, destroy by their influence; I. i.

STUCK, thrust; IV. vii.

SUBJECT, subjects, people; I. i.

SUCCESSION, future; II. ii.

SUDDENLY, immediately; II. ii.

SULLIES, stains, blemishes; II. i.

SUN, "too much i' the s.", probably a quibbling allusion to the old proverb "Out of heaven's blessing into the warm sun," = out of comfort, miserable; I. ii.

SUPERVISE, perusal; V. ii.

SUPPLIANCE, dalliance; I. iii.

SUPPLY, aiding; II. ii.

SUPPOSAL, opinion; I. ii.

SWADDLING CLOUTS, swaddling clothes (Ff. "*swathing*"); II. ii.

SWEET, sweetheart; III ii.

SWINISH, "with s. phrase," by calling us swine; I. iv.

SWITZERS, Swiss guards; IV. v.

SWOOPSTAKE, sweepstake (the term is taken from a game of cards, the winner sweeping or drawing the whole stake); IV v.

SWOUNDS, a corruption of *God's wounds;* an oath; II ii.

——, swoons, faints; V. ii.

TABLE, tablet; I. v.

TABLES, memorandum-book; I. v.

TAINTS, stains blemishes; II. i.

TAKE ARMS AGAINST A SEA, an allusion to a custom attributed to the Celts by Aristotle, Strabo, and other writers; "they throw themselves into the foaming floods with their swords drawn in their hands," *etc.*. III. i.

TAKES, affects, enchants; I. i.

TAKE YOU, pretend; II. i.

TARDY, "come t. off," being too feebly shown; III. ii.

TARRE, incite; II. ii.

TAX'D, censured; I. iv.

TELL, count; I. ii.

TEMPER'D, compounded; V. ii.

TEMPLE (applied to the body); I. iii.

TEND, wait; IV. iii.

TENDER, have a care for; I. iii.

TENDERS, promises; I. iii.

TENT, probe; II. ii.

TERMAGANT, a common character in the mystery-plays, represented as a most violent tyrant; III. ii.

TETTER, a diseased thickening of the skin; I. v.

THAT, that which; II. ii.

——, so that; IV. v.

THEFT, the thing stolen; III ii.

THEREABOUT OF IT, that part of it; II. ii.

THEWS, sinews; I. iii.

THIEVES OF MERCY, merciful thieves; IV. vi.

THINKING, "not th. on," being forgotten; III. ii.

THINKS'T THEE, seems it to thee; V. ii.

THOUGHT, care, anxiety; IV. v.

THOUGHT-SICK, sick with anxiety; III. iv.

THRIFT, profit; III. ii.

THROUGHLY, thoroughly; IV. v.

TICKLE O' THE SERE, easily moved to laughter; II. ii.

TIMBER'D, "too slightly t.", made of too light wood; IV. vii.

TIME, the temporal world; III. i.

TINCT, dye, color; III. iv.

TO, compared to; I. ii.

TO-DO, ado; II. ii.

VIDELICET, that is to say; II. i.

VIGOUR, "sudden v.", rapid, power; I. v.

VIOLET, emblem of faithfulness; IV. v.

VIRTUE, power; IV. v.

VISITATION, visit; II. ii.

VOICE, vote, opinion; V. ii.

VOUCHERS, "double v., his recoveries," "a recovery with *double voucher* is the one usually suffered, and is so denominated from *two* persons (the latter of whom is always the common cryer, or some such inferior person) being successively *vouched,* or called upon, to warrant the tenant's title" (Ritson); V. i.

WAG, move; III. iv.

WAKE, hold nightly revel; I. iv.

WANDERING STARS, planets; V. i.

WANN'D, turned pale; II. ii.

WANTON, effeminate weakling; V. ii.

——, wantonly; III. iv.

WANTONNESS, affection; III. i.

WARRANTY, warrant; V. i.

WASH, sea; III. ii.

WASSAIL, drinking bout; I. iv.

WATCH, state of sleeplessness; II. ii.

WAVES, beckons; I. iv.

WE, "and we", *i.e.* "as for us"; I. iv.

WEEDS, robes; IV. vii.

WELL-TOOK, well undertaken; II. i.

WHARF, bank; I. v.

WHAT, who; IV. vi.

WHEEL, refrain of a song; IV. v.

WHICH, who; IV. vii.

WHOLESOME, sensible; III. ii.

WILDNESS, madness; III. i.

WILL, "virtue of his will," *i.e.* his virtuous intention; I. iii.

WIND, "to recover the w. of me," a hunting term, meaning to get to windward of the game, so that it may not scent the toil or its pursuers; III. ii.

WINDLASSES, indirect ways; II. i.

WINKING, "given my heart a w.", closed the eyes of my heart; II. ii.

WINNOWED (*vide* "Fond").

WIT, wisdom; II. ii.

WITHAL, with; I. iii.

WITHDRAW, "to w. with you," "to speak a word in private with you" (Schmidt); III. ii.

WITHERS, the part between the shoulder-blades of a horse; III. ii.

WITHIN'S, within this; III. ii.

WITTENBERG, the University of Wittenberg (founded 1502); I. ii.

WONDER-WOUNDED, struck with surprise; V. i.

WOODCOCKS, birds supposed to be brainless; I. iii.

WOO'T, contraction of *wouldst thou;* V. i.

WORD, watch-word; I. v.

WORLDS, "both the w.", this world and the next; IV. v.

WOULD, wish; I. ii.

WOUNDLESS, invulnerable; IV. i.

WRECK, ruin; II. i.

WRETCH, here used as a term of endearment; II. ii.

WRIT, "law of w. and liberty," probably a reference to the plays written with or without decorum; II. ii.

YAUGHAN, "get thee to Y."; probably the name of a well-known keeper of an ale-house near the Globe; V. i.

YAW, stagger, move unsteadily (a nautical term); V. ii.

YEOMAN'S SERVICE, good service, such as the yeoman performed for his lord; V. ii.

YESTY, foamy; V. ii.

YORICK, the name of a jester, lamented by Hamlet; V. i.

YOURSELF, "in y.", for yourself, personally; II. i.

GLOSSARY

FOR

Macbeth

A ONE, a man; III. iv.

ABSOLUTE, positive; III. vi.

ABUSE, deceive; II. i.

ACHERON, the river of the infernal regions; III. v.

ADDER'S FORK, the forked tongue of the adder; IV. i.

ADDITION, title; I. iii.

ADDRESS'D THEM, prepared themselves; II. ii.

ADHERE, were in accordance; I. vii.

ADMIRED, wondrous-strange; III. iv.

ADVISE, instruct; III. i.

AFEARED, afraid; I. iii.

AFFECTION, disposition; IV. iii.

AFFEER'D, confirmed; IV. iii.

ALARM, call to arms; V. ii.

ALARUM'D, alarmed; II. i.

ALL, any; III. ii.

——, "and all to all," *i.e.* and we all (drink) to all; III. iv.

ALL-THING, in every way; III. i.

A-MAKING, in course of progress; III. iv.

ANGEL, genius, demon; V. viii.

ANGERLY, angrily; III. v.

ANNOYANCE, hurt, harm; V. i.

ANON, immediately; I. i.

AON, ANON, "coming, coming"; the general answer of waiters; II. iii.

AN'T, if it; III. vi.

ANTIC, grotesque, old-fashioned; IV. i.

ANTICIPATEST, dost prevent; IV. i.

APACE, quickly; III. iii.

APPLY, be devoted; III. ii.

APPROVE, prove; I. vi.

ARGUMENT, subject, theme; II iii.

ARM'D, encased in armor; III. iv.

AROINT THEE, begone; I. iii.

ARTIFICIAL, made by art; III. v.

AS, as if; II. iv.

ASSAY, "the great a. of art," the greatest effort of skill; IV. iii.

ATTEND, await; III. ii.

AUGURES, auguries; (?) augurs; III. iv.

AUTHORIZED BY, given on the authority of; III. iv.

AVOUCH, assert; III. i.

BABY OF A GIRL, (?) girl's doll; according to others, "feeble child of an immature mother"; III. iv.

BADGED, smeared, marked (as with a badge); II. iii.

BANE, evil, harm; V. iii.

BATTLE, division of an army; V. vi.

BEGUILE, deceive; I. v.

BELLONA, the goddess of war; I. ii.

BEND UP, strain; I. vii.

BENISON, blessing; II. iv.

BENT, determined; III. iv.

BEST, good, suitable; III. iv.

BESTOW'D, staying; III. i.

BESTOWS HIMSELF, has settled; III. vi.

BESTRIDE, stand over in posture of defense; IV. iii.

BIDES, lies; III. iv.

BILL, catalogue; III. i.

432

BIRNAM, a high hill twelve miles from Dunsinane; IV. i.

BIRTHDOM, land of our birth, mother-country; IV. iii.

BLADED, "b. corn," corn in the blade, when the ear is still green; IV. i.

BLIND-WORM, glow-worm; IV. i.

BLOOD-BOLTER'D, locks matted into hard clotted blood; IV. i.

BLOW, blow upon; I. iii.

BODEMENTS, forebodings; IV. i.

BOOT, "to b.", in addition; IV. iii.

BORNE, conducted, managed; III. vi.

BORNE IN HAND, kept up by false hopes; III. i.

BOSOM, close and intimate; I. ii.

BRAINSICKLY, madly; II. ii.

BREAK, disclose; I. vii.

BREECH'D, "having the very hilt, or breech, covered with blood"; (according to some "covered as with breeches"); II. iii.

BREED, family, parentage; IV. iii.

BRINDED, brindled, streaked; IV. i.

BRING, conduct; II. iii.

BROAD, plain-spoken; III. vi.

BROIL, battle; I. ii.

BROKE OPE, broken open; II. iii.

BUT, only; I. vii.

BY, past; IV. i.

BY THE WAY, casually; III. iv.

CABIN'D, confined; III. iv.

CARELESS, uncared for; I. iv.

CASING, encompassing, all surrounding; III. vi.

'CAUSE, because; III. vi.

CENSURES, opinion; V. iv.

CHAMPION ME, fight in single combat with me; III. i.

CHANCED, happened, taken place; I. iii.

CHAPS, jaws, mouth; I. ii.

CHARGE, "in an imperial c.", in executing a royal command; IV. iii.

CHARGED, burdened, oppressed; V. i.

CHAUDRON, entrails; IV. i.

CHILDREN (trisyllabic); IV. iii.

CHOKE THEIR ART, render their skill useless; I. ii.

CHUCK, a term of endearment; III. ii.

CLEAR, serenely; I. v.

——, innocent, guiltless; I. vii.

——, unstained; II. i.

CLEARNESS, clear from suspicion; III. i.

CLEPT, called; III. i.

CLING, shrivel up; V. v.

CLOSE, join, unite; III. ii.

CLOSE, secret; III. v.

CLOSED, enclosed; III. i.

CLOUDY, sullen, frowning; III. vi.

COCK, cock-crow; "the second c.", i.e., about three o'clock in the morning; II. iii.

COIGN OF VANTAGE, convenient corner; I. vi.

COLD, (?) dissyllabic; IV. i.

COLME-KILL, i.e., Icolmkill, the cell of St. Columbia; II. iv.

COME, which have come; I. iii.

COMMAND UPON, put your commands upon; III. i.

COMMENDS, commits, offers; I. vii.

COMMISSION, "those in c.", those entrusted with the commission; I. iv.

COMPOSITION, terms of peace; I. ii.

COMPT, "in c.", in account; I. vi.

COMPUNCTIOUS, pricking the conscience; I. v.

CONCLUDED, decided; III. i.

CONFINELESS, limitless, IV. iii.

CONFOUNDS, destroys, ruins; II. ii.

CONFRONTED, met face to face; I. ii.

CONFUSION, destruction; II. iii.

CONSEQUENCES; v. mortal; V. iii.

CONSENT, counsel, proposal; II. i.

CONSTANCY, firmness; II. ii.

CONTEND AGAINST, vie with; I. vi.

CONTENT, satisfaction; III. ii.

CONTINENT, restraining; IV. iii.

CONVERT, change; IV. iii.

CONVEY, "indulge secretly"; IV. iii.

CONVINCE, overpower; I. vii.

CONVINCES, overpowers; IV. iii.

COPY, (?) copyhold, non-permanent tenure; III. ii.

CORPORAL, corporeal; I. iii.

——, "each c. agent," *i.e.* "each faculty of the body"; I. vii.

COUNSELLORS, "c. to fear," fear's counsellors, *i.e.* "suggest fear"; V. iii.

COUNTENANCE, "be in keeping with"; II. iii.

CRACK OF DOOM, thunder at the day of doom; IV. i.

CRACKS, charges; I. ii.

CROWN, head; IV. i.

DAINTY OF, particular about; II. iii.

DEAR, deeply felt; V. ii.

DEGREES, degrees of rank; III. iv.

DELIVER THEE, report to thee; I. v.

DELIVERS, communicates to us; III. iii.

DEMI-WOLVES, a cross between dogs and wolves; III. i.

DENIES, refuses; III. iv.

DETRACTION, defamation; "mine own d.", the evil things I have spoken against myself; IV. iii.

DEVIL (monosyllabic); I. iii.

DEW, bedew; V. ii.

DISJOINT, fall to pieces; III. ii.

DISPLACED, banished; III. iv.

DISPUTE IT, fight against it; (?) reason upon it (Schmidt); IV. iii.

DISSEAT, unseat; V. iii.

DISTANCE, hostility; III. i.

DOFF, do off, put off; IV. iii.

DOUBT, fear, suspect; IV. ii.

DRINK, "my d.," *i.e.* "my *posset*"; II. i.

DROWSE, become drowsy; III. ii.

DUDGEON, handle of a dagger; II. i.

DUNNEST, darkest; I. v.

EARNEST, pledge, money paid beforehand; I. iii.

EASY, easily; II. iii.

ECSTASY, any state of being beside one's self; III. ii.

EFFECTS, act, actions; V. i.

EGG, term of contempt; IV. ii.

EMINENCE, distinction; III. ii.

ENGLAND, the King of England; IV. iii.

ENKINDLE, incite; I. iii.

ENOW, enough; II. iii.

ENTRANCE, (trisyllabic); I. v.

EQUIVOCATE TO HEAVEN, get to heaven by equivocation; II. iii.

EQUIVOCATOR, (probably alluding to Jesuitical equivocation; Garnet, the superior of the order was on his trial in March, 1606), II. iii.

ESTATE, royal dignity, succession to the crown; I. iv.

ETERNAL JEWEL, immortal soul, III. i.

ETERNE, perpetual; III. ii.

EVIL, king's evil, scrofula; IV. iii.

EXASPERATE, exasperated; III. vi.

EXPECTATION, those guests who are expected; III. iii.

EXPEDITION, haste; II. iii.

EXTEND, prolong; III. iv.

FACT, act, deed; III. vi.

FACULTIES, powers, prerogatives; I. vii.

FAIN, gladly; V. iii.

FANTASTICAL, imaginary; I. iii.

FARROW, litter of pigs; IV. i.

FAVOR, pardon; I. iii.

——, countenance, face; I. v.

FEARS, objects of fear; I. iii.

FEED, "to f.", feeding; III. iv.

FEE-GRIEF, "grief that hath a single owner"; IV. iii.

FELL, scalp; V. v.

———, cruel, dire; IV. ii.

FELLOW, equal; II. iii.

FILE, list; V. ii.

———, "the valued f.", list of qualities; III. i.

FILED, made foul, defiled; III. i.

FIRST, "at f. and last," (?) once for all, from the beginning to the end; (Johnson conj. "to f. and next"); III. iv.

FITS, caprices; IV. ii.

FLAWS, storms of passion; III. iv.

FLIGHTY, fleeting; IV. i.

FLOUT, mock, defy; I. ii.

FLY, fly from me; V. iii.

FOISONS, plenty, rich harvests; IV. iii.

FOLLOWS, attends; I. vi.

FOR, because of; III. i.

———, as for, as regards; IV. ii.

FORBID, cursed, blasted; I. iii.

FORCED, strengthened; V. v.

FORGE, fabricate, invent; IV. iii.

FORSWORN, perjured; IV. iii.

FOUNDED, firmly fixed; III. iv.

FRAME OF THINGS, universe; III. ii.

FRANCHISED, free, unstained; II. i.

FREE, freely; I. iii.

FREE, honorable; III. vi.

FREE, remove, do away; III. vi.

FRENCH HOSE, probably a reference to the narrow, straight hose, in contradistinction to the round, wide hose; II. iii.

FRIGHT, frighten, terrify; IV. ii.

FROM, differently from; III. i.

———, in consequence of, on account of; III. vi.

FRY, literally a swarm of young fishes; here used as a term of contempt; IV. ii.

FUNCTION, power of action; I. iii.

FURBISH'D, burnished; I. ii.

GALLOWGLASSES, heavy-armed Irish troops; I. ii.

GENIUS, spirit of good or ill; III. i.

GENTLE SENSES, senses which are soothed (by the "gentle" air); I. vi.

GERMINS, germs, seeds; IV. i.

GET, beget; I. iii.

GIN, a trap to catch birds; IV. ii.

'GINS, begins; I. ii.

GIVES OUT, proclaims; IV. iii.

GOD 'ILD US, corruption of "God yield us"; I. vi.

GOLGOTHA, i.e. "the place of a skull" (cp. Mark xv. 22); I. ii.

GOOD, brave; IV. iii.

GOODNESS, "the chance of g.", "the chance of success"; IV. iii.

GOOSE, a tailor's smoothing iron; II. iii.

GOSPELL'D, imbued with Gospel teaching; III. i.

GO TO, GO TO, an exclamation of reproach; V. i.

GOUTS, drops; II. i.

GRACED, gracious, full of graces; III. iv.

GRANDAM, grandmother; III. iv.

GRAVE, weighty; III. i.

GRAYMALKIN, a grey cat (the familiar spirit of the First Witch); I. i.

GRIPE, grasp; III. i.

GROOMS, servants of any kind; II. ii.

GULF, gullet; IV. i.

HAIL (dissyllabic); I. ii.

HARBINGER, forerunner, an officer of the king's household; I. iv.

HARDLY, with difficulty; V. iii.

HARMS, injuries; "my h.", injuries, inflicted by me; IV. iii.

HARP'D, hit, touched; IV. i.

HARPIER, probably a corruption of Harpy; IV. i.

HAVING, possessions; I. iii.

HEAR, talk with; III. iv.

HEART, "any h.", the heart of any man; III. vi.

HEAVILY, sadly; IV. iii.

gin Mary; a slight oath; III. vi.

MATED, bewildered: V. i.

MAWS, stomachs: III. iv.

MAY I, I hope I may: III. iv.

MEDICINE, "physician"; (?) physic; V. ii.

MEEK, meekly: I. vii.

MEMORIZE, make memorable, make famous I. ii.

MERE, absolutely: IV. iii.

MERE, utter, absolute: IV, iii.

METAPHYSICAL, supernatural; I. v.

MINION, darling, favorite; I. ii.; II. iv.

MINUTELY, "happening every minute, continual": V. ii.

MISSIVES, messengers: I. v.

MISTRUST, "he needs not our m.", i.e. we need not mistrust him: III. iii.

MOCKERY, delusive imitation; III. iv.

MODERN, ordinary; IV. iii.

MOE, more: V. iii.

MORTAL, deadly, murderous; I. v.

——, "m. murders," deadly wounds: III. iv.

——, "m consequences," what befalls man in the course of time; V. iii.

MORTALITY, mortal life; II. iii.

MORTIFIED, dead, insensible; V. ii.

MOUNCH'D, chewed with closed lips; I. iii.

MUSE, wonder: III. iv.

MUST BE, was destined to be; IV. iii.

NAPKINS, handkerchiefs; II. iii.

NATURE, "nature's mischief," man's evil propensities: I. v.

——, "in n.", in their whole nature; II. iv.

NAUGHT, vile thing: IV. iii.

NAVE, navel, middle; I. ii.

NEAR, nearer: II. iii.

NEAR'ST, OF LIFE, inmost life, most vital parts; III. i.

NICE, precise, minute; IV. iii.

NIGHTGOWN, dressing gown; II. ii.

NOISE, music; IV. i.

NORWAYS, Norwegians; I. ii.

NORWEYAN, Norwegian; I. ii.

NOTE, notoriety; III. ii.

——, list; III. iii.

——, notice; III. iv.

NOTHING, not at all; I. iii.

——, nobody; IV. iii.

NOTION, apprehension; II. i.

OBLIVIOUS, causing forgetfulness; V. iii.

OBSCURE, "o. bird," i.e. the bird delighting in darkness, the owl; II. iii.

ODDS, "at o.", at variance; III. iv.

O'ERFRAUGHT, overcharged, overloaded; IV. iii.

OF, from, IV. i.

——, with; (Hanmer, "with"); I. ii.

——, over; I. iii.

——, by; III. vi.

——, for; IV. iii.

OFFICES, duty, employment; III. iii.

——, i.e. domestic offices, servants' quarters; II. i.

OLD (used colloquially); II. iii.

ON, of; I. iii.

ONCE, ever; IV. iii.

ONE, wholly, uniformly; II. ii.

ON'S, of his; V. i.

ON'T, of it; III. i.

OPEN'D, unfolded; IV. iii.

OR ERE, before; IV. iii.

OTHER, others; I. iii.

——, "the o.", i.e. the other side; I. vii.

——, otherwise; I. vii.

OTHER'S, other man's; IV. iii.

OURSELVES, one another; III. iv.

OUT, i.e. in the field; IV. iii.

OUTRUN, did outrun; II. iii.

OVERCOME, overshadow; III. iv.

OVER-RED, redden over; V. iii.

OWE, own, possess; I. iii.

OWED, owned; I. iv.

PADDOCK, toad (the familiar

spirit of the second witch); I. i.

PALL, wrap, envelop; I. v.

PASSION, strong emotion; III. iv.

PATCH, fool (supposed to be derived from the patched or motley coat of the jester); V. iii.

PEAK, dwindle away; I. iii.

PENT-HOUSE LID, *i.e.* eye-lids; I. iii.

PERFECT, well, perfectly acquainted; IV. ii.

PESTER'D, troubled; V. ii.

PLACE, "pitch, the highest elevation of a hawk", a term of falconry; II. iv.

POINT, "at a p.", "prepared for any emergency"; IV. iii.

POOR, feeble; III. ii.

POORLY, dejectedly, unworthily; II. ii.

PORTABLE, endurable; IV. iii.

POSSESS, fill; IV. iii.

POSSETS, drink; "posset is hot milk poured on ale or sack, having sugar, grated bisket, and eggs, with other ingredients boiled in it, which goes all to a curd"; II. ii.

POSTERS, speedy travelers; I. iii.

POWER, armed force, army; IV. iii.

PREDOMINANCE, superior power, influence; an astrological term II. iv.

PRESENT, present time; I. v.

PRESENT, instant, immediate; I. ii.

PRESENT, offer; III. ii.

PRESENTLY, immediately; IV. iii.

PRETENCE, purpose, intention; II. iii.

PRETEND, intend; II. iv.

PROBATION, "passed in p. with you," proved, passing them in detail, one by one; III. i.

PROFOUND, "having deep or hidden qualities" (Johnson); III. v.

PROOF, proved armour; I. ii.

PROPER, fine, excellent (used ironically); III. iv.

PROTEST, show publicly, proclaim; V. ii.

PURGED, cleansed; III. iv.

PURVEYOR, an officer of the king sent before to provide food for the king and his retinue, as the *harbinger* provided lodging; I. vi.

PUSH, attack, onset; V. iii.

PUT ON, set on, (?) set to work; IV. iii.

PUT UPON, falsely attribute; I. vii.

QUARRY, a heap of slaughtered game; IV. iii.

QUELL, murder; I. vii.

QUIET, "at q.", in quiet, at peace; II. iii.

RAVELL'D, tangled; II. ii.

RAVIN'D, ravenous; IV. i.

RAVIN UP, devour greedily; II. iv.

RAWNESS, hurry; IV. iii.

READINESS, "manly r.", complete clothing (opposed to "naked frailties"); II. iii.

RECEIPT, receptacle; I. vii.

RECEIVED, believed; I. vii.

RECOIL, swerve; IV. iii.

——, "to r.", for recoiling; V. ii.

RELATION, narrative; IV. iii.

RELATIONS, "the connection of effects with causes"; III. iv.

RELISH, smack; IV. iii.

REMEMBRANCE, reminder; III. iv.

REMORSE, pity; I. v.

REQUIRE, ask her to give; III. iv.

RESOLVE YOURSELVES, decide, make up your minds; III. i.

REST, remain; I. vi.

——, give rest; IV. iii.

RETURN, give back, render; I. vi.

RONYON, a term of contempt; I. iii.

ROOF'D, gathered under one roof; III. iv.

Rooky, gloomy, foggy; (Jennens, *"Rocky"*); III. ii.

Round, circlet, crown; I. v.

——, "r. and top of sovereignty," *i.e.* "the crown, the top or summit of sovereign power"; IV. i.

——, dance in a circle; IV. i.

Rubs, hindrances, impediments; III. i.

Rump-fed, well-fed, pampered; I. iii.

Safe toward, with a sure regard to; I. iv.

Sag, droop, sink; V. iii.

Saint Colme's inch, the island of Columba, now Inchcolm, in the Firth of Forth; I. ii.

Saucy, insolent, importunate; (?) pungent, sharp, gnawing (Koppel); III. iv.

Say to, tell; I. ii.

'Scaped, escaped; III. iv.

Scarf up, blindfold; III. ii.

Scone, the ancient coronation place of the kings of Scotland; II. iv.

Scotch'd, "cut with shallow incisions"; III. ii.

Season, seasoning; III. iv.

Seat, situation; I. vi.

Seated, fixed firmly; I. iii.

Security, confidence, consciousness of security, carelessness; III. v.

Seeling, blinding (originally a term of falconry); III. ii.

Seems, "that s. to speak things strange," *i.e.* "whose appearance corresponds with the strangeness of his message" (Clar. Pr.); I. ii.

Self-abuse, self-delusion; III. iv.

Self-comparisons, measuring himself with the other; I. ii.

Selfsame, very same; I. iii.

Sennet, a set of notes on trumpet or cornet; III. i.

Se'nnights, seven nights, weeks; I. iii.

Sensible, perceptible, tangible; II. i.

Set forth, shewed; I. iv.

Settled, determined; I. vii.

Sewer, one who tasted each dish to prove there was no poison in it; I. vii.

Shag-ear'd, having hairy ears; IV. ii.

Shall, will; II. i.

——, I shall; IV. ii.

Shame, am ashamed; II. ii.

Shard-borne, borne by scaly wing-cases; III. ii.

Shift, steal, quietly get; II. iii.

Shipman's card, the card of the compass; I. iii.

Shough, a kind of shaggy dog; III. i.

Should be, appear to be; I. iii.

Show, dumb-show; IV. i.

——, appear; I. iii.

Shut up, enclosed, enveloped; II. i.

Sicken, be surfeited; IV. i.

Sightless, invisible; I. vii.

Sinel, Macbeth's father, according to Holinshed; I. iii.

Single, individual; I. iii.

——, simple, small; I. vi.

Sirrah, used in addressing an inferior; here used playfully; IV. ii.

Skirr, scour; V. iii.

Slab, thick, glutinous; IV. i.

Sleave, sleave-silk, floss silk; II. ii.

Sleek o'er, smooth; III. ii.

Sleights, feats of dexterity; III. i.

Slipp'd, let slip; II. iii.

Sliver'd, slipped off; IV. i.

Smack, have the taste, savor; I. ii.

So, like grace, gracious; IV. iii.

So well, as well; I. ii.

Sole, alone, mere; IV. iii.

Solemn, ceremonious, formal; III. i.

Soliciting, inciting; I. iii.

Solicits, entreats, moves by prayer; IV. iii.

Something, some distance; III. i.

Sometime, sometimes; I. vi.

Sorely, heavily; V. i.

TRAMMEL UP, entangle as in a net; I. vii.

TRANSPORT, convey; IV. iii.

TRANSPOSE, change; IV. iii.

TREBLE SCEPTERS, symbolical of the three kingdoms England, Scotland, and Ireland; IV. i.

TRIFLED, made trifling, made to sink into insignificance; II. iv.

TUGG'D, "t. with fortune," pulled about in wrestling with fortune; III. i.

TWO-FOLD BALLS, probably referring to the double coronation of James, at Scone and Westminster (Clar. Pr.); IV. i.

TYRANNY, usurpation; IV. iii.

TYRANT, usurper; III. vi.

UNFIX, make to stand on end; I. iii.

UNROUGH, beardless; V. ii.

UNSPEAK, recall, withdraw; IV. iii.

UNTITLED, having no title or claim; IV. iii.

UNTO, to; I. iii.

UPON, to; III. vi.

UPROAR, "stir up to tumult" (Schmidt); IV. iii.

USE, experience; III. iv.

USING, cherishing, entertaining; III. ii.

UTTERANCE, "to the u.", *i.e. à outrance* = to the uttermost; III. i.

VANTAGE, opportunity; I. ii.

VERITY, truthfulness; IV. iii.

VISARDS, masks; III. ii.

VOUCH'D, assured, warranted; III. iv.

WANT, "cannot w.", can help; III. vi.

WARRANTED, justified; IV. iii.

WASSAIL, revelry; I. vii.

WATCHING, waking; V. i.

WATER-RUG, a kind of poodle; III. i.

WHAT, who; IV. iii.

WHAT IS, *i.e.* what is the time of; III. iv.

WHEN 'TIS, *i.e.* "when the matter is effected"; II. i.

WHICH, who; V. i.

WHILE THEN, till then; III. i.

WHISPERS, whispers to; IV. iii.

WHOLESOME, healthy; IV. iii.

WITH, against; IV. iii.

——, by; III. i.

——, on; IV. ii.

WITHOUT, outside; III. iv.

——, beyond; III. ii.

WITNESS, testimony, evidence; II. ii.

WORM, small serpent; III. iv.

WOULD, should; I. vii.

WROUGHT, agitated; I. iii.

YAWNING PEAL, a peal which lulls to sleep; III. ii.

YESTY, foaming; IV. i.

YET, in spite of all, notwithstanding; IV, iii.